FAIR TRADE

D0023891

FAIR TRADE

MARKET-DRIVEN ETHICAL CONSUMPTION

**Alex Nicholls
and
Charlotte Opal**

Los Angeles | London | New Delhi
Singapore | Washington DC

© Alex Nicholls and Charlotte Opal, 2005
Chapter 5 © Whitni Thomas, 2005

First published 2004
Reprinted 2010, 2011

Apart from any fair dealing for the purposes of research or
private study, or criticism or review, as permitted under
the Copyright, Designs and Patents Act, 1988, this
publication may be reproduced, stored or transmitted in any
form, or by any means, only with the prior permission in
writing of the publishers, or in the case of reprographic
reproduction, in accordance with the terms of licences issued
by the Copyright Licensing Agency. Enquiries concerning
reproduction outside those terms should be sent to the
publishers.

SAGE Publications Ltd
1 Oliver's Yard
55 City Road
London EC1Y 1SP

SAGE Publications Inc.
2455 Teller Road
Thousand Oaks, California 91320

SAGE Publications India Pvt Ltd
B 1/I 1, Mohan Cooperative Industrial Area
Mathura Road
New Delhi 110 044

SAGE Publications Asia-Pacific Pte Ltd
33 Pekin Street #02-01
Far East Square
Singapore 048763

British Library Cataloguing in Publication data

A catalogue record for this book is available
from the British Library

ISBN 978 1 4129 0104 8
ISBN 978 1 4129 0105 5 (pbk)

Library of Congress Control Number: 20041012345

Typeset by C&M Digitals (P) Ltd., Chennai, India
Printed in Great Britain by the MPG Books Group
Printed on paper from sustainable resources

Let us spread the fragrance of fairness across all aspects of life.
Professor Shyam Sharma, TARA projects (Hanoi, 2004)

Contents

About the Authors

Dr Alex Nicholls, PhD (King's College, London) and MBA (Saïd Business School, University of Oxford), is a university lecturer in Social Entrepreneurship at the Skoll Centre for Social Entrepreneurship within the Saïd Business School, University of Oxford. He has worked extensively on Fair Trade as a writer and researcher for the last five years and has published articles and spoken at international conferences whilst continuing to teach and research on the topic.

Charlotte Opal, M.Phil and MBA (both as a Rhodes Scholar at Oxford University), is the New Products Manager at TransFair USA, the Fair Trade certification and marketing agency in the USA. She has worked in Zambia, Swaziland, Mexico, South Africa, and Belize and at the World Bank headquarters in Washington, DC.

Both authors have carried out Fair Trade consultancy work for commercial partners and the United Nations Development Programme. In 2000, the authors were jointly awarded first prize in The Guardian/Association of Business Schools' Award (Business and Society category) for their project work on new product development with Cafédirect.

Whitni Thomas, MSc (London School of Economics) is Head of the Access to Finance Initiative at NEF (the New Economics Foundation). Her work at NEF includes research and consultancy around improving access to finance for financially excluded individuals and for socially driven businesses. She is also an associate of Twin Trading Ltd, a leading Fair Trade organization based in the UK. She has worked in Mexico on international development projects, and spent six years as an investment banker for JP Morgan in New York and London.

Acknowledgements

There are so many people to offer our thanks to who have materially helped us in the writing and production of this book that space does not allow us to acknowledge them all here. A good number are, or have become, close friends. All are worthy of our sincere appreciation. The brave cohort of interviewees who gave of their time in helping us to research this book have played a huge role in giving this work relevance and deserve a special mention: Hamish Renton; Diana Gayle; Sarah Hoole; Bruce Crowther; Ian Bretman; Alistaire Menzies; Carol Wills; Steve Sellers; Kim Easson; Luuk Zonneveld; Paul Rice; Joe Osman; Pauline Tiffen; Rob Everts; Sophi Tranchell; Jeroen Kroezen; José Luis Zárate; Ben Huyghe; and Terry Hudgton.

Furthermore, many of our colleagues have also been invaluable in providing comments and thoughts on this book while it was in progress and we are greatly indebted to them: Professor David Waller; Dr Andrew Alexander; Peter Cullen; Dr Doug Foster; Dr Steve New; Dr Jesse Rothstein; Dr Tim Jenkinson; Mark Magers; and Katie Feiock. The (certified) award for patience and support goes to our editor, Delia Alfonso.

Alex Nicholls

Particular thanks also go to my academic 'patrons' – Jeff Skoll and Professor Anthony Hopwood – without whose material support this book could never have been written. My personal gratitude goes to my mother Catherine Nicholls for repeated investments (emotional and financial) in my academic vocation and to Adele, Sam, and Harriet for their love and support above and beyond the call of duty.

This book is dedicated to my father, Peter Nicholls.

Charlotte Opal

I would like to express my admiration for René Ausecha Chaux, Pedro Haslam, and the legions of others who risk life and limb to fight injustice. You are an inspiration and it is an honour to be 'fighting the good fight' with you. Many thanks also to Mark Magers, from TransFair USA, for allowing me to take brief breaks from said good fight to finish this book.

It is dedicated to my grandparents, Chet and Zee Opal, in loving memory of my father, Chet Brian Opal.

This book is a celebration of the extraordinary and inspiring work being done by Fair Trade campaigners, retailers, wholesalers, labelling initiatives, other support networks, and, above all, by heroic producers. We owe them our single biggest debt of gratitude.

Abbreviations

ATO   Alternative Trading Organization

EFTA   European Fair Trade Association

FLO   Fairtrade Labelling Organizations International

FTO   Fair Trade Organization (registered by IFAT)

IFAT   International Federation of Alternative Trade

MNC   Multinational Corporation

NEWS   Network of European World Shops

NGO   Non-Governmental Organization

NI   National (Certification) Initiative

SME   Small or Medium-sized Enterprise

US   United States of America

UK   United Kingdom

VC   Venture Capital(ist)

A NOTE ON CURRENCY CONVERSIONS

This book includes figures in US dollars ($), Canadian dollars (CA$) UK pounds (£) and Euros. The exchange rate calculations used at the time of writing (October 2004) are as follows:

Currency	Conversation Rate
€1	$1.23
€1	£0.69
$1	£0.56
£1	$1.79
CA$1	$0.79
CA$1	£0.44

PART ONE

The Rise of Fair Trade

Introduction

Fair Trade is …

More Money to the World's Poor

I used to live in a thatch hut with a mud floor. Now I have two concrete houses. And I have been able to educate my children. Sophia is at university in Belmopan and Laurence is a teacher. They had to work in a shrimp farm when they were younger, but my children now only go to school. We don't need them to work.

> Jeronimo Tush, Cocoa Grower, Belize (Sutcliffe, 2004: 20)

A Success Story

I am enormously pleased with the way things have gone in the past five years, because more and more organizations across the world have come forward and identified themselves as being Fair Trade organizations … and I think that indicates the degree of interest that there is in this rather special kind of trade that deliberately sets out to make a difference to the lives of marginalized people.

> Carol Wills, The International Federation of Alternative Trade (Interview, 2004)

A Rethinking of Global Trade

In the end, what Fair Trade is about is working with marginalized producers – people on the edge of the international trading system. It's bringing them in and building their sustainability, their understanding of selling and trading and allowing them to survive often in situations where they probably wouldn't. What Fair Trade brings is a long-term relationship and the ability to plan ahead. So it's about empowerment and the growth of output and quality for the groups and to get to a point where they no longer need to engage with the Fair Trade relationship.

> Diana Gayle, The Fairtrade Foundation (2003)

A Market Opportunity

We wouldn't be selling this stuff if there wasn't something in it for us in the context of sales benefits, the halo of Fair Trade, and brand benefits. So we started to get interested in it and we felt, frankly, that it was a sector that was ripe for something to happen. Growth is really fast – it is basically a start-up in food terms – it's not explosive growth, but it is rapid.

> Hamish Renton, Tesco UK (2003)

Consumer Empowerment

People see it as charity, but it is not, it is justice. We have to get rid of the charity way of thinking. I see Fair Trade as doing two things: one, it is helping people immediately and changing their lives; then, there is the bigger picture where it is a protest tool, a way of registering your vote. But now we are not boycotting something, we are supporting something positive.

Bruce Crowther, Fair Trade Towns Co-ordinator,
Fairtrade Foundation (2003)

Producer Empowerment

Fair Trade farmers will say that because they now have a prestige product in the market ... when they now go knocking on somebody else's door, whether or not it is a Fair Trade importer, they get received, whereas in the past they did not.

Kimberly Easson, TransFair USA (2003)

PREFACE

The world is changing fast. Perhaps never before in human history has the pace of technological and economic advances been so rapid. During the past thirty years the inter-connectedness of the 'global village' has become more and more apparent as the communications revolution and cheaper air travel have linked communities around the world. Mass migration and the increasing integration of previous generations of immigrants are changing the concept of nationality in many countries. Cultures have clashed, blended, and been synthesized into rich new combinations, and global brands have emerged to draw disparate consumers into common aspirations (see further Gabriel and Lang, 1995). The collapse of the 'Second World' planned economies in eastern Europe and the Soviet Union has also led to an increasing consensus over economic and political norms based around the US model of free market democracy and neo-liberal economics (the so-called 'Washington Consensus'). Some have referred to this trend towards global homogenization as 'the end of history' (Fukuyama, 1992).

Paralleling the cultural and technological innovations of recent times has been the development of global business on a scale undreamt of even at the height of the European imperial age during the eighteenth and nineteenth centuries. Today's corporations span the globe with interests across many nation states and supply chains that encircle the planet. The largest of these multinationals have turnovers equivalent to small independent countries. For example, WalMart – the world's largest company by market capitalization in 2003 – had a turnover in 2002 greater than the gross domestic product (GDP) of Turkey, Denmark, South Africa and many other countries (Young and Welford, 2002). As a result of this huge increase in the scope and influence of global corporations, consumers in the developed world have never before been offered such a range of products sourced from so many distant lands, and the profitability growth of many businesses is now increasingly driven by opportunities to seek out cheaper source materials and labour from around the global marketplace.

These dramatic changes have benefited many, both in the developing and developed worlds. However, the relentless onward march of globalization has also generated problems. In tandem with the retreat by government in many countries from traditional social welfare agendas, the growing economic muscle of multinationals has created losers as well as winners (Klein, 2000; Singer, 2002; Stiglitz, 2002). Whilst increases in overall global trade, global GDP, and foreign direct investment (FDI) have all helped improve life expectancies and the overall standard of living for many in developing countries, global inequality has also grown. Clearly, some in this global revolution are benefiting more than others. Indeed, many are not benefiting at all.

As protestors in Seattle, Doha, and Genoa have drawn attention to some Western consumers' growing disillusionment with the progress of development through global trade, Fair Trade has emerged as the most important market-based mechanism to improve the lives of producers in developing countries. Sales of Fair Trade products in Europe, North America and Japan have grown exponentially in recent years. Fair Trade bananas have a 50 per cent market share in Switzerland (AgroFair, 2004), and global sales of all Fair Trade products amounted to approximately £500m ($895m) in 2003 (Vidal, 2004), up from an estimated £335m ($600m) in 2002 (Leatherhead Food International, 2003). Fair Trade coffee is the fastest-growing segment of the speciality coffee industry in the USA and the UK (McCarthy, 2004). To date, these figures include the initially small, but rapidly growing, US market. If US market development follows the pattern of European markets – and there is evidence to believe that it may be moving even faster – global sales of Fair Trade will increase by a factor of 10–15 in the next few years. Therefore, it is far from fanciful to assume that global Fair Trade sales will top £1 billion ($1.8 billion) by 2007 (Demetriou, 2003).

As a result, addressing Fair Trade issues is now part of the agenda for most major European retailers, including Monoprix, Tesco, Migros, and Carrefour. Moreover, Fair Trade is now the subject of hundreds of global media stories each year and also forms an important part of both the taught programmes and research literature of several distinct academic disciplines, including development economics, finance, accounting, business ethics, marketing, buying, and retail operations. National governments and supra-national organizations, such as the United Nations and the European Commission, are also recognizing this important new model of trade.

Fair Trade attempts to address some of the key problems in the increasingly deregulated global marketplace by addressing the producers' needs, as well as those of consumers, big corporations and their shareholders. Fair Trade represents a new way to do business that looks holistically at the supply chain to address market failures and their social impacts at source, but which still acknowledges the need for profitability. Fair Trade is not about aid, charity, or just 'doing good': it is about recognizing the global community as having rights and responsibilities that extend across all of its stakeholders. Public demonstrations against perceived misuse of power by multinational corporations are now commonplace, and the public mood generally is clearly shifting towards a demand for more transparency and fairness in all areas of business activity. The rise of Corporate Social Responsibility (CSR) as a boardroom-level topic for discussion reflects this change in consumer sentiment and – in the wake of the Enron accounting scandal – seems unlikely to prove to be a flash in the pan (see further, Hilton and Gibbons, 2002). Furthermore, the exponential growth in sales of Fair Trade products across several countries also demonstrates the commercial viability and consumer appeal of a fairer approach to business activities. Thus, it is reasonable to say that the time has now come for a serious discussion of Fair Trade's development and future prospects.

WHAT IS FAIR TRADE?

The aim of Fair Trade is to offer the most disadvantaged producers in developing countries the opportunity to move out of extreme poverty through creating market access
(typically to Northern consumers) under beneficial rather than exploitative terms. The
objective is to empower producers to develop their own businesses and wider communities through international trade. Fair Trade offers a new model of the producer-consumer
relationship that reconnects production and consumption via an innovative supply chain
model which distributes its economic benefits more fairly between all stakeholders. Fair
Trade attempts to address the gross imbalances in information and power that typify
North-South supplier-buyer relationships by countering the current failures evident in
many global markets.

The Fair Trade model thus operates in stark contrast to the conventional international
supplier-buyer transactional relationship that aims to maximize return to the institutional
buyer through the establishment of a power imbalance in favour of the purchaser (though
not always the end-consumer). This may be done through controlling information flows,
thus exerting the influence of scale or scope, or via exclusive deals with wholesalers. Fair
Trade's proposition to consumers is that setting producer prices at a level where the producer can not only reach a basic standard of living, but also develop, is the only truly 'fair'
way to operate. Thus, trade becomes a developmental tool with many positive externalities.

In operational terms, Fair Trade is specifically defined by several key practices:

- *Agreed minimum prices, usually set ahead of market minimums.* Fair Trade prices are set taking
  account of local economic conditions to allow producers a living wage from their work.
  In the case of small-scale commodity production, the Fairtrade Labelling Organizations International (FLO) calculates a Fair Trade floor price, which covers the cost of
  production and provision for family members and farm improvements. If the world
  market price for a particular commodity (for example, coffee or cocoa) falls below this,
  Fair Trade importers pay the floor price, or otherwise the world market price. By guaranteeing a price above the cost of production, Fair Trade allows producers to plan
  ahead and invest in the future of their businesses. For estate-farm worker models of
  production (for example, tea, some kinds of fruit), the Fair Trade guarantee is that farm
  workers are being paid the legal minimum wage and that International Labour
  Organization (ILO) standards are followed. For other Fair Trade goods such as handicrafts or textiles that lack a certification process, the price is determined as 'fair' in a
  regional or local context through agreement, dialogue, and participation between
  wholesale buyers and producers. The price covers not only the costs of production but
  enables that production to be socially just and environmentally sound.
- *Focus on development and technical assistance via the payment to suppliers of an agreed social
  premium (often 10 per cent or more of the cost price of goods).* The social premium paid to
  smallholder producers and farm workers on top of the Fair Trade price for their
  goods allows them collectively to implement larger development projects, such as
  building schools or sinking new wells. Small-scale farmers are usually organized into
  democratic co-operatives that decide how the Fair Trade premia are to be spent, for
  example, on community projects, or else retained for co-operative business investments such as milling facilities, trade show participation, or new product development.

Farm workers must form an association that receives the social premium and votes on how to use it, for example as regards housing, pension funds, or in other social investments. Thus, Fair Trade ensures that producers move out of subsistence poverty through trade rather than aid, an approach that is more sustainable and maintains the dignity of producers.

- *Direct purchasing from producers.* Fair Trade aims to lessen the influence of brokers, consolidators and other agents in global supply chains and thereby to increase efficiency, reducing the number of margins within a value chain. This ensures more of the final price of the goods can return to the producer.
- *Transparent and long-term trading partnerships.* For many small producers consistency of income is vital for survival. Fair Trade ensures that importers sign long-term contracts so that producers do not suffer from the effects of buyers' short-term bias. This allows them to plan ahead and invest in new technology or planting that should ultimately increase their income and help them to develop their businesses.
- *Co-operative, not competitive, dealings.* Fair Trade fosters buyer-producer relationships built on mutual respect. This can ultimately be a more efficient way of delivering value to the consumer as it leads to a higher quality product and consistency of supply. It also provides an important element in the ethical positioning of Fair Trade products that has helped to drive their extraordinary sales growth.
- *Provision of credit when requested.* As importers generally have much easier access to credit than do developing country producers, importers are required to pre-finance up to 60 per cent of the total purchase of seasonal crops. This enables farmers to receive an advance for their crop even before it is exported, which will smooth their income streams.
- *Provision of market information to producers.* Fair Trade transactions acknowledge the market price of the goods in question and keep producers informed about market movements. As Fair Trade producers still typically sell the bulk of their produce to non-Fair Trade buyers, this is especially useful in their wider negotiations.
- *Farmers and workers are organized democratically.* Small-scale farmers must belong to a co-operative that is democratically organized and which practises one-farmer, one-vote systems. On Fair Trade estates and plantations, farm workers form democratically-controlled groups that manage the disbursement of the Fair Trade social premia.
- *Sustainable production is practised.* All farms and co-operatives must have resource management plans in place. Certain pesticides are prohibited on all farms. Many farms use Fair Trade premia to invest in organic certification, which demands a higher Fair Trade floor price.
- *No labour abuses occurred during the production process.* In all cases, child and slave labour abuses are prohibited and workers must be allowed to unionize.

In simple terms, then, Fair Trade represents a new approach to the buyer-supplier transaction which aims at equality of exchange within a partnership approach, underpinned by a developmental, rather than confrontational, agenda. Fair Trade recognizes the power discrepancy between the developing and developed worlds (Strong, 1996) and aims to forge long-term partnership relationships (Tallontire, 2000). A firm focus on the producer, rather than the consumer, has been central to Fair Trade – contracts aim to maximize returns to suppliers rather than buyer margins, within an agreed developmental structure (Barratt Brown, 1993). Furthermore, it appears to be working. As sales continue to grow, Fair Trade's dual aims of immediate poverty alleviation and more long-term producer development are having a measurable impact. As Carol Wills, Executive Director of the International Federation of Alternative Trade (IFAT) noted:

> From my own experience, particularly in places like Bangladesh, you can go into villages where the community is organized around a Fair Trade activity and a village near by which is not and the difference is great. And it's not just the practical things like savings and a house and more food, but it's in people's – especially women's – self-esteem and self-confidence. Fair Trade is so often associated in those parts of the world with group formation, doing more with the group than just production. Fair Trade offers a premium payment going back to the co-operative or plantation and the co-operative or plantation having a democratically-organized committee representative for everybody set up to decide what to do with the premium, so it can be used to build a school or pay for teachers or pay for a clinic or water pumps … strengthening the co-operative, building institutions, setting up credit unions and all that, that is making them stronger anyway when they are negotiating with other buyers.
>
> So, very broadly, consumers can say to themselves, my purchase is making a bit of a difference back in the producer community, but also it is being noticed, where I am buying the product, here in Switzerland, in Austria, in Italy, or Japan wherever, because it is getting so visible, that politicians are beginning to think what is this Fair Trade, what is it, is it some sort of free trade, what is it? (Interview, 2004)

KEY FAIR TRADE ORGANIZATIONS

FLO (http://www.fairtrade.net)

The Fairtrade Labelling Organizations International is the global umbrella organization for the 19 national Fair Trade certification initiatives. Its main objectives are:

- To guarantee the integrity of the Fair Trade mark and certification process.
- To facilitate the business of Fair Trade by helping to match supply and demand.
- To offer producer support and consultancy to improve their business strategies.

FLO inspects producer groups to certify them for compliance with Fair Trade standards, including democratic organization, financial transparency, adequate working conditions, and progress regarding social and community development goals. FLO and its members then licence companies to use FLO's Fair Trade mark to signify that for a given product the Fair Trade standards, including minimum pricing, credit provision, and long-term trade relationships, have been met.

IFAT (http://www.ifat.org)

Formerly the International Federation of Alternative Trade, IFAT now styles itself as 'The International Fair Trade Association'. IFAT is essentially a global trade association for Fair Trade producers and traders of both FLO-certified products and non-certified goods. Membership is open to both trading and non-trading organizations that satisfy the basic Fair Trade criteria, and current members span all continents. Application begins with a self-assessment process that must include existing IFAT members as referees. Once accepted into IFAT, members are liable to be externally audited on an ad hoc basis. There is also a fee for membership. The organization is structured as follows: an elected Executive Committee (to make strategic decisions and carry out planning); an appointed Secretariat (to act as a point of contact for the membership); the membership.

IFAT has three stated objectives:

- To develop the market for Fair Trade. IFAT works with its members to foster a positive environment for Fair Trade market growth and links its membership to other resources and support networks.
- To build trust in Fair Trade. IFAT has set up a monitoring system for its members to add credibility to their Fair Trade credentials. The monitoring process is in three stages: self-assessment against the standards for Fair Trade organizations; mutual review between trading partners; external verification.
- To speak out for Fair Trade. IFAT delivers the message of Fair Trade by developing and then communicating its own particular perspective on the current debates around trade and development, and by organizing yearly a World Fair Trade Day on the second Saturday in May.

IFAT launched the Fair Trade Organizations (FTO) mark in January 2004. This mark does not aim to compete with FLO certification, as it is specifically not a product mark. IFAT uses its established monitoring system to identify if an applicant can be awarded the FTO mark. Once an IFAT trading member has successfully met the requirements of the IFAT monitoring system they can be registered as a FTO.

EFTA (http://www.eftafairtrade.org)

The European Fair Trade Association is an advocacy and research body based in the Netherlands (Head Office) and Belgium (Advocacy Office). Established in 1990, EFTA is a network of eleven Fair Trade organizations in nine European countries: Austria, Belgium, France, Germany, Italy, the Netherlands, Spain, Switzerland and the United Kingdom. Members include Oxfam, Traidcraft, and Gepa. EFTA has two main objectives:

- To make Fair Trade importing more efficient and effective. EFTA builds networks of producers and support groups to encourage and facilitate the exchange of information and best practice.
- To promote Fair Trade to commercial and political decision-makers. EFTA co-ordinates campaigns and lobbying activities and publishes data to support the Fair Trade case.

EFTA publishes Fair Trade figures and analysis for Europe and a twice-yearly newsletter. It also contributes a significant research and advocacy document once a year: the EFTA Yearbook.

NEWS (http://www.worldshops.org)

The Network of European World Shops aims to promote Fair Trade by stimulating, supporting and linking world shops in Europe that retail Fair Trade products. It is a network of 15 national World Shop associations in 13 different countries, all together representing about 2,500 World Shops in Europe. NEWS also promotes and undertakes campaigns to increase consumer awareness of Fair Trade. Its specific activities include: the publication of a biannual 'NEWS!letter', the organization of a biennial European Conference and an annual European World Shops' Day. NEWS runs an office in order to give shape to all its activities.

Fair Trade Federation (http://www.fairtradefederation.com)

The Fair Trade Federation is a US-based trade association of Fair Trade wholesalers, retailers, and producers whose members are committed to providing fair wages and good employment opportunities to economically disadvantaged artisans and farmers worldwide. There is a membership fee scaled according to turnover. The Fair Trade Federation offers its members access to its trade network and members directory, as well as an in-house journal and links to Fair Trade events.

FINE

FINE is a discussion forum for FLO, IFAT, NEWS, and EFTA. It came into being as part of a process of recognition that the Fair Trade movement needed to be more coordinated strategically. To date the most pressing issue has been to address the role of certification in the future development of Fair Trade. Of particular importance is reconciling the many IFAT members who do not have access to FLO certification (but may have the IFAT FTO mark) – either due to scale or the product groups in which they operate being inappropriate – with Fair Trade's move into the mainstream consumer marketplace. This issue has yet to be resolved.

Certification

Another important part of the Fair Trade model is product certification. The first Fair Trade products gained credibility with customers by their selling location – typically world or charity shops such as Oxfam in the UK or Ten Thousand Villages in the USA. However, as Fair Trade groups developed new products and aimed to expand their outlets, it became evident that consumers would benefit from a certification label that identified a Fair Trade audit process for the product in question. In the Netherlands, the Max Havelaar Foundation – named after a fictional Dutch colonial officer stationed in Java who championed the cause of impoverished Javanese coffee farmers – began the first independent Fair Trade labelling initiative in 1988 (see Image 1). Oxfam then followed, in conjunction with Traidcraft, Christian Aid, New Consumer, the World Development Movement, and CAFOD, together establishing the Fairtrade Foundation, the UK's third-party auditor of Fair Trade practices for selected goods. In 1997, these and other national

Image 1   *Max Havelaar logo*
Reproduced with permission of the Max Havelaar-Foundation.

Image 2   *FLO Fair Trade mark*
Reproduced with permission.

initiatives formed the Fairtrade Labelling Organizations International (FLO), to pool certification and marketing resources amongst consuming countries.

Today many Fair Trade products are certified as such by the award of a Fair Trade mark authorized by one of the 19 international Fair Trade labelling organizations. In Britain, FLO's mark (see Image 2) can be found on many leading Fair Trade products, such as Cafédirect coffee, tea, and cocoa. This mark guarantees independent auditing of Fair Trade goods and offers consumers an important degree of reassurance when buying Fair Trade products, much as the Soil Association mark does for organic produce in the UK. Given that Fair Trade products are usually more expensive than other substitutes, due to the particular structure of their value chain, this reassurance is especially important (see MacMaolain, 2002, for a further discussion of labelling issues). In the USA and Canada the TransFair logo is used (see Image 3).

However, not all Fair Trade products bear this mark. Indeed Traidcraft, the largest single Fair Trade company in the UK, offers the majority of its products without it. This is not because they are produced outside of the Fair Trade guidelines, but rather it is as a result of the sometimes complex, expensive, and difficult process of acquiring the mark. FLO is responsible for establishing producer guidelines and minimum pricing in order for any

Image 3   *TransFair Fair Trade mark (USA)*
Reproduced with permission of TransFair USA.

product to carry the Fair Trade mark. This work is ongoing but time consuming and, with limited resources, only a few new product groups are certified every year. Therefore, the group of FLO certified products is not yet comprehensive, and is limited mostly to agricultural products. Thus, alternative trading organizations (ATOs) like Traidcraft or Oxfam, which sell a lot of 'fairly traded' goods – particularly handicrafts and textiles – cannot at this stage carry the Fair Trade mark on many of their products, because they have yet to be certified by FLO. Clearly, if the market for Fair Trade is to expand significantly in the future this problem must be urgently addressed (Nicholls, 2004). This matter is discussed in detail in Chapters 6 and 10.

THE FAIR TRADE 'ALTERNATIVE'

Fair Trade is defined by a range of quite distinct trading objectives and has an easily defined social mission. But, in what ways is Fair Trade really 'fair'? Clearly, the term 'fair' can be highly contested and is, inevitably, the matter of subjective opinion. Indeed, as Carol Wills of IFAT noted, there are even a number of basic semantic problems with the phrase:

> The word 'fair' wasn't the word that was used at all to start with, it was 'alternative'; that these types of organization were providing an alternative to conventional international trade which tended to marginalize small producers. I think alternative was rather a good word, because it was alternative in all kinds of ways: cutting out the middleman, trading directly (whereas we know that a lot of big businesses trade through a series of agents); alternative distribution channels; alternative work force, volunteers in many cases, and so on and so forth. But then the word went out of fashion in a lot of countries and tended to get associated with brown rice and sandals and beards and hairy legs and that sort of thing. It was just not seen to be the right word anymore. Well, the Fairtrade Foundation came in at the beginning of the 90s and the phrase 'Fair Trade' began to be more widely used ... But these are words and, of course, you have to think about language as well, because, of course, in English you have 'fair' and 'ethical' and there are shades of meaning between the two but there are other languages, such as Spanish or French, where there isn't actually a real word for 'fair'. The meaning gets slightly blurred and you cannot translate it at all in many countries in a way that means anything. (Interview, 2004)

'Alternative' trade does, indeed, provide an accurate (and translatable) description of the model that has become increasingly known as Fair Trade. However, Fair Trade genuinely offers the aforementioned fairness in a number of important ways. Firstly, by promoting a supply chain that delivers value to producer and buyer more evenly, Fair Trade clearly treats the former with greater fairness than conventional trade. Secondly, by requiring companies to conform to minimum guidelines to be able to make claims of independent certification of Fair Trade standards, competitors play on a more level and ethical playing field. Finally, by offering the consumer a transparent supply chain embedded in the product at the point-of-purchase, Fair Trade provides a fairer choice in store than many other products on offer.

The word 'fair' may indeed resonate best as Fair Trade moves into the mainstream and is no longer just an 'alternative'. As Paul Rice, Chief Executive Officer of the Fair Trade labelling organization TransFair USA, explained:

> The good news is that fairness is kind of a core American value – much more so than say, healthy eating, or organic food. We often compare ourselves to organics, and it's growing very fast, but I think there's something about fairness that's deeply ingrained in our history and our national

psyche. Americans love underdogs, and they want to feel like things are fair, and finding resonance with that core value system and giving people an opportunity to act on it in an effortless way – that is the key to our success. (Interview, 2004)

In summary, Fair Trade is not about charity, nor is it necessarily not-for-profit, but rather it represents a redefinition of profitable transactions encompassing and empowering all key stakeholders and, thus, offers a range of benefits unavailable from 'traditional' business models. Fair Trade today is a consumer-driven phenomenon, underpinned by the growth of 'ethical' consumption more generally. Fair Trade has moved from being purely an activist-led advocacy and empowerment model towards being a market-led commercial success story.

To some economists, Fair Trade is an aberration (see, for instance, Lindsey, 2004). Firstly, its price structure fails to obey the rules of a 'free market', setting price controls that are driven by humanitarian issues rather than the 'free' interaction of supply and demand. It is thus accused of fostering and indeed encouraging uncompetitive production. Secondly, 'ethical' consumer behaviour is seen as highly 'irrational', since it does not aim to maximize the financial utility of the purchaser (Fair Trade products generally sell at a premium) and thus does not conform to conventional market mechanisms.

However, Fair Trade is a unique solution to market failures in the global trading system. As a consumer choice movement, it is outside the scope of government regulation and thus cannot be criticized as an interventionist trade policy. And in addition, by correcting market failures to make the trading system work for everyone, Fair Trade is, in fact, a neo-liberal solution to problems with trade. Fair Trade works within an efficient capitalist system, rather than abandoning the liberal trade model entirely (Jones, 2004). These issues will be discussed in more detail in Chapter 2.

STRUCTURE OF THE BOOK

This book represents a new study of the strategic background to, and future of, the Fair Trade movement. Whilst a number of books and articles, both academic and mass-media, have considered aspects of Fair Trade (for example, Littrell and Dickson, 1999; Ransom, 2001; Young and Welford, 2002), only Barratt Brown (1993) considered the subject holistically, and this work focused primarily on the historical and developmental aspects of Fair Trade rather than the strategic or operational issues. Furthermore, Barratt Brown was writing at the very beginning of the emergence of Fair Trade as a commercially viable business model, and much has changed since then. Consequently, the time is now right for a thorough re-analysis of the Fair Trade phenomenon. This book explores all the key areas of current Fair Trade thinking and engages with a range of business and management disciplines including developmental economics, business ethics, corporate strategy, marketing, finance, and retail operations. There is an international perspective throughout.

The full range of Fair Trade issues is set out in the context of modern business. Central to the approach followed here is an exploration of the critical tension resulting from the key aim of Fair Trade to achieve co-operation rather than competition amongst the dynamic parties in a supply chain, whilst faced with the market-driven imperatives of neo-liberal capitalism. If Fair Trade is to represent a sustainable and scaleable commercial model then there must clearly be some integration with mainstream big business. Indeed, balancing the demands of being both 'in' and 'against' the market is a notable feature of Fair Trade. The challenge is often how to maintain mission integrity whilst also achieving mainstream commercial growth (Barratt Brown, 1993; Nicholls, 2002, 2004). It is argued that this is not only possible, but can also already be discerned in action around the world today.

The book is divided into ten chapters – in addition to this introduction – and falls into three broad parts. Part One (Chapters 1 to 3) explains the background to the rise of Fair Trade. Part Two (Chapters 4 to 7) covers the operational aspects of Fair Trade businesses. Finally, Part Three (Chapters 8 to 10) identifies the growing impact of Fair Trade and plots its likely future course, including a discussion of the important challenges facing it today.

Throughout the book, unless otherwise indicated, figures for Fair Trade sales will refer to FLO *certified* products only (see further Chapter 6). These are typically commodity foods like coffee, tea, bananas, and chocolate. This is because it is for these goods that the most reliable data can be found. They also now represent the bulk of the Fair Trade consumer market. However, it should be understood that the majority of Fair Trade lines, though not the majority of sales, consist of non-certified products. These are typically handicrafts (for a detailed discussion of the issues around these products see further Littrell and Dickson, 1999).

The first chapter sets the scene for the rest of the book, presenting key definitions and themes and establishing the historical and economic backgrounds to Fair Trade. The key drivers behind its emergence are identified, as are its main objectives and impacts. Some of the objections to Fair Trade are also explored.

Chapter 2 considers in detail the economics of Fair Trade. It shows the global market failures that provided the initial impetus behind Fair Trade and explains the Fair Trade model's approaches to make markets work more effectively. The importance of the positive economic externalities generated by the Fair Trade process is also established. Finally, the economic efficiency of the Fair Trade mechanism is discussed.

Chapter 3 establishes a philosophical context for Fair Trade by examining supply chain ethics. Firstly, it questions the boundaries of corporate responsibility in terms of companies' supply chain actions. Secondly, the philosophical milieu for Fair Trade is defined across a range of established ethical theories, most notably deontology and utilitarianism. The notion of social justice is identified as particularly important here and this is developed and critiqued in terms of Fair Trade operations. The chapter concludes by setting out the business responses to increased consumer interest in supply chain impacts.

Chapter 4 outlines the structural landscape and strategic options of the Fair Trade movement. It examines Fair Trade business structures, contrasting co-operative and competitive as well as for-profit and not-for-profit models, using the global coffee and banana industries as detailed case studies. The role and function of alternative trading organizations are discussed at length and the key strategic issue of mainstreaming is addressed. The Fair Trade value chain is also explored in contrast to more traditional supply chains and its advantages are set out. The challenges inherent in maintaining integrity whilst also growing commercially are considered, as Fair Trade first-movers position themselves for an environment in which Fair Trade moves into the mainstream and more traditional businesses enter the market.

Chapter 5 discusses the financial context of Fair Trade business development and falls into two parts. Firstly, it considers the financing needs of producers in the South and of other producer organizations more generally. Secondly, the chapter discusses the financial challenges and potential solutions for Northern market access organizations. This chapter in particular queries whether Fair Trade organizations must be seen as 'special cases' in terms of corporate financial structures, or whether conventional sources of funding can work for these new models of trade.

Chapter 6 explores the certification of Fair Trade products, beginning with the history of certification in Europe. The certification process is considered in detail, including its financial structure. The importance of certification to Fair Trade is established, whilst its limitations are also acknowledged. Two particular issues emerge for further discussion. Firstly, as Fair Trade grows in popularity the landscape for certification has become more competitive; these competitive threats are discussed in the wider context of challenges to advances in Fair Trade certification. Secondly, the tension between the current pace of market-driven new product development in Fair Trade and that of the certification and audit process is discussed. Finally, the various drivers of future Fair Trade new product development are also analysed.

Chapter 7 considers the marketing and selling of Fair Trade in both strategic and operational terms and first explores the marketing objectives for Fair Trade. It then sets out the marketing positioning which Fair Trade has adopted and considers the range of marketing communications options used for promotion. The development of Fair Trade marketing is analysed and three stages are identified. A social network model is used to demonstrate the importance of establishing connectivity between producer and consumer in Fair Trade marketing.

Chapter 8 sets out the current market for Fair Trade goods. It begins with a consideration of the 'ethical' consumer and Fair Trade consumers as a subset within this market segment. The chapter then goes on to define the sales landscape for Fair Trade products, first globally, and then in a country-by-country survey of the main markets. It also considers developments within Fair Trade retailing internationally. The role of supermarket own-label Fair Trade products is explored in a case study of Tesco PLC.

Chapter 9 explores the Fair Trade business model from the perspective of its impacts. The real value of Fair Trade to the producers is, clearly, in the impact it has on their lives in comparison with conventional trading relationships. This chapter summarizes existing research on monetary, non-monetary, direct and indirect impacts of Fair Trade, and explores the ranges of social impact metrics that are currently available to help define Fair Trade business success. Of particular importance is the Social Return on Investment model, and the chapter concludes with its application to a hypothetical Fair Trade co-operative case study.

Finally, Chapter 10 draws the book to a close by pulling together the various key arguments laid out in earlier sections whilst looking forward towards the various possible Fair Trade futures. A number of important emerging challenges for the continued development of Fair Trade are set out.

This book aims to appeal to academics and students, as well as practitioners, who are interested in business ethics, corporate social responsibility, stakeholder management, supply chain issues, developmental economics or international trade policy. Its structure allows readers to focus on specific aspects of business strategy and management and to understand their relevant Fair Trade contexts, as well as to gain a broader overview of the subject as a whole. Finally, this is not a book exclusively written for an academic audience: given the widespread consumer interest in ethical trade generally and the growing market for Fair Trade products in particular, this book endeavours to engage all ethically aware readers who are concerned about the human dimensions of global trade justice.

Having introduced the concept of Fair Trade, the discussion will now move on to explore the background to its phenomenal growth in recent years.

1

Fair Trade: The Story So Far

This chapter maps out the historical development of the international Fair Trade movement. The economic and social drivers behind the emergence of Fair Trade are then delineated and key objections to it explored. Fair Trade's aims and impacts are then outlined. The chapter concludes with a brief discussion of the likely future directions for Fair Trade.

Changing Lives

There's something about chocolate. It means different things to different people: a reward to yourself for a job well done, a thank you gift to a friend, a pick-me-up after a bad day. To cocoa farmers in Ghana, chocolate means their livelihood, and a future for their families. Farmers in Kumasi, Ghana, used to sell their cocoa to the government. They had little or no control over the price they received. Then in 1993, the Kuapa Kokoo Co-operative was formed. Today, it secures fair prices for over 60,000 members. Oxfam campaigns for farmers and manufacturers in poor communities to receive a fair price for the products they sell. Fair Trade organizations buy the cocoa at above market price. This extra money is given to farmers in the form of a bonus and some is spent on community projects.

Kuapa Kokoo means 'good cocoa farmers'. Their slogan 'Pa Pa Paa' means 'best of the best' – Kuapa Kokoo gives the best to its farmers and gets the best produce from its farmers. Kuapa Kokoo is owned by its members and is one of the few companies in Ghana that pays a yearly bonus. It also organizes meetings where farmers can take their own decisions without managerial intervention.

The farmers

I have been selling my cocoa crop to Kuapa Kokoo for two years now and things have improved for me already. Since Kuapa Kokoo gave the village its own scales, we have made more profit. When we sold our cocoa through the government, they weighed our sacks and told us what that weight was. We were often cheated. Having our own scales has made a huge difference to our income.

Susannah Gyamfinah, Fenaso Domeabra Village

I have my own cocoa farm and I rely on my children to help me harvest the cocoa. I have three children and two older children who are training to be seamstresses. They help me when they can because our family ties are strong.

Lucy Mansa

When the government was buying her cocoa, Lucy was rarely paid on time. As a result, she was unable to pay her children's school fees, and they went without an education. Now, through the Fair Trade bonus she gets from Kuapa Kokoo, she can send her children to school.

Source: Oxfam.org.uk

INTRODUCTION

Consumers clearly like Fair Trade – the Swiss spend an average of £6 ($10.74) per head per annum on Fair Trade products (Leatherhead Food International, 2003). Sales are growing fast worldwide, at a pace of 21 per cent in 2002 and to more than 40 per cent in 2003, for labelled Fair Trade products (FLO, 2003). The Fair Trade model is delivering significant developmental benefits to thousands of the poorest producers across the globe: the Fairtrade Labelling Organizations International (FLO) estimated that producers earned an additional $37m (£21m) in 2002 through sales of labelled Fair Trade products. However, why is Fair Trade necessary to begin with? In what ways has the market failed small-scale producers and farm workers?

As has already been suggested, there appears to be an inherent conflict between the current manifestation of 'free' global markets and Fair Trade (see further, Jenkins, 2002). Whilst this book will argue that the two are not, in fact, incompatible, the historical origins of the Fair Trade movement can still be seen in the negative consequences of the development of a distorted global market for trade.

Classical free trade theory has its origins in Adam Smith's and David Ricardo's theories of comparative advantage (see, for example, Krugman and Obstfeld, 1997). Under the theory of comparative advantage, countries export what they are relatively good at producing and they import what they cannot produce sufficiently. Mountainous Guatemala grows high-quality cloud-forest-grown coffee. Japan manufactures technologically advanced electronic products. Opening up countries to international trade allows Japanese electronics producers to import delicious coffee, and Guatemalan coffee farmers to access high-tech products. Under free trade, both parties are better off: international trade is thus a win-win situation in which everyone benefits.

Supporters of free trade insist that the unfettered movement of goods, services and finance between countries offers the most efficient model of transactional business. Inherent in this is the understanding that whilst some benefit, others will inevitably fail, but that this still works ultimately for the general good, weeding out the weak and inefficient.

Widespread attempts to liberalize world trade and to bring the benefits of free trade to all countries began after the Second World War. In a time of reconstruction and reconciliation, the General Agreement on Tariffs and Trade (GATT) – set up under the auspices of the newly formed United Nations in 1948 – endeavoured to arbitrate between international trade disputes via a series of 'rounds' of negotiations to promote free trade and international deregulation (Ransom, 2001). This loosening up of trade rules was accompanied by structural adjustment lending to developing countries by the International Monetary Fund and World Bank from 1960 to 1980, which was often tied to trade liberalization. During the 1980s, 42 countries received loans from the World Bank with the express purpose of reforming their trade régimes (Rodrik, 1992).

The volume of international trade has increased significantly over the last thirty years suggesting that GATT and its successor, the World Trade Organization (WTO), have had a considerable impact on generating free trade around the world (Rugman, 2002). Total trade in 2000 was 22 times the level in 1950 (Ransom, 2001). However, global inequality has also simultaneously grown – the share of the world's income distributed amongst the poorest 10 per cent fell by a quarter between 1988 and 1993, whilst the share going to the richest decile increased by 8 per cent (Dikhanov and Ward, 2001). By the late 1990s the poorest 20 per cent of the global population generated only 1 per cent of the global Gross Domestic Product, whilst the richest 20 per cent generated 86 per cent (Young and Welford, 2002).

Clearly, the benefits of increased free trade have not been evenly spread. In one aspect, this failure is macroeconomic. High levels of indebtedness caused countries to rely on export-intensive industries and to exploit resources in the short term, with minimal regard for long-term consequences. Colonial and development legacies have resulted in export earnings being highly concentrated in just a few, often primary commodity, industries, leaving countries' national incomes exposed to world price fluctuations (Timberlake, 1985). Furthermore, corruption in many developing countries can result in a failure to distribute export income equitably (Collier and Gunning, 1994).

But macroeconomics does not fully explain the failure of trade liberalization to distribute wealth evenly. The key conditions on which classical and neo-liberal trade theories are based are notably absent in rural agricultural societies in many developing countries. Perfect market information, perfect access to markets and credit, and the ability to switch production techniques and outputs in response to market information are fundamental assumptions which are fallacious in the context of agricultural producers and workers in many developing countries.

The absence of these microeconomic conditions can nullify or even reverse the potential gains to producers from trade. Whilst the theory of international trade as a win–win for all actors involved on a national level may be broadly correct, nevertheless, within developing countries market conditions are not such that producers can unambiguously be declared to be better off through trade. Agricultural producers in developing countries face several market imperfections that question the ability of trade to lift them out of poverty.

- *Lack of market access.* An export market free from importing-country interference through subsidies and tariffs may be considered 'free' and can function well for exporters, but if primary commodity producers cannot access these functioning markets, due to their remoteness and lack of transport, the benefits of this free market cannot be realized for them. To access markets, small-scale producers often rely on middlemen, who can collude to ensure that there is no competition for producers' goods and thus no fair market price for them (Rice and McLean, 1999).
- *Imperfect information.* A fundamental necessity for the functioning of any free market is 'perfect information', implying that producers and traders have access to knowledge about market prices. Remote producers with no access to radio, newspapers, or telephones cannot access information about prices, and are at the mercy of the middlemen who come to their often isolated farms.
- *Lack of access to financial markets.* Producers in developing countries have no access to income-smoothing devices like futures markets. A cocoa farmer living in a remote mountain village in Peru cannot call the London Coffee and Cocoa Exchange to lock in a set price for next year's harvest, because of communications difficulties and a lack of significant volume to trade. Peru's international cocoa exporters and the US's

chocolate ice cream companies can and do use futures markets to stabilize the cost of goods. Thus the cocoa farmer is left completely exposed to world price fluctuations, when a perfectly functioning futures market exists to protect him or her from these variations. Similarly, such a farmer has no access to insurance cover to protect his or her income from extreme weather conditions or political unrest.

- *Lack of access to credit.* Rural banks are either non-existent or do not lend in the small amounts that family farmers require. Thus, credit for farm machines and fertilizers is often available only through exploitative middlemen at extremely high rates of interest. Much as farmers are not able to access fair markets for their crops, they cannot access fair markets for credit.
- *Inability to switch to other sources of income generation.* In a perfectly functioning market, economic actors can switch easily from one income-generating activity to another in response to price information. This is clearly not the case for the world's poor. Even if isolated producers had access to price information, their ability to change their source of income is limited. The 1.2 billion people who live on less than $1 (£0.56) a day (IBRD, 2000) are extremely risk-averse. Switching from growing a crop that your grandfather grew to a higher-priced crop that no one in your village has ever grown before is an extremely risky activity. For families with no slack in their income and little by way of savings, risk-taking is not an option. A lack of access to credit or education about other income sources contributes to this inability to diversify income sources (Oxfam America and TransFair USA, 2002).
- *Weak legal systems and enforcement of laws.* Many developing countries have passed strict environmental and labour laws that are ignored by local authorities. Factory owners may bribe local officials to overlook pollution and labour violations. Countries that do enforce laws may see investments move to more lax régimes. Farmers with insecure land titles cannot use their land assets as collateral for loans to diversify into other areas of production, or to invest in technology improvements on their farms (deSoto, 2000).

Given these market imperfections, can the global trade system be made to work for everyone? Can the beauty of the win-win trade theory be made a reality? Fair Trade, in correcting the largest market failures in the global trading system, takes the theory much closer to reality. By providing a profitable relationship to all those in the supply chain – producers, exporters, importers, manufacturers, and retailers – Fair Trade is a sustainable, market-based solution to global trade failures. Consumers who choose to buy Fair Trade products can fulfil their desire to make the world a better place while still enjoying consumer goods. Somewhere between the anti-globalization protesters in Seattle and theories in economics textbooks lies a truly sustainable model for a trading system in which everyone benefits. Fair Trade represents such a model.

THE DEVELOPMENT OF FAIR TRADE

It seems as if somewhere about a year ago we stopped rolling this huge boulder up a hill and now it is going down hill. (Interview with Ian Bretman, 2001)

Historically, the commercial growth of the Fair Trade market can be seen as developing in four waves. In the first wave, the concept of Fair Trade began to take shape after the Second World War, when charities in Western Europe – most notably Oxfam – began to import handicrafts from producers in Eastern Europe to support their economic recovery. Simultaneously, the Mennonite Central Committee in the USA began to develop a market for embroidery from Puerto Rico by setting up the SelfHelp Crafts of the World organization that would later become known as Ten Thousand Villages.

In the second wave, alternative trading organizations (ATOs) like Traidcraft in Britain and Gepa in Germany emerged with the aim of offering producers the opportunity to trade with the developed world for the first time, without the control of middlemen who would inevitably squeeze prices at the beginning of the supply chain. Frequently, these ATOs had their basis in religious or other community-based organizations, working as 'social' entrepreneurs using a business mindset to address social problems (see further Bornstein, 2004; Leadbeater, 1997). During this period, Fair Trade products were sold mostly in catalogues and world shops.

The third wave of development involved naturally sympathetic retail businesses, such as the Co-operative Group in the UK and Wild Oats Markets in the USA, promoting Fair Trade products to a larger consumer base. ATOs launched more mainstream product categories and began to develop notable brands like Cafédirect and Divine Chocolate. The development of Fair Trade certification marks also helped bring the concept of Fair Trade in from the margins. Solidifying growth in the mainstream has characterized the fourth wave of Fair Trade development, as its success has encouraged the market entry of more traditional players, including Costa Coffee, Sainsbury's, Starbucks, and Sara Lee. Of particular importance here has been the emergence of supermarket own-label Fair Trade products, most notably in Tesco UK.

Over the past five years particularly there has been a huge increase in the market for Fair Trade products internationally. This has been driven by a number of different influences that can be grouped under four main headings: political, academic, cultural and informational (see Figure 1.1). Each driver is considered below. None of these influences has worked alone, but rather each has interacted with the others (and continues to do so) to create a general shift in opinion towards an understanding of the value of Fair Trade in the developed world. Perhaps the most significant influence has been the emergence of ethical consumerism and the mass-market associated with it, growing out of important cultural and informational changes in Western society (Nicholls, 2002).

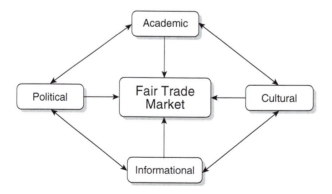

Figure 1.1   *Influences on the development of the UK Fair Trade market*
Source: Nicholls (2002)

CASE STUDY: A SHORT HISTORY OF OXFAM

During the Second World War, Greece was occupied by the Nazis. In 1941, the Allies imposed a naval blockade, and scarcely any food or medical supplies could get through, even to civilians. Famine quickly took hold. A national Famine Relief Committee was set up in the UK in May 1942 and support groups were formed throughout the country. They tried to persuade the British government to allow essential supplies through the blockade, and they raised funds for war refugees and displaced people across Europe. The Oxford Committee for Famine Relief (OX-FAM) met for the first time on 5 October 1942.

Many of the Relief Committees were wound down after the war, but the Oxford Committee saw a continuing need and enlarged its objectives to include 'the relief of suffering in consequence of the war'. Activity then centred on the provision of food parcels and clothing to Europe. From 1948 grants were made to projects in Europe and elsewhere and in 1949 the Committee's objectives were again broadened to 'the relief of suffering arising as a result of wars or of other causes in any part of the world'.

The 1960s brought great changes. Concern for the world's poor grew amongst the general public and the charity's income trebled over the course of the decade. The organization worked to present a different picture of poor people in the Third World: one in which they were portrayed as human beings with dignity, not as passive victims. Education and information materials explained the root causes of poverty and suffering, the connections between North and South, and the role of people in the North in creating, and potentially solving, poverty in the developing world.

Oxfam's overseas operations changed as well. The major focus of work, managed by a growing network of Oxfam field directors, became support for self-help schemes whereby communities improved their own water supplies, farming practices, and health provisions.

As Oxfam continued to expand its work throughout the 1970s, many new ideas and theories were put forward about development and poverty, including the decision to employ local people to oversee and work on projects. Oxfam's relief work in the Sahel in the late 1970s looked at the traditional ways by which communities existed – helping them to improve and refine their survival techniques, and making sure that local people kept control of the schemes they were involved in. The same principles of community involvement and control are still behind Oxfam's work today. In the 1970s it became clear that many of the problems associated with poverty required government and international action. Oxfam started – within the bounds set by charity law – to campaign on behalf of the people it worked with overseas and to talk to decision-makers who shaped policy on relevant issues.

Oxfam's network of shops run by volunteer groups around the country became one of the main sources of income in the late 1960s, selling donated items and handicrafts made by producers in villages where Oxfam ran development projects. Oxfam's shops are now a familiar sight on most high streets. Approximately 22,000 volunteers work in more than 830 Oxfam shops in the UK.

Oxfam Trading rapidly expanded its sales of fairly traded products during the 1970s and 1980s. A mail-order catalogue was also started, which boosted annual sales above £1 million ($1.8m) by the early 1980s. The program took the name 'Fair Trade' in 1996 (trading under the name 'Oxfam Fair Trade Company'), to bring it in line with the wider Fair Trade movement, which included campaigning for improvements in the terms of trade and conditions for workers.

Oxfam's largest ever response to a humanitarian disaster was in the Great Lakes region of Central Africa in the mid-1990s. But aid alone could not provide solutions to the political, economic and social problems of the region. In an effort to build a lasting peace, work on the ground was matched by international lobbying and campaigning aimed at the UN, the Organization of African Unity, and powerful governments worldwide.

During 1997 and 1998, Oxfam undertook a major review of the way it worked, its aims and how it fitted into the world around it. After assessing inefficiencies in its Fair Trade sourcing, Oxfam Fair Trade shifted from direct sourcing of Fair Trade products for its shops to buying from Fair Trade importers like Traidcraft, focusing efforts on helping producers to gain market access through development projects.

Thorough research, both within and outside Oxfam, helps the organization to focus on its core beliefs and to develop a strategy so that no matter how the world changes, it can respond and make a major impact on poverty and suffering. Whether donating, fundraising, campaigning, volunteering, or working 'on the ground' to implement project activities, Oxfam donors, supporters, staff, project partners, and participants are working together to overcome poverty and injustice.

Source: www.oxfam.org

Political Influence

The political context for alternative trade has changed significantly in the developed world during the past ten years (Murray and Raynolds, 2000). National and international campaigners and pressure groups, supported by charities and NGOs, have grown in power and membership with the result that the political climate for trade with developing countries is being redefined (Strong, 1996). There is a growing international consensus that 'trade not aid' is the best route to take in order to alleviate poverty in the developing world (see for example, Annan, 2001; Strong, 1996), as demonstrated by the United Nations Development Program's initiatives.

In the UK, the Ethical Trading Initiative, sponsored by the Department for International Development, has increased public awareness of ethical trading and encouraged British retailers to support Fair Trade products. This reflects a shift in values towards a greater concern for developing world issues (Strong, 1996). In addition there has been a new consensus emerging concerning the value of a 'stakeholder' approach to business transactions (Whysall, 2000a, 2000c). The stakeholder model emphasizes the importance of broadening the focus of a company's activities beyond immediate interest groups, such as customers and shareholders, to embrace employees, suppliers, the local community and even competitors.

Academic Influence

Paralleling the rise in consumer interest and demand, academic scholarship exploring Fair Trade has also extensively developed in recent times (Bird and Hughes, 1997; Gould, 2003; Moore, 2004; Murray and Raynolds, 2000; Nicholls, 2002, 2004; Nicholls and

Alexander, forthcoming; Raynolds, 2000, 2002a, 2002b; Renard, 1999, 2002; Strong, 1996, 1997; Tallontire, 2000, 2002; Whysall, 1998; Wright, 2004). This research field grew out of the debate concerning ethical business, in general, and green and environmental issues, in particular. There has been a shift from a concern about the sustainability of production and its environmental impact to an awareness of the social context of the process and trade justice. Fair Trade combines a discussion of global responsibility with business ethics in a framework centred on the individual worker's experience. The movement is from a consumer-focused discussion further down the supply chain to the producer: from 'us' to 'them'. The proliferation of business ethics courses and modules in UK academic institutions has supported the growth of ethical consumerism, as a new generation of senior managers, sensitive to the ethical business agenda, has increasingly influenced corporate behaviour (Bishop, 1992; Cowe, 2000; Sheridan, 2000).

Cultural and Informational Influence

The growth of ethical consumerism over the last thirty years provides the main driver behind the development of a Fair Trade market (Burke and Berry, 1974; Strong, 1997). A recent UK survey suggested that 65 per cent of consumers now judge themselves 'green or ethical consumers' (Guardian/ICM, 2004), although it should be acknowledged that there is often a discrepancy between what people say they will do and their actual behaviour. Nevertheless, according to the Co-operative Bank/NEF (2003), the UK ethical market was valued at £19.9b ($35.6bn) in 2002 with products specifically marketed as 'ethical' accounting for £6.9b ($12.4bn) (a 13 per cent growth on 2001). The result has contributed to a shift in consumer attitude to many brands. According to Clifton (2001), the key criteria for successful brands have changed significantly over the past thirty years. There has been a shift from pragmatic, price- and value-driven imperatives towards 'real values' – the bundle of meanings that suggest a brand is adopting a definable position in an understood moral or ethical framework (see Table 1.1).

This supports Fletcher (1990), who suggested that there has been a move away from the self-focused consumer of the 1970s and acquisitive consumer of the 1980s towards a new focus on values. As a subset of ethical trade, Fair Trade has also moved into the mainstream of modern consumerism. A survey for Oxfam in 1994 indicated that 81 per cent of consumers would buy products that were identified as giving a better deal to producers in developing countries. Furthermore, a MORI survey for the Fairtrade Foundation in 1999 showed that, once introduced to the concept behind Fair Trade, 68 per cent of consumers said that they would like to buy these products.

The main driver for this cultural shift has been the extraordinary rise in the volume of easily accessible information about global social issues, coinciding with the broadening of consumerism within all levels of society (Whysall, 2000b). This has come

Table 1.1 *Brand values 1970–2000*

Decade	Key criteria	Example
1970s	Low prices	Tesco
1980s	Higher added value	Armani
1990s	Real value	Asda
2000+	Real values	Body Shop

Source: Nicholls (2002)

about both as a result of increased media engagement with the broad subject (Strong, 1996), and also because of the growth in use of the Internet by interest groups to publish and disperse information about unethical corporate behaviour (Whysall, 2000b; see also for example, www. corporatewatch.org.uk; www.actionaid.org). The result is that the 'concerned' consumer now focuses on production and supply chain issues as well as the intrinsic properties of a product and the service package surrounding it. There has been a change in consumer attitude towards business ethics, largely driven by better information about the supply chain. The media and the Internet now regularly expose unethical business behaviour, and it is clear that such information damages the bottom line (Whysall, 1995).

Ethically sensitive consumers are no longer a small, if vocal, pressure group: rather, a third of the public now see themselves as 'strongly ethical' (Cowe and Williams, 2000). Furthermore, the main ethical issue of the 1980s – 'green' environmentalism – has now been broadened from a product focus into a more general concern over the entire production process, particularly highlighting the human/social element. Consumer focus has moved down the supply chain. The result of this increased consumer interest has been a dramatic rise in demand for Fair Trade products and an increased product range to satisfy this. The marketing and branding issues around Fair Trade are fully addressed in Chapter 7.

FAIR TRADE PRODUCT GROUPS

Until the 1990s, handicrafts and textiles dominated Fair Trade sales. Since 1991, however, food has taken over as the most important category in terms of sales volume and growth (this is discussed further in Chapter 8). This change is the result of a number of factors. Firstly, in contrast to many ATO-sold craft products, Fair Trade food positioned itself from the 1990s onwards as premium quality rather than ethically driven. Thus, it immediately appealed both to the multiple supermarkets and a broader customer base and could grow a new market quickly. Companies selling Fair Trade crafts and textiles (with the exception of People Tree, a Fair Trade clothing brand carried in Selfridge's department stores) did not reposition themselves to address new markets, preferring instead to consolidate their position with ATOs and world shops.

Secondly, the Fair Trade certification process is far better suited to commodity foods, such as coffee and tea, than to handicrafts or textiles. This is because the latter are far more diverse in terms of production techniques and specifications and it is, therefore, nearly impossible to devise and audit certification standards that can be broadly applied to them all (this issue is further addressed in Chapter 6). Consequently, crafts and textiles do not benefit from the marketing impact of a Fair Trade product logo. This reduces their appeal outside of their traditional ATO environment and limits their ability to differentiate themselves from other similar, but non-Fair Trade, products. This lack of brand value also undermines consumer trust in the Fair Trade element of their product proposition and diminishes customer purchase loyalty. Any attempt at premium price positioning also becomes more difficult.

The end result of the establishment of Fairtrade Labelling Organization International's (FLO) certification process has been – effectively – to isolate those producers whose products that do not qualify for certification from the various benefits offered by the mark, although most likely these producers do benefit from general consumer education about Fair Trade and the situation of the world's poorest producers. Many of these producer groups are members of the International Federation of Alternative Trade (IFAT). IFAT members recognize the value of a Fair Trade mark, although it is clear that any such logo applied to handicrafts would have to take the form of a brand rather than labelling statement, since product level auditing would be almost impossible. To this end, IFAT introduced a self-monitored Fair Trade Organization (FTO) mark in 2004 to recognize its members at an institutional, rather than a product, level. The future development of the relationship between a universal Fair Trade label and the full range of Fair Trade product categories is one of the most significant ongoing issues (this is returned to in some detail in Chapters 6 and 10).

In this book much of the focus will be on FLO-certified products and producers. However, it needs to be clearly stated at the outset that this is no reflection of the relative importance of FLO-certified products against non-certified categories. Rather, it reflects the simple fact that reliable figures, analysis and scholarly work are much more readily available for the former group than the latter. Nevertheless, non-certified product issues are included in the general discussion wherever appropriate.

FAIR TRADE OBJECTIVES

Fair Trade has three interlinked aims: to alleviate extreme poverty through trade; to empower smallholder farmers and farm workers to use trade relationships as a means of enhancing their social capital; and to support the wider campaign for global trade reform and trade justice. Crucially, Fair Trade addresses these objectives through a market-driven commercial model, rather than by charity or a developmental aid mechanism. This approach is ultimately more sustainable and empowers producers to develop livelihoods that avoid dependency.

In the case of the first aim, the progress of Fair Trade has been startling over the last ten years as sales have soared, more producers have registered, and markets have widened. The rapid growth in Northern markets of Fair Trade has transferred millions of dollars to disenfranchised producers in the developing world – Cafédirect alone returned £2.8m ($5m) in additional income to its coffee suppliers in 2003. One Costa Rican coffee producer explained that Fair Trade 'was like a revolution. Before, this house was not ours, now it is' (Ronchi, 2002). At the Korakundah tea garden in India, workers have used Fair Trade premia to establish a pension fund for retired tea pickers. As one tea picker from the garden testified, 'the difference the pension fund has made is like a blind man gaining sight'. The growth of Fair Trade and its impact on poverty reduction are discussed further in Chapters 8 and 9.

In terms of the second aim, the impact of Fair Trade premia and other, related, support and developmental work with producers has also generated significant benefits. The strengthening of farmer and farm worker organizations and their use of Fair Trade income to invest in community development projects can have even more impact than increasing individual's incomes. Organizations such as Traidcraft Exchange or the Day Chocolate Company have brought producers from the South onto a more equal footing with Northern businesses and markets. Such work has also produced powerfully positive social and economic externalities in terms of improved negotiating skills and community building. These externalities are explored further in Chapter 9.

In the case of the third aim, much has also been achieved. Fair Trade began as a campaigning issue driven by activists and maintains a powerful international network of lobbyists. In common with many such movements, Fair Trade has been highly inventive in promoting its message (the result of very limited marketing resources). Initiatives like Fair Trade Fortnight in Britain or the Fair Trade Towns campaign across Europe have been enormously successful in raising consumer awareness and also increasing sales. Fair Trade is now taught in school and university curricula, written about in academic and commercial media, and discussed at conferences and fora around the world. Similarly, populist campaigns such as Oxfam's 'Make Trade Fair' initiative are generating powerful grassroots action that is also media-friendly.

The growing political impact of Fair Trade groups such as the Fairtrade Foundation or IFAT is clear at both a national and international level. The symposium on Fair Trade that formed part of the 2004 UN Conference on Trade and Development (UNCTAD) meeting in São Paulo was an encouraging example of this. Fair Trade symposium topics included the social, environmental and economic impacts of Fair Trade; policy initiatives to expand Fair Trade; domestic Fair Trade; and solutions to the commodity crisis. Nearly 200 people attended the morning policy session, including many government officials. A highlight of the afternoon was the participation of the Brazilian Minister for Agrarian Development, Miguel Rossetto.

This event generated the São Paulo Fair Trade Declaration that actively challenged UNCTAD to support the management of world commodity markets and foster greater trade price stability and fairness (see case study, below). The declaration was signed by more than 90 Fair Trade organizations from 30 countries, was entered into the UNCTAD record, and was also hand-delivered to UN Secretary General Kofi Annan.

However, although Fair Trade is clearly driving change in many commercial supply chains and raising public awareness levels of the importance of trade justice, its measurable impact at a political level is less clear. Whilst sympathetic governments may endorse Fair Trade, there is limited evidence that it is forcing its way onto their policy agendas or driving institutional change. For example, whilst European Union trade tariffs on cocoa beans are set at zero, they are still 9.6 per cent in the case of cocoa butter or paste, and it is the latter that delivers the majority of the margin on the original commodity itself. Cocoa producers are thus penalized when they attempt to gain access to the main return from their crop. Therefore, it is clear that there will need to be a continued focus on the political aspect of Fair Trade – as well as its commercial objectives – if it is to play a part as an effective catalyst for change in global trade regulations. This issue is returned to in the final chapter of this book.

CASE STUDY: FAIR TRADE DECLARATION – UNCTAD XI, SÃO PAULO

It is often stated that trade has the potential to positively contribute to poverty alleviation, to sustainable development and to achieving the Millennium Development Goals. Experience has shown, however, that if not carried out in a fair and responsible manner, trade can, in fact, exacerbate poverty and inequality, undermine sustainable development and food security, and negatively impact local cultures and vital natural resources. Trade should not be seen as an end in itself but as a means to sustainable development.

We, members of the international Fair Trade movement and our allies, believe that in order to overcome the structural inequalities in international trade and finance policies, UNCTAD must reinforce its position as a UN agency, independent of the Bretton Woods Institutions. Its central focus should be the evaluation and promotion of policies to ensure that trade does, in practice, lead to sustainable development. UNCTAD should not be transformed into a technical assistance agency, existing merely to assist developing countries promote foreign investment and fulfil their commitments to the WTO and to other international financial institutions.

On the occasion of the UNCTAD XI Conference in São Paulo Brazil, we offer concrete proposals to UNCTAD member governments and other international organizations. The implementation of these proposals would contribute greatly to the promotion of a global trading system that truly works for poverty reduction and sustainable development.

Introducing Fair Trade

For more than forty years, the Fair Trade movement has demonstrated that trade can make a sustainable and significant contribution to improving the lives of producers and workers whilst protecting natural resources and the environment. From modest beginnings we have developed into a global network, bringing together several hundreds of thousands of small-scale producers and workers on plantations and in factories, thousands of trading and retail companies, NGOs and labelling organizations into an organized trading system reaching tens of millions of consumers.

Fair Trade is a trading partnership based on dialogue, transparency and respect, that seeks greater equity in international trade. It contributes to sustainable development by offering better trading conditions to, and securing the rights of, marginalized producers and workers – especially in the South. Fair Trade organizations (backed by consumers) are engaged actively in supporting producers, raising awareness and in campaigning for changes in the rules and practice of conventional international trade.

At present, the vast majority of businesses do not internalize the costs of their social and environmental impacts. By contrast, the Fair Trade movement believes that in order for trade to be sustainable, and not to distort markets, the full social, environmental and economic costs of goods and services must be taken into account. Whilst many governments and international bodies quote the rhetoric of sustainability, Fair Trade organizations have the experience of how to make this a reality.

Millions of people in 48 countries of Latin America, Africa and Asia benefit from Fair Trade relationships. In 2002, worldwide sales of Fair Trade products were estimated at over US$400 million [£224 million] and the market is growing rapidly. International sales grew in 2003 by an average of 43 per cent, including 61 per cent growth in the UK, 81 per cent in France and 400 per cent in Italy. In the USA, sales of Fairtrade certified coffee grew 93 per cent in 2003.

Producers, consumers and businesses are key to the success of Fair Trade, but governments and international institutions also have a critical role to play. True progress requires that the promotion of Fair Trade is carried out hand in hand with efforts to overcome structural inequalities in international trade and finance policies. Recognition of the right to food sovereignty, improved market access with remunerative prices for small producers, stable commodity prices, strengthening of regional agricultural zones as well as overcoming the debt and financial crises are some of the burning issues which need to be addressed.

Fair Trade demands to UNCTAD

1. Fair Trade producers, organizations and businesses have first-hand experience of the impact of the crash in commodity prices and have been in the forefront of providing solutions through technical support and a fair price to producers. Fair Trade is based upon principles of participation, fairness and equity in each daily transaction. In order to help overcome the structural inequities in the international trading system, we call on UNCTAD member governments to:

   • Reassert UNCTAD's role and leadership in the creation and management of multilateral mechanisms which will regulate world commodity markets, and foster greater stability and fair prices for farmers who make up more than half the world's population.
   • Promote the right of all countries, especially poorer countries, to promote food sovereignty and to protect and support vulnerable or emerging producer groups and economic sectors.
   • Promote South-South co-operation, especially in the area of information technology and biotechnology in order to bridge the information and technology divide.
   • Ensure that civil society organizations and producer groups are fully involved in the establishment and implementation of such mechanisms.

2. As a movement concerned with supporting marginalized producers and workers in the South, we call on UNCTAD member governments to:

   • Conduct research on the impact of mainstream trade (trade policy and corporate activity) and on the impact of Fair Trade on poor and marginalized groups in the South.
   • Address the impact of regional and bilateral trade agreements on small producers and on poor and marginalized groups in developing countries.
   • Strengthen the participation of small and medium sized enterprises in the policy-making process by providing capacity-building assistance and bolstering regional coalitions and partnerships.
   • Support the creation of small-scale producer credit and loan guarantee programs, along with business support services for producer organizations.

3. Given Fair Trade's proven track record of using trade as a tool to promote sustainable and equitable development we call on UNCTAD member governments to take into account the experience and lessons of Fair Trade in the following ways:

- Design programs to integrate Fair Trade into ongoing UNCTAD activities that seek to increase producer access to certification programs, information, technical assistance and Fair Trade markets in the North.
- Raise awareness among its members, both in the North and South, about the economic development and market opportunities that Fair Trade provides.
- Encourage and develop partnerships with the private sector, civil society and producer groups which encourage ethical sourcing practices and Fair Trade consumer education.
- Recognize the Fair Trade movement's definition of Fair Trade.
- Implement and promote Fair Trade and other ethical purchasing programs in UNCTAD offices and among member governments and other UN agencies.

Source: http://www.forumsociedadecivil.org.br/dspMostraBiblioteca2.asp?idBib=19

FAIR TRADE IMPACTS

Despite strong and growing consumer and producer support for Fair Trade, there remains the objection that the impact of this new trade model at a producer level is marginal at best, non-existent at worst. Whilst it is certainly true that reliable impact metrics in social accounting are still under development, it is also clear that the direct influence of Fair Trade has transformed many producers' lives. TransFair USA, for instance, estimates that in five years of activity in the USA, Fair Trade has returned over $30m (£16.8m) to coffee farmers in developing countries above that which they would have received in the conventional market (TransFair, 2004). However, the impact of the Fair Trade model goes beyond merely offering a fair price to producers, often encompassing important externalities and community benefits. The issue of Fair Trade social metrics will be further considered in Chapter 9.

Nevertheless, two further objections to Fair Trade are often raised. The first criticism is that the proportion of the final selling price of a Fair Trade product returned to the producer is actually very small. Whilst it is true that a typical Fair Trade chocolate bar only returns about 4 per cent of its final price to the producer, this can be twice as much as would conventionally go back down the supply chain. The fault that this return seems so small does not lie with the Fair Trade model, but rather reflects the typical supermarket product value chain where the initial commodity price represents only a small part of the total value-added of the final product. Multiple margins (producer/importer/wholesaler/processor/retailer and so on) ensure that input prices will always constitute the smallest part of the finished cost. What is more important to understand, therefore, is that the $1.26 (£0.71) per pound offered to Fair Trade coffee growers will typically be double what they would have received in the market. Whilst at a unit level this difference may seem marginal, at the aggregate level of a shipment it is very significant, particularly when it makes the difference between a sustainable and unsustainable livelihood for the producer. The composition of the Fair Trade value chain is discussed in greater detail in Chapter 4.

The second objection often levelled at Fair Trade impact is the suggestion that a more effective way of helping the poorest producers is through targeted developmental aid rather than trade. It is clearly the case that, according to the majority of aid charities, the bulk of each pound or dollar donated to them goes towards development projects. Indeed, it is not uncommon for this figure to be 80 to 90 per cent of each donation. In this simple sense, it is indisputable that £1 given to a development charity generates more immediate revenue for relieving poverty than £1 spent on a Fair Trade product. However, history suggests that this difference is not always reflected in impact. Unfortunately, whilst international aid, the main alternative to Fair Trade, can address sudden crises effectively, it often fails to offer a developmental path for the poor out of poverty and dependence on outside support (see Barrientos, 2000 and Johnston, 2002, for a discussion of the relationship between trade and development). Despite the good intentions of many aid agencies, the significant sums spent in poverty alleviation over the years often seem to have had little long-term effect. As Sutcliffe noted with respect to Belize

> While the Toledan [Fair Trade cocoa] farmers are hard to pin down on the relative fairness of different forms of trade, when it comes to aid, they have very clear opinions. Caytano Ico, secretary of the Toledo Cacao Growers Association, voices a typical opinion when he states, 'Aid is big business. There are over forty aid agencies in Toledo. But $25m (£14m) has been spent here in the past twenty years and it has had no effect. (Interview, 2004)

Because Fair Trade guarantees that a specific amount of money reaches the commodity producer, the impact can be much more direct. Again, Sutcliffe summed this up

> By comparison with the merry-go-round of international aid, the money from Fair Trade food passes through remarkably few hands on its way from your pocket to the pocket of a poor farmer. (Interview, 2004)

Consequently, it is increasingly felt that trade rather than aid is the best way to change long-term patterns of poverty (Annan, 2001). Because Fair Trade offers development through trade that is sustainable and market driven, but which works in partnership with producers, it represents a more effective mechanism for alleviating poverty than aid or macro-institutional economic intervention. It is also more attractive to producers as it preserves the dignity of their labour and helps raise their standing as international traders. Furthermore, because of its developmental focus, Fair Trade generates significant social as well as economic capital in producer communities (see Putnam, 2000, for a detailed discussion of the value of social capital). In addition, Fair Trade's active campaigning also addresses positive structural change in trade markets. As Carol Wills, Executive Director of IFAT, commented

> The focus of our Fair Trade advocacy program is helping producers understand the issues … organizing ourselves so that groups of people in Africa or other parts of the world globally can seriously prepare documents presenting a Fair Trade position on issues around agriculture or whatever it might be, because it is about trying to change the world trading system so that it is fairer. A truly free trading system might be to everyone's advantage, but at the moment it's not free and it's very much not fair, so we work together to help develop our understanding, build capacity, develop the positions, and then deliver the messages at the EU, at the World Trade Organization, at UNCTAD. (Interview, 2004)

Such positive externalities are a major additional benefit to the basic Fair Trade price guarantee and help ensure that the impact of Fair Trade goes far beyond the purely commercial.

CONCLUSION

Arising out of the perceived failure of liberalized international trade to bring benefits to the most disenfranchized producers in developing countries, Fair Trade is rapidly becoming the consumer standard for social responsibility in the sourcing of agricultural commodity products. Because Fair Trade is entirely a consumer choice model, it operates within the larger free trade model of unregulated international commerce. Fair Trade is not controlled or enforced by any government agency; rather it can be seen as just another product feature, like colour or size, albeit a very powerful one. Economists shy away from floor prices, but if consumers are willing to pay more for the Fair Trade guarantee of giving farmers a higher price, it is clearly their right to do so. Fair Trade actually increases the options and choices available to consumers, one of the key benefits of capitalistic systems. Steve Sellers, Chief Operating Officer for TransFair USA, described the Fair Trade model:

> It's very American – we're about money, and about the capitalist system and about freedom of choice, and we are saying, by God make your choice, just make an informed choice. Understand what's going on and then make a choice. Understand what's going on, open yourself to the notion of conscience, and then make a choice. (Interview, 2003)

Fair Trade also makes the free trade system work the way it is supposed to. By providing farmers with access to credit and information, it corrects market imperfections. As with any market, the more knowledgeable one's trading partner, the more they are likely to gain by negotiation. Transferring market knowledge to producers in developing countries will inevitably make them better off. So there are some losers in Fair Trade, namely brokers and middlemen, who had been relying on one-sided information flow and exploitation of farmers. But on balance, all actors within a free trade system should benefit from the increases in transparency, efficiency, and competitiveness that come from Fair Trade's expansion of the market power and knowledge base of primary producers.

The growing consumer demand for Fair Trade-labelled products has caught the eye of European supermarket chains hoping to position themselves as socially responsible corporate citizens. As a result, Fair Trade food market growth has been exponential, and new products are in line for certification each year. Indeed, Fair Trade has become part of the business plans of many importers, manufacturers, and retailers throughout Europe and North America. However, there still remain significant issues for non-certified handicrafts and Fair Trade textile producers. These artisans do not currently benefit from FLO labelling and have seen their market growth slow. Chapter 10 considers some future options for this important group.

This chapter has set out the case for Fair Trade. It has explained how Fair Trade differs from conventional models of international trade and why it is necessary. The history and development of the movement have been delineated and its objectives and impacts outlined. The next chapter explores the economic context for Fair Trade in more detail and considers some of the objections raised against it by the conventions of neo-liberal thinking.

2

The Economics of Fair Trade

Fair Trade is a development tool that uses existing capitalist supply chains to return more income to producers. It does this through improving free-market mechanisms as well as through non-market measures such as price floors. This chapter will outline the developing country market failures that Fair Trade attempts to address, and explain how Fair Trade pricing works within Fair Trade supply chains. It then outlines some positive externalities of Fair Trade that may not be measured through typical economic analysis, and examines whether or not Fair Trade represents an efficient transfer of wealth to impoverished producers.

INTRODUCTION

Poverty, environmental degradation, and rural-urban migration in developing countries are manifestations of problems with the global trade system. As Oxfam rightly points out, many of the developing nations' problems with agricultural exports are due to distorted markets in the USA and Europe, for instance in cotton, rice and sugar. Governments in the global North impose discriminatory tariffs which encourage developing countries to export primary commodities, by taxing such value-added processes as tea drying, cocoa bean processing and spice processing (Oxfam, 2002). But for such commodities as coffee, cocoa and tropical fruits, which for the most part do not grow in rich Northern climates, there must be other factors at work.

One of these factors is the improper functioning of the free market, which Fair Trade directly addresses. Many of the benefits associated with free market economics are best achieved in a free market environment. But, as introduced in Chapter 1, agricultural producers in developing countries rarely find themselves in a functioning free market. Several basic requirements for the operation of a free market are not met in rural areas of developing countries. Two of the basic principles of Fair Trade, direct trade with producers and the Fair Trade floor price, address these market failures very effectively.

This chapter will outline how Fair Trade corrects market failures by improving market access as well as information and credit flows. But while Fair Trade functions within the free market system, it is important to acknowledge that Fair Trade is specifically a development tool used to improve the lives and income of those people in developing countries who are involved in international trade. A critique of those aspects of Fair Trade that run contrary to the free market is thus included.

This chapter will also look at some of the external benefits of Fair Trade that do not necessarily enter monetary benefit calculations, yet contribute to better functioning of the market. The leadership development and empowerment of farm workers and smallholder farmers fostered by Fair Trade can improve the quality of democratic institutions and the functionality of the market itself. These external benefits will be further delineated in Chapter 9, which examines the impacts of Fair Trade on producers in developing countries.

MAKING MARKETS WORK

As introduced in Chapter 1, the basic principles of Fair Trade include (Barratt Brown, 1993):

- Direct purchasing from producers.
- Transparent and long-term trading partnerships.
- Agreed minimum prices.
- Focus on development and technical assistance via the payment to suppliers of an agreed social premium.

Within these four principles, direct trade and long-term trading relationships can improve the functioning of the export market for producers in developing countries, while the minimum price guarantee and payment of the social premium are more development-oriented mechanisms for improving the lives of farmers and farm workers. We shall examine each principle of Fair Trade and how it interacts with market forces in turn.

FAIR TRADE PRINCIPLE ONE:
DIRECT TRADE WITH PRODUCERS

One of the most important benefits of the Fair Trade model has nothing to do with the price floor and is thus perfectly compatible with a free market system: the requirement to work directly with producers, whether they are farming co-operatives, plantations, or small-scale craft manufacturers. Fair Trade importers must, wherever possible, buy directly from a farming co-operative, a farming estate, or local producer group. While estates, plantations, and large-scale craft and textile manufacturers have historically enjoyed access to export markets, small-scale producers are typically isolated from direct export access unless organized into co-operatives or similar group-selling structures.

The organization of small-scale producers into co-operatives or larger trading groups addresses several of the market failures outlined in Chapter 1. Simply improving the trading standards already increases producer income, by allowing them to capture more of the prevailing market price, even if they are unable to sell at the higher Fair Trade price. The major microeconomic market failures and how the Fair Trade requirement to work with co-operatives may address these are outlined in the following sections.

Lack of Access to Markets

Farmers in developing countries often live in isolated rural areas with few or no roads, and, with incomes generally well below £700 ($1,253) per year, do not own trucks or mules to take their product to the market. They are thus reliant on middlemen to come to their farms and buy their product. This link in the supply chain is the most exploitative, as competition by buyers is rarely achieved and, thus, farmers receive only one price offer. Middlemen (called *coyotes* in Central America; the word is also reserved for the middlemen who arrange transport for illegal labourers into the USA) will agree not to compete with each other on price, so that only one middleman comes to the farm gate to offer a price for the farmer's crop (see, for example, Nelson and Galvez, 2000).

Under a co-operative structure, farmer members own shares in an umbrella business organization, with equity ownership usually proportional to the amount of product they sell through the co-operative. This co-operative can pool farmer resources to own or rent a truck, which is used to travel to members' farms to collect product. Because the co-operative is owned by the farmers themselves and all co-operative profits are shared democratically according to the wishes of the farmer members, there is no incentive for this market access component to be exploitative. Co-operative membership allows small farmers to benefit from group selling and purchasing. Historically, only large estate own-ers and export companies who consolidated products from *coyotes* realized such benefits.

It should be noted that Mendoza and Bastiaensen (2003) found the *coyote* method of product consolidation and commercialization to be more efficient than a co-operative structure with its expensive bureaucracy. While it is true that *coyotes* may be more efficient at taking product to an export market than top-heavy co-operatives, this efficiency only transfers to higher prices for farmers if there is competition at the buying level. Because *coyotes* form buying cartels and effectively isolate suppliers from buyers, farmers do not benefit from competition for their product (they are subject to a 'monopsony' situation, with only one buyer). Thus, the intermediaries experience competition when selling their collected product to exporters, but the efficiencies are not necessarily passed back to the primary commodity producer.

For many Southern craft and textile producers there were simply no supply chain structures historically in place through which to reach Northern markets. Consequently, Northern alternative trading organizations (ATOs) have typically helped build such orga-nizations by encouraging producers to collaborate as trading groups, as well as support-ing non-governmental organizations (NGOs) that have grown up in local markets to help impoverished artisans and craftsmen bring their goods to market. Such producer-driven wholesalers typically share a strong sense of mission with Northern Fair Trade organizations. The usual point of market entry for craft products is via the large network of world shops found in Europe and, to a lesser extent, the USA.

Producers Lack Information About Prices

One of the assumptions of a perfectly functioning market is that participants have 'perfect information' regarding market prices. Coffee, for instance, is traded on public exchanges in London and New York. The prices set by world supply and demand through these exchanges are published daily in every major newspaper and in real-time on the Internet. Farmers with access to this information can adjust production and stocks accordingly.

But farmers in remote locations without access to telephones, radio news, newspapers, or the Internet cannot possibly know these up-to-date prices. They are reliant on the *coyotes* who visit them at the farm for market information. In the same way that these *coyotes* collude to prevent competition for farmers' supplies, price information is typically limited to the one middleman who visits the farm.

Once organized into a co-operative, however, farmers can pool their income to pur-chase a phone, fax, and Internet service to ensure access to current price information. Co-operatives can offer storage facilities and warehouse shelf-stable product during low-priced markets to protect themselves from market fluctuation, benefiting their farmer members by using information about future prices to control when they sell.

The power differential that exists between small farmers and traders can often be easily addressed through farmer organization and pooling of resources. Information disequilibria can be corrected by very small investment, as is shown in the case of cocoa traded in West Africa. In Ghana, the government is the sole exporter of cocoa beans but buys product from middlemen who consolidate beans grown by small family cocoa farmers. These middlemen visit remote farms and bring scales with which to weigh the farmers' beans. With no capital to invest in their own scales, villagers are at the mercy of middlemen with rigged scales. Kuapa Kokoo, a cocoa farming co-operative in Ghana, used co-op funds to purchase scales for villagers to check the middlemen's calculations (Carslaw, 2002). A village-level investment of £100 ($179) for scales thus protected the farmer members from this exploitative practice and they are now enjoying a larger income from middlemen. Their ability to purchase accurate technology and the price information gained through the co-operative's actions have improved their bargaining position considerably.

Producers Lack Information About Quality and Industry Requirements

The concept of perfect information applies to other elements of a business transaction besides price. Quality requirements and general industry knowledge are other important factors that change the value of a particular crop. However, small farmers with little direct market feedback or experience may not be able to capture such knowledge. If acting on their own, small farmers cannot interact directly with customers in the North to get feedback regarding quality and business capacity requirements. Language barriers are an obvious way that small farmers can fail to reach potential clients. By joining a large export co-operative, small farmers can pool resources to hire, for instance, an English- or German-speaking sales manager to better market their products.

An excellent example of how increasingly 'perfect' information can improve the bargaining position of small farmers is demonstrated through how Fair Trade coffee farmers interact with US importers. The Cecocafen Coffee Co-operative in Matagalpa, Nicaragua, has constructed a tasting (or 'cupping') laboratory and has trained 'cuppers' in the art of coffee quality testing. The co-operative can now send samples to US and European coffee importers with a description of the bean characteristics and have an informed discussion with buyers to receive feedback concerning quality and post-harvest techniques.

Co-operatives also pool resources to visit clients in consuming countries, develop sales relationships and learn more about the industry they supply. In May 2003, 96 coffee producers from 14 countries and 29 Fair Trade certified co-operatives participated in the Specialty Coffee Association of America's annual trade show in Boston, meeting with potential clients and attending industry educational events. The *Seattle Times* reported in June 2003 that small-scale coffee farmers from the Cepco Co-operative in Mexico visited the Starbucks headquarters to learn more about coffee quality assessment. The article quotes Jaime Hernandez, Cepco's Trade and Sales Manager: 'It is very interesting to be able to share and to see firsthand what an American (coffee) company is looking for' (in Batsell, 2003: C1). Co-operative structures and direct trade allow small-scale low-income farmers to deal directly with large traders in the North to address information imbalances in the trading system.

In a similar way, craft producers are increasingly looking to improve the quality of the information flows between themselves and their consumers to develop more effective marketing strategies. For example, the Asia Fair Trade Centre of Excellence was founded to act as a resource in helping to target new product development more efficiently. By drawing out consultancy expertise from successful Fair Trade organizations the Centre helps to spread best practice amongst smaller groups. In addition, it has supported a Fair Trade craft presence at the Bangkok International Gift Fair – a major international industry event – to connect small-scale producers and large Northern buyers. The latter has proved to be a qualified success over several years.

Producers Lack Access to Financial Markets

Many commodity exchanges also trade futures and options, contracts that involve trading a commodity at a later date for a price fixed today. Farmers benefit from locking in to a specific selling price for their crops at a future date (or an option to sell at a given price), because this makes their income predictable. If the market swings below the set future price, the farmer is guaranteed the future price. If the market rises above the future price, the farmer must sell at the fixed future price and does not benefit from the upswing in the market. With an option, a farmer could choose whether or not to sell his crop at the set price; if the market were to swing up, he would prefer to sell at the going market rate and thus would choose not to exercise his option.

Accessing these income-smoothing market solutions is virtually impossible for small farmers. Futures contracts are for large amounts of product, several times more than small farmers' annual output. While a typical subsistence cocoa farm may yield only a half ton per annum, futures contracts in cocoa beans on the London International Financial Futures and Options Exchange and the New York Board of Trade are in units of 10 metric tons (International Trade Centre, 2001). Trust among parties on the exchanges is built through relationships and exchange memberships, involving registration with the exchange and often audits – something that is not possible for a small-scale farmer, but is easily done by an export co-operative. Pooling production through a co-operative thus allows all farmer members to benefit from these financial markets and reduces their exposure to risk from price fluctuations. The issue of financial market access for Fair Trade is discussed in detail in Chapter 5.

Credit Markets Are Not Competitive

In a well-functioning market, actors can use loans to smooth income flows. A farmer can borrow money during the planting season for seeds and fertilizer, and pay the lender back, with interest, after he or she has sold the crop.

For many farmers in developing countries, the problem is not access to credit but rather a lack of competition in credit markets. Many small farmers rely on financing from the *coyote*, who might contract out a farmer's crop for next season. As this is the same uncompetitive *coyote* situation explained earlier, there are no competing finance offers, and financing rates can be as high as 100 per cent per annum (Bacon, 2004; Zárate (interview), 2003). Nelson and Galvez (2000) describe how these informal credit markets are biased against small farmers in rural Ecuador. Here, farmers buy goods that they need *al fiado* – on faith, or on credit – and are often expected to repay by selling their cocoa beans for a lower-than-market price. But whilst a formal credit system involves explicit interest rates and repayment schemes, the *al fiado* system is based on a social arrangement in which farmers are often exploited and a relationship of dependency is established. As the authors explain, '[i]n many cases, this mechanism means that farmers remain in a state of continued indebtedness which places the trader in a position to sell products and buy cocoa under increasingly favourable conditions' (p. 14). Large co-operatives can access competitive bids for formal loans and spread the benefits to their farmer members.

Unfortunately, even competitive bids for loans can sometimes be exorbitantly high in developing countries without properly functioning capital markets. The Fair Trade requirements recognize credit as a central issue for farmers with seasonal crops (especially coffee) who could benefit from loans out of the harvest season. As a result, one of the key Fair Trade standards for such seasonal crops is that the importer must provide up to 60 per cent of the contract amount if asked by the co-operative. However, anecdotal evidence suggests that sometimes co-operative leaders are afraid to ask Fair Trade importers for credit for fear that the buyer will go to a less-demanding co-operative and they will lose the sale. Chapter 5 will examine further the issue of producer access to credit.

Producers Cannot Easily Respond to Market Forces

A final element crucial to the proper functioning of a market is the ability of a market actor to change behaviour in the face of market forces. A Nebraskan soyabean farmer who sees that the price she can get for organic soyabeans is twice the price she is getting for her conventional beans can choose to start organic production. There are, of course, switching costs – she will have to learn how to farm organically and pay for organic certification. But if the price incentive is great enough, an average-income farmer in the North can choose to change production in the face of price and market information. She has access to credit to invest in a new crop, government and industry programmes that teach her how to convert to organic production, and a social safety net in case the experiment fails.

Now consider the case of organic cocoa beans. Since 2000, they have consistently traded at a 20 per cent premium to conventional cocoa beans. This should represent a reasonable incentive to a cocoa farmer to convert to organic production, as cocoa is not a particularly fertilizer- or pesticide-intensive crop. But for a cocoa bean farmer in West Africa whose family has been using artificial fertilizer for forty years, the costs and risks of switching to a higher-priced crop are daunting. New crops require an investment in seeds, technology and know-how that subsistence farmers can ill afford.

Even if the switching costs are low, poor producers can often be risk-averse, meaning that they avoid risk even if the potential rewards are extremely high. If a farmer is barely able to provide for his family's basic needs of food, clothing, and housing, he is going to be highly reluctant to switch to another income source with no proof of success. Farming non-organic cocoa beans may not have pulled his family out of poverty, but it may have always provided enough income for basic survival. But what if he were to stop using fertilizers, in order to gain organic certification, and his crop failed? His children might starve. The farmer is therefore extremely risk-averse: the threat of a possible large loss of income outweighs any potential benefits. This risk aversion hampers the functioning of the free market by reducing the ability of actors to change behaviour in the face of market signals. The organic certification decision is a parallel for crop-switching decisions faced by farmers all over the developing world; sugar farmers deciding whether to plant soya; coffee farmers deciding whether to plant cocoa and so on.

Risk aversion is, thus, a poverty problem. The main way that Fair Trade directly addresses this more subtle issue is through the guarantee of above-market prices which raise the income of producers. As farmers get higher incomes, they have more room to manoeuvre and might consider trying out new income-generating activities. Improved market information can also build producer confidence.

Yet an interesting indirect benefit of Fair Trade is the increase in knowledge transfer and the demonstration effect as a result of the required organization of poor workers and producers. The Fair Trade standards demand that small farmers be organized into co-operatives, and workers form representative bodies, in order to distribute the Fair Trade premia. This increased organization results in faster and more codified – often documented – knowledge transfer. Representatives of central co-operative organizations visit several villages with member co-operatives and are exposed to successful projects that they can then share with other co-operative members through formalized communication channels. Farm workers can pool their Fair Trade resources and start new joint business ventures, spreading the risk of failure amongst several members. An example of income diversification at a Fair Trade co-operative is illustrated in the case study below.

CASE STUDY: INCOME DIVERSIFICATION AT LA TRINIDAD

La Trinidad is a second-tier coffee export co-operative in Oaxaca, Mexico, owned by three smaller first-tier coffee co-ops, which sell their coffee to La Trinidad to export. With help from the Oaxacan NGO Fomcafé, La Trinidad has improved the quality of its production and recently started exporting 100 per cent of its members' coffee production on Fair Trade terms, allowing the 250 farmer members to earn roughly three times as much as they would have from local middlemen.

Because the co-operative recognizes the value of income diversification to reduce reliance on the coffee market, its members have voted to invest their Fair Trade premia in several different income-generation projects. One first-tier co-op in the village of Xanica opened a grocery store that earns them significant income and has the further benefit that now villagers do not have to walk two hours to the nearest store. The co-operative has set up a basic sugar mill and several beehives, using investment funds from the co-operative. The women's committee has organized a ceramics studio to produce tortilla plates. Some products will be sold locally in Xanica village, others in larger Mexican markets, and some abroad.

Coffee-farming village, Oaxaca, Mexico

La Trinidad earns enough through Fair Trade coffee sales to cover the costs of production and living, thus members are able to invest in projects that diversify their income stream so that they are not wholly dependent on coffee sales. Having several income streams and enough income to cover their basic needs makes the members of La Trinidad much more able to change production patterns in the face of market signals.

Source: Interview with Zárate (2003), after a site visit by the author to La Trinidad

Weak Legal Systems

Many developing countries have passed progressive wage and benefits laws, but rarely enforce them. According to Human Rights Watch (2002), Ecuador's Constitution and Labour Code provide adequate protection for freedom of association and prevent child labour. But Ecuadorian banana producers have captured an increasing share of the US market with low prices achieved through labour union intimidation and abuse of labour laws. Human Rights Watch interviewed 45 children who were working, or had worked, on Ecuadorian banana plantations, most having started at age ten or eleven. These children worked twelve hours a day on average, and were exposed to pesticides, sexual harassment, and extremely physically demanding and dangerous work:

Four boys explained that they attached harnesses to themselves, hooked themselves to pulleys on cables from which banana stalks were hung, and used this pulley system to drag approximately twenty banana-laden stalks, weighing between fifty and one hundred pounds each, over one mile from the fields to the packing plants five or six times a day. Two of these boys stated that, on occasion, the iron pulleys came loose and fell on their heads, making them bleed. (2002: 2–3)

Under Ecuadorian law, children aged under 14 years may not work, and children aged 14–18 years can only work a maximum of seven hours per day. Domestic laws decree a maximum weight that children can carry, and forbids that children undertake work that is hazardous or harmful, including handling toxic chemicals such as pesticides and 'tasks that are considered dangerous or unhealthy' (Minor's Code, Article 155(2), in Human Rights Watch, 2002). Yet these laws are obviously not being enforced. Human Rights Watch also found several cases of intimidation of union organizers and dismissal of workers who attempted to organize unions, also illegal under domestic law. A famous incident involving the night-time raid of a community of 150 banana workers on a Noboa-owned plantation in Ecuador who were attempting to unionize has resulted in no arrests or convictions, almost two years later. The government of Ecuador has found a competitive export strategy: a lack of enforcement of its labour laws. By ensuring low labour prices, Ecuador's banana industry has rapidly grown to supply 25 per cent of the US and European Union's banana imports (Otis, 2003).

This race to the bottom is encouraged by Northern retailers who demand ever-lower prices and whose customers may not realize the consequences on workers and the environment of price-squeezing farmers. The extremely low banana prices seen in discount retailers in the North do not cover minimum wages for workers on banana plantations. The Fair Trade minimum price guarantee is intended to ensure that the seller is earning enough to cover wage costs. Furthermore, FLO Fair Trade standards require farms and co-operatives who employ significant numbers of workers to abide by International Labour Organisation standards and domestic laws regarding the use of child labour, the right to organize, the use of dangerous chemicals and machinery, working hours, and other fundamental labour rights. FLO inspections verify that workers receive, at the very least, the country's legal minimum wage, or the local wage, whichever is higher. The Fair Trade process is, thus, an independent verification of wage and labour standards that may exist but which may not be enforced in producing countries.

Similarly, the International Federation of Alternative Trade (IFAT, the trade body for Fair Trade producers that largely represents non-FLO certified craft groups) Code of Practice specifies that Fair Trade working conditions should conform to 'local statutory regulations' and, further, stipulates that equal employment opportunities must be in evidence. It also supports 'concern for people' which focuses on ensuring a good quality of life for all producers.

FAIR TRADE PRINCIPLE TWO: LONG-TERM TRADING RELATIONSHIPS

The requirement of Fair Trade importers to sign long-term contracts is another way to smooth income and correct information failures. By locking in prices, farmers benefit from a predictable income flow, much like a futures market. Strong relationships with buyers encourage information exchanges regarding quality and logistical requirements that farmers whose product is sold on the 'faceless' commodities exchanges cannot enjoy.

However, long-term relationships are difficult to enforce through the Fair Trade system; most Fair Trade standards require only six-month to one-year purchase contracts. The first-mover Fair Trade importers (arguably, those most committed to the principles of Fair Trade) are likely to remain loyal to suppliers and work with them to overcome supply and quality problems – a buying system that is fundamental to the theoretical underpinnings of Fair Trade. But as the Fair Trade system expands and more traditional traders take part, these unenforceable practices are likely to fall by the wayside. A coffee importer experiencing problems with one Fair Trade co-operative may choose simply to switch suppliers once the long-term contract expires; with 300 coffee co-operatives to choose from, he has little monetary incentive to invest in improving the co-operative's supply problems. FLO standards do not codify what a 'long-term relationship' must be beyond the signing of a contract. IFAT does not include any explicit statement of the duration of trading relationships in its Fair Trade Code of Practice.

Other traders complain that not all actors in the Fair Trade system are committed to long-term trading. Unequal power relationships exist on the Northern end of the Fair Trade supply chain as well; large retail chains can push the risk burden of long-term relationships on to small Fair Trade importers. Retailers add and drop products with short notice, and are not necessarily interested in helping suppliers to correct problems. When interviewed in 2003 Tristan LeComte, president of AlterEco, a Fair Trade food importer in France, felt that 'supermarkets should be required to invest in long-term relationships, as well. Under the Fair Trade rules, I must sign a long-term contract with my suppliers, but the retailers can switch supply anytime they like. They may keep a Fair Trade product but switch to another Fair Trade importer, who works with different farms'.

Nevertheless, direct trade and long-term buying contracts help farmers increase the amount of the export price that is returned to them as well as allow farmers to access market information. Long-term buying can replace public commodities exchanges, which can be difficult to access and are not always sufficiently differentiated to reflect varying qualities and origins. While the nature of the trade relationship can be difficult to dictate, as Fair Trade grows, co-operatives (as with any other business actor) will in theory not forget which importers gave them the best terms and most assistance.

FAIR TRADE PRINCIPLE THREE: THE FLOOR PRICE

While the IFAT Code of Practice simply states that trading relationships should be characterized by 'equitable commercial terms, fair wages and fair prices', for nearly all Fair Trade products certified by FLO, Fair Trade standards require that all producers be paid a minimum price for their product, regardless of how low the market price goes.[1] If the market price rises above the Fair Trade floor price, the minimum Fair Trade price is the market price. Thus, the Fair Trade minimum price is always either the market price or the Fair Trade floor, whichever is higher. The Fair Trade floor price is intended to cover the costs of production and is loosely structured using the following formula:

Fair Trade floor price = cost of production + cost of living + cost
of complying with Fair Trade standards

Production and living costs are usually calculated individually for each country of origin or region (for example, Africa, Central America). Costs of production are intended to cover land, labour and capital costs of sustainable production and are calculated based on surveys of producers; an extra premium for certified organic production is included to cover the extra costs of investing in the transition to organic production and certification. The cost-of-living element is intended to ensure Fair Trade producers a decent standard of living, estimated through proxies such as real interest rates and daily or minimum wages. Costs of complying with Fair Trade standards include, for instance, those of belonging to a co-operative, organizing a workers' assembly, paperwork associated with inspections and reporting to FLO, attending world and regional Fair Trade assembly meetings and so on. Whilst some attempt is made to accommodate regional differences in costs of living and production, in the interest of simplicity averages must be taken here. For example, the Fair Trade floor price for Nicaraguan coffee is the same as for Costa Rican, despite the fact that Costa Rica's cost of living is much higher – GDP in Costa Rica is four times higher in terms of purchasing power than in Nicaragua (CIA, 2004).

For commodity farmer members of co-operatives, the Fair Trade floor price can be considered the equivalent of a minimum wage. It is intended to provide farmers with sufficient income to cover their costs of production and provide for their families. For estate owners who hire labour to work on their farms, the Fair Trade floor price is considered enough to pay workers the minimum wage or the local wage (whichever is higher) and provide decent working conditions. The Fair Trade standards for hired labour require that International Labour Organisation minimum labour standards are met regarding pay, worker safety, and so on and the standards ensure that this is possible through a guaranteed minimum price.

The concept of a minimum wage in commodity prices is not new. John Maynard Keynes defended it in the early part of the twentieth century:

Proper economic prices should be fixed not at the lowest possible level, but at the level sufficient to provide producers with proper nutritional and other standards in the conditions in which they live … and it is in the interests of all producers alike that the price of a commodity should not be depressed below this level, and consumers are not entitled to expect that it should. (Keynes, 1946: 167)

Keynes's is a moral argument that one should not assume that one could pay less for a product than the cost of its production, plus the cost of a decent standard of living for the producer.

In the neo-liberal model, however, consumers might pay prices below the cost of production if prices decrease in the face of increased supply. In the free market system, world supply and demand are kept in check by the movement of prices; when the supply increases (say, in a bumper harvest year), the price comes down and demand increases to soak up the extra supply, as illustrated in Figure 2.1.

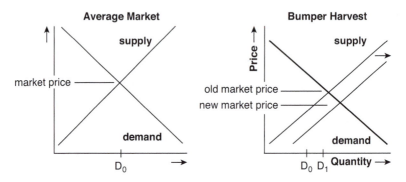

Figure 2.1 *Impact of a bumper harvest on market price*

If market prices have a lower limit on them because of a price floor, however, demand will not pick up and a surplus will result, as shown in Figure 2.2.

Neo-liberal economists would argue that the use of a price floor in the Fair Trade model is a fundamental hindrance to the efficient functioning of the free market. By keeping prices high through the Fair Trade price floor mechanism, farmers and producers cannot sell their surplus bumper crop because there are not enough willing buyers at the high price. The result is wasted product that could have been sold had the price been allowed to be lower, known as a 'dead weight loss'.

Whilst it is true that a price floor imposed on the entire market can in theory lead to excess supply, the reality is that Fair Trade products account for, at most, 1 per cent of the trade in their particular markets. Thus Fair Trade cannot be 'price-setting' because 99 per cent of world trade still operates under free market principles. Of course, as Fair Trade market share continues to grow, the price floor will eventually have some effect on the world market price and thus will create distortions. As Fair Trade gains market share, it will be necessary for the Fair Trade system to change in order to be more flexible during supply shocks, perhaps even abandoning the price floor mechanism after reaching a certain market share. A further option may be to increase the sophistication of the price floor mechanism by offering different floors based on quality and origin. This would give buyers more options for offering Fair Trade-labelled product whilst remaining competitive on price.

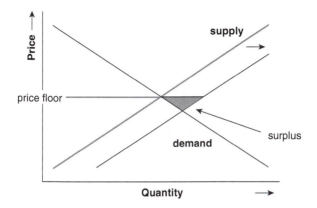

Figure 2.2 *Bumper harvest (supply shock) with price floor*

Finally, as consumer awareness of the needs of subsistence producers grows, it may be that demand curves will shift such that there is little demand for low-priced goods because consumers understand the negative implications for producers of paying low prices. In the Fair Trade market, this could already be the case in Switzerland where Fair Trade bananas had achieved a 50 per cent market share by 2004. In this scenario, the demand curve in Figure 2.2 would be much flatter, and the dead weight loss created by a price floor much smaller. These issues will be revisited in the final chapter, which discusses the implications for the Fair Trade model as Fair Trade moves into the mainstream and gains market share.

It can also be argued that a guaranteed high price encourages farmers to plant more and leads to a structural oversupply in agricultural markets. Again, because Fair Trade is such a minor part of global trade in commodities, it is unlikely that the price floor is currently sending a signal on an industry-wide level that would encourage farmers to plant more. But what about on a micro-level, for instance the case of a co-operative which is selling well on the Fair Trade market and thus receiving a higher-than-average price during a low-priced market? Unfortunately, scant data have been collected regarding the actual impact of price signals on individual farmers in the Fair Trade system. It could certainly be the case that farmers who have had success in the Fair Trade system plant more with the expectation that they will be able to sell their production at the guaranteed Fair Trade price. It could also be that as Fair Trade farmers learn more about the functioning of the free market, they decide it is in their best interests to diversify their income-generating activities and reduce their exposure to commodity price fluctuations. Changing the Fair Trade standards to require Fair Trade producers to diversify their income stream would ensure that farmers do not plant more in response to a guaranteed minimum price.

LeClair (2002, 2003) also flags the potential for artificially high prices to leave producers dependent on products for which no viable market exists outside the Fair Trade system. If the Fair Trade market were to go into decline, these producers would be left with fewer buyers and limited options for alternative sources of income. Again, requiring Fair Trade producer groups to diversify their income sources would remedy this potential threat to producer well-being. Some Fair Trade buyers, especially in crafts, limit the length of their contracts with individual producer groups to require them to 'graduate' to non-Fair Trade buyers (Humphrey, 2000). In this case, Fair Trade could be seen as a safety net whilst producers develop the capacity to diversify their income sources and learn to make higher-quality products that can command high prices outside of the Fair Trade system.

ARE SUPPLY AND DEMAND CURVES RELEVANT IN DEVELOPING-COUNTRY AGRICULTURE?

While the beauty and simplicity of the classical economic model is very attractive, its applications are beginning to be challenged by economists. Daniel Kahneman, one of the two 2002 Nobel Prize winners in economics, has a significant body of work challenging the fundamental notion of economic actors as 'rational' (Princeton, 2002). Several recent experiments have shown that consumers frequently engage in 'irrational' behaviour, such as choosing a scenario in which they receive a low reward if it means they are getting more than their neighbour, rather than a higher reward that is lower than their neighbour's. Non-monetary factors such as competition and relative success thus come into play in what seems like straightforward economic decision making.

Similarly, several factors specific to developing-country agriculture detract from the effectiveness of the classical economic model in explaining supply and demand responses to price.

Supply Factors

In the classical economic model, falls in world prices will reduce supply, as producers do not find it worth their effort to produce if they are receiving a lower price. But agricultural supply cannot respond to price information in the same way. First, once planted, sugar cane will grow no matter how low the sugar price on the New York Board of Trade falls – it does not reduce its output in response to world commodity prices. In order to minimize losses, sugar farmers will harvest this cane as long as it covers their marginal cost of harvesting (for instance labour, processing and transport), even if it does not cover the cost of prior investment in the harvest. The lower price may not cover the costs of yearly maintenance of the crop, but it makes sense for the farmer to get whatever income he or she can (Lindsey, 2004).

The short-term supply response to agricultural price changes can thus have a significant time lag. But agricultural supply has long-term supply constraints as well. A farmer can respond to a high world vanilla price by planting more vanilla vines, but it takes three to five years for those vines to produce export-quality vanilla beans, by which time the price may have fallen again. In coffee and cocoa, futures markets can correct for these time lags by locking in future pricing. But many commodities (bananas, spices, and so on) do not have futures markets, and as discussed above, small-scale farmers in developing countries do not usually have access to these futures markets anyway. The time lag inherent in some agricultural commodity production introduces a price volatility that cannot always be traded away, thus supply curves do not respond to price changes in the straightforward manner depicted in Figures 2.1 and 2.2.

Furthermore, commodity farmers in developing countries are usually members of the poorest sectors of society and are struggling to survive without government-provided social safety nets. Faced with falling market prices, 'the only way to maintain income is to increase the volume of output' (Oxfam, 2002: 159). Thus in response to a lower world sugar price, farmers might choose to increase supply and plant more rather than pull up plants. This contributes to an increased world supply, further depressing prices.

Demand Factors

It is also possible that world demand for finished agricultural products is rather inelastic in response to changes in commodity prices because the commodity cost represents such a small portion of the end retail price to consumers. If that were the case, the demand curve in Figure 2.2 would be more vertical, and the surplus produced by the price floor would be lessened.

To take a $1 chocolate bar as an example, the cocoa component of the end price of the bar might be only $0.02. The price of cocoa beans is but a minor element in the price of the finished product: cocoa beans must be roasted, ground and mixed with milk, sugar, and other ingredients. The bars are then moulded, packaged and delivered to stores. If a bumper crop led to an oversupply of cocoa and the price dropped to $0.01 for the same amount of cocoa, the end retail price of the chocolate bar might drop only to 99 cents (assuming the same recipe). A halving of the price of cocoa beans thus would result in only a 1 per cent drop in the retail price, which might not affect demand very much. Conversely, a doubling of the world price for cocoa beans would result in only a $0.02 (or 2 per cent) increase in the retail price, which again would most likely have a minimal effect on demand.

Maseland and de Vaal (2002) found that the price elasticity of the product in question determines the relative benefit of Fair Trade to producers. If demand for the product is relatively inelastic, the product will be exported even if the price of the raw material is high, thus producers are not hurt much by the increased selling price. For many Fair Trade products, the producer price is but a small fraction of the end retail price – according to Lindsey (2004), for instance, the cost of coffee is only 5 to 7 per cent of the price of a cup in Starbucks – thus the demand curves can be seen to be relatively inelastic. It could be argued that it is just these products (labour-intensive, with inelastic demand curves) that should be the focus of Fair Trade schemes.

FAIR TRADE PRINCIPLE FOUR: THE SOCIAL PREMIUM

In addition to the Fair Trade minimum price, Fair Trade standards require the payment of a social premium to the co-operative or farm worker organization. The social premium is added regardless of organic or quality product features and must be spent by the co-operative or farm worker organization on social development projects in the grower community. FLO inspections check that the social premium was earmarked for and spent on social development projects chosen by the community. This social premium is a fundamental aspect of Fair Trade pricing and is the essence of using Fair Trade as a business-oriented development strategy. Figure 2.3 shows the Fair Trade prices for cocoa beans as compared to the world market price from 1960 to 2003. The Fair Trade price floor

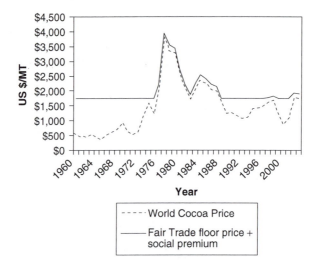

Figure 2.3   *World market price of cocoa beans vs. Fair Trade price, 1960–2003*

for cocoa beans is $1,600/MT (£896), and the social premium is $150/MT (£84). Thus when the world market price is below $1,600/MT, the Fair Trade minimum price is $1,750/MT (£980). When the world price rises above $1,600 (as it did in the early 1980s), the Fair Trade minimum price becomes the world market price *plus* the $150/MT social premium.

If the fair price is to be compared with a minimum wage scheme, one can translate the social premium to a savings rate component of a minimum wage calculation. To simply cover the costs of living and production with compensation does not allow those living on minimum wages to invest in retirement, or health care, or education; in other words, they must be completely dependent on government or community support for all savings and investment in bettering their lives. In developing countries in particular, government is usually poor at delivering these services, and local communities often do not have the resources. The Fair Trade social premium, therefore, is the guarantee that producers earn a little extra to invest in improving their social condition or the quality of their natural environment. In fact, Fair Trade co-operatives and worker organizations must jointly decide on projects to be funded with the social premium and demonstrate to inspectors the progress on such projects and how they benefit the community. Including a social premium in the calculation of the minimum Fair Trade price could be explained as a way of ensuring a savings rate amongst farming communities.

Adding on the social premium to a market price that has risen above the Fair Trade floor, however, is more difficult to justify. Take, for example, the case of cocoa beans. The world market price for cocoa beans averaged US$1,941/MT (£1,087) in the first six months of 2003, well above the Fair Trade floor of $1,600/MT (£896). The social premium for cocoa beans in the Fair Trade system is $150/MT (£84). If Fair Trade cocoa co-operatives were to sell their beans on the world market for $1,941, they would earn well above the Fair Trade floor price that is intended to cover their cost of production ($1,600/MT) plus the $150 to invest in social development projects. $1,941 would thus seem like a 'fair' price. Yet under the FLO standards, the co-operative must receive from Fair Trade importers the $150 social premium *in addition to* the $1,941 world market price. Fair Trade importers are thus always paying more than their competitors, even when the market price is high and the farmers are earning more than what is considered a 'fair' price.

Requiring Fair Trade importers to pay the social premium even when the market is high represents an attempt to offer farmers incentives to sell to the Fair Trade market, even when non-Fair Trade market prices are high, to ensure the sustainability of the market. This approach may be seen as paternalistic towards producers, suggesting that they might not realize that Fair Trade represents a better long-term solution because it protects them from downturns in the market. However, the 'time discount' for subsistence producers is relatively high, and it is possible that they would favour a high-volume high-priced contract with a non-Fair Trade actor and discount the importance of a low-volume, high-priced contract to a Fair Trade importer, despite the future benefits of selling to Fair Trade importers in low-priced markets. In this scenario, they would sell everything to the non-Fair Trade importer, Fair Trade actors would not be able to buy product, and the Fair Trade market would be harmed. Keeping Fair Trade prices higher than the market will reduce the likelihood of this occurring. As the Fair Trade market grows and producers have been in the system for a longer period of time, this price incentive could be phased out of Fair Trade standards. It should be noted that the IFAT Code of Practice effectively sidesteps the issue, by not including any statements about social premia.

The social premium represents the 'development agenda' aspect of Fair Trade and could be fairly criticized as being contrary to the free-market system. It represents a direct transfer to the producer in a developing country to be used for development projects. Insofar as the producer organization (the farmer-owned co-operative or the worker organization) decides how it wants to spend the social premium, it is a more 'empowered' system of wealth transfer in the name of development. FLO monitors that the co-operative or worker organization plans and votes on its investment projects through democratic processes, but does not make judgments as to the value of the chosen use of the social premium. This contrasts starkly with other development projects that are Northern-funded, but also largely Northern-developed and Northern-run (as is the case with most bilateral and multilateral donors and lenders, including the UN, World Bank, and bilateral development agencies such as the US Agency for International Development and the UK's Department for International Development).

In summary, several aspects of Fair Trade, including direct trading, improved information flows and access to credit make the free market system work better. But Fair Trade is not an entirely free-market system because of both the price floor mechanism and the social premium transfer. Fair Trade must thus be seen as a development project for transferring wealth from consumers to the developing world through market-based mechanisms. Besides wealth transfer, there are external social benefits which are more difficult to measure in monetary terms but are nonetheless significant. These external social benefits are considered next.

EXTERNAL BENEFITS OF FAIR TRADE

Whilst many of the benefits of Fair Trade involve improvements to the functioning of the free market, there are also external and development benefits. Non-Fair Trade farmers in Fair Trade communities benefit from the multiplier effects of extra income to Fair Trade farmers, as well as community projects like roads, clinics and schools built with Fair Trade social premia. The information gained by Fair Trade farmers through long-term direct Fair Trade relationships helps them capture more value in non-Fair Trade negotiations. But another important benefit is the empowerment of peasant farmers and low-wage workers who are required to organize and interact directly with the market as part of the Fair Trade standards. We will introduce the concept of empowerment here and then revisit non-monetary externalities of Fair Trade in Chapter 9, which examines the existing literature regarding the monetary and non-monetary impacts of Fair Trade on producers and their communities.

Organization and Empowerment: Workers

Fair Trade was originally developed to help family farmers and craft producers access trade routes and earn a fair price for their product, and the original FLO standards reflect this bias towards small-scale producers. The system has developed, however, to include workers in developing countries who do not own the means of production but are employed by large land or factory owners. The fair price guarantee ensures that employers can pay fair wages and provide decent working conditions. But the Fair Trade system also requires that the importer pay the Fair Trade social premium directly to a democratically elected 'Joint Body', made up of worker representatives and management. The Joint Body allows worker representatives to discuss, with management, the use of Fair Trade social premia and to vote on projects that will benefit the entire community.

The direct developmental benefits of the social premium can be seen quite easily. Joint Body organizations on tea estates, for instance, have created micro-credit funds, invested in electrification of tea-picker housing and started organic vegetable gardens to improve nutrition among farm worker families (see www.TransFair USA.org and www.fairtrade.org.uk). But the indirect benefits are also numerous. Participation in a Joint Body often represents the first time that workers have made community development decisions which can be supported financially in a significant way. The fact that workers discuss and take decisions independent of management is a development goal of Fair Trade that encourages leadership and empowerment, specifically addressing the issue of 'paternalism' in developing countries' agricultural sectors.

Paternalism in the agricultural sector refers to situations in which all work, wages, transport, housing, health care and education are provided by the farm owner or manager. Workers live in housing provided for them by the plantation owner, often isolated from towns. They are thus often reliant on the owner for transport to shopping, schools, health clinics, and entertainment options. Under paternalism, many of the farmer's obligations to the worker cannot be formalized or enforced by a contract as they take the form of a 'gift relationship' (Leholo, 1996: 4). All decision making is undertaken by the management, and can result in both good and bad outcomes for workers.

Because of the unequal power relationship and lack of knowledge of rights on the part of the workers, paternalism is generally an undesirable state for worker-management interactions. But while Fair Trade buyers might seek to minimize paternalism, formalizing all such 'gifts' might introduce conflict between workers and managers. Workers might enjoy getting these services for 'free', and management might feel that they can make these decisions for their illiterate uneducated workers better than they can themselves; for some managers workers are like children (hence the term 'paternalism'). The Joint Body structure, which requires that management have minority representation on the board, attempts to address the delicate nature of these often centuries-old community relationships.

The distribution of the social premium is the main function of the Joint Body. Under the FLO standards it is expected that wages, working conditions, and related issues will be addressed by unions, not the Joint Body:

> If one or more independent and active trade unions exist in the sector and the region, FLO expects that the workers shall be represented by (a) trade union(s) and that the workers shall be covered by a Collective Bargaining Agreement within one year after certification. (FLO, 2004: 4)

In practice, however, the leadership, independence and empowerment fostered by the Joint Body within the Fair Trade system can have spill-over effects into the areas normally addressed by unions, such as wages and working conditions. FLO's hired labour standards have been criticized for failing to adequately support labour unions. The standards do not, for instance, specify the certification implications if workers do not unionize despite the presence of independent trade unions in the region. Plantations with large social premium income (for instance, Fair Trade banana plantations in Ecuador) have well-funded Joint Bodies and farm workers may not find it necessary to join a union, as their wages and benefits are guaranteed by the FLO inspection and their income and well-being are improved by the social premium.

In an environment of severe union intimidation and labour abuses such as characterizes the Ecuadorean banana industry, having the most progressive plantations choose not to unionize hurts those workers who are not part of the Fair Trade system and who would benefit from a more powerful union movement. In this way, farm worker empowerment and income increases can actually have negative external effects on farm workers outside of the Fair Trade system. Requiring Fair Trade farm workers to unionize, however, would negate the empowerment and self-determination that are the intended aims of Fair Trade's involvement with farm workers.

Organization and Empowerment: Co-operatives

The Fair Trade requirement that small farmers get organized into export or sales co-operatives guarantees that farmers become engaged in the development of their businesses or communities. It also allows small farmers to voice their opinions collectively, often increasing their power at the national government level. This is an especially noticeable benefit in countries in which landed elites have often been the only rural voice listened to at national tables.

La Trinidad Co-op leader Salomón Garicía presents organizational structure to members in Oaxaca, Mexico

In El Salvador, for instance, a member of the Apecafé Coffee Co-operative was recently elected to the national coffee board, the first time that a small peasant farmer has been a member of the most important national industry group. In Ghana, the Kuapa Kokoo Co-operative has started an organic cocoa-farming project in open defiance of the Ghana Cocoa Board, which fears that organic farming will introduce pests into the national crop.

The cultural differences between small family farmers and large estate owners are marked. Co-operative members often cannot speak English or other languages helpful for making international sales. Latin American or African plantation owners may have attended university in Europe or the USA and learned to swap jokes and stories over beer and cigars with buyers in the local sports bar, but small family farmers almost certainly have not. The co-operative model allows small peasant farmers to pool resources and invest in one of their own learning such skills, or to hire outside sales-people with the necessary knowledge. At the Specialty Coffee Association of America annual convention in Boston in 2003, small family farmers mingled at a party for ven-dors to Dunkin' Donuts, the USA's largest chain of coffee and doughnut shops. Dunkin' Donuts had recently announced the introduction of Fair Trade Certified espresso drinks into all of its stores in North America, and farmers were there to make sales and intro-duce themselves.

The co-operative model also allows leaders to shine through formalized recognition and fostering of leadership talents, as well as providing resources with which to imple-ment their ideas. In civil-war-torn southern Colombia, one such co-operative leader has stood up to local revolutionary groups to recapture control over their farming. René Ausecha Chaux, General Manager of the Cosurca Coffee Co-operative in southern Colombia, is slowly converting co-operative members from growing coca leaf (used to manufacture cocaine) to growing coffee for the Fair Trade market:

> It is precisely the lowest coffee prices in decades that are driving farmers to plant coca and poppy. Farmers do not want to be part of the illegal economy; they would rather farm some-thing like coffee, which they are proud to sell. But the low world price does not give them this option. The only legal crop which can compete with coca production is Fair Trade coffee. (Interview, 2002)

Ausecha Chaux is teaching farmers to switch from coca production to coffee, and in the meantime gaining more Fair Trade sales for his co-operative. He estimates that since 1993 over 400 acres of coca plants have been switched to coffee production and 1600 acres of coca crops have not been planted because farmers were earning enough from Fair Trade coffee sales (TransFair USA, 2002a).

Ausecha Chaux's strategy is very dangerous, as local guerrilla and paramilitary leaders rely on money skimmed off illegal coca leaf sales to fund their operations. But according to him 'the FARC [guerilla] are turning a blind eye, because they know that we are des-perately poor and they cannot squeeze much more from us. They also need our political support, as peasants, and thus understand that they must let us be part of the formalized economy, which is what we want' (2004). Because Ausecha Chaux has the power of 650 coffee-farming families behind him, he can achieve social change in a way that an unor-ganized peasant farmer cannot.

It is important to note, however, that empowerment is not necessarily an essential element of farming co-operative structures. Mendoza and Bastiaensen (2003), for instance, claim that co-operatives can copy the 'vertical and clientilistic modes of organization' (p. 43) that form the basis of dependency and underdevelopment in Nicaragua. Co-operatives where management defines its members as ignorant and in need of protection are certainly not interested in the empowerment of farmer members. Whilst FLO inspects co-operative management for adherence to the co-operative's election policies and democratic structure, it cannot force management to devolve more power to the electorate, or even ensure management turnover. Mendoza and Bastiaesen propose that Fair Trade organizations should 'certainly not take the assumed advantages of co-operatives for granted' (p. 43).

THE EFFICIENCY OF FAIR TRADE

Leaving aside the potential external and non-monetary benefits, the main purpose of Fair Trade is to guarantee that more money reaches the world's poor farmers. But how efficient is this transfer of wealth? Certainly the most efficient way to increase someone's income is to hand them money directly (LeClair, 2002), rather than hand extra money to a retailer, who hands some of it to a distributor, who hands some of *that* to a coffee roaster, who hands some of *that* to an importer, who pays a coffee farmer in Peru. Every link in the chain takes a margin, leaving less in the hands of the coffee farmer.

Whilst there is scant formal research regarding exactly how efficient this wealth transfer is, anecdotal evidence would indicate that Fair Trade is a very inefficient way to give money to poor farmers. In the USA, an extra 20 cents (14p) per pound paid for organic Fair Trade bananas would guarantee a minimum of 5 cents (3.5p) per pound, a return of only 25 per cent to the producer.[2] One Oxfam craft project had a return of 33 per cent to producers (Redfern and Snedker, 2002), whilst Stecklow and White (2004) found that Border's bookstores were charging $4 (£2.24) extra per pound of organic Fair Trade coffee over organic non-Fair Trade. Of that $4, farmers might get $0.61 (£0.34), only 15 per cent of the extra paid by the consumer.[3]

But the most dismal return found was between Nescafé and Cafédirect, a Fair Trade brand found in many UK supermarkets. Mendoza and Bastiaensen's (2003) comparison of the returns to Nicaraguan coffee farmers through Fair Trade versus conventional marketing chains found that in 1996 with a high-priced coffee market consumers paid $1.63 (£0.91) per pound extra for Cafédirect over Nescafé, but the Nicaraguan coffee farmer saw only $0.03 (£0.02) extra, a return of just 2 per cent. In 2001 with a low-priced coffee market, however, farmers earned 18 per cent of the extra cost paid by Fair Trade consumers because retail prices paid for the two brands had not changed that much, but farmers earned much less from Nescafé sales with the world price so low.

Why are income returns to farmers through Fair Trade so inefficient? One reason is that the importing and retail industries work on a margin basis, adding 25, 30, even 50 per cent to their costs and then selling on to their clients. Thus the higher the cost of goods (and Fair Trade ingredients are automatically higher-cost), the more money gets added on to the selling price, translating into a larger price difference between Fair Trade and non-Fair Trade at the retail level rather than at the farm-gate level. Stecklow and White (2004) claim that supermarket chains may even charge higher margins on Fair Trade goods than on non-Fair Trade goods because they know that consumers are expecting to pay more for Fair Trade in the first place. If this is true, it is unlikely that the practice will survive as Fair Trade grows, as the marketplace will become increasingly competitive and consumers will become more aware of what other companies are charging for similar products. But industries that operate on a margin basis, such as retail, will always multiply the effect of higher Fair Trade costs in the end retail price.

Furthermore, according to Mendoza and Bastiaensen (2003), Fair Trade marketing chains are more inefficient than conventional marketing chains partly because they have higher capital costs, but also because they are small and their overheads are thus spread across a lesser volume. They found, for instance, that Cafédirect spent more than three times as much per pound on advertising as did Nescafé. Fair Trade products might, then, be stuck in a vicious circle whereby inefficient high-cost marketing chains keep Fair Trade sales low, which does not allow companies to capture the scale economies that would help them lower costs.

It would seem then, that on one level it is correct to say that to say in the end it is better to give £1 to Oxfam [a leading UK charity] than to spend £1 on a jar of Cafédirect, because in all likelihood Oxfam's development projects return more of that £1 to people in developing countries than does Cafédirect. But whilst returning more money to poor farmers is the primary aim of Fair Trade, it is not the only aim. As outlined in this chapter, there are several external benefits to producers from participating in Fair Trade, beyond the monetary variety. There is also, perhaps, a psychological benefit to consumers in participating in a more ethical supply chain. As Wills points out, aside from knowing that a bit extra has got back to the farmer, consumers know that their purchase 'is also being noticed, where I am buying the product, here in Switzerland, in Austria, in Italy or Japan or wherever' (2004). Consumers might value the sending of such a signal that they are interested in returning a fair price to developing country producers.

It should be noted that whilst Fair Trade is a development project, it operates within normal capitalistic structures and thus should not be compared to a charity. Perhaps a perfectly rational economic actor would understand the inefficiencies of Fair Trade and remember to donate to Oxfam the money saved by buying Nescafé instead of Cafédirect. But, more likely, consumers make decisions to give money to charity separate from their supermarket purchases. LeClair (2002) notes that direct contributions are difficult to solicit because their reward is only psychological, as opposed to a Fair Trade purchase of a physical product that the consumer will use, which has both psychological and physical benefits. If supermarket purchase and charity donation decisions are indeed made separately, then any Fair Trade return to producers can be seen in addition to that charitable giving which consumers were already doing. It could even be the case that Fair Trade, by raising the visibility of the realities of daily life in developing countries, increases donations to charities.

Finally, to calculate a true measurement of return to farmers per retail dollar or pound spent on Fair Trade, all of the external benefits to both Fair Trade and non-Fair Trade producers must be measured. It may be the case that when these more indirect benefits are taken into account, the return on Fair Trade purchases rivals returns to charitable donations. This is discussed further in Chapter 9.

FAIR TRADE: IN AND AGAINST THE MARKET

As we have shown, Fair Trade attempts to correct market failures by requiring direct trade and improving information flow to historically disadvantaged producers. Table 2.1 outlines the core elements of the Fair Trade model and how they address both market failures and the broader issue of poverty in the developing world. However, not all Fair Trade principles

Table 2.1 *Developing-country problems and Fair Trade solutions*

Issue/market failure	Fair Trade solution
Small farmers lack information about prices.	Farmers must be organized into co-operatives; can pool resources to access information.
Smallholder farmers lack information about market requirements.	Farmers must be organized into co-operatives; can pool resources to send co-operative leaders to visit trade shows and clients to learn about quality requirements. Direct long-term relationships are required; clients more likely to share information.
Smallholder farmers lack access to financial markets.	Farmers must be organized into co-operatives; can pool production to access futures markets.
Smallholder farmers lack access to credit.	Importers must pre-finance up to 60 per cent of seasonal crops.
Smallholder farmers are risk-averse and do not diversify.	No direct solution – raising incomes through Fair Trade may decrease risk-aversion.
Weak enforcement of labour law in producing countries.	Standards require that producers adhere to ILO standards regarding minimum wages, child labour, working conditions, freedom to join unions.
World prices not covering costs of production.	Fair Trade floor price guaranteed no matter how low the world price falls.
In effort to lower costs, less sustainable production methods are used in the developing world, harming workers and the environment.	Fair Trade floor price covers costs of sustainable production. Environmental standards prohibit certain chemicals and land over-use; premium required for certified organic products.
Farmers and farm workers in the developing world are poor.	Fair Trade guarantees minimum or regional wages for workers and price floors for smallholders. Social premium guaranteed, which must be spent on development projects to improve well-being of farm workers and smallholder farmers.

coincide with a perfectly free market. Fair Trade has a specific development goal of increasing income to producers in developing countries, with minimum wage (price floor) and social premium elements as the primary mechanisms for achieving this goal.

It is worth noting, however, that Fair Trade is a consumer choice trading model that operates entirely within the free market system. If consumers choose to distort the free market system by giving more money to developing country producers when they purchase Fair Trade products, even if the end producer does not get all of the extra price they pay at the supermarket, it is their right as independent economic actors to do so. Fair Trade does not involve any sort of government regulation. As part of their international development agendas, town, city, and even national governments have chosen to support Fair Trade through assisting Fair Trade activist groups and through purchasing Fair Trade products, but have not required consumers to do so by law. Thus as long as consumers fully understand the system, they are making a free choice to engage in a trading practice – 'Fair Trade' is a subset, then, of 'free trade'.

Because Fair Trade does function within a broader free market trading system, it is important to gauge how Fair Trade will affect the free market as the movement grows. Although Fair Trade is not yet a significant enough factor in the supply chain to affect world prices and supply, there certainly exists an incentive for over-production of commodities through the distorting impact of the price floor. If Fair Trade continues to grow and eventually becomes a dominant market force, the issue of distorting price-setting incentives must be addressed. These issues will be considered in the final chapter. But as an interim solution to the problem of desperate rural poverty, a lack of access to competitive markets and an over-reliance on mono-cropping resulting in a single source of tradable income, Fair Trade stands out as a shining example of how the world's poor can earn enough to become rational economic actors and begin to think about diversifying their income and switching out of primary commodity production.

This chapter has examined the economic context of Fair Trade principles and highlighted those aspects of the Fair Trade model that fit within a broader free trade model, as well as those aspects that could be considered more interventionist. The strengths and shortcomings of Fair Trade as an economic model will be revisited in the final chapter. Recognizing that Fair Trade is essentially a consumer choice model, we will now examine it within the broader context of consumer interest in ethical trade.

NOTES

1. A notable exception is tea, whose prices vary greatly based on quality. In the case of tea, the estate owner is paid the agreed price and a separate social premium is paid directly to the tea-workers' organization.

2. Assuming a $1.75 (£1.21) social premium plus $0.25 (£0.17) market differential extra per 40-lb. box; often the market differential is much higher.

3. Assuming market price of organic coffee stands at $0.90 (£0.62) per pound and Fair Trade floor price for organic coffee is $1.41 (£0.97). 1 lb. of roasted coffee requires 1.2 lb. of green coffee.

3

Supply Chain Ethics

This chapter explores the nature of the ethics of supply chain management as a context for the rise of Fair Trade. Firstly, it fills in the background to the current ethical discussion of supply chain actions and secondly, the nature of corporate responsibility in supply chains is reviewed. This is followed by a discussion of the philosophical frameworks that may be applied to supply chains and their analytical implications for Fair Trade. The key issues of social justice and human rights are explored in terms of their relationship to trade. Finally, business responses to the emerging ethical agenda are considered.

INTRODUCTION

In recent years there has been a trend towards framing business activities in terms of ethical behaviour. Under increasing scrutiny from consumers and the media, companies have had to re-evaluate the success of their operations by measures beyond profitability and efficiency alone. The concept of the double – or triple – bottom-line is now widely applied to capture not only conventional financial metrics, but also to include environmental and social impacts (Elkington, 2001). This shift in thinking has also lead to the development of strategic corporate social responsibility within many major businesses, underpinned by greater transparency and supply chain accountability (Hartwick, 2000; Hughes, 2001). The proliferation of academic courses in Business Ethics further demonstrates this change in the commercial landscape (Bishop, 1992; Cowe, 2000; Sheridan, 2000).

Much current discussion concerning the ethics of business centres on the nature and impact of the extended global supply chains that characterize many large-scale companies (Diller, 1999; Zadek, 1998). The result of rapid developments in technology, allied to the reduction of trading barriers in developing countries, these new supply chains have offered enormous cost savings whilst also vastly increasing the number and range of stakeholder groups impacted – sometimes indirectly – by corporate actions. Since the scope and actions of complex global supply chains often remain obscure to customers (and, indeed, on occasion to corporations themselves), the incentives for ethical behaviour have typically been small. The result has been a string of corporate scandals, consumer exposés and boycotts over the past ten years (e.g. Whysall, 1998, 2000a).

The main ethical objections to global trade between North and South centre on the drive towards maximizing end margins via a leveraging of the enormous power and information asymmetries between developed world corporate buyers and developing world producers/manufacturers. The key issues may be summarized as follows:

- Producers will be paid below subsistence prices if the market will tolerate it.
- Producer/manufacturer working conditions are not the responsibility of the ultimate buyer (particularly under conditions of sub-contracting).
- Labour rights enforcement is the responsibility of the local legal system.
- Short-term contracts are more efficient than long-term commitments.

The business response to consequent scandals has been a new focus on 'ethical trade' increasingly driven by consumer boycotts and unfavourable media attention (see for example, Barrientos, 2000). This has taken the form of an acknowledgement by business of the company's responsibility to behave towards all its stakeholders in a way congruent with the expectations of civil society. Fair Trade falls within this larger range of ethical business actions, representing its most clearly defined and stringently observed manifestation. Over recent years, the issue of ethical trade has become increasingly important to many global businesses (although what is expected from ethical trade is not always clearly defined), and the pressure on companies to behave transparently and responsibly with stakeholders – particularly suppliers – has grown significantly. Whilst Fair Trade fits into a tradition of activist-led ethical trade that predates consumer-driven corporate social responsibility, there is still a clear link between the broad notion of an ethical supply chain and the role of Fair Trade in reconnecting consumer and producer across wide geographical distances.

Today, Fair Trade is both an activist and a consumerist movement. On the one hand it has been driven by campaigners who frame the perceived inequality in trading relations between developing and developed worlds as an ethical issue to be addressed. On the other hand, it has a place within a wider range of issues driven by the growth of consumerism where individuals have asserted their right to know more about the actions of the corporations with which they interact, and about the nature of the products they buy, as part of a broader reaction against their historically passive role in the marketing relationship. As a consequence, business has had to respond by taking more responsibility for its actions via greater accountability and transparency and often because of this by behaving in more ethical ways.

THE RISE OF CONSUMER AWARENESS OF
SUPPLY CHAIN ISSUES

As companies have increasingly sought out lower cost sources of goods and services through extended, global supply chains and the 'industrialization' of the buying process, there has been no commensurate development of supply chain governance (Lang, 2003). This has left many producer and manufacturer groups with little or no leverage in the negotiation process. Furthermore, as distribution chains have lengthened and widened the strategic control exerted from the centre of organizations over them has also loosened (often as a result of low-cost outsourcing). The move towards outsourcing and the quest for low cost alternatives to local production have increased many companies' profitability, but sometimes at the expense of other externalities such as poor working terms and conditions for the new manufacturing/production groups, increased risk at the start of the supply chain and environmental and social degradation. NGOs have been working to expose these issues for some time, but it is only in the last ten years or so that consumers and the media in developed countries have begun to share their concerns. Such campaigns have had a widespread impact with consumer boycotts of Nike and Nestlé having had particular impact.

A whole new literature critiquing global business has emerged, spearheaded by Naomi Klein's *No Logo* (2000), and ranging from the populist such as Moore (2001, 2003) and

Roy (2002), to the more academic such as Rosenberg (2000), Stiglitz (2002), Legrain (2002) and Singer (2002). At the same time, effective pressure group activity, such as that associated with the so-called anti-globalization movement, has grown, culminating in large set-piece demonstrations outside major political events, such as those witnessed at the Seattle round of the World Trade Organisation talks in 2001. These events have helped to spark a broader public debate about the impact of global trade that has now reached such a critical mass that it is of interest to major corporations. Furthermore, organized groups such as the World Social Forum (established in reaction to the perceived unaccountability of the powerful World Economic Forum) are both positioning themselves against the business 'establishment' and its institutions and developing new policy initiatives to highlight the needs of the developing world. The World Social Forum has grown from attracting some 20,000 participants to its first meeting in Brazil (2001) to a gathering of over 100,000 in Mumbai three years later. At the latter there were representatives from over 130 countries and keynote speakers included a Nobel Laureate economist.

Consumer and activist concerns over the actions and impacts of global businesses have taken a number of forms, focusing on a range of issues from sustainability and eco-friendliness to human rights and workplace conditions. However, a unifying theme has been the changing nature of the modern supply chain and its constitution in the free market system. Central to this new model has been a perceived return to a proto-Marxist conceptualization of the (now distant) worker as an expendable and exchangeable unit of production. It is argued that free trade acts at its most efficient when it allows business to seek out the most efficient unit of production from the global labour market and thus cut costs (for itself and its end consumers) and improve profits for its shareholders. That the most efficient units of production tend to be found in the low wage lightly regulated labour forces of many developing countries has maximized the impact of this new direct foreign investment, but has also demanded working conditions that do not always benefit its citizens overall. Undoubtedly, the increasingly global markets for goods and services that have emerged over the last ten years have improved overall the lives of many in developing countries and have contributed towards rising standards of living and life expectancy in many regions. However, the question remains whether the full range of impacts of such advances is acceptable to consumers in the developed world.

The phenomenal growth in demand for Fair Trade products over recent years suggests that consumers in developed countries are becoming more aware of, and sensitized to, the plight of citizens in the developing world. There would appear to be an increasing sense of connectivity between consumers in the North and producers in the South as the human effects of global trade are better understood and more widely discussed. In many ways, it is this growing sense of connectivity that has provided one of the main market drivers for the rapid expansion of Fair Trade. As Steve Sellers, Chief Operating Officer of TransFair USA, commented:

> I think that a lot of people are not simply self-interested and I think that a lot of people really are coming to understand the interrelated nature of the globe and so I think that people really do care about the quality of the coffee bean ... but I think they also care about the quality of other people's lives. It's hard anymore to neglect what Marx in the 1840s or 1850s called 'commodity fetishism': the notion that a commodity is not simply an apple that exists in a vacuum in space and magically appears in your grocery store, but that an apple is, in fact, the product of a series of relations of production from the tree to your store. (Interview, 2003)

Such a shift in the public perception of global relationships is also supported by survey work carried out by the Department for International Development (DFID, 2002) that suggests that 73 per cent of British consumers are 'concerned' about poverty in the developing world and that 69 per cent agree that such poverty is a moral issue for them. Interestingly, respondents felt that poverty in the developing world could have consequences that affected them personally (42 per cent) and could damage the interests of the country as a whole (66 per cent). Chief amongst these negative impacts were the putative costs of providing aid/cancelling debt (29 per cent) and the potential for increased immigration (29 per cent). Clearly, British consumers' emerging sense of connectivity with the developing world has not always been framed in positive terms.

The survey respondents were also critical of big business and private investors, with 43 per cent agreeing that they made little or no contribution to alleviating poverty. Similarly, 43 per cent also felt that 'working for a fairer world trading system' was one of the three key paths to reducing poverty in developing countries. Finally, 46 per cent of the sample agreed that buying Fair Trade goods was a way to reduce developing world poverty (this option came second only to charitable donations at 63 per cent). Indeed, DFID had already set the promotion of Fair Trade as one of its Millennium Development Goals.

That there is growing interest in and concern about the actions of corporations and their relationships with producers is indisputable. However, before considering the ethical context of this shift, the relationship between corporations and supply chains will be critically considered.

Responsibility in Supply Chains

From the outset it must be understood that the ethics of supply chain management remain highly contested. The consumerist argument suggests that companies are accountable for the actions and interactions within their own supply chain, primarily because, unlike other externalities generated by a business, the supply chain is an integral part of its operations and thus a defining feature of its character as a company. However, as New (2004) pointed out, allocating corporate responsibility across an international supply chain can be highly problematic.

First, there is the question of whether it is appropriate to allocate ethical responsibility to a corporation at all – namely, can a company be seen as a moral agent? The nature of incorporation does clearly establish a company as having a distinct legal identity with attendant rights and responsibilities, but it is one that is quite distinct from its employees (Chryssides and Kaler, 1993: 226). Thus the company is not a representation, at least in legal terms, of the people within it. This state of affairs might logically suggest that a company cannot, therefore, be seen as having any of the social responsibility associated with individual citizens and is, thus, effectively divorced from accountability for the intentions and actions of its managers. This is analogous with an argument that suggests it is not the gun but the gunman that is responsible for the result of a shooting. This argument is supported by the fact that it is impossible to punish the company itself for perceived wrong-doing: any punitive action taken against a business in effect damages individuals associated with it – employees, shareholders, suppliers and so on – rather than the corporation itself. Of course, individual employees and shareholders can also benefit from perceived wrong-doing, for instance through increased profits gained through squeezing supply chains, but it can be difficult to assign causality, especially if the perceived wrong-doing happened generations before.

The counter argument suggests that, in fact, the actions of a corporation closely reflect the decisions of an organized hierarchy of individuals within it. Indeed, this is the purpose of a well-structured and effective organization. Furthermore, if strategic planning is implemented successfully, a company will pursue specific aims even if individual personnel change. In this sense the corporation has a life of its own with particular corporate intentions and, it may be argued, particular attendant social responsibilities. That a number of examples of corporate malfeasance, for example the fraudulent accounting practices at Enron, are the result of the emergent properties of 'corporate culture' that coalesce somewhere between the individual and company level responsibility, further emphasizes the methodological difficulties of assigning moral responsibility in business situations (see further Micklethwait and Wooldridge, 2003).

Nevertheless, if we accept that a corporation can accept ethical responsibility for its actions (and this is not always the case) then the next issue is how this responsibility can be articulated across a modern supply chain. As New (2004) noted the key factor here is the causal link between the corporation's strategic intentions and their playing out across a supply chain's actual operations. Many supply chains function as hierarchies with various actors responding to drivers higher up the chain from themselves (this is the typical buyer-supplier relationship), thus an understanding of supply chain causality incorporates important variables as relativities in information and power.

Supply chain information is increasingly embedded in modern products, often through provenance. Indeed, Fair Trade has focussed much of its marketing effort on promoting the specifics of product origin and the nature of production. With modern management information systems firmly in place in multi-nationals, most supply chains are closely monitored to establish efficiency. In such conditions, responsibility for the nature of the supply chain may be fully allocated to the corporation since there can be no recourse to a defence based on ignorance of working or environmental practices. However, a second issue of power is also significant here.

The tendency to outsource elements of global supply chains has, in some cases, loosened control from the organizational centre of the chain's operation. If the strategic goal is entirely outcome-driven then there need be no mechanism in place to audit each stage of the supply chain for its broader performance. Clearly, then, accountability by a firm for its supply chain activities may be seen in terms of power over and information about elements of the chain itself. Indeed, a lack of power or information has been a common defence in corporate supply chain scandals: Nike's main defence when exposed as a buyer of sweatshop-produced goods was that this criticism be directed at the manufacturers of the goods rather than Nike as the corporate buyer. The fact that consumers remained unimpressed by such an argument is significant, as it rests on a perception of Nike's power and information very different from that presented by the company itself.

Thus, it can be seen that the allocation of responsibility across a global supply chain remains a complex and contested matter. The next section will develop the critique of supply chain ethics by setting out the philosophical context of trade. Application of the discipline of philosophical discourse below will establish the terminology for a subsequent discussion of Fair Trade as part of the ethical supply chain movement.

THE PHILOSOPHICAL CONTEXT

Philosophy may be understood as the use of reason and logic to explore and better understand the 'truth' of reality, particularly the patterns of cause and effect within our experience. Recourse to the philosophical context of 'ethics' at this point will allow a deeper understanding of a variety of analytic approaches to corporate behaviour and to Fair Trade within it. Such analyses will demonstrate a range of interpretations of what is ethical business behaviour and will highlight the potential impact of Fair Trade actions to enhance corporate reputation in each of them.

> Ethics deals with the good life for humankind. Morality in contrast is a concern for justice, which is making restitution if wrongs are done. Ethics, in these terms, can be thought of as developmental whereas morality is judgemental. (Fisher and Lovell, 2003: 30)

There is sometimes a degree of confusion over the meaning of 'business ethics' and its connection, if any, with concepts of morality. However, the basic definitions of each found in any dictionary offer immediate help. For example, the *Concise Oxford Dictionary* defines 'moral' as 'concerned with goodness or badness of human character or behaviour or the distinction between right and wrong' and 'ethics' as 'the science of morals in a human context' (1990). Therefore, as regards business ethics literature, 'morality' is usually seen as an absolute interpretation of (corporate) behaviour in terms of its human implications and outcomes, good or bad. Business ethics itself may be seen as the scientific study of such behaviours. However, a consideration of the wider philosophical study of ethics – the science of morality – offers a broader range of perspectives on corporate actions and may be used to explore the various moral contexts of Fair Trade.

The philosophy of ethics may be broadly divided into two main schools of thought: consequentialism and deontology. The former is concerned with the implications of actions with reference to the good that they can generate. In other words, what matters in terms of making an ethical judgement is the effect of actions alone. The latter is centred on the primacy of principles with reference to what is accepted as right or wrong from established and agreed standards and does not take into account the consequences of actions at all. This dichotomy of thought can be seen in the critiques of supply chain management that have led to the evolution of Fair Trade. From a consumerist perspective, the ethical objection to modern supply chains is consequentialist and rests on the outcomes as experienced by key stakeholders such as producers and factory workers. However, for many activists, the argument is largely a deontological one, based around an *a priori* and absolutist sense of social justice and fairness in trade. This will be explored in greater detail below.

These two positions on ethical behaviour can further be broken down into either individual or institutional contexts. At the one extreme, ethics may be seen as part of the project of self-development through understanding personal responsibility and acquiring judgement. At the other, institutional frameworks cast ethics as something to be seen as fixed and external to the individual, but as a structure to which the individual may turn for guidance (see further Fisher and Lovell, 2003: 69; Petrick and Quinn, 1997: 48). Following the work of Fisher and Lovell as specified here, Figure 3.1 demonstrates this framework of ethics. Each quadrant will be considered in terms of its general implications for supply chain ethics and particular relevance to Fair Trade.

Quadrant 1: Virtue Ethics

This quadrant features ethics that are based on principles as applied to individuals. 'Virtue' here represents the 'means' not the 'ends' that can generate a 'good' life for an individual person. Thus, unethical means can never be justified by ethical outcomes and a virtuous action cannot be so described if it has been carried out with unethical intentions. Such

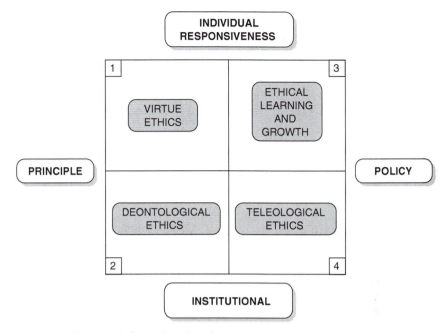

Figure 3.1 *Framework for ethical theories*
Source: Fisher and Lovell (2003)

philosophy is, therefore, described as 'non-consequentialist'. Aristotle (384–322 BC) is most often associated with this kind of thinking.

Virtue ethics centres on a set of predefined internal characteristics, rather than external imperatives, that governs ethically good behaviour and allows the individual to make the 'right' choice of action. The four chief virtues established by Aristotle's mentor, Plato, were: courage, wisdom, self-control and justice. Of these, Aristotle gave primacy to justice, but it has also been argued more recently that wisdom must be applied to temper justice (Fisher and Lovell, 2003: 75). Furthermore, the meaning of virtue is often highly contested and subject to cultural interpretation – there is a considerable difference in the definition of virtue between Homeric Greece, Christian Europe and the Muslim Middle East, for example. Another criticism of virtue ethics is that it can cast people in a purely instrumental role as mere articulators of established codes of behaviour – essentially denying free will. Furthermore, MacIntyre (1982) would argue that without an appropriate institutional context, any concept of 'the good' could not be pursued at all.

A virtue ethics analysis of Fair Trade would prove ambivalent. Such an approach would endeavour to consider trade in the context of individual behaviours viewed as virtuous at the time. Thus, the importance of social norms in the Aristotelian world-view might suggest that unethical trade that damages the environment or hurts children is no longer acceptable in the consumer marketplace, but would be less clear about the developmental and economic context of Fair Trade. The virtue or otherwise of the 'free' market is thus less clear-cut. Moral relativism, or the acceptance that different ethical boundaries apply in different contexts or cultures, further challenges assertion of the absolutes of virtue ethics. This is discussed further below.

Nevertheless, the virtuous individual is an identifiable actor in the development of ethical and Fair Trade. Bruce Crowther, the Fair Trade Towns Co-ordinator at the Fairtrade Foundation, explained his involvement as a simple matter of personal ethics responding to global injustice:

> Well, I've been an Oxfam campaigner for nineteen years; I came on the BandAid bandwagon. And the simple reason I do this is because a child dies every 3.4 seconds from poverty. It is the greatest injustice in the world today and I cannot live with that fact and do nothing. People say, 'you must be really depressed', well, it is only depressing if you do nothing about it. So you have to do something about it – it is not about alleviating your conscience, but simply any decent person would do something. There isn't a choice … Well, my mother brought me up to be caring and it's in the genes. I just have a feeling for justice. When I first got on the BandAid bandwagon religion did not come into it and I did it just because such poverty is immoral. (Interview, 2003)

Whilst the manifestations of such a response to the global supply chain can be critiqued (for example, it could be suggested that Fair Trade does not work to alleviate the problem of trade injustice), the ethical context of its inception in virtue ethics is clear. Virtue ethics may explain the actions of pioneers and leaders in a range of social movements, from peaceful political protest (Ghandi, Luther King), to civil reform (Wilberforce, Nightingale) and modern social entrepreneurship (Muhammad Yunus at the Grameen Bank). In each case an extraordinary and driven individual drew on a belief set and personality to bring about ethical and practical change.

Quadrant 2: Deontological Ethics

Central to an understanding of the deontological world-view is the work of Immanuel Kant (1724–1804). Kant's philosophy argued that all genuinely ethical behaviour must be driven, *a priori*, by a set of universal principles and that the outcomes of such behaviour are largely irrelevant to how they must be judged. Again, such thinking is non-consequentialist. Kant further explained his concept of guiding principles as being 'duties' or the bounding concepts that define what is right. To be truly ethical such duties must also be carried out with free will. The key to a full understanding of Kant's 'duties' lies in his development of the idea of a 'categorical imperative' or, in other words, a defined principle that must always be obeyed. A categorical imperative can be defined by its universality, namely that it may be understood by all reasoning people to be a standard code of conduct of equal impact, whether it is applied to the doers, receivers, or observers of an action (Fisher and Lovell, 2003). This is in contrast to hypothetical or conditional imperatives that may be tested or qualified by circumstances.

Application of the categorical imperative approach is itself highly contested. Various attempts have been made to modify Kant's original premise (Beck, 1959; Bowie, 1999; De George, 1999). Nevertheless, the model of principle-based ethics has in some ways become more relevant in the increasingly fractured post-modern experience of citizens in developed nations (hence the growth of formalized religion in many parts of the world).

Of particular importance in this deontological tradition are theories of justice and rights. As has already been noted, Aristotle established justice as an important virtue ethic within individual behaviour. Closely allied to such deontological thinking is the philosophy of Natural Law, which proposes an objective moral order above human law. This set of ideas centres on a notion of inalienable human rights and proposes that there is an objective moral order that goes beyond human law. Typically this philosophical approach expands virtue ethics' focus on justice to form an ethics of human rights. A group of eighteenth century political philosophers led by John Locke and including Paine, Rousseau and Wollstonecraft developed these notions of social justice, based around the concepts of liberty and equality, as an argument against the despotic governments and monarchs of the time and sowed the seeds of the democratic tradition in Europe and North America. Natural Law established three key human rights initially: life, liberty and property. More recently these have been much expanded upon to include other rights (to employment, for instance) and freedoms as well (for example, of association: see Dworkin, 1977).

Three key statements of human rights have emerged from the Natural Law tradition of thinking: the American Declaration of Independence (1776), the French Declaration of the Rights of Man (1789) and the United Nations Declaration of Human Rights (1948). The philosophical contribution of Natural Law in establishing an ethics of social justice and human rights has been highly influential in the development of the Fair Trade movement.

More recently theories of justice have been further explored, most notably by Nozick and Rawls. Nozick (1974) adopted a libertarian position that attributed primacy to so-called negative freedoms, by which he meant an individual's freedom *from* any particular stricture. From this perspective, there should be few restrictions on individual activity outside those established by law and the role of government is cast as enabling rather than restricting, with a main responsibility to uphold property rights. Nozick further developed a theory of 'entitlement' that established the ethical context of legal ownership as central to notions of justice in society. In Nozick's view equality of opportunity is an ethical irrelevance in the development of individual well-being – it is the responsibility of everyone to create and pursue their own opportunities within the law. The law, in turn, is ethically charged with then protecting and preserving that which each individual has achieved for themself.

A very different philosophical tradition may be discerned in the work of Rawls (1971). Rawls developed a theory of distributive justice that imagined a society in its 'original position' where members were unaware of their individual characteristics or how these could generate social advantages or disadvantages for them. In the original position individuals are unaware of where they live or under what government and have no knowledge of their personal skills or failings. In such a state, encapsulated by Rawls as lying behind a 'veil of ignorance', each individual if offered the choice of which type of society in which they might live would rationally choose that which offers the best conditions for all in order to assure that they also benefit from such a system. This represents the most effective risk-minimizing response. Thus, Rawls's theory demonstrates a rational approach to justice and fairness that can be based, ultimately, on self-interest. However, his model does not permit one individual to prosper at the expense of another and thus refutes Nozick.

In a Kantian analysis, Fair Trade stands as a manifestation of a normative categorical imperative that establishes the need to treat others fairly (as one would wish to be treated) and to avoid exploitation. The asymmetry in power and information that exists between North and South would only strengthen the Kantian argument. However, it could be argued that the impact of international trade itself answers the imperative – offering direct foreign investment and access to new markets to developing countries that materially improve livelihoods – and that the exact contractual terms agreed are of less importance. Finally, applying Rawls's theory of justice also supports an ethical interpretation of Fair Trade, since it would argue that no one would choose to be exploited or paid below-subsistence prices for their produce. Few choose to starve.

An understanding of deontological and Natural Law ethics provides an interesting lens through which to examine some key Fair Trade actors. The activist campaigners behind the earliest alternative trading organizations (ATOs) were driven by a clear sense of the injustice of modern trading conditions between North and South. As Steve Sellers of Transfair USA noted in 2003.

> I think it is two-fold. We certainly stress quality, because we think quality is important, but there's also a very straightforward social justice argument. The fact is that when you eat rice it really did come from somewhere, when you drink tea it did come from some place. We feel strongly that there is a strong moral component to this. As a human being, you, I, all of us, should be concerned with all the other human beings who are involved in this process. So, putting quality totally aside, there's a moral and ethical imperative to understand and educate yourself about what's happened and then to act on that and to take into account consciously the series of human beings who exist from that farm to us here.

The virtuous individual, then, should aim to address the inequality of modern trade between the developed and developing world through personal action. This can apply as much to the NGO activist as it does to the conscience-driven consumer, insofar as the motivation for action in both cases is driven by personal principle, not institutional outcome. Similarly, deontology demands that the principled corporation address issues of fairness and justice in all its dealings. At an institutional level, the role of Fair Trade organizations has been both to develop a commercial model of social justice and to act as advocates for the rights of farmers in the South.

Linked to deontology, and of considerable importance in the development of the Fair Trade movement, has been the philosophy of organized religion, particularly Christianity. In the UK, Christian groups were behind the establishment of both the Fairtrade Foundation and Cafédirect and in Europe, the largest ATO, Gepa, is run by four Christian organizations. Fair Trade in the USA was pioneered by Christian Mennonite organizations selling crafts sourced through charitable and missionary activities in the developing world. Furthermore, a number of key actors in the UK Fair Trade movement express strong religious beliefs. Bruce Crowther, architect of the Fair Trade Town campaign, explained that his own personal motivation was framed by the actions of Quakerism:

> I had no idea about Quakers before. An example was the slave trade abolition – I knew nothing about it – but it turns out that Quakers were the people that started that. Another example was Oxfam – I was startled to find out that it was founded by Quakers and still has incredible connections. But Quakers don't shout about themselves. Another example that fascinated me was Mahatma Ghandi's visit to the Lancashire cotton mills – his movement against the cotton mills was a really significant step. They thought he would be lynched by the cotton workers, but he managed to convince them that, yes, you will be poor, because you will be out of work, but people are dying in my country because of what is happening here. And then I found out that it was a Quaker that invited him to go. (Interview, 2003)

In the USA, faith organizations have embraced the Fair Trade movement. The Catholic Relief Services (CRS) is organizing its churches to serve Fair Trade coffee at church and educate their membership about Fair Trade. According to Joan Neal of CRS, '[i]t's important for us to help Catholics to be able to do their day-to-day living, and live out principles of Catholic faith, which call us to be people of justice.' Jonathan Frerichs of Lutheran World Relief explained his organization's interest in Fair Trade: 'Coffee is basically of sacramental stature in the Lutheran Church. There's very little said about where it comes from.' Fair Trade, he says, 'lifts up the farmer again and again. That's why it feels so solid in churches' (in Zazima, 2003).

Similarly, there is a longstanding tradition of philanthropy and ethical trading associated with other religiously motivated families in the UK, such as the Lewises (founders of the John Lewis Partnership), the Cadburys, the Peabodys and the Sainsburys. The Christian tradition of helping the poor clearly fits well with the fundamental strategy of Fair Trade although, crucially, Fair Trade rejects the charity model in favour of empowerment through trade and development.

CASE STUDY: TEN THOUSAND VILLAGES

Ten Thousand Villages is a not-for-profit program of the Mennonite Central Committee (MCC), the relief and development agency of Mennonite and Brethren in Christ churches in North America. Ten Thousand Villages began in 1946 when Mennonite Central Committee (MCC) worker Edna Ruth Byler of Akron, PA, visited MCC volunteers who taught sewing classes in Puerto Rico. They were looking for ways to improve the lives of their students, many of whom lived in poverty. Byler brought several pieces of embroidery home to sell to friends and neighbours. In the early 1970s, the flourishing project moved out of Byler's basement and became an official MCC program.

For over fifty years the Ten Thousand Villages program of MCC was known as SELFHELP Crafts of the World. This alternative trading organization became officially known as Ten Thousand Villages in 1996. In 2004, Ten Thousand Villages had over 180 stores across North America.

The organization has the following founding principles:

- To work with disadvantaged artisans.
- To purchase from craft groups that are concerned for their members and promote member participation.
- To pay fair prices for handicraft and to do so promptly.
- To pay up to half the value of a handicraft order when it is placed and the balance when the items are shipped to North America. This provides operating capital for artisans to purchase raw materials and for craft groups to pay workers.
- To offer consumers handicrafts that reflect and reinforce rich cultural traditions.
- To promote Fair Trade.
- To use marketing strategies and messages consistent with the company's mission and ideals including: responsible lifestyle choices; efficiency; Christian ethics.
- To work with volunteers in North American operations wherever possible.

Ten Thousand Villages provides vital fair income to Third World people by marketing their handicrafts and telling their stories in North America. Ten Thousand

Villages works with artisans who would otherwise be unemployed or underemployed, providing sustainable income through Fair Trade. This income helps pay for food, education, health care and housing. Thousands of volunteers in Canada and the United States work with Ten Thousand Villages in their home communities. In 2003, total sales were $14.6m (£8.2m), up from $12.6m (£7.1m) in 2002, and net income was $442K (£248K), up from $8.4K (£4.7K) in 2002. The organization is a member of the International Federation of Alternative Trade (IFAT).

Source: http://www.tenthousandvillages.org

Quadrant 3: Ethical Learning and Growth

This set of ideas suggests that individual ethical decision making can only come about by a process of development and self-awareness set in the context of defined ethical ends or 'policies'. Thus, self-knowledge through learning can be both the means to achieve ethical outcomes and an ethical goal in itself. This philosophical approach is consistent with the extensive and growing self-development management literature that aims to improve company performance through developing individual staff members. Clearly, mission statements and company policy mean little if they are not articulated through the business by its staff and their interactions with stakeholders. In this way, an ethical trading code of conduct has little value unless it is accompanied by training and education across the whole company about its meaning and operational impact.

The implication of this approach for Fair Trade is to stress the need for education in propagating the Fair Trade message. This can be seen as either an issue for raising consumer awareness or organizational sensitivity. The Fairtrade Labelling Organisations internationally and the local Fair Trade organizations in each member country (such as the Fairtrade Foundation in the UK and TransFair in the USA) have a responsibility to increase the levels of consumer understanding of Fair Trade and generate publicity to make the market grow and to raise awareness. This is the advocacy function at the heart of much Fair Trade marketing. A wide variety of techniques are evident such as: product focus (the annual Fair Trade Fortnight in the UK); public relations (celebrity endorsements); traditional media marketing (the UK Co-operative Group's Christmas 2003 television advertisements) and educational campaigns (such as the Reading International Solidarity Centre's work, focussed on citizenship classes in schools in the Reading area). Retailers also have a role to play in educating consumers, but acknowledge that this must be done in collaboration with other Fair Trade partners. Hamish Renton, Project Leader of 'Food You Can Trust' at Tesco, commented:

It's the business of the Fairtrade Foundation, we think, to grow the awareness of the category, and what we're doing is growing the category on the shelf. What we are trying to get across to people is the variety, what we're sourcing from where: there are a few good messages in there. Some are sponsored by the brands, telling how long they've been there and so on. And in the end you have some examples of what it does – people we've helped. It's probably nothing that anyone else hasn't done, but we think we know our customers better than anyone, therefore, we know the tone of voice that they will respond to. (Interview, 2003)

Within companies, the role of ethical educator may fall to senior managers who are championing ethical or Fair Trade goods. Many large retailers now have specific ethics or sustainability managers charged with monitoring internal ethical standards; in such cases this individual would develop internal training and communications models to explain and promote the Fair Trade model. The role of company codes of conduct discussed further below is also significant here.

Quadrant 4: Teleological Ethics

In this quadrant lie consequentialist theories that rely on an institutional context to both achieve and define their ethical ends. One such context is the stakeholder model. Here the impact of business decisions is framed by the effect they have on all the parties linked to them. Thus, an ethical approach to decision making in this context involves considering (and perhaps even consulting) all stakeholders first (see for example, Whysall, 2000c).

Perhaps the most famous of all teleological theories is utilitarianism. This world-view was championed in the nineteenth century by the British social reformer Jeremy Bentham (1748–1832) and took a 'consequentialist' approach to actions that stressed the importance of outcomes for the general good. Thus, the overall utility of an action (that is, how far it can ensure the maximum good or happiness for the maximum number of people) determines its ethical value. Such an approach requires the outcomes of action to be somehow measured in terms of happiness. Thus, a major issue with this theory lies in first, defining what is meant by happiness and then in establishing how it can be measured. There is always the danger that a utilitarian approach will focus on a single 'good' outcome rather than the common good. Such narrow vision is often a feature of target-based activities and can ultimately lead to a distortion of overall outcomes.

Nevertheless, a utilitarian approach has great value in assessing supply chain relationships, as it factors in economic externalities beyond simple transactional accounting. Therefore, a teleological analysis of a contractual agreement would not only measure outcome happiness by final profit, but would include its impact on all stakeholders in providing an ethical measure of its worth. So, if one party benefits at the expense of another, utilitarianism would look to explore the nature of these balancing utilities and judge if there was a net 'good' achieved overall. In the case of a trading arrangement where one party makes a profit by buying commodities at a below-subsistence price (resulting in starvation for the producer), it is clear that a utilitarian analysis would define this as unjust and unethical.

In this quadrant lies the consumer movement supporting the emergence of Fair Trade into the mainstream. The consumer in developed markets is increasingly framing the wider impact of a corporation's activities as part of its core performance – a focus on outcomes that is clearly teleological. Thus, there is a growing demand for corporate accountability that goes far beyond the legal boundaries of the company and extends to its broader influence across its network of social and economic connections. A range of boycott campaigns in recent years ranging from the political (Shell) and humanitarian (Nestlé) to the social (Nike) and economic (WalMart) demonstrates this. There is now a widespread perception among the public that the pressures of globalization and hyper-competition are negatively impacting supply chain dynamics (see for example, Hutton et al., 2001).

In tandem with this, the growing consumer concern about global actions by corporations has been reflected in increased media scrutiny of business operations such that aspects of corporate activity that could once be kept hidden are increasingly being made public. The diffusion of digital communication such as the Internet has changed fundamentally the way the public views the world. Information from around the globe passes rapidly across boarders and allows activists and pressure groups to highlight corporate wrong-doing to millions at the click of a mouse. These opportunities for rapid global dissemination of information have proved instrumental in furthering the cause of anti-globalization protesters and have helped generate damaging brand associations for many major businesses. This teleological concern on the part of consumers in the developed world has provided the context in which activists have been able to promote Fair Trade and watch it grow.

However, there is an interesting corporate perspective here too, best described as 'ethical pragmatism'. Companies are increasingly recognizing the value of adopting proactive, rather than reactive, ethical policies. Such an approach to supply chain management can have a positive value both inside and outside of companies. For internal stakeholders (employees) ethical behaviour can generate a positive corporate culture that improves staff retention as well as offering improved management of whistle-blowing situations. With respect to external stakeholders (consumers, policy/law makers, suppliers, media, professional bodies) ethical behaviour offers positive marketing, strengthened negotiation positions and damage limitation in difficult situations.

Furthermore, some ethical policies such as practicing good environmental husbandry can have a long-term commercial benefit as they can protect the sustainability of important suppliers. Tesco, currently the largest UK supermarket, has launched an extensive range of own label Fair Trade products. Hamish Renton, Project Leader of Tesco's 'Food You Can Trust' program, explained the rationale behind such a bold move:

> It was simply listening to customers. Every year we do a UK brand review that is the UK's largest quantitative and qualitative customer listening exercise. My understanding is that it is a huge number of customers that it touches from accompanied shops to surveys, and [Fair Trade] was emerging as a trend. Eighty per cent of customers were focussed on their world, but 20 per cent were more ethically motivated and 20 per cent of 16 million is quite a lot of people actually and we have a good enough offering, do we do a good enough job? It really stemmed from there. But don't discount the possibility that underneath it all we might just be nice people and want to do some good things. You only have to look at our CSR agenda, the fact that we were the first to do 'computers for schools' – it raised eight million quid – I set up our 'five-a-day' pro-gramme on fruit and veg for cancer research a couple of years before the government got into it; we do 'Race For Life' every year. In terms of corporate citizenship, Tesco get ticks in all the boxes, so don't discount that as a motivating factor as well. (Interview, 2003)

Diana Gayle, Marketing Officer at the UK's Fairtrade Foundation, reinforced this point, noting that the business case for Fair Trade can be part of a larger corporate social responsibility strategy:

> I very much believe that the way companies can engage with Fair Trade doesn't have to be just launching a product with the Fair Trade mark on it, there are a number of ways they can engage with it. Whether it's looking at how Fair Trade can be part of a company's wider CSR [Corporate Social Responsibility] agenda, so for example, it is so much part of companies' ethos that they will switch to recycled paper or whatever, similarly switching to Fair Trade or sustainable purchasing should be part of their strategy. (Interview, 2003)

Finally, even from an activist perspective Fair Trade can work in a utilitarian way as a powerful and sustainable model of poverty alleviation through trade, not aid. One of the key arguments for the long-term value of Fair Trade is that it can break the dependency culture by which many poor communities become trapped through aid programmes.

When applied to the concept of Fair Trade, the range of philosophical approaches supports its ethical value. From a utilitarianist viewpoint, Fair Trade offers the mechanism by which a great good can be offered to the majority of the population (that is, those living in the developing world). From a Kantian perspective, Fair Trade presents the choice to do what is right in terms of relieving poverty and dependence on aid – often quite literally saving lives in the process. The philosophical background to Fair Trade therefore spans consequentialism, deontology, Natural Law and religious ethics. Indeed, Fair Trade is congruent with a variety of interpretations of the moral response to injustice such that it effectively defies criticism from an ethical/philosophical perspective.

RESPONSES TO SUPPLY CHAIN ETHICS

Despite the theoretical debate over supply chain responsibility noted above, the fact is that consumers are increasingly apportioning such responsibility to corporations, driven at least in part by their perceptions of the ethical imperatives of justice and Fair Trade. As a consequence, a number of business responses can be discerned. The main focus of such responses has been on the production/manufacturing element of the supply chain, as this is the part of the chain in which many stakeholders perceive much of the negative effect of global trade (largely uncovered by consumer activists). These responses may be categorized into external and internal according to their locus of accountability, namely whether they are framed by actors outside the company (that is, government, trade unions, international bodies and so on) or within its strategic management structure (see Figure 3.2). Along this spectrum fall national and international legislation, international codes and regulations such at the United Nations' Global Compact, informal agreements between civil society and business such as the Ethical Trading Initiative in the UK, and finally, self-policing codes of conduct. Fair Trade is situated towards the middle of the spectrum encompassing both external regulation (through certification, for example) and voluntary corporate strategy (such as Tesco's own label).

At one end of the spectrum are external responses including legislation and regulation at an institutional level. At one extreme are national laws that protect workers from exploitation and danger. The majority of developed countries have, for example, health and safety legislation to control working conditions and other laws that protect workers from unfair wages or overly long hours. The trade union movement also has an important

Figure 3.2 *Spectrum of business responses to ethical trade*

role to play here. In addition, some transnational legislation is emerging to protect workers, most notably the European Convention on Human Rights.

In terms of external regulation, there are a number of global bodies that have addressed issues of supply chain inequality. These regulatory initiatives are positioned in the middle of the spectrum of business responses to ethical trade, as they are external frameworks that require internal corporate co-operation to have any affect. Examples include the International Labour Organisation (ILO), the United Nations Global Compact and Social Accountability International.

The ILO was created in 1919 to address 'injustice, hardship and privation' in international working conditions via the establishment of International Labour Standards (ILS). In 1944, the ILO's mandate was broadened to include social policy and civil rights issues with the incorporation of the Declaration of Philadelphia into its constitution. The ILO effectively functions via international treaties with signatory governments on its conventions (that should be interpreted as binding) and recommendations (which take the form of non-binding guidelines). In addition, the ILO issues codes of conduct and other resolutions and declarations that aim to express normative working practices and conditions.

There are four areas covered by the eight 'fundamental' ILO conventions. These focus on basic human rights (and link closely with the theory of Natural Law):

- Freedom of association.
- Abolition of forced labour.
- Workplace equality.
- Elimination of child labour.

These are considered as a *sine qua non* of membership of the ILO. Currently, there are 175 member states in the organization, of which 99 have ratified all four fundamental areas covered by the conventions. These include the European Union, Japan, much of Africa, some Latin American and a few other Asian countries. The United States and China have only ratified two of the key areas.

The ILO enforces its conventions by both ratifying an individual country's labour laws (subject to regular review) and by investigating specific allegations against a member state. However, the ILO has no legal recourse to prosecute, rather it acts as a watchdog for unjust behaviour.

Further along the spectrum are two United Nations' initiatives. The first is the Universal Declaration of Human Rights (1948) that featured some specific labour-related articles. These included: Article 4 calling for the abolition of slave labour; Article 23 establishing the universal right to work, the free choice of employment, and safe working conditions; Article 24 setting out the right to holiday and leisure time within work. In 1999 the United Nations built on this with the launch of the Global Compact, an initiative in 'voluntary corporate citizenship'. In the Compact, businesses around the world were challenged to join together with UN agencies and labour and civil rights groups to support nine principles of human rights, labour, and the environment based around the Universal Declaration. To date over 1,300 companies worldwide have signed up to the Compact. However, the Compact does not represent an enforceable set of regulations, rather it aims to catalyze sound corporate citizenship.

At the external end of the spectrum, some also argue that the World Trade Organization represents another important institutional player in developing improved labour conditions, as it can play a crucial role in bringing the benefits of global trade to the poor. However, the collapse of the Doha round of negotiations in 2003 called such optimism into serious doubt. Global trade inequality is the key driver behind Fair Trade and the current market mechanisms simply do not help alleviate this. However, the call for greater trade barrier liberalization amongst developing countries (who do, broadly speaking, have more tariffs in place than the developed world) often fails to address the grossly distorting Northern trade barriers, such as the vast agricultural subsidies enshrined in the European Union's Common Agricultural Policy (which amount to as much as the entire gross domestic product of sub-Saharan Africa). The decision by the G22 group of developing countries (including India, Brazil and China) to end their involvement in Doha early on suggests a growing realization that the WTO does not offer a viable forum to pursue their own trade interests.

Another important international initiative is Social Accountability International (SAI). SAI is a USA-based non-profit organization set up to develop and implement voluntary and verifiable social accountability frameworks with a particular focus on workplace standards. In 1996 the SAI developed the Social Accountability 8000 (SA8000) standard in tandem with a range of stakeholders. SA8000 is modelled on ISO (International Studies Organization) frameworks and is based on ILS (International Labour Standards). It promotes management action to improve workplace conditions. The code was established by the Council on Economic Priorities Accreditation Agency and was designed to be an independently audited assessment of a company's ethical and social behaviour. The code addresses nine areas of employment practice, including forced labour, child labour, health and safety and working hours. However, it has no guidelines on producer prices although it does discuss worker remuneration:

> Wages paid for a standard working week must meet the legal and industry standards and be sufficient to meet the basic needs of workers and their families; no disciplinary deductions. (SA8000, 2004)

The code is not enforceable by national law and is yet to be widely accepted by business.

Yet further along the spectrum, moving closer to internal accountability, lies the UK-based Ethical Trading Initiative (ETI) (Blowfield, 2002). The ETI represents an innovative coalition of businesses, NGOs, trade unions and government (the UK's Department of International Development) aiming to improve trading conditions for all stakeholders. The rationale for its development was a widespread perception of abuses of the labour force in global supply chains, particularly via sub-contracting that hides the real workers and the conditions in which they operate, in the context of weak government and ineffective labour laws in some developing countries. ETI defines itself as:

> A ground-breaking initiative which brings together a range of organisations from all parts of society with the aim of helping to make substantial improvements to the lives of poor working people around the world. As consumers of the goods they produce we all have a stake in this unique and innovative initiative. The ETI aims to develop and encourage the use of a widely endorsed set of standards, embodied in codes of conduct, and monitoring and auditing methods which will enable companies to work together with other organisations outside the corporate sector to improve labour conditions around the world. (ETI, 2004)

The ETI specifically addresses the issue of ethical sourcing and locates responsibility as well as power across the supply chain. It has a 'base code' that closely follows the ILS which consists of nine provisions:

- Employment is freely chosen.
- Freedom of association and the right to collective bargaining are respected.
- Working conditions are safe and hygienic.
- Child labour shall not be used.
- Living wages are paid.
- Working hours are not excessive.
- No discrimination is practiced.
- Regular employment is provided.
- No harsh or inhumane treatment is allowed.

The aim of the ETI is 'to ensure the rights and improve the conditions of workers through good supply chain management' (ETI, 2004). It is not an auditing organization – it exists to share learning that can improve international labour standards. There are currently 31 UK companies engaged with the ETI, mostly in the retail sector. A specific criticism that has been levelled is that it does not address the potential inequalities within the buyer-supplier relationship (Hughes, 2001). This is, of course, the role of Fair Trade.

At the 'internal' extreme of the spectrum resides corporate responses to ethical trade. Companies are increasingly attempting to offer greater transparency in their activities, principally in the form of self-policing codes of conduct for suppliers/producers and more values-driven mission statements that strive towards an 'ethical' approach to operations. Eighty-five per cent of US companies have some form of internal code of conduct and many large-scale UK firms have followed suit.

Business writers have also responded to growing consumer concern about 'globalization'. Hilton and Gibbons (2002) lead the fight back, claiming that multinational business can be more benign than has been presented by activists and 'anti-globalizers'. Setting out an agenda to bring 'social values to consumerism and capitalism, not destroying one in favour of the other' (p. xvii), they argue that social leadership can be good business and that the CSR mindset is now a *sine qua non* of big business strategy. Clearly, the ethical path can make sense for all stakeholders and it is the case that there has been a movement towards inclusion and social accountability evident in the corporate sector, either reactively or proactively.

However, despite many multinational retailers developing codes of conduct, there remains firm evidence of widespread labour abuses at the bottom of the supply chain. Oxfam's labour report 'Trading Away Our Rights' (2004) revealed that there is a widening gap between statements of corporate social responsibility and the reality of supply chain behaviours. The report highlighted the difficulty that suppliers of large multinationals have in reconciling the competing imperatives of the buyers who want both socially responsible manufacturing standards and the lowest prices. In a highly competitive market, it will always be the latter than ultimately drives business decisions. Furthermore, there is lack of consistency and transparency in the ethical trading standards and metrics of social impact and performance that are typically employed in corporate codes of conduct reporting.

Young and Welford (2002) carried out a survey of UK retailers and demonstrated that most had some form of trading code of conduct in place. However, none satisfied their 'five star' ethical trading rating and only eight merited a 'four' or 'three' star rating, meaning that they had both a publicly available trading code of conduct in place and that it was independently verified. More than 80 per cent of the survey did not use external social auditing.

Central to the credibility of internal ethical accountability is the concept of social auditing. Zadek (1994) described the social audit process as having much in common with the traditional financial audit in that, to be credible, an impartial and external party must carry out the process. However, he also identified some key differences between the two: first, that the social audit is driven by the agendas of the full range of stakeholders who engage with the business under scrutiny rather than simply those of the shareholders; second, that the analysis should encompass behaviours as well as impact or effects. Thus, the process has a functional universality as well as a values-based sensitivity. Of course, such an approach is fraught with problems, not least in finding a convincing mechanism through which to reconcile economic quantitative data with more qualitative value-based information. In an analysis of the social auditing process at Traidcraft, a leading UK Fair Trade organization, Zadek (1994) noted that a holistic approach worked best, one that avoided trying to reconcile different data into a single metric or benchmark. Such an approach generated interesting tensions around the concept of 'fairness'. Suppliers tended to judge Traidcraft on its behavioural performance (that is, the transparency of it dealings) rather than solely on the volume of trade generated (some suppliers saw their sales go down but still felt fairly treated).

There are a number of other criticisms that have been levelled at internal codes of conduct:

- They actually reduce, rather than increase, the level of corporate ethical behaviour as they remove uncertainty about what is appropriate behaviour and can encourage a lowest-common-denominator approach.
- They negate individual ethical responsibility in business and allow managers to justify their own actions in corporate terms.
- They are expensive to set up and audit effectively and may, therefore, lack institutional support.
- They do not effectively control corporate actions – only legal regulation can achieve this.

Above all, as a result of being both voluntary and self-policing, corporate codes of conduct are often criticized for being an easy option and acting as mere ethical window-dressing. Hutton et al. summed up these objections: 'part of the critique of some of the emerging voluntary codes of conduct and voluntary social accounting and reporting processes are indeed that they are a means of reducing the structural obligation corporations have' (2001: 116).

Codes of conduct aside, companies have also responded to the changing ethical climate for purely commercial reasons. The Quality-Ethics Matrix (Figure 3.3) demonstrates how ethical products can be conceptualized as part of a wider offer to the consumer. The matrix has as its axes quality/price and ethics, each expressed in quadrants as either low or high. When applied to Tesco, currently the UK's leading supermarket, quadrants 1 and 2 represent two established propositions based around quality/price: the *finest* and *value* ranges. The ethical positioning of these is low. In quadrant 3, high quality/price and high ethics, lie organic produce and existing Fair Trade brands such as Cafédirect. This is a familiar trade off for consumers and a potentially lucrative market for retailers. However, the innovative offer lies in quadrant 4, low price/quality and high ethics, and here is the space for Fair Trade own-label products that are cheaper than existing Fair Trade brands. Indeed,

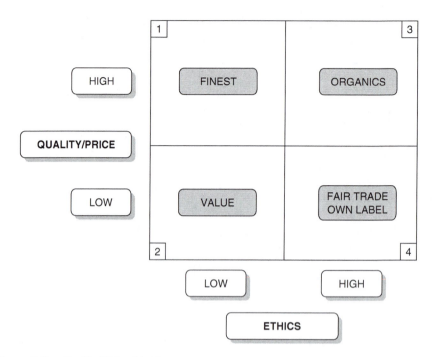

Figure 3.3   *Quality-Ethics Matrix*

there is potential here for a Fair Trade *value* range that stretches the price positioning of Fair Trade further and thus could open up entirely new markets. For Tesco, exploiting the ethical aspect of certain products allows them to offer more choice, expand their market and 'do the right thing'. Thus, ethical trading and commercial opportunism can success-fully mix.

CONCLUSION

This chapter has argued that supply chain ethics can be conceptualized within an estab-lished philosophical tradition that considers the nature of society and the individual cit-izen's responsibilities within it. Corporations are part of society, not separate from it, and they are increasingly adopting a role as 'good citizens' (whether proactively looking for marketing value or reactively under consumerist pressure). Fair Trade sits at the heart of this new relationship between business and civil society.

However, the use of ethical frameworks also adds complexity to the debate. As has already been noted above, the theory of ethical relativism reminds us that ethics can be culturally bounded. Namely, ethical models may not function similarly in different cultures or across wide geographical areas. One major objection to business ethics is, thus, that it attempts to impose in a paternalistic fashion the mores of one culture onto another – the best example of which is child labour. If it is already commonplace for children to work in a developing country to help their family survive (and local laws permit this), is it appropriate for a corporation in the developed world to stipulate that it will not employ them? From a utilitarian perspective, perhaps not: from a deontological one, certainly yes.

Indeed, the ILO's constitution enshrines the principle of relativism, stating that international labour standards be set with 'due regard to those countries in which climatic conditions, the imperfect development of industrial organisation, or other specific circumstances make the industrial conditions substantially different' (www. ilo.org/public/english/about/iloconst.htm).

Furthermore, when Zadek (1994) brought together ethical philosophy and business thinking in a discussion of ethical trading, he identified four 'lenses' through which it could be interpreted:

Economic Utilitarianism

This interpretation views a consumer's attitude to ethics as being bounded by an individual economic utility curve that simply balances personal morality with economic factors such as price in an instrumental way. Thus, a consumer justifies the higher price of a Fair Trade product by the personal 'value' of the moral gesture made in its purchase.

Social Psychology

This interpretation centres on the concept of the self-construction of identity through external factors such as purchase decisions within a social or group context. Thus, the individual 'buys' a sense of self as part of their social identity. This is discussed further in Chapters 7 and 8.

Reciprocal Ethics

Anthropology suggests that trade traditionally represented an attempt to establish bonds between communities and that ethical trade offers an opportunity to return to a sense of connection between consumer and producer that has been lost in the modern supply chain. This also has a marketing value.

Transcendent ethics

The fourth of Zadek's paradigms acknowledges the spiritual and humanist traditions of ethics that focus on altruism and the negation of the ego through a surrender to an external system of behaviour. This approach acknowledges the spiritual roots of some Fair Trade activists.

Clearly, then, an ethical interpretation of trade is a complex and contested matter. Nevertheless, Fair Trade counters many of the ethical objections to the modern supply chain and corporate sourcing strategy. In stark contrast with much of global buying practice, it offers suppliers a liveable and sustainable price, secure contracts, and developmental partnerships. By focusing its strategic objectives on both ends of the chain – quality products for consumers, quality of life for producers – Fair Trade ensures that the key stakeholders are acknowledged and protected.

Fair Trade fits into a range of philosophical traditions within supply chain ethics, answering both the deontological imperatives of the activists and the utilitarian demands of ethical consumers, whilst also embodying the supremacy of justice in both the Aristolean and Natural Law frameworks. That the Fair Trade movement has its roots in Christian activism only serves to underline its philosophical credentials. But, in the spirit of Bentham, it must also be remembered that Fair Trade is also highly practical in its delivery of better standards of living to producers and protection of the environment in sustainable practices.

This chapter has explored a variety of perspectives on supply chain ethics. First, it suggested that consumers are increasingly aware of the actions of corporations throughout their supply chain actions and, as a consequence, are demanding more information about the details of production of goods they purchase. As a result businesses are looking to demonstrate social responsibility in their dealings with suppliers. However, the chapter went on to acknowledge that attributing responsibility in modern supply chains can be problematic. Next, a philosophical context for supply chain ethics was developed based on the application of both consequentialist and deontological approaches to ethical behaviour. Fair Trade was critiqued in these terms. Finally, the chapter examined the range of responses to international supply chain issues that have developed.

The first part of this book has established the background to the rise of Fair Trade and set it in both an economic and philosophical context. Part Two explores Fair Trade operations including finance, certification and marketing. However, Part Two begins by looking at the industry structures and business strategies that have brought Fair Trade to market.

PART TWO

Fair Trade Operations

4

Fair Trade Industry Structures and Business Strategies

This chapter analyses the structure of the coffee and banana industries and outlines the development of Fair Trade in each industry's supply chain. It then describes the business structures, missions and strategies of leading alternative trading organizations (ATOs) that were amongst the founders of Fair Trade, using case studies as examples. Finally, the interaction between ATOs and traditional players as they compete in an increasingly mainstream Fair Trade market is discussed.

INTRODUCTION

The first three chapters of this book have provided a background to the economic and ethical contexts for the development of Fair Trade. A unique subset of a broader ethical trade movement, Fair Trade grew out of a desire to correct market imperfections and link producers with consumers through direct trading relationships. It has grown into a development movement with the aim of improving the lives of the world's poor by increasing their income and civic empowerment.

Part Two will examine how the Fair Trade system works in practice, focusing on how its structures and strategies have changed to accommodate growth and the entry of new players, as well as examining challenges to such growth (for example, access to finance). This first chapter will analyse the industry structures of the two most important Fair Trade products, coffee and bananas, and investigate how Fair Trade actors entered these markets and influenced the supply chains.

The two industries offer interesting contrasts. Both are concentrated in that three to four companies buy the majority of the world's production, but coffee offers more opportunities for product differentiation through different flavours, origins, growing regions and brands, whereas bananas are more commoditized. The two crops are grown very differently and thus Fair Trade standards have developed to accommodate the needs of the poorest actors within each supply chain. In coffee, Fair Trade works only with small producers organized into co-operatives, as they represent 50 per cent of the world's production and probably an even larger percentage of 'speciality' coffee production, grown on small shaded plots in distinct regions that produce their own flavour characteristics in the coffee bean. Because of their perishable nature and sensitive supply chain logistics, export bananas are grown mostly on large plantations that employ hundreds of farm workers. In bananas, then, Fair Trade addresses the development needs of both small producers and farm workers by operating two models of direct trade, one for co-operatives and the other for organizations of farm workers. After examining these two industries and how Fair Trade started and developed within each of them, we will turn to the strategies of the various businesses involved with Fair Trade. Fair Trade was started by a number of Alternative Trading Organizations (ATOs) that were engaged in direct and fair trading relationships with producers in the global South. The concept has now grown to include mainstream brands and businesses. An in-depth look at ATOs' strategies and their corporate structures will focus on how they have adapted to reflect the presence of larger players with other competitive advantages such as economies of scale, strong brand names and wider distribution.

The term 'ATO' encompasses several meanings (Littrell and Dickson, 1997, 1998). The origins of Fair Trade lie in creating 'alternative' trade patterns to secure higher incomes for the world's poorest producers, who were not necessarily benefiting from 'business as usual'. As Fair Trade enters the mainstream, however, the systems set up by ATOs are no longer viewed as 'alternative'. More and more mainstream companies are adopting Fair Trade practices on at least a few of their products, and many high street supermarkets now carry Fair Trade products. The term 'ATO', however, continues to serve a useful purpose in distinguishing those companies that were set up with the express purpose of delivering Fair Trade benefits to producers from second-mover companies who have adopted Fair Trade in the face of consumer pressure to meet a market opportunity, or only apply Fair Trade to some of their products. In general, ATOs conform to the following characteristics:

- All or nearly all products are traded according to Fair Trade principles, including fair pricing, direct trade, long-term relationships and credit provision in all ATO sourcing.
- Nearly all ATOs have adopted the Fairtrade Labelling Organisations International (FLO) certification system on products for which standards exist.
- ATOs' mission statements include commitments to Fair Trade and several ATOs are structured to return the maximum amount of income to farmers, even above the Fair Trade minimum. Maximizing profit is not their primary or even secondary goal. This aspect of ATOs can still be considered 'alternative' in modern Anglo-American capitalistic corporate governance.

In this context, the umbrella term 'ATO', therefore, covers privately held companies, worker-owned co-operatives, companies limited by shares, partly-producer-owned companies, and not-for-profits. In fact, the only thing that ATOs share is their commitment to reducing poverty through improving the terms of trade for the world's poorest producers and each organization has a different idea of the best way to operationalize this strategy. Nevertheless, the term is useful and necessary. ATOs represent the origins of Fair Trade, and as such are an essential part of the story of the development of the Fair Trade system, its certification and impressive growth.

COFFEE

Coffee was the first labelled Fair Trade product sold in the North and continues to be the highest volume and highest value product for most national Fair Trade markets. As the first and most important Fair Trade-certified product, the development of Fair Trade within the coffee export industry illustrates the development of Fair Trade itself (Rice, 2001).

This section will first examine the structure of the traditional coffee export industry, and how small-scale farmers typically market their product, and then describe the development of the Fair Trade model as an alternative to the traditional system. In creating the Fair Trade model, ATOs identified the points in the coffee export chain where poor farmers could capture more value and reconfigured trade and power relationships to ensure higher returns to primary producers. This critical analysis of trade relationships and correction of information and power imbalances characterizes the development of Fair Trade models in all products.

Industry Structure

The global coffee roasting industry is relatively monopolistic, with five companies, Kraft, Nestlé, Sara Lee, Procter & Gamble, and Tchibo, buying almost half of the global supply of green coffee beans (Gresser and Tickell, 2002). Eight transnational corporations control the export of more than 50 per cent of the world's coffee production (Bacon, 2004). Yet the coffee-growing industry is extremely diffuse, with 20 to 25 million farmers and farm workers earning a living from the crop (Gresser and Tickell, 2002; Rice and McLean, 1999). Seventy per cent of the world's coffee is grown on plantations of less than 25 hectares, and estimates of the world's production grown by very small family farmers (that is, less than five hectares) average at around 50 per cent (Bacon, 2004; Gresser and Tickell, 2002; Rice and McLean, 1999). Nearly all coffee is grown in developing countries, with Brazil, Vietnam, Colombia and Indonesia accounting for over 60 per cent of world production (ICO, 2004). Coffee is therefore a crop that is extremely important to the developing world, yet importers' concentrated buying power means that the supply chain is largely controlled by transnational coffee exporters and roasters rather than by the millions of farmers and farm workers who grow the beans.

It was not always thus. From 1962 to 1989, producing and consuming nations jointly controlled supply through the International Coffee Agreement, which aimed to keep coffee prices relatively high and stable (within a range of $1.20 to $1.40 per pound or £0.67 to £0.78 per pound) by setting export quotas for producing countries (Bacon, 2004; Gresser and Tickell, 2002). But the agreement fell apart when the USA pulled out in 1989, leading to an increase in world supply and a decline in prices from $1.16 (£0.65) per pound in 1988 to $0.52 (£0.29) per pound in 2003 (ICO, 2004), below the costs of production for most small farmers, especially in Latin America (Gresser and Tickell, 2002; Rice and McLean, 1999).

Aside from facing declining world coffee prices, small coffee farmers are also disadvantaged in global coffee trade relationships as outlined in Chapter 2. After coffee cherries are picked, they are milled to remove the beans from the surrounding cherry ('wet processing'), dried and then milled again to remove the dry parchment from the coffee beans ('dry processing'). Because small farmers do not produce enough individually to merit investment in either milling process, they generally sell their coffee in whole cherry form. And because small coffee farmers are often isolated from markets, they must sell their coffee cherries to middlemen who visit their farms, called *coyotes* in Latin America. The *coyotes* then consolidate small farmers' production and sell either directly to transnational-owned mills, or to independent mills, who process the cherries and then sell to transnational brokers and exporters (Oxfam and TransFair USA, 2002). Figure 4.1 summarizes the traditional coffee supply chain, and the relative concentration of actors within it.

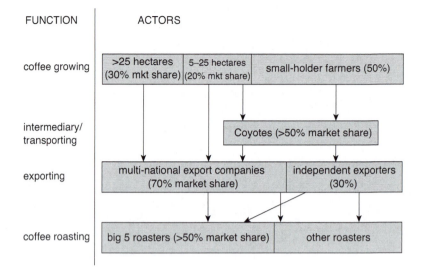

Figure 4.1   *Traditional coffee supply chain*

Small farmers' isolation translates to a lack of access to markets, price information, futures exchanges and technical assistance – structural market failures that are present no matter what the world coffee price may be. The Fair Trade coffee movement grew out of a desire for Northern coffee consumers both to guarantee a decent price for producers and to ensure producers access to the market information they were missing, thereby reducing their isolation and allowing them to capture more of the value in the supply chain.

Fair Trade in Coffee

Beginning in the 1980s, some small-scale coffee roasters in the North started to import directly from co-operatives of family coffee farmers at above-market prices. These ATOs were pioneers in what we know today as Fair Trade coffee. To address the isolation of small coffee farmers, coffee ATOs imported directly from farmer-owned co-operatives. Coffee producer co-operatives perform the *coyote* function by consolidating members' production, but because the co-operative is owned by the farmer members, the profits normally retained by the *coyote* are instead captured by the farmers themselves. Because some of the most serious exploitation happens at the farmer-*coyote* link as discussed in Chapter 2, cutting out the latter allows the farmers to capture much more of the value chain. The Fair Trade system also required the co-operatives to own or at a minimum control the milling process in order to be able to export directly, further increasing farmer power. Figure 4.2 depicts the role of the co-operative in the Fair Trade coffee supply chain.

Whilst direct trade with co-operatives is an essential element of the original Fair Trade model, Fair Trade coffee importers also developed a minimum price intended to cover small farmers' costs of production, pegged (not coincidentally) at the bottom of the target range set by the International Coffee Agreement. The minimum Fair Trade price was later modified to vary across regions, include a premium for organic certification, and to designate a 'social premium' to be spent on community development projects. The floor

Figure 4.2   *Fair Trade in the coffee supply chain*

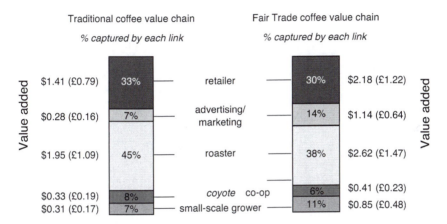

Figure 4.3   *Traditional vs. Fair Trade coffee value chain (low-priced coffee market)*
Source: Adapted from Mendoza and Bastiaensen (2003)

price for Central American Arabica coffee (a high-quality bean), for instance, is $1.21 (£0.68) per pound plus a $0.05 (£0.03) per pound social premium. The $0.05 per pound is added on to the market price if the market rises above the floor price of $1.21 per pound.

The result of these two key elements in the Fair Trade value chain is much higher incomes to coffee farmers, especially in periods of low world market prices. Figure 4.3 compares the value chain for traditional coffee and the Fair Trade coffee value chain. By removing the *coyote* from the chain, the Fair Trade chain allows the small-scale grower to capture a higher percentage of the retail price: typically 11 per cent *vs.* only 7 per cent from the *coyote*. Because the farmers own the co-operative exporter, they also retain the 6 per cent normally captured by intermediaries. Fair Trade thus allows farmers to capture higher percentages of the value added in traditional coffee marketing chains. Furthermore, because Fair Trade offers a guaranteed minimum price to co-operatives, the actual financial return to farmers is also higher (as is the end retail price to consumers).

Whilst ATOs operated successfully in the coffee trade for several years, Fair Trade in Europe and the US remained a niche market until the emergence of certification and independent Fair Trade labelling in the late 1990s (see further Chapter 6). The entry of certified Fair Trade coffee in the USA followed the emergence of the 'speciality' coffee industry through the exponential growth of coffeehouses, led by Starbucks. The speciality coffee industry focuses on high-quality beans and emphasizes origin countries. Thus, its members are especially interested in direct linkages with producers and are willing to pay more for high-quality coffee, aspects which led this sector to be natural first-adopters of Fair Trade. The 1,200-plus speciality coffee roasters in the USA (Rice and McLean, 1999) vary in size and usually carry several different blends of coffee, thus it was relatively easy for these companies to experiment with Fair Trade origins and offer one or more Fair Trade blends. Fair Trade coffee has benefited from this association, as speciality coffee is the fastest-growing segment of the US coffee market (SCAA, 2004). However, the European speciality coffee market is much smaller, which some suspect may limit the market share potential of Fair Trade coffee in Europe.

Mainstreaming Fair Trade Coffee

Recently, a combination of consumer and shareholder pressure coupled with the success of ATOs and smaller roasters with marketing Fair Trade coffee has resulted in a number of larger coffee roasters, including Procter & Gamble and Starbucks, entering the Fair Trade market. In April 2000, Starbucks announced that it would start to serve Fair Trade coffee in all of its company-owned cafés in the USA. Since then, Starbucks has expanded its offering of Fair Trade coffees to its university foodservice accounts and to 20 countries worldwide. Its purchases of Fair Trade coffee have grown from 650,000 pounds in 2001 to 1.1 million pounds in 2002 and 2.1 million pounds in 2003. Procter & Gamble launched a Fair Trade coffee offering on-line under its Millstone brand in late 2003, and the product arrived on grocery store shelves in late 2004. In 2000, Costa Coffee became the first UK café chain to offer Fair Trade coffee, and Marks & Spencer announced in September of 2004 that it would serve only Fair Trade coffee in its 198 Café Revive outlets, representing an 11 per cent market share of the UK-branded coffee bar market (Fairtrade Foundation, 2004d).

In the USA, Green Mountain Coffee Roasters, a publicly traded company with $116.7m (£65.4m) in sales in 2003, converted its organic coffees to Fair Trade. Having gained organic certification in 2000, it has seen Fair Trade become an increasingly large share of its business, from almost 7 per cent in 2001 to over 12 per cent in 2003. Green Mountain's Fair Trade volume increased by 92 per cent in 2003 (TransFair USA, 2004), compared with overall company growth of 15.3 per cent (GMCR, 2003). The company has set a goal of increasing Fair Trade coffee sales to be at least 25 per cent of total company sales by 2008. Green Mountain has introduced a line of certified Fair Trade coffees into hundreds of supermarkets in the USA, including Publix in Florida and Georgia, Harris Teeter in the mid-Atlantic region and Wegman's in the North. Green Mountain can be seen as representing a new era of mainstreaming Fair Trade coffee; rather than one product offering, Green Mountain usually offers at least five flavours, ensuring that consumers can find a Fair Trade product that satisfies their taste requirements.

The entry of multinational corporations (MNCs) and the mainstreaming of Fair Trade represent a big potential growth opportunity for the latter, providing Fair Trade coffee growers with access to new markets, channels and customers and making it possible for thousands more coffee farmers to benefit from Fair Trade. This mainstreaming also presents new challenges to both ATOs and the Fair Trade system. As will be discussed below, ATOs like Equal Exchange in the USA (see their case study below) must continue to adapt their business models to respond to potential new competitors, and the Fair Trade certification system will have to balance opportunities for growers with the preferences of traditional companies for their existing supply chain relationships. For instance, large companies may prefer to work with brokers and intermediaries rather than directly with Fair Trade co-operatives, decreasing the importance of Fair Trade's direct link between farmers and roasters.

While in Europe Fair Trade coffee has been slow to get past the 5 per cent market share level (Kocken, 2002), the success of the model and the increase in consumer awareness has required the large coffee MNCs to address the problems of poverty amongst coffee producers. In September 2004, Nestlé, Sara Lee, Kraft and Tchibo signed a 'Common Code for the Coffee Community' to improve working and environmental conditions on coffee farms. The code requires producers to pay minimum wages, cease using child labour, allow union membership and to follow international environmental standards (Williamson, 2004). Annemieke Dijt, a Director at Kraft, said that the company had recognized that 'consumers of mainstream coffee now see the conditions under which coffee is produced as more important than in the past' (in Williamson, 2004: 1). The success of Fair Trade coffee has encouraged activist groups and consumers to apply the Fair Trade model to other commodities, including bananas, to which we now turn.

CASE STUDY: FAIR TRADE COFFEE
EQUAL EXCHANGE, USA

Image 1   *Equal Exchange logo*
Reproduced with permission of Equal Exchange.

Equal Exchange, founded in 1986 near Boston, Massachusetts, is a pioneer in the US Fair Trade movement. A 100 per cent Fair Trade coffee importer and roaster since its inception, Equal Exchange adopted the international Fair Trade certification model and 'Fair Trade Certified' logo for its coffees in 1999, after thirteen years of importing Fair Trade coffee. The company diversified into Fair Trade teas in 1998, cocoa in 2002 and chocolate bars in 2004.

Mission statement: Equal Exchange

> To build long-term trade partnerships which are economically just and environmentally sound, to foster mutually beneficial relations between farmers and consumers and to demonstrate through our success the viability of worker-owned co-operatives and Fair Trade.

Besides purchasing all of its coffee, tea and cocoa on Fair Trade terms, the company is set up as a worker-owned co-operative, to prove that alternative business structures can

FAIR TRADE

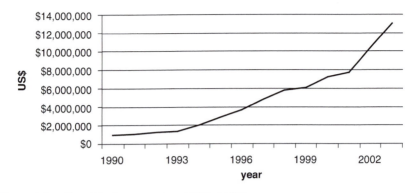

Equal Exchange Sales Growth, 1990–2003

Figure 4.4 *Equal Exchange sales, 1990–2003*
Source: Equal Exchange (2003)

be successful. After working for Equal Exchange for one year, workers can buy one share of Class A stock, gaining access to a 'one share, one vote' system that sets everyone on equal ground, from the company founders to newcomers. The worker-owners' approval is required for major decisions such as new product launches or a change in the company's location. Worker-owners elect the company's board and hold six out of nine seats.

According to Jonathan Rosenthal, when he, Rink Dickinson and Michael Rozyne founded Equal Exchange, 'we had a simple dream: to create a small worker-controlled business dedicated to spreading economic fairness instead of just making a profit. Thirteen years into our experiment, we have achieved far more than we ever thought possible. We're a proven alternative to conventional business, building a better way of doing business and hope for a more just world' (Equal Exchange, 1999: 2). The company is certainly proving that Fair Trade sourcing can be a win–win situation for business: sales reached $10m (£5.6m) in December 2002. Figure 4.4 shows the company's explosive sales growth. Equal Exchange won the Natural Product Expo's Socially Responsible Business Award in 1999 and the 2000 Business Ethics Magazine Award for Stakeholder Relations.

In response to entry into the Fair Trade market by several more traditional companies, Equal Exchange has emphasized its status as a 100 per cent Fair Trade ATO which has been following Fair Trade practices for over fifteen years. Historically strong in natural food stores and food co-ops, Equal Exchange has seen recent success in mass-market retailers such as Stop & Shop and Shaw's in the Northeast of the US, and Albertson's in the Northwest, as mainstream consumers become more educated about Fair Trade. An innovative approach to faith-based organizations, including providing training materials directly to places of worship, allowed them to capture a sympathetic niche market. Through the company's partnerships with the Catholic Relief Services, the Mennonite Central Committee, the Unitarian Universalists, Lutheran World Relief and the American Friends Service Committee, sales to faith-based organizations reached $2.6m (£1.5m) in 2003, 20 per cent of total sales.

Sources: Equal Exchange (2002, 2003); Everts (2004)

BANANAS

The best-selling produce item in Northern supermarkets, bananas are the fourth most consumed food product in the world (Chambron and Smith, 1997). As consumer demand in Northern consumer countries has grown, the pursuit of increased yields and profit in export banana production has been plagued with abuses of land and people, especially in Latin America (Raynolds and Murray, 1998). Fair Trade's success in changing the nature of coffee marketing and increasing returns to coffee farmers led NGOs and consumer activists to consider applying the model to banana production (Orchard et al., 1998). This section will describe the structure of the international banana industry and investigate the development of the Fair Trade model within this context.

Industry Structure

Like coffee, bananas are grown almost exclusively in the developing world. Most bananas are actually consumed in country: total world production averaged 92 million metric tonnes from 1998 to 2000, yet only 11.7 million of these were exported to consumer countries in the North (Arias et al., 2003). The global banana export industry is highly concentrated, with just three companies, Dole, Del Monte and Chiquita, accounting for 55 to 60 per cent of world trade and two other companies, Fyffes (in the European Union) and Noboa (in the USA), controlling up to a further 25 per cent in some markets (Arias et al., 2003; Smith, 2004). The end result is an ogopolistic industry in which five MNCs control almost the entire consumer market from farm to distribution.

Unlike coffee, which can be stored for at least a year after milling and before roasting, bananas are edible only up to one month after being picked. The banana export industry is therefore much more vertically integrated than the coffee industry, in order to increase efficiencies of getting product to market (Van de Kasteele, 1998). Large banana MNCs own, or control through long-term relationships, the plantations where bananas are grown, the packing plants where the fruit is washed and put into boxes and the ships that take the boxes to the Northern consuming countries. Upon landing in the USA or the European Union (EU), the MNCs sell the fruit either directly to large supermarkets or to independent ripeners (bananas are shipped green and ripened to order in 'ripening rooms' where ethylene gas is pumped in to turn them yellow), who service smaller chains and independent retail outlets.

In order to reduce the amount of time from harvesting to shipping, banana production has evolved from smallholder production to large monocrop plantations of hundreds of hectares of banana plants. The concentration of plants leaves them highly susceptible to disease, especially a black fungus known as *Sigatoka* which has spread to banana plantations throughout Central America and threatened their entire crops (Arias et al., 2003). These tropical pests and diseases can be fought only by frequent application of powerful fungicides and chemicals, thus the growing of bananas has become concentrated on large plantations which can be aerially sprayed. At an annual cost of $1000 (£560) per hectare to fight *Sigatoka* in particular, large plantations can achieve scale economies in spraying and fungicide application that small farmers cannot (Ploetz, 2001).

Figure 4.5 depicts the industry structure of the global trade in bananas. The vast majority of export bananas are grown by MNCs or independent plantations and then sold to MNCs for export to the North. Because of the complex logistics, small farmers grow less than 10 per cent of export bananas, mostly in the Caribbean. These smallholder farmers

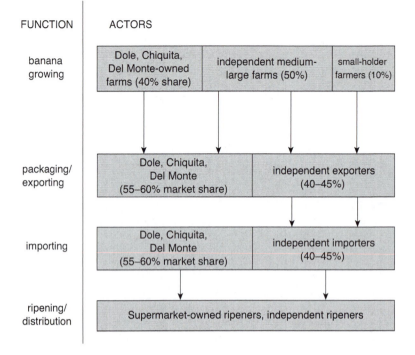

Figure 4.5   *Conventional banana supply chain*

can sell to independent or (more rarely) MNC exporters, or to their own co-operative, which can either export directly or sell to MNC or independent exporters. The power of traditional banana marketing, then, lies with the large companies that control export, import, and often the growing as well.

Because supermarkets typically carry only one brand of bananas, any company that can undercut a competitor and provide lower-cost bananas to a retailer can capture large volumes of business. Each banana box lost to a competitor represents empty cargo space on multinational-owned ships, increasing inefficiencies for the MNCs (Roozen and van der Hoff, 2003). Moreover, consumers are extremely brand aware, but are not particularly brand loyal (Jain et al., 2003; Roozen and van der Hoff, 2003). The result is a highly competitive buyers' market, in which supermarkets can exercise power over the MNCs to extract margin in what is essentially a commodity industry.

Survival mechanisms employed by the large multi-national banana companies are numerous:

• *Signing long-term contracts* with retail chains locks suppliers into providing a steady volume of bananas at a set price for one to two years. Rather than each store buying bananas daily from their local distributor, long-term contracts are negotiated at the corporate level for hundreds of stores at the same time. As the volumes represented are significant, these long-term contracts are extremely price competitive (Arias et al., 2003). In the USA, long-term banana contracts are a relatively new addition to the produce industry and have allowed MNCs to consolidate market share.

- *Bundling* is the practice of offering one product only in conjunction with another. For instance, a banana company might offer organic bananas to a large retail chain at a relatively low price, but only if the chain signs a long-term contract to buy non-organic bananas from the company as well. Suppliers thus capture both markets at once and benefit from their size by being able to offer a variety of products. In the USA, Dole and Del Monte offer retailers several fruits and vegetables that they are able to bundle with large banana contracts. Chiquita is also adopting this practice.

- *Blocking independent companies' access to transportation logistics.* Because MNCs often control the banana shipping lines, independent banana exporters sometimes have a difficult time accessing space on banana ships, even when empty space is available.

- *Downward pressure on prices paid to growers.* Most important in the Fair Trade context, the price offered to growers has been steadily decreasing as powerful retailers squeeze the MNCs (EIU, 2003). To keep wages down, many plantations have resorted to skirting labour laws by hiring temporary workers and employing union intimidation tactics, with several documented cases in Ecuador.

The three big banana MNCs have recently been diversifying out of plantation ownership, to reduce their exposure to weather and political risk (Otis, 2003). They still, however, sign long-term contracts with independent growers and thus in effect control the entire supply chain. They are thus isolated from labour disputes on individual farms, yet control the quality and supply logistics whilst still exerting pressure on independent suppliers to lower prices.

Effects of the Industry Structure on Farmers and Farm Workers

The intense price competition amongst MNCs to gain supermarket business has resulted in their moving sourcing away from high-wage unionized countries like Costa Rica and Panama to Ecuador, Brazil and Cameroon, where wages are lower, labour laws loosely enforced and working conditions are poor (EIU, 2003). Ecuador has become the world's largest exporter by ensuring that its prices are only 40 to 60 per cent of the price for bananas from Central America (Otis, 2003). Dole now sources over one third of its bananas from Ecuador (Arias et al., 2003), up from 19 per cent a decade ago (Otis, 2003).

Only five of Ecuador's 5000-plus banana plantations are unionized. Even where unions do exist, increasing indirect sourcing on the part of MNCs reduces their power to negotiate better wages and working conditions. When MNCs sell off their plantations and turn to sourcing from independently owned plantations, unions are no longer able to negotiate directly with MNCs. Farm prices increasingly depend on the power farm owners have vis-à-vis the MNC to set prices (Smith, 2004), creating an oligopolistic buying situation and discriminating against small plantations and small farmer co-operatives. The result has been an average annual decline in the real price of imported bananas of 1.4 per cent between 1973 and 2001 (Smith, 2004).

What is the effect of this downward price pressure on farmers and farm workers in the developing world? Human Rights Watch, a New York-based NGO, found that on Ecuador's banana plantations 'the wages of two working and fully paid adults may not be sufficient to provide for their family, in which case, the added salary of a child may be sought to supplement the family's income' (2002: 15). Their investigation of working conditions on export banana farms found children working in hazardous conditions, exposed to pesticides, heavy labour and even sexual harassment. The shifting of purchases to Ecuador has resulted in downward pressure on wages and labour standards in Central America. According to Otis (2003), banana exporters in Guatemala and Honduras are increasingly turning to non-unionized farms.

FAIR TRADE ENTERS THE BANANA INDUSTRY

Against this backdrop of lower prices to banana farmers, reducing the wages they are able to pay their workers, and a lack of enforcement of labour laws in important origins like Ecuador, in 1996 consumer activists in Europe turned to the Fair Trade coffee model for a consumer choice-based solution to the problems faced by the world's small banana farmers and farm workers.

Consumer activism in the banana sector has a long history. The major MNCs are accustomed to reacting to consumer outrage over media stories exposing the exploitation of the workers who grow their favourite fruit. In the 1990s, media in the North reported on a lawsuit brought by ex-workers against Chiquita, Del Monte and Dole for health problems such as sterility and skin deformities that allegedly developed from their exposure to dangerous pesticides whilst working on MNC-owned banana farms (Arias et al., 2003). Many consumers have a lasting latent impression of banana MNCs' unethical dealings in the 'banana republics' of Central America during the Cold War. But except for Chiquita, which in the 1990s began to work with the New York-based NGO Rainforest Alliance to improve environmental and working conditions on company-owned banana farms, MNCs' response to allegations of worker abuse was largely reactive. And because Chiquita did not publicize its Rainforest Alliance program amongst consumers or guarantee a minimum price to struggling banana farmers, it was not perceived by consumers as a way that they could personally influence banana industry practices through their purchase decisions.

In response, the Dutch NGO Solidaridad (which had been instrumental in launching the Max Havelaar Fair Trade certification label in the Netherlands – see Chapter 6) founded AgroFair in the mid-1990s. AgroFair is an ATO working in the Fair Trade fresh fruit sector; its mission is to improve the prices received by banana farmers in developing countries. In addition to being a model for industry through its innovative producer ownership structure (see their case study following), AgroFair also introduced the concept of minimum Fair Trade pricing to the banana industry. FLO had not yet begun certifying bananas, so AgroFair devised its own environmental and social standards and calculated the minimum cost of sustainable production, taking into account the lower yields incurred by the prohibition of dangerous pesticides. Its initial work became the foundation for the Fair Trade banana standards adopted by FLO in 1997 for international certification of Fair Trade bananas.

CASE STUDY: CORPORATE STRUCTURE AT AGROFAIR, NETHERLANDS

AgroFair

Image 2 *AgroFair Logo*
Reproduced with permission of AgroFair Benelux.

Created as an ATO from the beginning, AgroFair was founded by Solidaridad, a Dutch non-profit which helped pioneer the original Max Havelaar Fair Trade label in the Netherlands, and a coalition of fruit farmers and farming co-operatives in Ghana, Ecuador and Costa Rica, whose investment capital was provided by Solidaridad. The Dutch company Ambtman, one of the few remaining independent banana ripeners in Europe, was initially one-third owner but its shares were later bought out by Solidaridad and the company restructured, such that the producers were 50 per cent owners but receive 100 per cent of the profits.

Aside from benefiting directly from European sales, AgroFair's producer-owners are involved in the sales and marketing strategy of their product in Europe through their board membership. Banana producers' involvement in sales and marketing is a fairly novel idea. Uniban, the Colombian union of banana growers, has a sales and market-ing operation, and the Noboa family in Ecuador has also succeeded in selling their Bonita-brand bananas from their enormous plantations into Europe and North America. But the majority of North-South trade in bananas is dominated by three large MNCs: Dole, Del Monte and Chiquita. These companies are headquartered in the North but their increasingly vertical integration has resulted in their ownership of enormous growing operations in developing countries. As Nico Roozen of Solidaridad explains in his description of the origins of AgroFair:

> With the traditional players, you can see a trend: western companies are integrating the sup-ply chain, getting closer and closer to the global South. They do not focus only on selling bananas – they also dominate production and logistics. What AgroFair is doing can be called 'reverse supply chain integration': the Third World producer is integrating the supply chain in his own interest. The producer is dedicated not only to growing product, but to orga-nizing logistics, and having at the same time a voice and vote in the sales strategy. In con-trast to normal opinion, AgroFair has shown that involving Third World producers in business structures, making them co-responsible for the marketing strategy, is a viable aspi-ration. (Roozen and van der Hoff, 2003: 159)

Figure 4.6 shows the current ownership structure of AgroFair, which has expanded since its founding to include other NGO partners, including Twin Trading in the UK and CTM, an Italian Fair Trade importer which does not use the FLO logo or certi-fication system. The holding company has three sales divisions, one in the UK (AgroFair UK), one in the Netherlands (AgroFair B.V.) and AgroFair Italy. AgroFair B.V. maintains all purchasing and logistics centrally. The AgroFair Foundation provides grants and loans to producer groups for quality improvements.

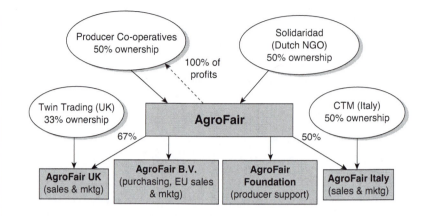

Figure 4.6   *AgroFair corporate structure*

FLO-certified producers who maintain a stable trade relationship with AgroFair for more than one year are invited to join the producer ownership co-operative, which has now expanded to include growers from Peru, Burkina Faso and the Dominican Republic.

Source: Roozen and van der Hoff (2003)

The Fair Trade banana model developed by AgroFair, and later adopted by FLO, applied to both co-operatives of small family farmers and plantations that employed farm workers. Both models use two familiar Fair Trade components: a Fair Trade *minimum price* designed to cover the costs of sustainable production (including ensuring fair wages and decent working conditions for farm workers), and a *social premium* to be spent on development projects.

Figure 4.7 shows how the Fair Trade model works for banana co-operatives. In this model, small farmers who do not produce enough to export directly sell their bananas to a farmer-owned co-operative, which prepares the bananas for export. The co-operative then either exports independently or sells the bananas to an exporter. The importer pays the minimum Fair Trade price (or market price, whichever is higher) and the social premium directly to the co-operative. The co-operative then returns some income to the producers and retains the rest for development projects, business capacity building, technical improvements, organic conversion and other co-op projects. The farmer-owners of the co-operative vote for how much of the Fair Trade income they would like distributed as opposed to retained in the co-op, and also vote for what projects they would like to see implemented.

The Fair Trade model for plantations is depicted in Figure 4.8. In this supply chain, the importer or exporter works with a plantation that has been inspected to ensure that working conditions and wages comply with Fair Trade standards. The importer must pay the Fair Trade minimum price (or market price, whichever is higher) to the plantation, so that it earns enough to cover the costs of complying with the Fair Trade labour and environmental standards. The importer pays the social premium directly to a worker-controlled group called a 'Joint Body', rather than to the plantation owner. The Joint Body is elected by the farm workers and controls the distribution of the social premium, which must be

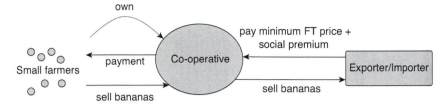

Figure 4.7   *Fair Trade banana supply chain – co-operative model*

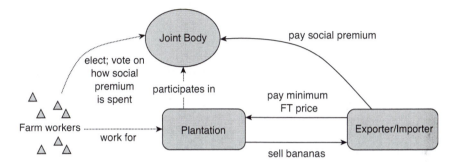

Figure 4.8   *Fair Trade banana supply chain – plantation/farm worker model*

spent on community development projects to benefit the farm workers and their families. Plantation management sit on the board of the Joint Body but the farm workers must have the majority of the votes.

While the Fair Trade coffee supply chain cuts out middlemen to return a higher percentage of the end retail price to primary producers, unlike coffee the influence of middlemen in the export banana industry is not significant. Therefore, the primary benefits to banana farmers and farm workers come from the minimum Fair Trade price, which allows plantation owners to earn fair wages and small-holder farmers to earn a decent standard of living, as well as the social premium. The Fair Trade minimum export price in Ecuador is $0.13 (£0.07) per pound, which can be as much as 60 per cent higher than the going market price. In addition, farm workers and co-operatives earn $0.04 (£0.02) in social premium per pound sold. Thus, instead of reconfiguring the value chain by cutting out middlemen, Fair Trade raises the price paid to producers. The result is usually higher retail prices to consumers, although some importers, distributors and retailers may take lower margins to keep prices down.

The Influence of Fair Trade in the Banana Industry

AgroFair's initial entry into the European market met with many difficulties. The European Union has a complex system of country import quotas for bananas, designed to protect banana farmers in former French and British colonies in Africa and the Caribbean. Importers must have licences from the EU to import bananas, which are granted to importers based on last year's trading volume. Three per cent of licences granted each year are to new entrants, but only companies that have previous experience of importing other fruits into Europe are eligible. AgroFair, then, found itself unable to access banana import licences from the EU, despite intensive lobbying and a postcard-mailing campaign –'Give Fair Trade bananas a fair chance'– organized by EUROBAN, a network of NGOs lobbying for sustainable banana production and trade (Chambron and Smith, 1997). AgroFair was forced to buy licences from existing licence-holders, increasing their costs on a product that already required a high Fair Trade export price.

AgroFair's first bananas appeared in the Dutch market in November of 1996 with much success and were carried in 70 per cent of supermarkets. AgroFair quickly ran into supply problems, including a difficulty in accessing space on shipping lines which were largely controlled by MNCs, and even in buying insurance for such small volumes of risky product. Relying on only a few producers and origins made AgroFair especially vulnerable to weather and transportation risks (Roozen and van der Hoff, 2003).

Despite its initial difficulties, AgroFair became profitable in 1999–2000 and now sells Fair Trade-labelled fruit into major supermarket chains in Switzerland (Migros and Co-op supermarkets), Belgium (Carrefour, Colruyt), the Netherlands (Laurus), Denmark, Italy, Austria, Sweden and the UK (the Co-operative Group). Its offerings now include Fair Trade mangoes and pineapples, launched in 2002. And in February 2004, the Co-op supermarket chain in Switzerland announced that all of its bananas would be Fair Trade certified, with AgroFair as the primary supplier. The result is an almost 50 per cent market share for Fair Trade bananas in that country (AgroFair, 2004; Smith, 2004). Figure 4.9 shows the growth of AgroFair sales. Whilst AgroFair's core business is Fair Trade, the company does sell non-Fair Trade fruits for logistical reasons (for example, to fill a container-load), to provide a market to farmers, or to test out supply chains for future Fair Trade sales (Kroezen, 2004).

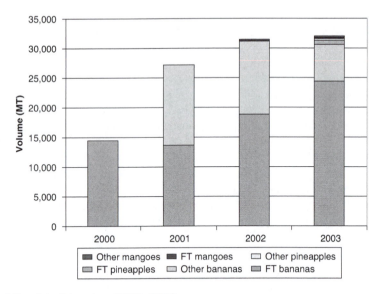

Figure 4.9 *AgroFair sales, 2000–2003*
Source: Kroezen (2004). Note: FT sales include non-FLO labelled sales to CTM in Italy.

Without a doubt, Fair Trade's entry into the European banana market has transformed the global banana industry. NGOs, activists and Fair Trade marketing organizations have educated their constituencies about the need for Fair Trade and AgroFair provided an outlet for educated consumers to vote for Fair Trade with their purchasing dollars. The success of Fair Trade fruit, particularly in the UK and Switzerland, has forced the multinational banana companies to consider offering Fair Trade or some other form of socially responsible fruit. Fyffes, the world's fifth-largest banana importer, registered with FLO to offer Fair Trade bananas to European retailers. Dole, as the primary supplier to the Co-op, lost £1.2 million pounds of banana sales per week to AgroFair's Fair Trade program (AgroFair, 2004), representing at least £11.2m[1] ($20m) in annual revenue lost by not being able to supply the Co-op with Fair Trade fruit. The company eventually began working with FLO to source Fair Trade bananas for some of its European customers (Horowitz, 2004). Dole and Del Monte are pursuing Social Accountability International certification for their company-owned farms in response to growing pressure from educated consumers and retailers. Similarly, Chiquita estimates that 56 per cent of its sales in Northern Europe were to 'customers who had either inspected our farms or formally asked questions about our social and environmental performance' (2002: 10). The company deems 42 per cent of its German sales, 47 per cent of its Dutch sales, 69 per cent of its UK sales and 76 per cent of its Swiss sales to be at risk in the absence of its various social and environmental certification programs (Chiquita, 2002).

Ben Huyghe, AgroFair's Sourcing Manager in charge of purchasing and logistics, is proud of the impact that AgroFair and Fair Trade have had on the banana industry:

> In general, we have to conclude that – I see it myself when I go to the tropics – multinational corporations are slowly improving conditions, both social and environmental. If multinationals adopt the basic ideas of Fair Trade in their basic corporate standards, then maybe you don't have to see the success or the impact of Fair Trade on the amount of Fair Trade volume sold, but maybe on the whole sector, related to the Dole-owned farms, Chiquita-owned farms, and Del Monte-owned farms for example. (Interview, 2004)

FROM ALTERNATIVE TO MAINSTREAM

Having examined the industry structure for the two highest volume Fair Trade products, we now turn to examine more closely the actors within the Fair Trade supply chain. As the first-movers in Fair Trade, the ATOs were pioneers in experimenting with direct trade and returning more income to farmers on a large scale. The success of the Fair Trade model they developed has encouraged the entry of larger, more traditional businesses into the Fair Trade market. What are the implications for the ATOs of the mainstreaming of Fair Trade? We shall examine first the structure and mission of some leading ATOs and then turn to their strategy and mainstream businesses, and what this strategy, structure and interaction mean for the future of Fair Trade.

Alternative Trading Organizations

> It is a stark fact that the price MNCs now pay for coffee is at a desperate 30 year low. Cafédirect has proved that even in such a crisis, we can pay more, offer upfront credit and development support to farmers – and still make a profit. As a company, we face all the usual stresses of a conventional business – like cash flow, 'just in time' supply chain management, fluctuating interest and exchange rates. And on top of that, we meet stringent Fair Trade criteria that conventional businesses would not countenance. This is not just an alternative way of doing business. It transforms business ethics. (Newman, 2002: 4)

ATOs are, of course, 'alternative'. They are businesses and not-for-profit organizations that attempt to turn normal capitalistic relationships on their heads. Aside from their mission to source inputs according to Fair Trade standards and norms whenever possible, ATOs often employ stakeholder models of corporate governance, including producer ownership, and many have a mandate to act as leaders in the industry, thereby encouraging competition. What kind of business wants to increase its cost of goods? What kind of business measures success by increasing returns to its suppliers? What kind of business actually hopes that competitors will enter its niche markets? ATOs are a unique breed in the multinational-dominated world of global trade.

ATO Corporate Structure

Many ATOs were founded by charities or religious groups (for instance, Gepa in Germany, Traidcraft in the UK and SERRV and Ten Thousand Villages in the USA) and consequently many are not-for-profits. In 2000, 38 per cent of the members of the Fair Trade Federation, the ATO membership organization in North America, were not-for-profits (Fair Trade Federation, 2002). A variant on this model is for not-for-profits to hold guardian shares in a for-profit ATO, to ensure that the social mission is not compromised. This is the model followed by Traidcraft PLC, the trading arm of the Traidcraft Foundation, and Cafédirect, the UK's leading Fair Trade coffee brand, which was co-founded by four ATOs. Both of these companies recently issued share offerings, but public shareholders have limited voting rights and charities retain guardian shares, structures that ensure that the social mission of the ATO is not compromised.

Producer ownership is another feature of the corporate structure of many ATOs. AgroFair in the Netherlands is 50 per cent owned by fruit co-operatives, with the remainder in the hands of a Dutch not-for-profit. In 2004, Equal Exchange in the USA sold $100,000 (£56,000) worth of Class B (non-voting) shares to one of their long-term coffee co-operative sources in Oaxaca, Mexico. Sometimes this producer ownership becomes integral to the ATOs' brand meaning. A good case in point is the Day Chocolate Company in the UK, which is 30 per cent owned by Kuapa Kokoo, a Fair Trade cocoa farming co-operative in Ghana (see Purvis, 2003). Two members of the co-operative sit on the 11-member board of Day Chocolate, having the effect of 'producing a clear focus on the developing world, to which the benefits of fair trade should accrue' (Davies and Crane, 2003: 84). This producer ownership element is entrenched in the structure of the organization. According to Managing Director Sophi Tranchell when interviewed in 2004, 'our ownership structure is our unique selling proposition', which results in the need to be carefully balanced when raising finance for expansion. For instance, to maintain 30 per cent producer ownership could involve bringing in new equity from Northern investors which could dilute the shares of current Northern investors (including amongst others, The Body Shop), whilst bringing in more producer-owners could in turn dilute Southern shares.

Other models of ATO corporate governance exist of course. AlterEco in France, for instance, is privately held. As discussed previously, Equal Exchange in the USA is actually a worker-owned co-operative, much like its producer partners. Equal Exchange has a progressive internal compensation structure whereby the highest-paid employee may not earn more than three times the pay of the lowest-paid employee (Equal Exchange, 2003). The co-operative has 370 outside shareholders, representing $2m (£1.1m) in equity, but their shares do not increase in value and their return is targeted to be on average only 5 per cent.

ATO structure and mission are often unique in the business world and whilst this does not force them to be small scale (Gepa in Germany had a turnover of $41.2m (£23m), in 2002), it does make it difficult for ATOs to access working capital and investment for expansion. ATOs are generally reluctant to incorporate venture capital or public shareholders into their structure for fear of diluting the social mission or producer ownership components of company structure (Thorpe, 2004). Furthermore, traditional lending institutions may not be equipped to assess risk for a company one-third owned by cocoa farmers in Ghana, with higher costs of goods than its competitors and slim profit margins. Equal Exchange's operating profit margin, for instance, ranged between 2.9 per cent and 5 per cent from 2000 to 2003. Equal Exchange Co-Director Rob Everts when interviewed in 2004 thought that access to capital remained one of the primary challenges to ATOs. We will revisit the issue of financing ATOs in Chapter 5.

ATOs as Models for Industry

ATOs have experimented with several models of corporate governance, to prove to traditional companies that for-profit companies can be structured in atypical ways. Several ATOs also aim to act as catalysts for change in their respective industries by proving that products can be sourced in a more ethical way. In the UK, Traidcraft (see their case study following) includes the concept of being a model for other businesses in its mission statement. The company created a groundbreaking social audit system with the UK's New Economics Foundation, which was revised and adopted by the Body Shop in 1995 (Redfern and Snedker, 2002).

CASE STUDY 1: ALTERNATIVE TRADE ORGANIZATION – TRAIDCRAFT PLC (UK)

Image 3   *Traidcraft logo*

The Traidcraft Foundation was created in 1979 to exhibit 'the Christian principles of love and justice in international trade' (Redfern and Snedker, 2002: 5). The Foundation started Traidcraft Exchange, a non-profit consulting firm that provides training and information to producers to help them access Northern markets whilst retaining a guardian share in Traidcraft PLC, a for-profit trading company that imports Fair Trade handicrafts and food.

An ATO dealing only in fairly traded products (carrying the FLO logo on all products for which standards exist), Traidcraft PLC has five principal aims:

- To tackle poverty by providing a market for Fair Trade producers to supply.
- To demonstrate that it is possible to run a commercially sustainable business on Fair Trade principles.
- To root Traidcraft in the realities of trade, giving greater substance and credibility to advocacy and campaign work.

- To educate consumers about Fair Trade by presenting them with Fair Trade products.
- To provide a moral choice for consumers, enabling them to exercise their purchasing power in accordance with ethical criteria to help the poor in the developing world.

Traidcraft PLC works closely with Traidcraft Exchange to identify Fair Trade products suitable for the UK market. Traidcraft's sales channels reflect its origins as a Christian-oriented ATO: 50 per cent of its sales come through a network of 'Fair Traders', volunteers who sell Traidcraft products at churches and market stalls. While crafts and handmade goods made up the bulk of Traidcraft's initial business, Traidcraft's recent success can be attributed to the growth of the labelled Fair Trade foods sector in the UK, as some 59 per cent of its revenues came from food in 2003.

As one of the four founding members of Cafédirect, currently the UK's leading Fair Trade coffee brand, Traidcraft recognizes the power of the mass-market in marketing its products. Its GeoBar, a line of energy snack bars containing Fair Trade chocolate, honey, sugar and dried fruits, is sold in all major UK multiples and accounts for 20 per cent of its sales. Its tagline, 'The energy to make a difference', enforces the Fair Trade message.

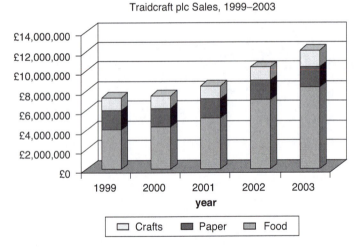

Figure 4.10   *Traidcraft sales growth, 1999–2003*

Traidcraft's success in the Fair Trade sector is significant. The company was profitable in 2002–3 for the sixth consecutive year, earning £425,000 in pre-tax profits on £12 million of trading. Traidcraft's five-year sales growth is shown in Figure 4.10.

Yet despite this success in both the retail and grassroots marketing segments, according to Redfern and Snedker, Traidcraft's impact on poverty through sales growth was 'neither an explicit nor an implicit goal for the organization' (2002: 6). Traidcraft's primary goal is not to create a large multi-national agency that alleviates poverty through Fair Trade, but rather to show that a better model of trade is possible and to encourage other companies to follow Traidcraft's example by introducing ethical sourcing into trading behaviour. Traidcraft was the first publicly limited company in the UK to produce 'social accounts', which report the social impact of the company's activities. The accounts aim to prove that companies can earn a profit whilst sourcing responsibly and having a positive impact on producers in developing countries.

Sources: Traidcraft website (www.traidcraft.org); Traidcraft (2002); Traidcraft (2003); Fairtrade Foundation website (www.fairtrade.org.uk)

Like Traidcraft, The Day Chocolate Company includes in its mission statement not only the mandate to sell Fair Trade chocolate, but to act as a model for other businesses (presumably, competitors in the £3.6 billion UK chocolate industry) to change their trading practices. According to Managing Director Sophi Tranchell, Day's 'mission within chocolate is to be a catalyst to the industry, and what we are is the threat of a good example. We have heard (other chocolate companies) say they cannot trace supply chains and where products have come from ... we are showing them that we can take it back to each village. Other chocolate companies are having to respond ... and if we get the mainstream producers to change their strategy a little then we have achieved something' (in Davies and Crane, 2003: 4). Day joined the Biscuit, Cocoa, Chocolate and Confectionery Alliance, a UK industry trade group, to increase its power and voice within the confectionary industry.

This particular ATO mission has the interesting effect of encouraging competition. In theory, an ATO with the goal of changing the industry would be pleased to put itself out of business if it had, indeed, become such a role model that traditional players switched to Fair Trade supply chains. According to Rink Dickinson, co-founder of Equal Exchange in the USA: 'Believe it or not, we want more, not less competition. That's because we know these farmers and their struggles. They urgently need more importers to pay a just price. So we encourage our fellow roasters to expand on the modest Fair Trade programs they've announced so far' (Equal Exchange, 2000: 1). As mainstream players enter the Fair Trade market, ATOs may consider repositioning themselves, or even exiting if they feel that their goal in changing the rules of trade has been reached. We examine the business strategies of the various mainstream and ATO actors in the following section.

GOING MAINSTREAM

Fair Trade success in the late 1990s and early 2000s was the culmination of almost forty years of ATO engagement with producers in developing countries. Tallontire (2000) outlines the emergence and development of ATOs. In the 1950s and 1960s, when Fair Trade was just beginning, ATOs mainly consisted of charities and religious organizations selling products made by communities with which they were working on development projects. The 1970s and 1980s saw Fair Trade sales develop amongst politically motivated consumers in the North, especially from groups in the global South with solidarity movements growing around revolutionary political activities.

But the products sold by ATOs were largely focussed on the producer rather than consumer demands – a strategy which was not largely successful. By the mid-1990s, ATOs had built up big losses and were plagued with inefficiencies. Traidcraft had lost more than £300,000 ($537,000). The management consultancy McKinsey & Co., when studying Oxfam's Fair Trade supply chain in 2000, found that in the case of one particular product that could sell for £20 ($36), Oxfam had to spend £30 ($54) in getting it to market. Oxfam was thus losing £10 ($18) on each sale. And of that £10 ($18), only £3 ($5) was getting to the producer; the rest was the cost of field consultants, logistics and shop ownership (Redfern and Snedker, 2002).

The 1990s saw a change of focus on the part of ATOs to reposition their offering towards what would sell with more mainstream consumers. Some ATOs went bankrupt or closed their doors. Oxfam pulled out of direct Fair Trade sourcing and now buys Fair Trade products for its stores from other ATOs (it continues to help producers in developing countries access markets, but no longer buys directly from them). But other ATOs began to thrive with a new focus on the customer. Traidcraft reached profitability and in 1991 partnered with Oxfam, Equal Exchange UK (completely separate from Equal Exchange USA) and Twin Trading to launch the Fair Trade coffee brand Cafédirect, aimed at the UK mass market. The Day Chocolate Company, as shown in their case study below, was founded in 1997 to create a competitively priced Fair Trade chocolate bar able to hold its own in the mainstream marketplace.

CASE STUDY 2: ALTERNATIVE TRADE ORGANIZATION – THE DAY CHOCOLATE COMPANY (UK)

Image 4   *Divine chocolate logo*

Image 5   *Dubble Bar chocolate logo*
Reproduced with permission of The Day Chocolate Company.

In 1997, the Ghanaian co-operative of small-scale cocoa farmers, Kuapa Kokoo, voted at its annual general meeting to invest in a chocolate bar to be sold in the UK market. The Body Shop, Twin Trading (an ATO which provides financing for Fair Trade businesses and co-operatives) and Christian Aid (a UK development charity) all supported the initial start-up sales and marketing firm called The Day Chocolate Company. The Department for International Development, the UK government's ministry-level development agency, guaranteed Day Chocolate's initial start-up loan of £400,000 ($716,000) from the NatWest bank.

Mission Statement of the Day Chocolate Company

- Take a quality affordable range of Fair Trade chocolate bars into the mainstream chocolate market.

- Raise awareness of Fair Trade issues amongst UK retailers and consumers of all ages.
- Be highly visible and vocal in the chocolate sector and thereby act as a catalyst for change.
- Pay a Fair Trade price for all the cocoa used in the products.

Day's main consumer-facing brand, Divine chocolate, was launched in the UK mass market in 1998. Despite its atypical ownership structure (see above), Divine was deliberately positioned as a mainstream chocolate bar to compete against such well-known brands as Cadbury and Nestlé, rather than as a gourmet or organic chocolate to be sold only in speciality and health food shops. Its 45g bar and 100g bar were priced at 45p ($0.81) and 99p ($1.77) respectively, within range of other impulse confectionary buys. Sainsbury's introduced Divine into 70 stores in 1998, and after a successful 'Stock the choc' postcard campaign organized by Christian Aid, added another 270 stores. The Divine brand can now be found in 5,000 shops in the UK, and the range includes several flavours, including Divine Dark, as well as such seasonal products as Easter eggs, advent calendars and Christmas coins.

In October 2000, Day launched the Dubble chocolate bar, the first Fair Trade product aimed at the children's market. Dubble is co-branded with Comic Relief, a well-known charity in the UK, and Comic Relief earned a position on Day's board when Dubble was launched. Dubble is tied to a range of educational tools and child-oriented marketing materials, including a dedicated kids' website, 'Dubble Agents' toolkits for children and links between children in schools in the UK and Ghana. Day Chocolate have achieved impressive distribution of Dubble and in the process have taken Fair Trade into virgin territory, such as the Blockbuster Video chain, all major supermarkets, regional confectionary distributors and independent shops.

In March 2000, the Co-op chain of supermarkets in the UK launched a co-branded Co-op/Divine private label chocolate bar and in November of 2002 converted its entire range of own-brand chocolate to Fair Trade. In its press release announcing the launch, the Co-op indicated that it wished to 'start a race amongst major UK supermarket groups anxious to demonstrate they care and are keen to establish their ethical credentials'. The product even replaced the mainstream Yorkie bar in some stores.

In 2002, Starbucks converted all of its own-brand chocolate to certified Fair Trade, co-branded with Divine. Divine, Dubble and the Day Chocolate Company's private label ventures are thus firmly planted in the mainstream UK confectionery-buying markets. Working with schools, product giveaways and celebrity endorsements have allowed Divine to leverage a small amount of money to achieve a high degree of publicity. Divine's cost of goods is higher than traditional chocolate companies, but unlike the larger chocolate companies they can build brand loyalty (without spending huge sums on advertising) by structuring the Divine and Dubble brands around the Fair Trade message. The company reached profitability in 2003. In all, sales have grown from £1m ($1.79m) in 2001 to a projected £5m ($8.95m) annual turnover by autumn 2004.

Sources: Mayoux (2001); www.jusbiz.org; www.divinechocolate.com; Social Enterprise Coalition (2003); www.co-op.co.uk; Davies and Crane (2003); Curtis (2004); WorldAware (2002); Tickle (2004); Co-op Group (2004)

As Cafédirect gained market share (reaching over 7 per cent of the roast and ground and 3 per cent of the instant coffee UK market), Fair Trade bananas took off in Switzerland and other Fair Trade success stories started to appear, the more traditional players had to take notice and act. Because most supermarkets sell only one or two brands of bananas, a retailer who introduced a Fair Trade banana often replaced a mainstream brand entirely. In coffee, mainstream brands have been slower to react because the potential threat to Fair Trade brands is smaller – Nescafé does not necessarily lose shelf space when Cafédirect is also stocked.

The success of Fair Trade bananas in particular amongst supermarkets has attracted such mainstream brands as Dole to enter the Fair Trade market in Europe. Indeed, because of the complexity of the supply chain, some mainstream retailers in Europe prefer to work with established international logistics experts like Chiquita and Dole. But the participation of these companies is highly controversial for some Fair Trade consumers and industry participants. Many traditional supporters look to the historical reputations of banana MNCs for past mistreatment of workers, low prices to producers and unfair trading practices with competitors, and mistrust these companies' current support for and compliance with Fair Trade principles.

The solution preferred by FLO is to require established brands to use new brands on their Fair Trade products so that consumers will not confuse all of MNCs' practices as being Fair Trade – a phenomenon known as 'fairwashing'. But changing the brand name does not reduce these companies' market power, and smaller Fair Trade companies who have more expensive shipping costs, or who cannot bundle non-Fair Trade with Fair Trade and reduce delivery costs, are finding it difficult to compete. Whilst Fair Trade certification guarantees only that a fair price was paid to the producer, some ATOs want certification of fair business practices throughout the supply chain. The International Federation of Alternative Trade (IFAT), whose membership includes many non-FLO registered Fair Trade producer groups, addressed this issue by introducing a Fair Trade Organization mark in 2004 to identify the overall business performance of Fair Trade ventures. This new mark goes some way towards offering the consumer a more holistic assurance of a Fair Trade organization's business practices and standards, although IFAT's registration and verification process is not as stringent as the FLO's product-level certification (see further Chapter 6).

Supermarkets are also beginning to offer Fair Trade as a way to differentiate themselves from their competitors, especially discount retailers. Rather than engaging in a race-to-the-bottom and lowering their retail prices to compete with discount retailers, mainstream supermarkets can offer value-added Fair Trade and 'maintain an arguably more ethical stance' (EIU, 2003: 2). But this strategy may be short-lived as well. Growing consumer demand for Fair Trade will attract even discount retailers into the market. Demand for Fair Trade bananas in Europe was estimated to have reached 10 per cent in 1997 (European Commission, 1997); market share for Fair Trade bananas in Switzerland reached 50 per cent in the spring of 2004 (Smith, 2004). Indeed, simply offering Fair Trade is not good enough; retailers are now competing on how many varieties of Fair Trade products they can offer to prove their commitment.

Whilst mainstream coffee and chocolate brands may be slow to adopt Fair Trade practices, a quick way for a supermarket to increase its Fair Trade offer is through the development of own-label Fair Trade products. When the Co-operative Group, a UK supermarket chain, converted its own-label chocolate bars to Fair Trade, year-on-year sales increased 25 per cent despite a small price rise. There were more promotions on branded non-Fair Trade chocolate in the Co-operative Group that year, but these products' sales decreased by 1 per cent (Tickle, 2004). If the Fair Trade chocolate market continues to grow, the big chocolate brands will have to take notice of these trends.

According to Moore (2004) nine out of the top ten best-selling Fair Trade products in the Co-operative Group in 2002 were own-label. But that does not necessarily mean that when mainstream and private labels enter the market, ATO sales must decrease. When the Co-operative Group's own-label chocolate was introduced, priced at 39p ($0.70) for a 45g bar, sales of Divine Fair Trade chocolate, priced at 45p ($0.81), doubled (Hudgton, 2001). All ATOs profiled in this chapter have been growing exponentially despite, or perhaps because of, the entry of new mainstream players.

Nevertheless, the change from 'alternative' to 'mainstream' is not going to be easy for all players. Those companies that align themselves as models for different ways of doing business, or as 100 per cent Fair Trade, must consider what it means to be part of what is becoming a mainstream movement. Rob Everts, Co-Director of Equal Exchange USA, finds distinguishing Equal Exchange as an ATO to be particularly important as mainstream companies doing small amounts of Fair Trade enter the market. In a 2004 interview, Everts identified 'the desire to distinguish ourselves from mainstream companies doing small amounts of Fair Trade' as a challenge facing the company as an ATO. Moore (2004) fears that the Fair Trade movement will be diluted by the admission of mainstream companies with one or two Fair Trade offerings, or that by becoming mainstream the 'soul' of Fair Trade may be lost.

Another worry is that if Fair Trade is a passing trend, its long-term growth may not be safe in publicly held companies. As discussed earlier, ATOs' ownership and decision making have largely been structured to ensure that their social mission can never be compromised. But second-movers that engage with Fair Trade purely because they see a market opportunity cannot necessarily be trusted to keep their Fair Trade products on board if consumer interest flags. Green & Black, the first UK company to have a chocolate product certified by FLO, dropped Fair Trade certification on some of its products after the company's founders sold their majority stake. Cafédirect, whose current Managing Director came from the Body Shop, was careful to float public shares in the company on an ethical exchange rather than one of the public stock exchanges (Thorpe, 2004).

Kelly (2003) states that it may be true that organic ingredients could be 'genetically encoded' into a company and thus would be protected from erosion when a company turns public, but it may be less true for things like employee benefits which are less important to consumers. Where does Fair Trade fall? As a consumer-facing label, it is up to the core Fair Trade movement to make sure that Fair Trade remains 'top of mind' and that consumers continue to look for their label and seek out their goods when they make purchases. These threats and potential directions as Fair Trade enters the mainstream will be reviewed in more detail in the final chapter.

CONCLUSION

This chapter has shown that by working in and against the market, Alternative Trading Organizations have managed to create a trading system that empowers the poorest actors in global food supply chains through direct trade linkages and minimum pricing, returning more of the value of products to primary producers (Raynolds, 1994, 1997). ATOs have developed rapidly in the past twenty years, moving from supplying niche market products driven by what producers could make, to offering high quality mainstream products that have taken market share from more traditional players. Their success has encouraged competitor brands to re-examine their supply chains and address worker and farmer poverty, both by launching Fair Trade products and through their own company initiatives. The entry of mainstream players will require ATOs to rethink their business strategies as they compete for Fair Trade market share with companies that have scale economies and competitive advantages in distribution and brand awareness.

One of the major challenges to growth for producers and ATOs (as for many small businesses) is access to credit and financial instruments. Having introduced the business strategies of several of the key Fair Trade actors, the next chapter will discuss an essential element in operationalizing Fair Trade, that of finance.

NOTE

1. Based on $20 (£11.20) wholesale price per box to supermarkets.

5

Financing Fair Trade

Whitni Thomas

This chapter reviews the role of finance in Fair Trade. First, it examines the weak agricultural financial markets in which most producers in the South operate and considers their difficulties in accessing finance. It looks at how Fair Trade and the provision of pre-finance address some of the financing needs of small-scale farmers. Second, this chapter considers the capital challenge for Fair Trade companies in the North, and in conclusion explores whether new forms of capital are needed to enable the Fair Trade sector to reach scale. Although all Fair Trade producers need access to capital and have varied financing needs, this chapter focusses primarily on the Fair Trade producers, exporters and importers that deal in 'soft' commodities, such as coffee and cocoa. Fair Trade artisans that make handicrafts also need access to capital but their varied financing needs are not covered in detail here.

INTRODUCTION

The Fair Trade market is going from strength to strength. From a small mainly grassroots movement, it has done what was unimaginable twenty years ago. Fair Trade has caught the attention of the mainstream: mainstream consumers, mainstream retail outlets and thus mainstream corporations. The buyers of Fair Trade products are no longer just activist-shoppers, naturally sympathetic to the Fair Trade message. Consumer demand is real and the retailers appear to be on-board, so why are there so few Fair Trade products on our shelves? The answer to this question is a complex one. Chapter 6 underlines that the Fair Trade certification process for new products is costly and complex, thus discouraging new product development. Chapter 7 shows that marketing is one of the sternest challenges that Fair Trade groups face today. Fair Trade organizations need to move beyond attract-ing ethically aware consumers to achieve a more mass-market appeal. In some countries this is already happening, but it requires much more sophisticated marketing and brand-building strategies than have been used in the past. This chapter argues that another bot-tleneck to the development of the Fair Trade market is access to finance for both producers in the South and Fair Trade organizations in the North.

One of the cornerstones of the Fair Trade philosophy is provision of pre-finance to pro-ducers. Fair Trade importers usually advance up to 60 per cent of the invoice amount months before the product is actually received, although the real proportion varies. This dramatically increases the working capital needs of these importers. Some Fair Trade companies also commit to working directly with co-operatives to help them increase the quality and consistency of their products and access international export markets. This producer support and development is costly. Fair Trade organizations that try to open up new markets for producers invest large amounts of time developing products that can be sold under the Fair Trade label. They collaborate with the Fair Trade certification bodies to develop the certification process for these new products. All of this is resource and capital intensive. Fair Trade companies in the North then package and market the products to consumers and retailers. This marketing and brand building also requires capital investment. Each of these steps, which are indispensable to the process of growing the Fair Trade market, requires access to finance.

FINANCING THE NEEDS OF PRODUCERS IN THE SOUTH

Chapter 1 identified six market imperfections faced by small-scale producers in developing countries. Two of these are lack of access to financial markets and lack of access to credit. This section looks at both of these challenges in turn. First, this section provides an overview of agricultural financial markets in developing countries. Second, it looks at what financial products small-scale farmers need. Third, it considers how the pre-finance mechanism inherent to the Fair Trade model seeks to address some of the failures of rural financial markets. And finally, this section explores other financing needs of small-scale producers such as access to capital for long-term investment and to income-smoothing devices like futures instruments.

Agricultural Financial Markets in Developing Countries

To appreciate some of the challenges that Fair Trade producers face when trying to access finance, one must first understand the contexts in which they operate and, in particular, the financial infrastructures of developing countries. This section focusses on agriculture finance and access to credit for small-scale farmers. Generalizing the varied situations of countries from such diverse regions as Latin America, sub-Saharan Africa and Asia masks much variation, but the rural financial systems of developing countries do share a number of characteristics.

Rural financial systems are a subset of a country's financial infrastructure. But rural finance, and agricultural credit in particular, present distinct and significant challenges (see Dorward et al., 2001; FAO/GTZ, 1998, 1999; IADB, 1998).

- *Lenders face high transaction costs.* These transaction costs stem from serving areas with typically low population density and dispersed inhabitants. Making site visits to potential clients is both time and resource intensive for bank staff. Visiting bank branches can also be a burden on potential borrowers if they live in more remote regions and have to travel great distances. Lack of information about potential borrowers can be more acute in rural settings. It is difficult for lenders to assess the risk of lending to rural borrowers as many have no formal credit history, nor can they present a track record of cash-flow generation from their activities. Difficulty in gathering this information increases transaction costs.

- *Most prospective borrowers have no collateral.* Land is the preferred form of collateral for rural lending. But in many developing countries proving property rights in rural areas can be challenging. In certain instances, small-scale farmers might not have the title to their land or it may not be registered with the proper authorities. Other assets such as equipment, inventory and livestock are more difficult to use as collateral: such assets need to be valued, properly insured against theft and disaster, and the lender would need assurance that these assets could not be moved.

- *Agricultural contracts are seasonal and of long duration.* This is especially true of contracts tied to crop farming. During the long period between sowing and selling, it can be difficult for farmers to make interest and loan repayments as they incur costs tied to harvesting, storage and marketing. After the crop is sold and the debt repaid, there is a window of time when most farmers will not need credit. This presents a challenge for lenders. Potential clients will request credit around the same time of year (before planting, in order to buy seed and fertilizer, pay expenses related to land preparation and so on). There will be months of uncertainty during which many borrowers will struggle to meet interest and principal repayments, but once the crop is harvested and sold, the debt will be repaid and no credit taken out for a couple of months. The finance provider is then faced with a need to invest this excess liquidity. Lending for crop farming requires flexible finance mechanisms which are challenging to provide on a sustainable basis.

- *Banks are typically faced with a mismatch between the duration of deposits and loans.* Rural savers are likely to withdraw their savings at the time of greatest need-before the harvest. The timing will coincide with when the demand for loans is greatest, making it virtually impossible for lending institutions to match the timing of deposits and loans.

- *Lenders face covariant risks.* In agricultural lending, it is very difficult for lenders to diversify their risks. Even in regions where different crops are grown, certain production risks are the same across a given region: weather patterns, pest infestations and so on.

Through the years, successive governments and international development agencies have sought the best way to tackle the challenge of rural finance provision. From the 1950s to the 1970s many developing countries, in particular in Latin America, adopted a strategy of state-directed rural credit (IADB, 1998). Pressure was applied on commercial banks to open branches in rural areas and in many countries the state created agricultural development banks. Most state-capitalized development banks provided loans at below-market interest rates. Agricultural development banks were mainly created for political reasons and were never meant to operate in a self-sustainable manner. The performance of loan officers was typically based on loan disbursements rather than loan portfolio quality. This led many banks to make sizeable loans to well-established larger farmers (FAO/GTZ, 1999). A World Bank report (Braverman and Guasch, 1989) found that 5 per cent of farmers received 80 per cent of the credit disbursed in Asia and Latin America. Large farmers benefited from state subsidies, thus increasing inequality in rural areas (IADB, 1998).

In the 1990s, financial liberalization and reforms prevailed in many developing countries. Commercial banks closed their unprofitable rural branches and state-sponsored rural credit programmes were unwound. Subsequently, the availability of rural credit decreased and where available, its cost increased with the demise of subsidised interest rates (FAO/GTZ, 1998, 1999; IADB, 1998). Of course, for many small-scale farmers, access to formal credit was never an option to begin with. But financial liberalization has made access to formal credit even further beyond the reach of many small farmers.

There are various types of finance provider other than formal lenders who also extend credit. Table 5.1 details the different types of lender present in most developing countries.

Table 5.1   *Typology of lenders*

Formal lenders	Semi-formal lenders	Informal lenders	Interlinked credit arrangements
Agricultural development banks	Credit unions	Relatives and friends	Input suppliers/crop buyers
	Co-operatives	Moneylenders	
Rural branches of commercial banks	Village or semi-formal community banks	Rotating savings and credit associations	Processing industries
Co-operative banks	NGOs		
Rural banks/ community banks			

Source: FAO/GTZ (1999)

In Latin America most rural borrowers, especially small-scale farmers, are dependent on semi-informal, informal and interlinked credit arrangements to meet their financial needs (IADB, 1998). The situation is more acute in sub-Saharan Africa, where the collapse of formal lending programmes has left a gap in seasonal finance that is not being filled by semi-formal, informal or interlinked credit providers (Dorward et al., 2001; IADB, 1998).

Microcredit methodologies have emerged in the last twenty years as promising instruments to alleviate poverty through extending small loans to groups considered by formal lenders as unbankable. However, microcredit's success has been severely limited in rural environments (with the notable exception of Bangladesh) and for agricultural lending in particular. Whilst several different models exist, microcredit in developing countries typically relies on group guarantees as a substitute for collateral. Of prime importance is keeping risk in check. Loan amounts are kept small and of short duration with well-designed repayment incentives to do so. Such methodologies can be used in certain instances for livestock farming but are not easily applied to lending for crop farming. Furthermore, agricultural credit does not naturally apply to group lending (Dorward et al., 2001).

Interlinked credit arrangements, also called 'interlocking transactions', are 'an institutional arrangement whereby buyers of a crop provide inputs on credit at the beginning of a season and recover the input and credit costs when subsequently purchasing the crop' (Dorward et al., 2001: 5). In some countries, interlinked credit arrangements are available to farmers in crop production as long as the crops being cultivated are cash crops. But these credit arrangements are not typically available for subsistence agriculture. Fair Trade farmers are in the cash-crop-production business and often have access to credit through middlemen who buy their crops. These seasonal loans are tied to exclusive buying arrangements, which can be a welcome source of capital, but they have severe drawbacks. As Dorward et al. (2001) noted, if farmers have few alternative income sources and there are scant numbers of traders available, the latter may capture an undue share of the benefits in these transactions. This has been the complaint of many small-scale producers in developing countries.

The traders or middlemen concerned have a bad reputation in many developing countries and are known as 'coyotes', 'piranhas' or 'sharks' in various places. But they provide an indispensable link between producer and consumer. They play many roles: trader; moneylender; transporter; packer and distributor (Barratt Brown, 1993). The risk comes when power is concentrated in their hands and there is little competition, thus they can take advantage of the producers they buy from, particularly if these producers are in a weak bargaining position (Rice and McLean, 1999). This is especially true when it comes to access to finance for small-scale farmers in countries with a virtually non-existent rural financial infrastructure.

As Dorward et al. (2001) noted, the conditions under which interlinked credit arrangements can work efficiently are quite restrictive. There needs to exist:

- Strong incentives for traders to increase the volume that they process.
- Competition between traders to protect farmers' bargaining positions.
- High returns to seasonal input use.
- Some form of information sharing between traders, which allows them to penalize defaulting borrowers by denying them access to credit based on the borrower's prior experiences with other lenders.
- Some minimum scale of transactions (suggesting relations with larger-scale farmers, local assembly agents or farmer groups).

In liberalized markets such conditions are normally found only with cash crops showing significant economies of scale in marketing or processing. But even when these conditions exist, traders may also be credit constrained themselves.

This overview of the state of the financial infrastructure in developing countries has shown that for many small-scale farmers access to basic banking services is severely limited. The next section reviews which financial products the agricultural sector needs to access in order to function effectively. A review of how the Fair Trade model tries to address some of these requirements then follows.

An Overview of Financial Products Needed by the Agricultural Sector

As with any business sector, the agricultural sector has diverse financing needs stretching beyond access to credit. These needs vary as well depending on the actor within the agricultural sector. The agricultural sector is made up of small farmers, farmers' co-operatives (which group the farmers together to give them better operating leverage), large private farmers, exporters, agribusinesses and traders. The actors involved in Fair Trade include mainly the farmers themselves and the co-operatives or exporters which they work through, since Fair Trade aims to help producers capture more value by shortening the supply chain. Northern-based Fair Trade organizations do not transact directly with individual small-scale farmers. This would be unwieldy, costly and impossible to manage. In the case of Fair Trade crops grown by small-scale farmers, importers buy from exporters who are usually organized democratically in the form of co-operatives. These co-operatives are typically a regrouping of smaller co-operatives, known as second-level or third-level co-operatives.

Table 5.2 summarizes the financing needs of small-scale farmers and co-operatives/exporters and shows that farmers and farmers' co-operatives have a vast range of financing needs spanning savings, leasing, working capital, term financing and equity to insurance products. As the previous section showed, the financial market infrastructure in developing countries leaves most of these needs unmet. The financing needs detailed in Table 5.2 are similar whether the farmers and the co-operatives are operating in Fair Trade markets and open markets or just on the open market. This is because, with very few exceptions, Fair Trade co-operatives or exporters only sell a small amount of their crops on Fair Trade terms. The volume varies depending on the commodity and size of the co-operative. For example, the Peruvian coffee co-operative COCLA sold 16 per cent of its coffee in 2002 to the Fair Trade market.

The next two sections review farmers' financing needs and how some of these can be met through the Fair Trade model of operation.

Table 5.2 *Financial products needed by exporters and farmers*

Type	Description
Savings	Formal savings opportunities are instrumental to risk mitigation for farmers
Leasing	To buy farm machinery, irrigation equipment, livestock, processing equipment and to make land improvements
Pre-harvest working capital	To buy agricultural inputs – seeds and fertilizer – and to prepare the land
Pre-export working capital/trade finance	To finance the period from harvest to shipping, known as 'pre-finance'
Term finance	To buy farm machinery, irrigation equipment, livestock, processing equipment and to make land improvements
Equity	To invest in the co-operative and build its capacity
Insurance	To insure against crop failure and price fluctuations

Pre-finance in the Fair Trade Model

In a fully functioning financial market, co-operatives/exporters would be able to finance their working capital from local banks. They would, for example, sell their receivables to a bank for a discount in exchange for receiving the money up-front (invoice discounting) or perhaps arrange an overdraft facility secured on these receivables. But the same access-to-finance problems that plague individual small-scale farmers also plague the exporting organizations and co-operatives they partner. This has led to the provision of pre-finance acting as the lynchpin of the Fair Trade model. Whilst the provision of pre-finance to producers is generally accepted to be part of the Fair Trade way of doing business, it is not always available. The Fair Trade Labelling Organizations International (FLO) only inserts a pre-financing requirement on the part of buyers into some of their product requirements, not all of them. In addition, producers have to ask buyers to make the pre-finance available to them. However, almost 90 per cent of the International Federation of Alternative Trade (IFAT) members provide pre-finance or advance-payment services to producers. About 27 per cent also provide loans to their producer partners (Fair Trade Federation and IFAT, 2003).

The term 'pre-finance' is used to refer to different types of finance and as such is often misunderstood. Pre-finance is the provision of pre-export credit. Pre-export credit is a loan provided to an exporter based on a percentage (usually up to 60 per cent) of the value of the goods bought. This enables the exporter to receive part of the payment up front with the balance settled once the goods arrive at their destination[1]. Figure 5.1 shows where pre-export/trade financing, generally referred to as 'pre-finance', fits in with the crop cycle.

Whilst today few buyers provide finance as early on as the harvesting/treatment stage, the original pre-finance clause in the early Fair Trade certification process contemplated that it would be provided at this stage.

There are two mechanisms through which Fair Trade importers (the buyers) provide this pre-finance, either internally or externally. In practice, most buyers use a mix of both methods to finance their purchase, thus spreading the risk.

Internally   The buyer advances a portion of the invoice prior to receiving the shipment. A buyer's ability to finance this from their own cash flow varies from organization to organization and also on the time of year. Figure 5.2 illustrates how this works.

Externally   For example, through a one-off finance facility or a line of credit. The buyer sets up a line of credit with a financial provider. Then, as each order is made, the finance provider lends a certain percentage of the invoice amount to the seller. When the buyer

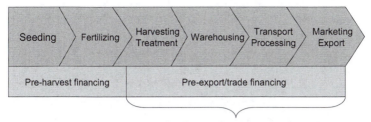

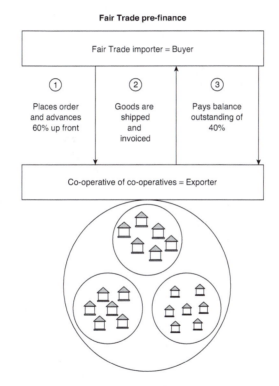

Figure 5.1   *The crop cycle and pre-finance*

Source: Adapted from Varangis et al. (2004)

Figure 5.2   *Pre-finance provided by the buyer*

receives the goods and is ready to settle the invoice, he pays the full amount to the finance provider. The lender keeps the amount advanced, deducts the amount of interest owed and pays the balance to the seller. Figure 5.3 illustrates how this mechanism works.

In some cases the interest on the pre-finance loan is borne by the buyer, but in most cases that cost is passed on to the exporter. The main benefit of pre-finance under Fair Trade terms is that the credit is available on affordable terms. Because the volumes that exporters and co-operatives sell on Fair Trade terms are usually just a fraction of their overall volume, most providers of pre-finance also provide finance to co-operatives/ exporters for sales to non-Fair Trade buyers. Finance providers to small-scale and Fair Trade co-operatives are reviewed in the following section, after a case study on one specialist Fair Trade finance provider, Shared Interest.

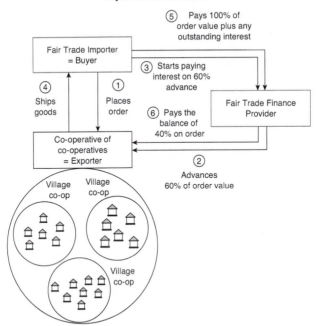

Figure 5.3   *Pre-finance provided through a specialized lender*

CASE STUDY: SHARED INTEREST

Shared Interest is a lending co-operative with around £23 million invested by some 8,500 individuals in Britain who understand the problems people in the South experience in getting access to credit. Founded in 1990 to address the credit needs of the Fair Trade sector, Shared Interest offers credit to Fair Trade producers and buyers against their orders. In 1997, Shared Interest entered into a strategic alliance with IFAT and since then has been focusing on providing credit to IFAT's Northern and Southern members.

To enable producers to access additional credit and to consolidate orders from all buyers to all producers, Shared Interest has developed a clearing-house system. By joining the clearing-house system, a buyer is able to access credit in order to finance prepayments to producers and to accommodate the period after shipment before goods are sold to their final customers. Once a producer has joined the clearing house, they are given an export credit facility and can request credit of up to 80 per cent of the order value from clearing-house buyers. This credit can come in the form of pre-finance from the buyer, however, it is also available if the buyer does not offer any pre-finance or to complement the buyer credit and the seller can access up to 80 per cent as an export credit. Shared Interest also offers term loans to producer organizations who wish to purchase an asset.

Many Northern-based Fair Trade organizations have buyer facilities with Shared Interest. The arrangement works because there is a community of people willing to invest some of their savings in Shared Interest. These investments are not deposits and Shared Interest is explicitly not a bank. This implies that saver capital is 100 per cent at risk. Shared Interest members buy withdrawable share capital in a range from £100 to £20,000, with the average investment being around £2,000. The interest paid on their deposits is low, typically 4 per cent below the UK's base rate. One third of members waive their right to 'interest'. Shared Interest loans are typically unsecured, which means that they rank behind other lenders. This enables Fair Trade organizations to use their assets as security to access others sources of working capital.

Shared Interest does not finance start-ups. It normally requires that a business has been trading for a minimum of three years and is (or is likely to be) profitable. Over the last twelve years, Shared Interest has suffered six losses; three were coffee producers, one a food producer, one a mixed handicraft/food buyer business and the last was a handicraft distributor. But Shared Interest has never lost any money for its investors and it limits its portfolio to around 15 per cent reliance on coffee. Foodstuffs represent half of its trade finance transactions, with the other half represented by handicrafts. Shared Interest is now branching out from working with IFAT-only members to work with producers in other areas, such as the food producers who are on the FLO's (Fairtrade Labelling Organizations International) register.

Safia Minney, founder of The Fair Trade Company in Japan, says of Shared Interest:

It's great to have someone who has taken the leap of imagination to provide credit for Fair Trade organizations to enable small-scale producers to get more benefit for their work. To us, Fair Trade should keep alive traditional skills and promote environmentally friendly production processes. In the face of all the barriers small-scale producers and small companies face, helping to provide credit makes the miracle of Fair Trade possible. Fair Trade is at least as much about empowering the consumer as it is about empowering the producer. (Interview, 2004)

Sources: Finance for Fair Trade, a Shared Interest pamphlet; 2003 Shared Interest annual report

Today there are a number of organizations that dedicate a portion of their resources to providing finance to Fair Trade producers and to small-scale farmers and co-operatives; some of which are listed in Table 5.3. This has not always been the case and the pre-finance 'methodology' that has emerged has evolved over the years. These finance providers are as heterogeneous as the Fair Trade sector itself. The loan funds come from international development non-governmental organizations (NGOs), environmental NGOs, foundations, social banks and Fair Trade buyers themselves. Most do not target their lending exclusively to Fair Trade contracts but focus on supporting small-scale farmers or sustainable agriculture.

It is worth noting that in some countries, there are also government-sponsored schemes that support the larger well-known Fair Trade producer groups like UCIRI in Mexico, by granting them access to credit. This enables these co-operatives to access credit at reasonable rates.

Other Financing Needs of Producer Organizations

While it is difficult to generalize the varied situations of Fair Trade producers in different countries, Table 5.4 attempts to summarize the availability of financial products for small-scale farmers in developing countries.

Table 5.3 *Overview of pre-finance providers*

Organization	Main activity	Products supported
CORDAID *NGO*	Provides pre-finance to small-scale producers, not just Fair Trade and organic.	Fair Trade and organic coffee but looking to work in other commodities. Also microfinance and housing work.
Douqué Coffees *Fair Trade buyer*	Leading buyer of coffee. Provides pre-finance to the exporters it buys from. Sometimes funds their sales to other buyers.	Coffee.
Ecologic Finance *Environmental NGO fund*	Provides affordable credit to rural producer co-operatives located in environmentally sensitive areas of Latin America.	Sustainable agriculture, non-timber forest products, renewable energy and ecotourism.
ForesTrade *Fair Trade buyer*	Fair Trade importer that provides pre-finance to the exporters it buys from.	Fair Trade and organic coffee, spices.
Green Development Foundation (GDF)	With funding from DOEN Foundation, provides pre-finance to 11 coffee co-operatives.	Fair Trade and organic coffee, sustainable tourism.
Oikocredit *Ecumenical development co-operative society*	Lends only in the South. Favours large medium-term loans, does not do much pre-finance.	Some coffee co-operatives, but also supports microcredit, women-led and environmental initiatives.
Rabobank Foundation	Lends to small-scale coffee co-operatives through GDF. Mainly trade finance. Some risk management work.	Coffee (through GDF), cocoa and cotton. Also supports microcredit initiatives.
Shared Interest *Specialist finance provider*	Lends mainly to the Fair Trade buyers but also to exporters. Until recently buyers and exporters had to be IFAT members, but Shared Interest is now branching out to work with FLO-registered producers. Also provides finance against exporters' non-Fair Trade sales.	Foodstuffs and handicrafts. Coffee limited to 15 per cent of portfolio.
Triodos – Fair share fund	Provides pre-finance to lower risk exporters.	Mainly coffee.
Triodos – DOEN fund	Manages money from DOEN which it lends to Fair Trade and organic coffee producers. Medium risk borrowers.	Mainly coffee.
Triodos – HIVOS fund	Manages money from HIVOS which it lends to Fair Trade and organic coffee producers. Higher risk borrower.	Mainly coffee.
TWIN Trading *Fair Trade buyer*	Fair Trade importer. Provides pre-finance to the exporters it buys from.	Mainly coffee and cocoa but looking to work in other commodities.
Verde Ventures *Environmental NGO fund*	Provides debt and equity financing to support conservation-oriented businesses in Conservation International's priority areas.	Loan fund dedicated to sustainable coffee but has also supported one other Fair Trade initiative in cocoa.

Source: Adapted from Rosenthal (2003)

Table 5.4 *Summary of availability of financial products*

Type	Availability
Savings	Varies by country.
Leasing	Very limited. Property rights and legal framework in most developing countries make use of leasing difficult, especially in rural areas.
Pre-harvest working capital	Unclear. In some situations, co-operatives have set up credit unions to make savings and loans available to individual farmers. Kuapa Kokoo, a Fair Trade cocoa co-op in Ghana, is one such example.
Pre-export working capital/ trade finance	Available for Fair Trade sales. Also available for other sales by the stronger co-operatives. Smaller co-operatives always find it more challenging to access finance while the better established ones are well-catered for. But coffee prices have been low and stable in the last four years – what will happen if prices peak and volatility returns?
Term finance	Very limited. In most countries, banks are reluctant to lend to farmers and farmers' co-operatives. Some organizations lend directly to co-operatives in the South (Oikocredit, CreditoSud) but availability is limited and terms and process are generally perceived as onerous by borrowers.
Guarantees	Limited. But some organizations like Oikocredit and Twin Trading will guarantee loans made by local banks.
Equity	Availability of outside equity is limited. Co-operative members usually contribute a nominal amount of capital to become members, but due to low available assets this capitalization is generally minor.
Insurance	Extremely limited. Mostly on pilot project scale only. Fair Trade contracts provide *de facto* insurance against price volatility but this only covers tiny volumes.

Availability of pre-finance credit is generally good for stronger co-operatives/ exporters but fewer have access to term finance. Medium-term loans are necessary for investment in warehouses, transport and processing equipment. For some co-operatives, their relationship with Fair Trade buyers has been instrumental in getting them access to medium-term finance. Some organizations such as Oikocredit (an ecumenical development co-operative society), Creditosud (an Italian social bank) and Shared Interest try to fill this gap, either through direct lending or the provision of guarantees to local banks. Lending and borrowing in a foreign currency are not ideal and provision of local lending needs to be developed.

Another challenge is the lack of risk management instruments that small farmers and co-operatives have access to and know how to use. Clearly, Fair Trade sales provide one type of insurance by naming a guaranteed price and thus eliminating price volatility. But for the rest of their crops, farmers and exporters are typically left at the mercy of price fluctuations. For the producer, this leads to an inability to plan crops, allocate resources or obtain credit. In facing such volatility, risk-averse low-income farmers typically adopt lower yield lower-risk production technologies and shift from cash crops to subsistence crops. For the co-operatives/exporters, price volatility leads to an inability to forecast cash flow properly, obtain credit or protect from financial loss. For the banks lending to agriculture, this leads to high levels of risk in lending combined with high levels of default due to client losses (Varangis et al., 2004).

There exists a full range of formal financial instruments and trading mechanisms to hedge price volatility and risks, but only 2 per cent of positions held on the derivatives market can be attributed to developing countries (International Task Force, 1999). Within developing countries, it is incredibly difficult for small farmers to access hedging instruments. This is due to a lack of knowledge and capacity in understanding how to use these and is also due to the fact that most risk-management brokers will not deal with small farmers and co-operatives because of the very high transaction costs that arise whilst dealing with unknown and multiple counterparties. Even in situations where the infrastructure does exist, the standardized instruments may be inappropriate because of contract size, basis risk or currency exposure (Lewin et al., 2004).

Many co-operatives will buy crops from their members at a set price. They bear the greatest risk between the time they buy the crops and when they are able to sell them. Training co-operative managers to do back-to-back trading whenever possible in order to minimize this exposure is one simple way of increasing their capacity to manage risk. The International Taskforce on Commodity Risk has undertaken a number of pilots working with co-operatives/exporters in different countries to train them to make use of hedging instruments. Whilst progress has been made, it has been slow and the results of some pilots have been mixed. For many farmers the cost of insurance (against price volatility) proves too high. Price volatility and lack of insurance mechanisms look set to remain a feature of the plight of small-scale farmers in developing countries for some time yet.

SUMMARY OF FAIR TRADE FINANCE IN THE SOUTH

Small-scale farmers and the co-operatives/exporters they partner face severe problems accessing the financial products they need to function effectively. This is true of all small-scale farmers in developing countries, whether they are able to sell some of their crop on Fair Trade terms or not. But the co-operatives that sell on Fair Trade terms do gain two distinct advantages: access to pre-export finance (or pre-finance) and a minimum amount for a crop, the latter acting as price insurance for their Fair Trade sales. Fair Trade buyers and other organizations have been instrumental in increasing the amount of credit available to co-operatives. This is especially true in the case of coffee, where many more loan funds exist today to help co-operatives meet their funding needs.

The Fair Trade connection has also helped some co-operatives access other forms of longer-term capital and to receive funds for development projects. However, there is less evidence that Fair Trade has improved access to finance at the individual farmer level. Small-scale farmers struggle to access credit and the other financial products they need. The creation of credit unions within co-operatives is one way to increase the provision of finance directly to the farmers. Both Kuapa Kokoo in Ghana and CEPCO in Oaxaca, Mexico, for example, have done this.

The Fair Trade sector can and should continue to try and address the financing needs of its Southern partners. Co-operatives could be encouraged to on-lend funds to their members. But it is clear that for the financial needs of small-scale farmers in developing countries to be met, a much greater change needs to take place. This change in the financial infrastructures of agricultural finance in developing countries is systemic in nature and, to a great extent, beyond the Fair Trade sector's powers to enable.

FINANCING FOR NORTHERN-BASED MARKET ACCESS ORGANIZATIONS

The previous section outlined the financing needs of Fair Trade producers based in the South. This section looks at access to finance for the Fair Trade organizations that buy from these producers and help them to access Northern markets. The first part of this section provides an overview of how Northern-based Fair Trade companies have financed their growth and how the choice of business model has influenced their access to finance. The second part considers whether the difficulties in accessing finance for these companies are inherent in the fact that they are engaged in Fair Trade activities or whether it is linked to other factors. The third part draws conclusions on the role of access to finance in supporting the growth of the Fair Trade sector.

The Experience of Northern-based Fair Trade Companies in Accessing Capital

The organizations that partner with producers to help them to access Northern markets form a heterogeneous group. They are rooted in different philosophies and have emerged from various backgrounds: faith-based, co-operative principles/mutualism, activism/solidarity and trading/commercial amongst others. Each Fair Trade company approaches Fair Trade in its own manner and seeks to improve producers' positions in the supply chain in a slightly different way. Many Fair Trade organizations are small, whilst others have grown through the years to be bigger operations. But on the whole, most Fair Trade companies fall into the small and medium sized enterprise (SME) category[2].

Table 5.5 summarizes research and interviews with nine Northern-based Fair Trade companies. Financing arrangements differ depending on the business structure of the Fair Trade organization, history, governance/ownership structure, philosophy and location. This sample of Northern-based Fair Trade organizations highlights the diversity of the Fair Trade sector. The companies' annual sales range from around £560,000 ($1m) to over £34m ($60m). Many were founded in the 1990s but one was founded in the late 1970s. One is faith-based, several are based on co-operative principles, two are partly producer-owned, several are entrepreneurially driven by their founders and two are owned or partly owned by the shops through which they distribute their products.

Almost all of the organizations have buyers' facilities with Shared Interest. These lines of credit are usually complemented by other short-term credit facilities or invoice discounting arrangements. Few, if any, have access to long-term debt from commercial banks. Some, such as The Day Chocolate Company and People Tree, have been able to raise some unsecured subordinated debt. Equity financing has come as a mix of ordinary and preference type shares. A couple of the organizations (People Tree and Tropical Wholefoods) have only had their founders as a source of equity. Others have expanded their equity base through widely held alternative share offerings (for example, Traidcraft, Cafédirect and Claro). Others, such as La Siembra and Alter Eco, have approached

Table 5.5 *Financing sources for nine Fair Trade companies*

	Traidcraft	Cafédirect	Day Chocolate	People Tree	Tropical Wholefoods	La Siembra	Alter Eco	Claro	CTM
Main products	Food & beverages, crafts, clothing, speciality paper	Coffee, tea, drinking cocoa	Chocolate bars, drinking cocoa	Clothes, accessories for the home	Dried fruit, snack bars	Chocolate bars, drinking cocoa, cocoa powder	Coffee, tea, chocolate, cocoa, olive oil, fruit juice, sugar	Chocolate, dried mango, dried pineapple, rice, cashew nuts, cocoa powder, household goods	180 products, largely food but some crafts
Turnover	£13.8m/ $24.7m, 2003/2004	£17m/ $30.4m (est.), 2004	£5.2m/$9.3m (est.), 2003/ 2004	£0.9m/$1.61m (est.), 2004	£1.4m/ $2.5m (est.), 2004	C$1.7m/ $1.3m/£0.75m 2003/2004	€5m/$6.2m/ £3.5m (est.), 2004	CHF16m/ $12.6m/£7m, 2002/2003	€50m/ $60.3m/ £34m, 2003
Location	UK	UK	UK	UK/Japan	UK	Canada	France	Switzerland	Italy
Structure (voting rights)	Public limited company. Ordinary shareholders have full voting rights but Traidcraft Foundation owns guardian share	Public limited company. Twin Trading, Equal Exchange UK, Oxfam & Traidcraft own 40% and a guardian share, with small investors owning 55% and producers 5%	Private limited company. 53% owned by Twin Trading, 33% by Kuapa Kokoo and 14% by the Body Shop	Private limited company. Wholly owned by founder	Private limited company. Owned by four founders/ partners	Workers' co-op, owned by staff	Société anonyme. 22% owned by 6 private investors, 8% by institutional investor and 69% by trust as 'Fair Trade friends'	Originally an import co-operative, then converted to a limited company	Second level co-op of 130 co-ops, owned by CTM shops
Year started	1979	1991	1998	Parent company founded 1992	1992, merged with FM Foods in 2001	1999	1999	1997, predecessor founded in 1977	N/A

(Continued)

Table 5.5 (Continued)

	Traidcraft	Cafédirect	Day Chocolate	People Tree	Tropical Wholefoods	La Siembra	Alter Eco	Claro	CTM
Distribution channels	47% Fair Trade volunteers, 28% supermarkets/ wholesale, 12% mail order, 13% independent retailers	Mainstream supermarkets, catering outlets	Mainstream supermarkets in the UK, through SERRV in the USA	Catalogue	Independent shops, health food stores, some supermarkets	Independent shops, health food stores, some supermarkets	Mainstream supermarkets	150 franchized shops, 300 other world shops, organic and health food shops and EFTA partners	50% through 250 of own shops, 35% supermarkets, 10% independent shops, 5% export
Debt financing	Overdraft facility, Shared Interest facility	Overdraft facility, Shared Interest facility	Overdraft facility guaranteed by DFID, invoice discounting facility, subordinated shareholder loans	Shared Interest facility, bank debt personally guaranteed by founder, unsecured two-year loan note bought by consumers	Shared Interest facility, invoice discounting facility	Line of credit with local co-operative bank, Shared Interest facility	Two credit facilities with French banks; does not work with Shared Interest	Shared Interest facility, plus other debt on its balance sheet	N/A
Equity financing	5,500 shareholders. £5m in ordinary shares marketed to the public but unlisted	Over 4,500 shareholders. £5m in ordinary shares marketed to the public but unlisted	Conservation International (debt but quasi-equity), Body Shop, Christian Aid, Twin Trading	Founders' own money	Founders' own money	CA$375,000 ($296,000; £165,000) of preference shares from 75 investors	Around 20 individual investors, a couple of institutional investors	1,200 shareholders: 127 Claro world shops, 1,000 private individuals, 40 parishes, clubs, charities, etc.	Through individual co-op members

outside equity investors on a more limited basis. Given low to non-existent dividend yields on the shares and the fact that all the shares in these Fair Trade organizations are unlisted, it would appear that most shareholders invest in Fair Trade companies because of the social value they see in the Fair Trade model.

Table 5.5 shows that the experiences of Fair Trade organizations are incredibly varied. The best way to understand their respective approaches to raising finance is to look at their experiences on a case-by-case basis. The following sections highlight the experiences of three Fair Trade companies in starting up their businesses and accessing finance as they have grown their operations.

The first case study is that of France Alter Eco. It aptly illustrates how the organization was founded and has grown with outside equity investment. It also highlights the example of a Fair Trade organization whose management feels that it has not been constrained in accessing finance. The second case study is that of Cafédirect. Its story underlines how a by now large and profitable Fair Trade company struggled to raise finance in the early years. It also shows how it can be difficult to raise outside equity on terms that are in line with a Fair Trade company's ethos. The last case study is that of La Siembra in Canada, highlighting how the choice of operating model, as a workers' co-operative, has limited its access to outside equity from institutional sources. It also shows how a Fair Trade company can successfully elicit the imagination of small investors.

CASE STUDY: FRANCE ALTER ECO

France Alter Eco, a *société anonyme* founded in 1999, is projected to turn over €5 million ($6.2m; £ 3.5m) in 2004. Its initial business model was to use profits generated through Fair Trade stores to support other development projects. To attract the capital needed for the project, the founders published an article in a personal finance publication in April 1999 detailing their store concept. They received phone calls from about 20 potential investors. France Alter Eco was founded with the support of 15 independent investors with €100,000 ($124, 000; £70,000) of equity and a €100,000 line of credit. These individuals invested between €2,970 and €74,700 ($3681–92,500; £2078–52,200) each in ordinary share capital. Alter Eco was turned down by ten other banks before finally being given a line of credit by Crédit Cooperatif, a co-operative bank that specializes in supporting charities, social enterprise and co-operatives. Credit was provided in exchange for personal guarantees and security.

Alter Eco's retail outlet was opened in November 1999. Initially, the company bought all of its goods through established Fair Trade importers like Oxfam Belgium and Solidar'Monde in France, but later on started to build direct links with producers for around 20 per cent of its products. Today Alter Eco buys 70 per cent of its goods directly from producer groups and 30 per cent from Fair Trade importers like Claro of Switzerland and Oxfam Belgium. Despite the store's initial success, sales per square foot in the first year were deemed too low for the store concept to be franchised.

The Alter Eco team changed its approach and in May 2001 closed the store, deciding instead to focus its efforts on mainstreaming Fair Trade products in supermarket chains. Alter Eco started working with Monoprix in September 2001 to develop a range of Fair Trade food goods. Monoprix invested time and energy in their partnership with Alter

Eco and helped them to develop their quality, health and safety testing, as well as packaging for the new products. In April 2002, Alter Eco launched 13 products in Monoprix stores nationwide. In 2003, it introduced ten new products. Alter Eco's products are now also listed nationwide in Leclerc, System U, Cora and Match supermarkets. It also has some regional/local referencing in Carrefour, Intermarché, Champion and ATAC.

Alter Eco has increased its capital base since its founding. The original 15 investors hold 69 per cent of the issued share capital. ESFIN Participations, a fund dedicated to investing in socially-driven ventures, holds 8.8 per cent. ESFIN has capped its potential upside at a maximum of 12 per cent. The remaining 22.2 per cent is held by six individuals. Alter Eco is currently raising additional capital from institutional investors (co-operative banks, social funds and so on) as dealing with individual investors has proved very time-consuming. In the long term, Tristan Lecomte, Alter Eco's President and founder, hopes that Alter Eco will be producer-owned at up to at least 40 per cent.

Lecomte believes that Fair Trade companies are not very different from mainstream businesses in terms of profit and loss. Whilst margins are thinner, these are compensated for by lower marketing costs. A Fair Trade company can keep marketing costs low if it plays on its Fair Trade image and is able to gain good free press coverage. But Lecomte believes that cash flow management is more challenging for a Fair Trade company. To provide the pre-finance it offers producers, Alter Eco works through its two banks to get access to credit. Alter Eco continues to have a good working relationship with its house bank, Crédit Cooperatif, and Crédit Cooperatif's mother company, Banques Populaires. It also has a line of credit with the Caisse d'Epargne. Lecomte does not believe that the two banks treat Alter Eco any differently than other enterprises. It must be noted, however, that unlike UK banks French banks will lend to Alter Eco on the basis of a letter of intent from a large supermarket, such as Monoprix, promising to stock their goods.

Sources: Interviews with Tristan LeComte (2003, 2004)

CASE STUDY: CAFÉDIRECT

Cafédirect, founded in 1991 by Equal Exchange UK, Traidcraft, Twin and Oxfam, has grown into the leading UK Fair Trade company. The founders' aim was to get small producers a better price for their crops and to provide greater opportunities for their communities. Cafédirect's range has expanded from a single coffee product in 1991 to a portfolio of 41 products, including gourmet coffees, specialty teas and drinking chocolate. Its turnover in 2004 is projected to be around £17 million.

Cafédirect was financially supported by its founders for over twelve years as the company found it difficult to negotiate outside sources of investment. The founders provided ordinary equity and preference shares as well as loans to the company. The preference shares paid a maximum of 10 per cent in dividends. The loans had no fixed repayment date, were recallable at three months' notice and paid interest at 2.5 per cent over base. The one outside loan that was secured in Cafédirect's early years was guaranteed by the Dutch foundation HIVOS. Cafédirect also agreed a Shared Interest unsecured credit line which has grown from £600,000 to £1 million. Cafédirect has an overdraft facility with Triodos Bank that has increased from £130,000 to £500,000 over the years. It has fixed and floating security over Cafédirect's stock and debtors.

But with sales growth in the last couple of years averaging between 20 and 30 per cent per annum, the company's need for working capital has increased rapidly. As Shared Interest limits its exposure to any one company and to coffee in particular, Cafédirect was not able to increase its Shared Interest line of credit in keeping with its sales' growth. With a concentrated debtor book and a lack of fixed assets with which to secure further debt, Cafédirect could not obtain additional debt to its overdraft and revolving credit facilities. In any event, what the company really needed was an equity injection in order to fund its permanent increase in working capital and to invest this capital in the growth of the business and the development of new products and new sales channels.

In 2002/2003, Cafédirect's board explored the possibility of raising venture capital, but some of the founders were concerned about the financial prerogative that a venture capitalist would inject into the business. In 2003, the company decided to raise capital through an alternative share issue in order to invest in its brand, repay borrowings, fund working capital and invest in computer systems. Cafédirect successfully raised £5 million ($8.7m) of equity from new investors in the first half of 2004. The share issue was oversubscribed. The company's shares are not listed on an exchange, rather willing buyers and sellers are linked up through Ethex, a matched bargaining system arranged on a periodic basis by the brokering bank Triodos.

The share prospectus makes it very clear that Cafédirect is first focussed on reinvesting in the company and supporting its producer partners, and second in providing investors with a fair financial and social return. As part of the share issue and ownership changes, the founders decreased their stake to 40 per cent and producer partners were given the option to buy up to 5 per cent of the company's equity. The balance of 55 per cent is held by 4,500 mainly small investors. It would appear that the investors who have bought into Cafédirect and its story have done so primarily for social return. In spite of Cafédirect's track record and profitability, surprisingly none of the UK ethical funds bought any Cafédirect shares in the recent share offering.

Source: Cafédirect, 'The future in your hands', share issue prospectus, 2004.

CASE STUDY: LA SIEMBRA

La Siembra, a worker-owned co-operative, was founded in 1999 and turned over C$1.7 million ($1.3m; £750,000) in the year ended 31 May 2004. It was the first organization to certify and distribute Fair Trade organic cocoa and sugar in North America. It sells its chocolate bars, baking cocoa and drinking chocolate both under its brand 'Cocoa Camino' and under private label. La Siembra is located in Ottawa, Canada, and supplies consumers using manufacturing facilities in Ontario and Switzerland.

Three friends working in international development founded La Siembra with C$15,000 ($11,850; £6,600) borrowed from 15 people. La Siembra negotiated a C$15,000 line of credit with the Desjardins Group which the founders personally guaranteed. At the beginning it sourced organic cocoa from the Organic Commodity Project. The founders mixed and tinned the cocoa themselves in a church basement after working their day jobs. They sold the tins of cocoa powder and drinking chocolate to local shops and cafés. In its first year, La Siembra turned over around C$40,000

($31,600; £17,600) and sold 25 to 30 cases of cocoa a month. As the project grew in scale, the founders felt it needed full-time commitment and more capital.

The current owners/managers bought into La Siembra in September 2000. They invested C$26,000 ($20,540; £11,440) into the business and negotiated an increase to C$30,000 ($23,700; £13,200) in a personally guaranteed line of credit. They outsourced the manufacturing and began a relationship with a cocoa co-operative in the Dominican Republic. In early 2001, the managers decided to raise C$270,000 ($213,300; £118,800) to diversify La Siembra's range and break into the chocolate bar market. Their bank agreed to provide La Siembra with a C$110,000 ($86,900; £48,400) line of credit if it were matched with equity. The managers networked amongst friends and family and set up an initial investors' meeting as a result of which they received around C$35,000 to C$40,000 ($28,045–$31,600; £15,400–£17,600) of investment. Their second investors' meeting yielded C$15,000 to C$20,000 ($11,850–$15,800; £6,600–£8,800) of investment in the company. The Canadian Worker Co-operative Federation and the Canadian Investment Alternative Co-operative were not interested in providing equity, but made subordinated loans to La Siembra totalling C$80,000 ($63,200; £35,200). With C$95,000 ($75,050; £41,800) in equity and quasi-equity raised, the bank increased the line of credit to C$110,000 ($86,900; £48,400) and removed the personal guarantee element.

In January 2002, La Siembra collaborated with TransFair Canada to establish the first North American Fair Trade certification for cocoa and sugar products. La Siembra has partnered with Equal Exchange in the USA to produce their own-branded hot cocoa (launched autumn 2002), cocoa powder (launched 2003) and chocolate bars (launched autumn 2004). Equal Exchange now represents around 25 per cent of La Siembra's sales. The partnership works especially well as both organizations are based on co-operative principles. As Kevin Thomson of La Siembra said: 'The co-operative link is really what started that relationship'. In summer 2003 La Siembra launched its products in Loblaws, Canada's largest supermarket chain.

In autumn 2003, La Siembra arranged a US$80,000 (£44,800) buyer's credit facility with Shared Interest. And in 2003/2004, La Siembra successfully raised new capital of around C$200,000 ($158,000; £88,000). The management team is planning a new offering in 2004/2005 for another C$200,000. This new capital will be used to support the company's growth and development of new product lines. The preference shares sold to outside investors earned a 1.3 per cent dividend in 2003. Whilst raising money from individuals is resource-intensive, La Siembra continues to rely on this method and has been holding investor meetings in big towns. Typical people who come to these investor meetings are between 30 to 50 years old, with most of them in their thirties. They are environmentally and socially conscious. The majority are there because they know someone who works for La Siembra or who has already invested, or they have tried the products. La Siembra has had some success with institutional investors: one co-operative insurance company has invested C$30,000 ($23,700: £13,200) in the business and it has been approached by an environmental investment fund interested in investing in the company. But this would have meant changing its structure from a worker's co-operative in order to give the fund a board seat. The management team would not contemplate changing its co-operative structure in order to raise capital as they believe that it is intrinsic to who they are.

Sources: Interviews with Colin MacDougall and Kevin Thomson, 2004

Table 5.6 *Illustrative growth stages of a business*

Seed capital	Start-up capital	First round venture capital	Second round venture capital	Private equity	IPO/trade sale
100% equity funded	100% equity funded	Mainly equity funded	Mainly equity funded	Larger equity base	Broad equity base
No debt	Maybe asset finance (hire purchase, mortgage)	Asset/trade debt, secured overdraft	Asset/ trade debt, secured overdraft	Unsecured debt might now be available	Asset/trade debt, secured and unsecured debt typically available
Personal savings Credit card debt Home mortgage	3 'F's: 'Friends, Fools & Family' Angel investor	Incubator-type VC Provides services and expertise along with equity	Broaden investor base because initial VC cannot provide the further capital needed for growth	Private equity placement with high net-worth individuals. Passive money, little interference in management of company	Entrepreneur typically loses control
Entrepreneur owns 100%	Entrepreneur owns 90%	Entrepreneur owns 60%	Entrepreneur owns 40%	Entrepreneur owns 30%	Entrepreneur can sell out eventually

Fair Trade Businesses' Access to Capital: The Same Challenges as Any Other Enterprise?

Table 5.5 and the three case studies of the previous section have highlighted the varied experiences of Fair Trade businesses in accessing finance. But can any common thread be found amongst these organizations' respective experiences? And are any commonalities to do with the enterprises' individual business models/stages of growth, or are they inherent to operating in the Fair Trade sector?

Many Fair Trade businesses are SMEs, and raising capital is difficult for small enterprises in most countries. In trying to raise debt finance, SMEs are often confronted with a lack of assets to offer as collateral for accessing secured debt. Because of their size and limited track record, most SMEs are also unable to access unsecured loans. There is no one financing path that small enterprises may follow as they grow, but there are a series of steps that they might take. Table 5.6 illustrates how a small enterprise might grow sufficiently to float on a public stock market.

Table 5.6 is an illustration of how a company might grow; not all companies will go through each of these stages. Many companies are not suitable for venture capital as it is typically reserved for businesses with high growth potential. Some companies may never require outside equity and might remain as privately held businesses. Others might be able to generate enough cash flow internally to support the growth of the business. What Table 5.6 does show is that as a company increases in size, refines its business model and establishes a good track record, outside finance becomes more readily accessible.

Most Fair Trade companies find accessing finance challenging. As the case studies showed, it is difficult for Fair Trade companies to raise debt in addition to that which can be secured on their assets. Most Northern-based Fair Trade companies are import/marketing organizations that have few assets apart from their stock. And even for those that have developed a brand name, most debt providers will not value the brand in considering the company's assets. Because they are import organizations, managing a Fair Trade company's stock levels is particularly important and can be challenging. Fair Trade companies have gone bankrupt in the past because of diversifying too quickly and not adequately managing inventory levels. Of course, this is no different than would be the case for a mainstream SME that specialized in importing and marketing goods. What is different is that working capital management is more difficult in Fair Trade companies because of offering pre-export finance to their suppliers. Fair Trade companies do not want to 'squeeze' their suppliers because they treat them as fully-fledged partners and not just suppliers. Unfortunately, though, many Fair Trade companies that sell through supermarkets – like Cafédirect – typically get squeezed on the other side by the retailers who stretch out payment terms. This is not as much of an issue for Fair Trade companies that rely on their own distribution outlets.

It is also challenging for Fair Trade companies, for example, to raise mainstream outside equity through venture capital as there might be contradictions with either the Fair Trade company's governance structure (for example, a workers' co-operative) or with the social prerogative of the business. Whilst many Fair Trade companies have raised equity from individual investors, this is time-consuming and takes time away from running the business. There also appears to be a lack of institutional equity capital available for Fair Trade businesses. Fair Trade companies suffer from the same difficulties in raising equity that social enterprises in the UK and socially driven businesses in other countries have suffered from. Because of this, there is an initiative underway to create an investment fund dedicated to Northern-based Fair Trade companies. Its success remains to be seen.

CONCLUSION

We live in a world where access to capital is crucial. Capital spurs innovation and enables companies to invest in their businesses. Capital is no less important in the Fair Trade sector; Southern and Northern based Fair Trade partners need access to finance to invest in their operations. The situation in the South is made more difficult by the inadequate agricultural financial infrastructure in most developing countries. Whilst components of the Fair Trade model such as the provision of pre-finance and the minimum price help to work around some of these problems, the Fair Trade model of trade alone cannot address the deficiencies of agricultural financial markets in the South. A much deeper systemic change needs to take place to provide access to financial services, especially credit, for small-scale producers in the South.

The situation for the North is somewhat different, as Northern-based Fair Trade organizations operate in countries with seemingly fully functioning financial markets. Those who believe that banking and capital markets should operate in a transparent and efficient manner would argue that Fair Trade companies' difficulty in accessing capital is due to the weakness of their businesses, and of course there are some Fair Trade companies whose inability to raise capital is due to unprofitable business models. Whilst varied, many Fair Trade organizations' business models are not weak or flawed; they operate in a similar fashion to other double bottom line businesses or Corporate Social Responsibility initiatives that have added on a social imperative to their business model. The difference is one of emphasis. Most Fair Trade businesses are trying to empower small-scale farmers in developing countries and are doing so through commercial means. Many are profit-driven but do not believe in extracting this profit by paying their suppliers an unfair price. They also reinvest the profit earned to create a stronger business and help producers.

Whilst some Fair Trade companies have had the opportunity to raise commercial capital, those companies which have raised outside equity have done so from socially motivated investors. The managers of the companies involved prefer to partner with individuals with similar working practices. Unfortunately, tapping small amounts of equity from numerous individual investors is time-consuming and costly. A better solution needs to be found to channel much-needed funds to Fair Trade companies in the North. Institutional sources of equity for socially driven businesses continue to emerge. The development of these is critical, as better access to capital will enable Fair Trade companies to develop new products to be sold in the North, providing access to new and bigger markets for producers in the South. Realizing the future potential of Fair Trade depends on more capital being made available to the sector.

This chapter has explored some of the financial issues for Southern producers and Northern ATOs. The next chapter will set out the details of the Fair Trade certification process.

NOTES

1. In practice, once shipping documents for the consignment are received by the buyer.
2. Defined by the European Union as a turnover of less than €50m ($62m; £35m) or assets of less than €43m ($53m; £30m) with less than 250 employees.

6

Fair Trade Certification

Having examined the need for Fair Trade to correct market imperfections and some specific examples of how Fair Trade business and finance actors have incorporated Fair Trade into global supply chains, we now turn to the involvement of third-party Fair Trade certification labels. This chapter will discuss the history of Fair Trade certification in Europe and its evolution into a global system of standards and trade audits, primarily under the umbrella of Fairtrade Labelling Organizations International (FLO). FLO's governance structure and the financing of certification are presented, as well as a critique of decision making in terms of growth and new product development. In addition there will be some final discussion of the role of other monitoring initiatives, particularly the system employed by the International Federation of Alternative Trade (IFAT) for craft and textile producers.

INTRODUCTION

The origins of Fair Trade lie in personal relationships between importers and co-operatives and in consumer trust of brands and companies' sourcing practices. Alternative trading organizations (ATOs; as in Chapter 4, the term 'ATO' will be used here to describe those companies that were set up with the express purpose of delivering Fair Trade benefits to producers) have historically maintained very close ties with producer groups, conducting visits to personally determine whether the groups involved are well-governed and will truly benefit from Fair Trade practice. Consumers in turn have trusted the ATO's promises of fair and direct trading relationships.

Beginning in the late 1980s, ATOs and Fair Trade retailers realized that by sharing a mark that identified their Fair Trade business practices, they could benefit from joint marketing and education around the Fair Trade label and grow more quickly (see 'Why Certify' on the next page). They could also protect their own promise of fair trading practices by subscribing to the same broadly recognized standards and submitting to independent audits of their transactions with producers. Various labelling initiatives sprang up all over Europe, led by the Max Havelaar Foundation in the Netherlands (Kocken, 2003), named after a fictional character in Dutch literature who supported the plight of Javanese coffee farmers. According to Redfern and Snedker, these labelling initiatives 'started from a position that businesses were fundamentally bad and therefore not to be trusted. The only way that they could be allowed to market products with a Fair

Trade label was through an intricate rule-based certification system' (2002: 7). Yet throughout this period of national labelling ATOs remained the most loyal supporters of labelling and certification; 'fundamentally bad' businesses had still not entered the niche Fair Trade market.

Formalization of the Fair Trade process into a label relied on one important principle: independent third party standard-setting and certification. Non-profits who licenced the use of the label had to guarantee that producer groups were democratically organized and transparent and that the importer paid the Fair Trade price to them. These national standard-setters and certification agencies became known as Fair Trade labelling national initiatives (NIs). NIs were generally founded by ATOs or non-profits, and to this day many remain governed by long-standing members of the Fair Trade community. Anti-poverty groups including Oxfam, CAFOD, World Development Movement, ChristianAid and the ATO Traidcraft, for instance, founded the Fairtrade Foundation in the UK. Members from these organizations make up the Board of Directors and Trustees of the Fairtrade Foundation (Fairtrade Foundation, 2002).

From 1989 until 1995, independent national Fair Trade labels coexisted in Europe, the USA, Canada and Japan (Ghillani, 2002; Levi and Linton, 2003; Thomson, 1999). Realizing that economies of scale could be reached by jointly monitoring producer groups and co-ordinating standard setting, discussions amongst NIs started with the aim of forming an internationally co-ordinated inspection and labelling system. In 1997, the 17 existing NIs joined together to form FLO, which rapidly became the largest social certification system in the world, covering the most products in the most countries. It is now headquartered in Bonn, Germany, and has field offices and networks of independent inspectors in Africa, Central and South America and Asia. More recently new NIs are applying for, or have achieved, FLO membership, including groups in Australia, Mexico and Spain.

WHY CERTIFY?

Those companies that choose to open their financial accounts and submit to an audit of their supply chain, much less pay a fee for the privilege of doing so, must see some value in third-party certification. Certainly, the consumer benefits from having only one phrase and one logo to understand when searching for socially responsible products. Many companies worry about 'label fatigue' with consumers seeing too many labels on the shelf and not trusting any of them. 'Sustainable', 'organic', 'kosher', 'shade grown', 'locally grown' and so on, can clutter packaging and confuse brand meaning. But third-party certification is often necessary for consumers to trust 'credence' characteristics that they cannot see or experience, such as environmentally friendly production practices or fair prices paid (Grolleau and Ben Abid, 2001).

Companies also find that using a label that other companies are promoting helps their own sales of Fair Trade products. Any Fair Trade marketing undertaken by a competitor increases brand equity behind the Fair Trade label and benefits all products that carry the label. This is true for non-competitor products as well: a tea drinker might first learn about Fair Trade when purchasing bananas and then see the Fair Trade logo in the tea aisle of the grocery store. Competitors are even joining forces to promote logos together. In April 2004, TransFair USA announced the creation of a joint marketing fund to which licensed companies could contribute for the generic marketing of TransFair USA's 'Fair Trade Certified' seal, tied to a product category rather than a brand (Rice, 2004). Companies could request specific geographic regions in which they would like the label promoted, but no brands would be featured.

But perhaps the most important reason for a company to seek third-party certification is to achieve scalability to grow beyond a local market. Coffee is an excellent case in point. In the USA, the speciality coffee industry includes only a few regional or national companies: the vast majority of membership consists of over 2000 'micro' roasters, who roast coffee frequently and in small batches for local delivery. The retailers and café owners know the roasters and have personal relationships with them based on trust. If the local roaster claims to be paying a fair price to the coffee co-operatives he or she sources from, the clients with whom the roaster or the sales staff have personal relationships are inclined to believe him or her, and pass this faith on to their customers.

If a coffee roaster wishes to expand his or her business beyond a small circle of trust, however, they will find that their word does not carry as much weight with those customers they cannot meet personally. Personal trust cannot be easily scaled – once the relationship becomes distant and impersonal, the brand must spend valuable equity ensuring trustworthiness rather than other brand claims like quality or uniqueness. At the opposite end of the spectrum, consumers might be sceptical of ethical claims made by large multinational companies. Third-party certification ensures consumers that the promises made by the company concerning its ethical dealings have been verified by an outside agency and carrying the certification seal adds to brand equity while letting the brand work to convey other messages (Grolleau and Ben Abid, 2001).

Fair Trade Governance: FLO

FLO International exists to improve the position of the poor and disadvantaged producers in the developing world, by setting the Fair Trade standards and by creating the framework that enables trade to take place at conditions favourable to them. (Mission Statement, FLO, 2002)

Reflecting its roots as a consumer organization seeking to align the interests of Southern producers and Northern companies, FLO's Board of Directors consists of six NI representatives, four producer representatives (one African, one Asian, one Latin American-coffee and one Latin American-non-coffee), one ATO representative and one commercial trader representative (representing more mainstream business). Each group elects its representatives at its membership meetings and via e-mail nominations and voting. The board meets quarterly to review financial statements and decide on major policy initiatives and strategic directions for Fair Trade labelling worldwide. Three committees report to the board: Standards and Policy, Certification, and Appeals (which handles certification

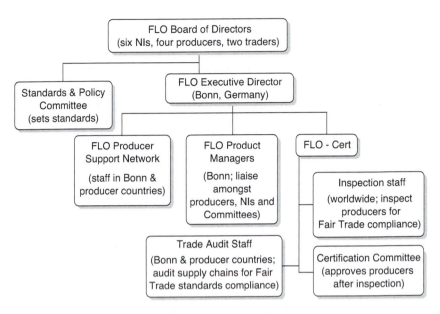

Figure 6.1   *FLO governance structure*

appeals). Finally, the board nominates a director who hires staff to carry out FLO's day-to-day activities. These fall into three categories:

- Inspecting producers' compliance with Fair Trade standards and auditing Fair Trade transactions, carried out by FLO-Cert.
- Organizing business facilitation by co-ordinating producers and traders to match supply and demand, carried out by FLO's product managers.
- Supporting FLO producers by providing market information and connections to NGOs that help with producer quality improvements and organizational capacity building, carried out by the FLO Producer Support Network.

Figure 6.1 depicts the main bodies in FLO and how they interact with each other. Each actor and their main duties will now be discussed in turn.

Fair Trade Standard-setting

FLO carries out its mission to provide market access to the world's poorest producers by developing Fair Trade standards for producer groups and terms of trade and then enforcing these standards by inspecting producers and conducting audits of Fair Trade supply chains. The standards for coffee producers were inherited from NIs when FLO was formed and have been the basis for creating standards for dozens of other products that are now certified by FLO.

FLO's Standards and Policy Committee is responsible for setting producer and trade standards for Fair Trade products. The Committee meets five to six times a year and consists of two FLO staff as well as representatives from three NIs, one commercial trader, one

ATO, one producer group and one independent body (historically, an NGO or alternative financer involved with producer issues).

Fair Trade standards can be divided into three parts:

- *Producer organizational requirements.* There are two sets of generic product group standards, one for co-operatives of small-scale family farmers and one for plantations. Family farmers not structurally dependent on hired labour must be organized into democratically run co-operatives with transparent accounting for the dispersal and use of Fair Trade income. Plantations wishing to be certified must have a democratically elected worker body that can distribute the Fair Trade premium in an equitable and transparent manner.

- *Sustainable production requirements.* These consist mostly of environmental standards regarding sustainable production and vary by product. In general, producer groups are not allowed to use certain pesticides classified as dangerous by the UN and the Pesticide Action Network and drinking water sources and endangered resources must be protected.

- *Trade standards.* These regulations govern relations amongst Fair Trade producers, exporters and importers. They include the Fair Trade minimum price but also the requirement for credit-provision and long-term relationships between producers and importers. Some Fair Trade products, namely bananas, have very strict standards regarding payment terms, quality requirements and dispute resolutions.

The Standards and Policy Committee must approve producer and trade standards for new products as well as changes to existing standards. The Committee thus receives proposals for the following: draft Fair Trade standards for new products (including Fair Trade price floor calculations); changes to price floors for existing products; changes to elements of current Fair Trade standards, including environmental and trade standards. If the Committee decides that a particular decision might have implications for the strategic direction of FLO, requests for clarification can be made to FLO's board of directors.

Producer Inspection and Certification

Once the Standards and Policy Committee has approved Fair Trade standards for a particular product, producers must be inspected for compliance. Producer groups sign up for an inspection visit by a FLO-trained inspector, who spends one to two weeks on site, depending on the size of the applicant group. Producers already in the system are re-inspected on an annual basis and any certified group may also receive surprise visits by FLO inspectors at any time. FLO inspection processes are described below.

After visiting the producers, the FLO inspector writes a report assessing the group's compliance with FLO standards for that product. The report is given to the FLO Certification Committee which judges whether the group complies with the Fair Trade standards for that particular product. Like the Standards and Policy Committee, the Certification Committee meets five to six times per year and is made up of FLO staff as well as representatives from three NIs, one commercial trader, one ATO, one producer and one independent body (historically, an NGO or alternative financer involved with producer issues). FLO-certified producer groups who do not pass re-inspection have a chance to appeal the decision of the Certification Committee with the Appeals Committee (made up of FLO Board members and specially appointed experts, depending on the case), whose decisions regarding producer compliance are final.

Fair Trade Inspections

A FLO inspection of, for example, a 9,000-member coffee co-operative would involve an inspector spending a few days with the co-operative management checking the books and accounting systems and then random inspections of members' farms to ensure compliance with FLO's environmental standards. The inspector would also conduct random interviews with farmer members to determine whether or not the voting structure and frequency of voting match the co-operatives' bylaws and that the co-operative's financial statements also match up with what was actually dispersed to farmers.

At the opposite end of the scale and in the case of smaller suppliers a FLO inspector would generally spend one week on, say, a small banana plantation. The inspector would examine the bank records of the Worker Association (Joint Body) and check this financial information using interviews with farm workers. Wage information and freedom of association checks would also be done by interview. The inspector would also visit neighbouring farms to determine regional average wages and check that farm workers on the applicant farm receive at least that amount. Because FLO banana standards have strict limits on aerial spraying of pesticides on banana farms, FLO inspectors also look at the records of aerial spraying companies to check that these are consistent with those on the farm.

Trade Audits

Once standards have been set, producers have been inspected for their compliance with these and the inspection reports approved by the Certification Committee, exporters, importers and manufacturers of those products (called, collectively, 'traders') can apply to participate in the Fair Trade system. These traders agree to be transparent about their Fair Trade transactions by reporting purchases and sales of Fair Trade ingredients to FLO and/or NIs right up until the Fair Trade label is placed on the final consumer package. This audit provides the guarantee that whenever the Fair Trade label appears, the Fair Trade minimum prices were paid and FLO's trading standards were followed.

With the exception of the USA, the main FLO office carries out all of the trade audit functions amongst producers, exporters and importers, with oversight by the Certification and Appeals Committees.[1] Once an importer has purchased the product, the audit trail is then tracked by the particular NIs involved in the supply chain, as outlined below. The companies who buy Fair Trade certified inputs from FLO authorized traders must be licenced by the NI of the consumer market in which they wish to sell Fair Trade products. These companies are called 'licensees' and include such companies as Aroma, licenced by Max Havelaar Switzerland to sell roasted Fair Trade coffee to McDonald's, and Starbucks, a licensee of TransFair USA.

In 2004, FLO's audit and certification functions, including co-ordination of producer inspections and training of inspectors, were officially split off into a subsidiary of FLO called FLO-Cert. FLO-Cert is seeking to obtain ISO-65 status as an independent certification organization (much like an organic certification agency). For the first time, FLO-Cert charged producers and traders for inspections and trade audits with the goal of eventually covering all of its inspection and audit costs.

As illustrated by the example below, the FLO method of Fair Trade product certification is retrospective (see Figure 6.2). Mistakes are often caught many months after they have occurred. The degree of reporting and bureaucracy must be kept in balance: the label is a guarantee of fair prices paid, but too much paperwork discourages potential business and can lead to late or infrequent reporting, which weakens the guarantee. FLO and its members constantly review the trade audit process with their stakeholders to ensure that the need for auditing all transactions is balanced with the need for business efficiency.

A FLO Trade Audit Illustration: Cocoa

Once a cocoa co-operative has been inspected by FLO-Cert and the inspection report approved by the Certification Committee for compliance with Fair Trade producer standards, FLO-licenced traders may start to purchase from them under Fair Trade terms and market the cocoa beans as Fair Trade.

- A cocoa bean importer in Switzerland, registered with FLO for Fair Trade reporting, submits a purchase order for Fair Trade cocoa beans to a FLO-certified co-operative in the Dominican Republic.
- The co-operative contracts for Fair Trade cocoa beans to be transported to the dock on a specific date. The price quoted must be at least the Fair Trade minimum price. If the co-operative asks for pre-financing from the importer, the latter must pay up to 60 per cent of the purchase price at the time the contact is fixed. (Pre-finance provision is one of the particular cocoa trade standards, and is also required for other seasonal crops like coffee. For year-round crops, credit requirements are different – fruit importers, for instance, are not required to provide advanced credit, but must pay producers within 48 hours of receipt of goods.)
- The co-operative reports to FLO the name of the importer, ship date, container number and price paid for the shipment. This is generally done semi-annually.
- The importer sends FLO the shipment date, container number and proof of price paid. Most importers aggregate shipment information and submit quarterly reports to FLO.
- The importer can now process the cocoa beans and market the resulting chocolate mass as Fair Trade Certified. The importer sells the Fair Trade chocolate to a candy bar manufacturer in England, who is licenced by the

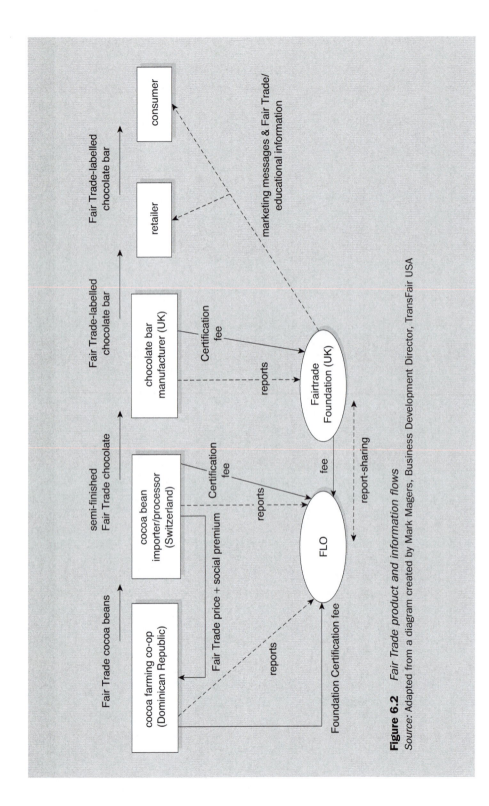

Figure 6.2 *Fair Trade product and information flows*

Source: Adapted from a diagram created by Mark Magers, Business Development Director, TransFair USA

Fairtrade Foundation (FTF), FLO's member in the UK, for Fair Trade reporting and label usage.

- The importer sends FLO a report of the sale of the chocolate to the English manufacturer, including the name of the cocoa co-operative from which the cocoa beans were purchased, as well as the container number.
- The English manufacturer reports the purchase of chocolate from the Swiss company to the FTF, and pays them a per-pound licence fee for the use of the Fair Trade logo. (These trades are generally aggregated into quarterly reports.)
- The manufacturer packages the chocolate bars with a wrapper featuring the FLO logo and claiming that the product is Fair Trade. The product is sold to thousands of retailers.
- FLO sends the FTF copies of the Swiss manufacturer's reports, showing details of sales of Fair Trade chocolate to FTF's members in the UK. The FTF checks that the quantities of purchases and sales match up with what the manufacturer reported as Fair Trade purchases.
- FLO checks the quarterly purchase reports of the Swiss cocoa bean importer against the semi-annual reports of Fair Trade sales sent by the cocoa bean co-operative in the Dominican Republic.
- If the product which carries the Fair Trade logo does not trace back to at least the Fair Trade price paid to the co-operative, it is up to FLO or the FTF to decide whether the party at fault loses its Fair Trade licence and is no longer able to trade under Fair Trade conditions, or if the situation can be remedied by either an immediate wire transfer to the co-operative or a product recall.
- The Fair Trade premium earned by each co-operative (in the case of cocoa, the $150/MT (£84) received above the world market or Fair Trade floor price) is totalled for the year. In the following year's FLO producer co-operative inspection, this amount must be accounted for and shown to have been used on social development programs undertaken by the co-operative.

FINANCING THE FAIR TRADE CERTIFICATION SYSTEM

Until 2003, the Fair Trade system was funded almost entirely by companies in consuming countries and by external grants and loans from charitable foundations. National Fair Trade labelling initiatives collected certification fees from their licensees (companies licenced by FLO or a NI to use the Fair Trade certification mark on prod-ucts), on either a per-pound basis or as a percentage of the selling price. From these fees and any fundraising efforts, they covered their own operating expenses and paid dues to FLO based on the pounds of Fair Trade product sold in their particular markets. FLO received this money from its National Initiative members and supplemented its budget through its own fundraising.

In 2004, FLO introduced an inspection fee for producers who wished to remain in or enter the Fair Trade system. Co-operatives and farms are required to pay FLO an initial inspection fee (or renewal fee, for currently certified producers) and once approved for entry into the Fair Trade system, must pay FLO an annual inspection renewal fee plus a variable fee based on pounds sold under Fair Trade conditions. The Fair Trade producer members of FLO's board voted unanimously to introduce inspection fees, after seeing that FLO's financial constraints prevent it from expanding the producer base or reacting to consumer demand for new Fair Trade products (Rice, 2004). At the multi-stakeholder Fairtrade Forum in London in September 2003, Fair Trade producer representatives expressed support for the introduction of inspection fees, stating that Fair Trade was the only certification system which directly translated into higher income for farmers and that paying to be part of the Fair Trade system would strengthen farmer involvement and encourage them to invest in making Fair Trade a success.

In 2004, FLO also started to charge other actors in the system, including exporters, importers and processors, an annual registration fee and per-pound fee. (Those companies already registered with National Initiative members of FLO are, in general, already charged fees by the National Initiatives and are therefore not double-charged.) All fees are intended to deter non-serious producers and businesses from entering the system and to capitalize a Fair Trade certification system that was unable to grow at the speed of the market. Whilst there are as yet no publicly available projections of the income FLO will gain from charging producers and companies for inspection and membership, at a minimum fee of €500 (£345; $615) with 315 producers and 249 traders (FLO, 2002), FLO could expect to receive an extra €282,000 (£195,000; $347,000) at the very least, even with no new actors entering the system. This would amount to 16 per cent of FLO's overall 2002 expenditures – a meaningful contribution to the capitalization of the FLO system.

Business Income vs. Donations

FLO and its member NIs are excellent examples of the new breed of hybrid not-for-profit organizations, falling under the broad heading of social enterprises, that derive a significant proportion of income from charging for business services, rather than donations from individuals, foundations and/or corporations. FLO and its members charge licenced companies a combination of annual and volume-based certification fees. As outlined in Table 6.1, this business income contributes to the overall budget of the organizations, allowing them to both audit the supply chain and certify Fair Trade products carrying the label, as well as market the concept of Fair Trade to consumers, press and businesses.

The contribution of business income varies widely, from 93 per cent of Max Havelaar Switzerland's latest budget, to only 27 per cent of Max Havelaar France's budget, and 34 per cent of that of TransFair USA. Some NIs are supported by their governments' development agencies – Max Havelaar France, for instance, received more than 40 per cent of its 2002 budget from the French Ministries of Foreign and Social Affairs as well as the European Union, down from more than 60 per cent in 2001. TransFair USA receives no government support, but achieves substantial capitalization from loans and grants, including a program-related investment from the Ford Foundation and a grant from the Rockefeller Foundation. This funding is essential in the present climate with little real venture capital available to fund social entrepreneurship.

The first three sections of this chapter have focussed on the FLO model of Fair Trade product certification. Whilst the FLO system is the largest social certification system in the world, not all companies choose to use it for consumer-facing claims of social responsibility.

Table 6.1 *National labelling initiatives' business income, 1999–2003*

Agency	Total annual expenditures	Proportion funded by fee for service				
		2003	2002	2001	2000	1999
FLO (2002)	€1,700,000; US$2,091,000; £1,173,000		61%	69%		
FLO members						
Fairtrade 35% Foundation UK (2002)[1]	£884,327; US$1,582,954		60%	45%	39%	35%
Max Havelaar France (2002)	€1,076,808; US$1,324,473; £742,997		27%	19%		
Max 92% Havelaar Switzerland (2003)[2]	CHF3,964,342; US$3,132,067; £1,744,310	93%	95%	89%	83%	92%
TransFair Canada (2003)	CA$342,201; US$270,338; £150,568	63%	64%			
TransFair Germany (2002)[3]	€1,094,704; US$1,346,486; £755,346		57%	60%	57%	
TransFair USA (2002)	US$1,600,000; £896,000		34%	53%		

[1] Funded by certification fees and sale of promotional items. Fiscal year was March–March until March 2002; then they switched to yearend, therefore 2002 figures are from March–December 2002 only; 2003 figures are for January–December 2003.

[2] Using 2003 SwFr–$–£ exchange rate. Other exchange rates listed on page viii.

[3] The available figure for 2000 did not separate Rugmark (a non-profit run by TransFair Germany) expenditures from Transfair fair Trade labelling activities. The same ratio of Rugmark expenditures as was spent in 2001 (17 per cent of total) was removed from the 2000 expenditures figure to estimate the Fair Trade budget for that year.

Sources: Fairtrade Foundation (2003a); Fairtrade Labelling Organisations (2002); Max Havelaar France (2002); Max Havelaar Switzerland (2000, 2001, 2003); TransFair Canada (2003); TransFair Germany (2001, 2002); TransFair USA (2001, 2002b)

The next section will discuss other paths that companies take, including promoting their own company programs, adopting other third-party certification or registration systems and implementing industry codes of conduct. As these can all be considered competitive threats to the Fair Trade labelling system, they will be analysed further in the final chapter which discusses the future of Fair Trade certification.

OTHER MODELS

The FLO model of product certification is expensive for companies to adopt because of both minimum price requirements and certification fees. The FLO system is also limited in that it certifies products rather than company trading practices. Because this system cannot satisfy all actors, some companies have adopted other methods of verifying or supporting their claims to social responsibility, including: promoting their own company programmes; adopting other third-party systems; implementing industry codes of conduct. This section will discuss each in turn.

Promoting Individual Company Programmes

In response to consumer concerns about extreme poverty and environmental degradation on the farms from which their foods are sourced, some companies have chosen to promote programs they have with individual producer groups and non-governmental organizations in source countries, rather than subscribe to international Fair Trade standards on all of their products (Rice and McLean, 1999). In the USA, Starbucks, the Organic Coffee Company and Allegro Coffee Roasters all produce consumer materials describing education, economic development and health projects that they support with profits from the sale of their coffees. Chiquita recently announced the establishment of a nature reserve in Costa Rica in co-operation with Monoprix, a leading Swiss supermarket chain (Chiquita, 2004).

At the other end of the spectrum are companies who think that the Fair Trade label does not go far enough to describe overall company business practices. FLO and its member National Initiatives certify products, not companies, but it is certainly possible that not all consumers understand this and associate the Fair Trade certification seal with the entire company's dealings, rather than just with those products that carry the seal. The halo effect that a certification seal can have on a brand is not uncontroversial. Some members of the Fair Trade community call it 'fairwashing', a play on the term 'greenwashing', defined by the Concise Oxford Dictionary as 'misinformation disseminated by a corporation so as to present an environmentally friendly public image'. As discussed in Chapter 4, some companies that carry only Fair Trade products can find themselves competing with companies that certify only a certain percentage of their lines as Fair Trade. These companies could, in theory, subsidize their Fair Trade lines with profits from non-Fair Trade sales and thus have more promotional dollars available to promote their Fair Trade lines, an unfair competitive situation vis-à-vis the 100 per cent Fair Trade companies.

In the USA, a small group of coffee roasters became so disillusioned with perceived 'fairwashing' by other companies involved in the Fair Trade certification system that they decided to drop third-party certification altogether. In April 2004, Dean's Beans Massachusetts, Larry's Beans in North Carolina, Just Coffee in Wisconsin and Café Campesino in Georgia all pulled out of the TransFair USA certification system (Rogers, 2004; Walker, 2004). As the Just Coffee website explains:

> When the mission-based Fair Trade companies ... started educating consumers about Fair Trade, the big commercial roasters scoffed. They saw Fair Trade as a small and passing fad. [Then] a funny thing happened. People got behind Fair Trade. Now a few years later the conventional roasters are lining up to access the Fair Trade label. The problem is that they want to do this without changing their business practices ... still buying the bulk of their coffee paying low market prices while they use the Fair Trade label on the miniscule amount of 'Fair Trade' coffee they purchase. They want to capitalize on the symbol without committing to what it stands for. (Just Coffee, 2004)

The roasters mentioned who have pulled out of the certification system have apparently not abandoned the Fair Trade concept; Just Coffee makes its purchase contracts with coffee co-operatives available on its website for customers to audit themselves, and the Dean's Beans website states that the company buys its coffee only from FLO-certified co-operatives at the international Fair Trade price, although this claim is of course not independently verified. It remains to be seen whether these companies can gain market share without third-party certification of Fair Trade practices. Whilst some consumers may bother to go to these companies' websites to do the independent verification of Fair Trade practices themselves, it is likely that as consumer awareness of third-party verification grows these companies will not be able to grow beyond a certain regional customer circle of trust. Nevertheless, according to Rogers, the rift 'demonstrates how some small companies feel cheated by larger corporations for infringing on their market niche, even when all parties involved insist they are working toward the same goal' (2004: 12).

Whilst for the moment these cases seem self-contained and do not appear to threaten consumer perception of Fair Trade labelling, they do highlight the growing tension between ATOs and mainstream companies that enter the Fair Trade market. It may be the case that FLO will be unable to keep all of these diverse actors under the same certification umbrella and more companies may break away and potentially launch their own certification label. Creating a second label that would indicate overall company practices, to sit alongside the product certification label, is one solution to this rift that will be addressed in the final chapter.

Some ATOs have decided not to get involved with third-party certification at all. The major example in this case is the Italian ATO, CTM Altro Mercato. This group represents ATOs and world shops in its home market and has built a strong own-label brand over several years. Having created considerable domestic brand loyalty, the company decided that it did not need FLO's label for its products that would qualify and would solely use its own label instead. To date this has had no significant effect on sales as the business has gone from strength to strength (see case study below).

CASE STUDY: ALTRO MERCATO

The CTM Altro Mercato consortium was founded in 1988 in Bolzano, Italy, with the goal of offering solutions to address the inequality between North and South. As of 2004, CTM Altro Mercato was the largest Fair Trade organization in Italy and the second largest worldwide. It comprises 130 organizations (associations and co-operative societies) that manage 260 world shops throughout Italy. These organizations act as alternative traders as well as informing and educating their local public about trade issues.

CTM Altro Mercato has the goal of becoming a key promoter of a solidarity economy that generates initiatives aimed at the self-development of marginalized producers at both the international and local levels. Specifically, the consortium offers a wide range of goods made by small producers in the South that are marketed by a network of not-for-profit organizations.

CTM Altro Mercato has developed over 200 food and 3,000 handicraft products directly imported from 150 producer partner organizations worldwide. The consortium also offers social audit research and training for key partners in the solidarity economy.

In 2002/3, the consortium generated €32.3m (£22.2m; $39.7m) in sales, a 49 per cent increase on 2001/2. Food accounted for more than 60 per cent of total sales, with handicrafts making up the balance.

The strength of the CTM Altro Mercato brand in Italy is such that the consortium has made a strategic decision not to carry the Fairtrade Labelling Organizations International (FLO) label on any of its products, even those for which it is eligible. However, CTM Altro Mercato is a member of the International Federation for Alternative Trade (IFAT) and through IFAT became a registered Fair Trade Organization (FTO) in 2004.

Source: Altro Mercato promotional literature, 2003

Other ATOs use FLO's labelling where standards exist, but rely on the strength of their own brands to send an ethical message to consumers when no independent certification is available. Carmenère wine co-branded by the Co-op retail chain and Traidcraft in the UK is a good example of this. In 2001 the Co-op wanted to source an own-label Fair Trade wine, but no independent FLO standards existed at the time. The group therefore developed a partnership with Traidcraft, a trusted ATO in the UK, to source and brand the product, thereby using Traidcraft's reputation to support the product's Fair Trade credentials in place of the FLO mark (Nicholls, 2004). FLO has since developed wine standards and Traidcraft has adopted that certification for its wines, but continues to rely on the strength of its brand for crafts and other products that FLO does not yet certify.

Individualized company programs are attractive in that the company controls the amount of money used and the nature of the project, rather than having to implement third-party-determined standards. But educating consumers about company-specific programs reduces the amount of money and opportunities for supplying consumers with other features of a particular brand. The Fair Trade logo can encapsulate a socially responsible message for the brand, leaving space to send other messages to consumers. Furthermore, weak systems can leave a company-specific label open to scandal, but the alternative of rigorous inspection and audit systems and standards is expensive to create. It is probably more cost-efficient for an individual company to rely on the FLO system, with its network of inspectors in over 40 countries in the developing world, to inspect producer groups for labour conditions, democratic organization and environmental impact of production. Judging by the number of new companies, including mainstream brands like Dole and Millstone coffee (owned by Procter & Gamble), signing up with FLO and its member NIs, the trend to let the Fair Trade label carry the primary social sourcing message seems to be stronger than that of promoting company-specific programs.

Adopting Other Certification Systems

Fair Trade actors are worried, however, about the growth of other social certification systems and labels. Whilst some, such as the Social Accountability International and International Standards Organizations are business-facing rather than consumer-facing, a few consumer-facing labels are emerging, the most important of which are Utz Kapeh and the Rainforest Alliance. In Europe, the Ahold supermarket chain founded the Utz Kapeh label in 1997 to signify 'certified responsible' coffee sourcing for its own-label coffee products. The label grew out of the recognition that direct-sourcing in coffee created to comply with Eurep-Gap food safety requirements could also serve to address consumer concerns about isolation of coffee farmers. Today, Utz Kapeh-certified farms must meet minimum wage and working condition requirements, as well as environmental standards (Utz Kapeh, 2004). The system has no minimum price requirement, so it is relatively cheap for companies to adopt and several European coffee roasters have implemented the code.

In the USA, the environmental not-for-profit Rainforest Alliance has had recent success in working with large multinationals like Kraft and Chiquita to certify producers and branded products. Whilst the Rainforest Alliance standards for farms focus primarily on environmental stewardship and management, they do include wage and working conditions standards similar to Utz Kapeh (Rainforest Alliance, 2004; Rice and McLean, 1999). Like Utz Kapeh, there is no minimum price requirement for products to be certified by the Rainforest Alliance, thus it is once again a less expensive way for companies to answer consumers' concerns about sustainability than to achieve Fair Trade certification.

Both Utz Kapeh and the Rainforest Alliance have begun limited forays into other markets, with Utz Kapeh working with Ahold-owned supermarkets in the USA and Rainforest Alliance certifying a Kraft-brand coffee, as well as some bananas, in Europe. Both marks have less consumer recognition than Fair Trade labels, yet their close alliance with multinational corporations may supplement their consumer marketing efforts. The Rainforest Alliance certifies coffee, bananas, citrus, cocoa, ferns, cut flowers and tropical woods, which positions them to compete with FLO in offering a 'lifestyle' option. Utz Kapeh works only with coffee producers and roasters. Neither label guarantees the extra income to farmers and farm workers that the FLO model ensures, nor is producer empowerment a stated goal of either certification model.

Finally, the registration model promoted by IFAT, a trade association of Fair Trade producers and importers, mostly of handicrafts, represents yet another option for companies to work with an independent third party to support claims of social responsibility. IFAT has created a 'Fair Trade Organization' (FTO) mark, positioned to be a company, rather than a product, label. The mark is verified by self-reporting, assessment of practices by other IFAT members and IFAT monitoring of a percentage of its members each year (IFAT, 2004c). Whilst the FTO mark was not necessarily designed to compete with the FLO product mark and rather aims to identify companies that are mission-driven and follow Fair Trade practices in all their dealings (IFAT, 2004d), companies could choose to replace the FLO product mark with the broader IFAT organization mark. FLO and IFAT are currently investigating the integration of their various standards and codes of conduct to avoid a split in labelling which would confuse consumers.

Adopting Industry-wide Codes of Conduct

Throughout the history of the modern corporation, consumer scandals have pushed market leaders to join with their competitors in the adoption of industry-wide codes of conduct (sometimes with the involvement of national governments in consuming countries, as was the case with the dolphin-safe tuna label in the USA). As discussed in Chapter 4, the recent decision by four leading coffee companies, representing some 80 per cent of the international coffee market, to implement a 'Common Code for the Coffee Community', which requires coffee farm workers to receive fair wages and working conditions as well as protecting their right to join unions, most likely came about because of consumer awareness of the plight of the world's coffee farmers, thanks in part to consumer education undertaken by Fair Trade organizations (Williamson, 2004).

According to Tallontire (2002), one of Fair Trade's most important contributions has been to influence the behaviour of mainstream companies when sourcing their products. An endgame in which the coffee industry adopts a minimum standard that improves the lives of the world's coffee farmers is no mean feat and should be seen as a measure of the success of Fair Trade. But most industry codes of conduct (and, indeed, the Common Code for the Coffee Community) focus on the performance of the supplier, not the trading relationship between supplier and buyer (Tallontire, 2002). Codes of conduct generally do raise the bar for business, but rarely do they represent the most progressive of practices, rather they can be seen as a compromise between a low-bar and high-bar approach to business ethics.

Because codes of conduct are generally not promoted to consumers directly, it is unlikely that these can be seen as a threat to the growth of the Fair Trade model. If the code of conduct is so successful that Fair Trade is no longer needed in producer communities, one would argue that Fair Trade actors would be satisfied to declare their objectives accomplished and not view that (unlikely) outcome as a competitive situation. The issue of codes of conduct has also been addressed in Chapter 3 in the context of ethical trading more generally.

Other Models – Threats to FLO Certification?

As Tallontire explains, the profusion of ethical claims and labels may erode the progress Fair Trade certification has made in positioning itself as the best option for ethical consumption:

> The increasing trend for conventional companies to espouse ethical principles – from ethical sourcing of supermarkets to cause-related marketing whereby companies donate a percentage of the consumer price to a charity or environmental group – has also created increased competition for fair trade products. The increasing number of ethical claims in the market place may cloud the fair trade message to consumers. (Tallontire, 2002: 18)

Yet despite some dissenters and groups that choose not to engage with the system, international Fair Trade certification is growing exponentially, both in volume and in number of products certified. Since 1997, FLO's members have approved price and trading standards for 14 mostly agricultural products, including coffee, tea, cocoa, sugar, honey, fresh fruit, dried fruit, rice, fruit juices, wine, cut flowers, nuts, spices and sports balls. Meanwhile, imports of other fairly traded products have continued to grow without the potential benefit of an independent monitoring and auditing system. Fair Trade labelling has moved from being a radical solidarity movement to a mainstream trend in retail.

Table 6.2 and Figure 6.3 show the growth of Fair Trade-labelled products in consuming countries. The growth rate of Fair Trade-labelled products rose from 11 per cent in 1998 to 22 per cent in 2001 and 42 per cent in 2003. TransFair USA, operating in the Fair Trade market with the largest potential volume, grew steadily at around 40 per cent from 1998 to 2002, and by a whopping 85 per cent in 2003 (Rice, 2004). FLO and the European Fair Trade Association estimate retail turnover to have grown 24 per cent from 2001 to

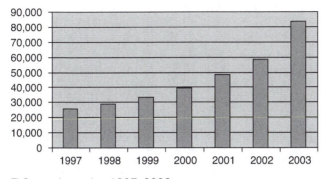

Figure 6.3 *FLO member sales 1997–2003*
Source: Fairtrade Labelling Organizations (www.fairtrade.net)

Table 6.2 *Average growth rates in Fair
Trade-labelled products*

Product (MT)	Growth rate (%)	Years
Total FLO labelled	18	1997–2002
Cocoa	18	1997–2002
Sugar	19	1997–2002
Honey	8	1997–2002
Coffee (roasted)	8	1998–2002
Orange juice	39	1999–2002
Tea	17	2001, 2002

Source: Fairtrade Labelling Organizations International. Available at:
http://www.fairtrade.net/sites/products/products_02.html.

2002, totalling an estimated €260 million (£179m; $319m) in 2002 (EFTA, 2001;
Ghillani, 2002).

Exponential growth rates in Fair Trade-labelled products can be attributed to several
factors, including new product launches, large untapped markets in speciality grocery and
competition amongst manufacturers and retailers regarding Fair Trade offerings. The
growth of current Fair Trade products, as mainstream brands and retailers adopt them,
will be discussed in Chapters 7 and 8. The development of new Fair Trade products
described in the following section offers an interesting insight into Fair Trade governance
and highlights the tensions first discussed in Chapter 4 between traditional Fair Trade
companies and mainstream companies entering the Fair Trade certification system.

FAIR TRADE CERTIFICATION: NEW PRODUCT DEVELOPMENT

Several forces drive new product development within the Fair Trade system. Retailers in
Northern countries might demand new products to broaden the Fair Trade category.
Consumer activist groups might ask for Fair Trade certification in response to negative

media attention around working conditions or pricing in particular industries. ATOs and NGOs who have been working with particular producers might ask that their products get certified. Broadly, research and development into Fair Trade standards is shaped both by consumer/activist groups (an advocacy-driven approach to growth) and by industry and retailers (a market-driven approach). Keeping these demands in balance is a central concern of Fair Trade stakeholders and the benefits and limitations of each approach are discussed below.

Advocacy-driven Growth in Fair Trade Certification

Northern imports of non-labelled fairly-traded products have long encompassed more than just 'solidarity' coffee. Starting in the 1980s, as NGOs became more interested in market-driven development projects, several fairly-traded products began to appear in Northern markets. Exportable products were sometimes the outcome of development projects that invested in quality improvements, new technologies or market access for crafts and commodities producers. The NGOs or ethically-minded businesses that had invested in such projects also tasked themselves with finding markets for these products. Often the sales outlet was through world shops and catalogues such as SERRV and Ten Thousand Villages in the USA, Gepa in Germany and Oxfam Fair Trade and Traidcraft in the UK. The trading practices behind these products were not third-party monitored but the products were nevertheless considered Fair Trade by consumers familiar with the retailers and brands.

Amongst food products, one example is Fruits of the Nile, a Ugandan-based NGO supported by Tropical Wholefoods Limited, a private for-profit UK company. Fruits of the Nile provides subsidized solar driers to Ugandan villagers, who dry excess fruits and vegetables during harvest season, when not all fruit can be consumed locally or exported. Tropical Wholefoods was created as an importer for dried Ugandan fruits and buys much of the product exported by Fruits of the Nile (it now also imports dried fruits and nuts from Burkina Faso, Pakistan and other developing countries). Tropical Wholefoods was able to penetrate the UK natural foods market and source own-label product for Oxfam, Traidcraft and others, creating a market for a value-added product manufactured by Ugandan village co-operatives. Villagers now earn a higher income through the fair prices paid by Tropical Wholefoods. According to Jane Nawuliro of the Tukolelere Wamuy Women's Association in Uganda:

> Originally I was earning my living by running a sewing machine. I was living in a rented room with my family. When I started solar drying I realized it was paying more than the sewing business. I sold my only sewing machine and put the money into fruit drying. Now I do not regret anything. I managed to buy a piece of land, constructed a semi-permanent house with bricks, and now me and my family are happier. My house has solar electricity which runs some of the driers during the day; and during the night it provides light, operates a television and a radio. I have provided employment to a number of women in my neighbourhood. (Tropical Wholefoods, 2003)

Another example of a producer group with strong Fair Trade ties is the Eswatini Kitchen, a jam and jelly factory in Swaziland in Southern Africa. A British volunteer set up this project to help women and marginalized community members (such as the handicapped) gain employment. The ingredients are grown by Swazi farmers and processed by a women-owned co-operative. The Eswatini Kitchen also sells baskets woven by rural women and wooden spoons carved by handicapped villagers who are often ostracized by their communities and can rarely earn cash income. Profits from the sale of all of these products support youth centres for AIDS orphans and street children (AlterEco, 2003; SERRV International, 2003). Eswatini Kitchen's products are sold in the North by such ATOs as AlterEco and SERRV International.

In order to reward NGOs and ethically-minded importers for investing in marginalized producer groups, Fair Trade stakeholders who buy from these groups often pressure FLO to prioritize products produced by groups like the Eswatini Kitchen and Fruits of the Nile for standard-setting. The FLO Fair Trade certification mark lends legitimacy to trusted brands like Traidcraft and Tropical Wholefoods, which source from these projects, and allows producer groups to expand their buying circle by accessing other importers interested in Fair Trade-labelled products. Because the primary motivator for standard-setting and certification in this case is lending legitimacy to successful Fair Trade partnerships, growth of this type can be considered supplier-driven in the introduction of new products. Whilst market considerations are taken into account (these producer groups already have willing buyers in the North), potential market demand and growth are not the primary motivators.

Problems with Advocate/Supplier-driven Growth

> The model [Fair Trade] is predicated on 'let's find the poorest guy in the world that makes widgets; now let's go to the West and find a market for those widgets'. (Interview with Hamish Renton, 2003)

Supplier-driven growth in Fair Trade certification lies at the heart of the Fair Trade activist movement. Its earliest participants originally intended Fair Trade to help the world's most marginalized producers access export markets. ATOs have participated in the Fair Trade movement since its inception and are asking FLO to be rewarded for their ethical practices by having their preferred suppliers prioritized for inspection. Relying solely on a supplier-driven strategy, however, threatens to marginalize Fair Trade as a movement by not allowing it to grow at the same pace as demand is growing.

One could argue that any supplier development project that is truly compliant with the spirit of Fair Trade can expand only very slowly unless key structures are already in place, including democratic producer organizations, quality controls and a capacity for technology dissemination. Otherwise, in order to increase supply new producers must be educated in terms of export quality requirements, co-operative decision making and business capacity building. By focusing only on producers who have been isolated from world markets and marginalized in the world trading system, Fair Trade organizations are limited to sourcing from producer groups that require long-term investment in business capacity-building.

Furthermore, the highly intensive technology investments and direct trade relationships that characterize the types of projects discussed above result in significant benefits, but for limited numbers of participants. Five hundred farmers benefit from the solar driers at Tropical Wholefoods' Fruits of the Nile Project in Uganda. Two hundred women and 20 handicapped villagers are employed by the Eswatini Swazi Kitchen and 200 street children and orphans benefit from the profits generated by the business. These and similarly intensive projects do not lend themselves to large-scale rapid growth in response to increases in demand from Fair Trade consumers in the North. Emphasizing small niche producers and markets does not take full advantage of the opportunities available through mainstream retail.

Finally, producers who have enjoyed a successful export relationship with ATOs may be more used to importer relationships that are flexible regarding language, quality requirements and failure to meet contract specifications. Mainstream traders are most likely less willing to work with producers as they improve their business knowledge and product.

Those who argue against advocacy-driven growth claim that limiting the expansion of Fair Trade threatens to deter businesses that see Fair Trade as a high-growth strategy and leaves them as a marginalized 'alternative' movement. By focusing on what Northern consumers want and then certifying producers based on market demands, FLO could ensure that its scarce product development resources are being spent on areas which will impact the highest number of producers. These market-oriented Fair Trade stakeholders are calling for market-driven growth in Fair Trade certification.

Market-driven Growth in Fair Trade Certification

As the Fair Trade market in the North has grown, demand for a wider variety of Fair Trade products, origin countries and producer groups has also grown. Recent trends show retailers to be some of the strongest forces pushing for more Fair Trade certification and new product development, as evidenced by the following data points:

- Swiss retailers, including Migros and the Co-op, asked Max Havelaar (the national Fair Trade labelling initiative/FLO member in Switzerland) to develop Fair Trade standards for cut flowers, introduced to the Swiss market in 2001.
- Tesco, currently the UK's largest supermarket retailer with a 29 per cent market share, announced in 2003 that it intended to double the volumes of Fair Trade products sold in Tesco stores. Tesco was the first to launch Fair Trade roses and several fruits and vegetables in the UK market.
- After launching a Fair Trade own-label coffee in 2002, Wild Oats Markets, a chain of 100 natural food supermarkets in the USA, saw bulk-bin coffee and packaged own-label coffees increase 20 per cent, despite a rise of approximately 10 per cent in the average retail price. The success of their Fair Trade coffee program led Wild Oats to source Fair Trade tea, fruit and chocolate products (Odak, 2003).

As will be discussed in Chapter 8, launching new Fair Trade products can rejuvenate retail brands by attracting press and consumer attention, and having a wider product range gives retailers more interest in educating their staff and customers about Fair Trade. Retailers also view the offering of Fair Trade products as a way of protecting their margins on competitive products, as consumers are willing to pay more for Fair Trade products. The success of Fair Trade in mainstream retail in Europe has resulted in a strong pull from retailers who want a wider variety of Fair Trade products, resulting in demand-driven growth in Fair Trade certification.

Because the demand is driven by a perceived market opportunity, the sales and growth potential for demand-driven Fair Trade supply is very promising. When demand is retail-driven especially, the likelihood of project success is high. As the supplier positioned closest to the end consumer, retailers are most likely to know consumers the best: a retailer who spots a Fair Trade market opportunity is probably correct. A retailer-initiated project is also more likely to succeed because the retailer is generally committed to project success and will help sell and market Fair Trade products to their consumers through promotions and point-of-purchase marketing materials.

Interestingly, 'traditional' retailers and manufacturers entering the Fair Trade market are also concerned with getting their preferred suppliers inspected and certified by FLO. Rather than switch suppliers to producer groups already on the FLO register, these buyers sometimes prefer that their existing supply chains become compliant with FLO standards and become certified. Because this type of supplier-driven growth does not focus on helping marginalized producers gain a more equitable footing in the world trading market, but rather seeks to legitimize pre-existing trade relationships, it can be differentiated from ATO-related advocacy-driven growth. This tension between working with marginalized groups (which may be more difficult for mainstream companies and retailers to cope with) and inspecting groups that already have market access is discussed further below.

Problems with Demand-driven Growth

Critics of a Fair Trade growth model that relies too much on market information and high-growth partners worry that short-term market growth strategies are sacrificing the long-term viability of the Fair Trade system. First, growing suppliers and traders faster than the certification system can realistically audit producers and supply chains exposes the certification system and its independent guarantee to failure and possible scandal, damaging the integrity of the Fair Trade mark and weakening the entire system. Similarly, rushing through standards development for new Fair Trade products risks having price floors or trading standards which are not fully researched and thus do not truly ensure the sustainable development and fair prices that consumers associate with the Fair Trade label.

Second, a product development strategy which focusses on high-growth companies who see Fair Trade as a potentially lucrative market risks tying the Fair Trade system too closely to those which are not necessarily interested in Fair Trade practices for the long term. If Tesco, a publicly-traded UK supermarket chain, perceived a drop in consumer demand for Fair Trade products, would Tesco spend money to convince consumers to continue to buy these products? As Fair Trade is not a core part of Tesco's mission, this may be unlikely. A true ATO, however, can be counted on to support Fair Trade through lean times. ATOs also work generally with producers to develop the quality of their product and improve their business skills, whereas conventional companies are content to engage with producers who have already passed the FLO certification system and thus do not need further investment (Tallontire, 2002). As discussed in Chapter 4, many Fair Trade stakeholders distrust the motivations of large publicly-traded companies for investing in Fair Trade and worry that supporting high-growth companies at the expense of smaller ATOs compromises the long-term viability of the Fair Trade movement.

Tensions Between Supply and Demand-driven Growth

Table 6.3 summarizes the key differences between advocacy or supply-driven growth in Fair Trade product development and demand-driven growth.

Table 6.3 *Characteristics of supply vs demand driven growth*

Supply- or advocacy-driven growth	Demand-driven growth
Sourcing from projects in which key Fair Trade stakeholders have invested; Fair Trade standards development and inspection are a 'reward' for ethical dealings in the past.	Sellers would like to see their current preferred suppliers become Fair Trade certified, rather than buy from different sources which may already be on the Fair Trade register.
Focusing on products whose production processes are characterized by high levels of exploitation (for example, diamonds).	As long as FLO's rules are followed and the product can be labelled, mainstream sellers are not particularly concerned with the types of producer projects supported.
Products must have proven market success, usually evidenced by the product selling already into Northern markets.	High growth potential as perceived by Northern retailers and manufacturers.
Rigorous standards and certification criteria must be developed to ensure integrity of the Fair Trade mark.	A limited understanding on the part of sellers of the Fair Trade requirements of producer groups and price floor calculations.
	Speed of supply growth is extremely important.

One can see fundamental tensions between these two approaches to new product development and supply growth within the Fair Trade system. First, although suppliers to ATOs must demonstrate proven market success to be eligible for Fair Trade certification, their markets are not chosen based on future potential expansion and the producers are not, as discussed above, necessarily able to grow quickly, even if there is a potential for growth in demand.

Second, mainstream end-stage suppliers can have little patience for the methodological approach to Fair Trade taken by its key stakeholders, such as the requirement for a robust calculation of the price floor, for instance. Retailers are accustomed to a three- to six-month product development cycle. As their expertise does not lie in Third World development, they can be unsympathetic to those Fair Trade requirements that slow down the product development process, such as the principle of helping the poorest, most marginalized producers who might not be ready to export and the need to calculate a price floor based on detailed cost of production data. Moving slowly enough to address all of these principles perfectly can mean lost opportunities. Developing new Fair Trade products is risky enough for retailers. Terry Hudgton, Corporate Marketing Manager at the Co-operative Group supermarket chain in the UK, commented when interviewed in 2001:

> It's nothing like developing other own-brand products. It's far more involved, there's far more sensitivities, and actually far more things can go wrong and fall down at the last minute than they can with standard products. [It] is very much different from a retailer saying 'I will launch a can of beans'; come hell or high water they will be able to source a can of beans from somewhere. If one supplier lets them down another supplier will be there waiting in the wings. That's not generally the case for Fair Trade.

In many ways, the fundamental tension between development-oriented supply and market-oriented demand is a healthy one. Development projects that encourage the supply of products for which there is no market should not be encouraged by the Fair Trade system. Market orientation of product development allows producers to tap into growing value-added market opportunities recognized by Northern players and is thus more sustainable in the long term. But one of the success drivers of Fair Trade, mainly the perception of consumers that Fair Trade makes a positive measurable difference in the lives of Third World commodity producers, would be compromised if only the 'easiest' producers and products were certified. The path to fastest growth is the past of least resistance: working with established supply chains in industries which are relatively easy to develop standards for means that Fair Trade is not targeting those Third World producers who are the most exploited. Thus keeping the tension between producer need and looking for growth markets ensures marketability whilst improving the lives of farmers who need Fair Trade the most.

This tension is unnecessarily increased, however, by the under-capitalization of the Fair Trade labelling and certification system. To begin, with FLO's funding structure does not allow for dynamic growth. FLO's income consists of a fee-for-volume paid by the national labelling initiatives in each of the 19 member countries of FLO. The fees calculated are undertaken at FLO's 'Meeting of Members' in May and are relevant for sales starting the following January. For example, TransFair USA, the US Fair Trade labelling initiative and member of FLO, achieved 85 per cent sales growth in 2003. The fees it pays for 2004, however, were calculated at the May 2003 meeting and were thus based on 2002's sales volume. TransFair USA's 2003 income grew due to its extremely high sales growth, but this growth will not be reflected in FLO's accounts until 2005. The dynamic growth achieved in Fair Trade markets cannot be captured by FLO in this retrospective system, thus resources are allocated relative to the areas with high historical sales and not necessarily in those areas with the most positive growth potential.

Second, FLO's fee calculations are undertaken on a cost-accounting basis and thus discourage investment in new product development. Fees per volume are calculated by dividing the cost of certifying the product (including price research, market research and product management) by the total volume sold in that year. For new products, with a very low initial trade volume and high start-up costs, the fee-per-volume is very high and then decreases as more volume is sold and economies of scale are achieved (the per-transaction cost of auditing a trader with 100 transactions is significantly lower than the per-transaction cost of monitoring only 10 transactions by that trader, as the audit reports are all filed together and the relationship costs are balanced over more trades). Thus national Fair Trade markets interested in a particular new product must pay extremely high fees to FLO in the initial stages of a product launch and business development. As the market grows, the fee lowers, significantly benefiting second-movers.

Whilst this cost-accounting approach is fiscally sound for a not-for-profit without access to investment capital, FLO's undercapitalization makes it difficult to commercialize a new product line because of the short-term need to recover initial investment in the product. The creation of a new product development fund would allow FLO and its members to pool resources in order to invest in standards development and allow them to repay investment more slowly. This capitalization of the Fair Trade certification system would allow it to respond more rapidly to dynamic growth, whilst still keeping in place the checks and balances that ensure that Fair Trade standards are met in certification priorities and standards development.

CONCLUSION

Fair Trade has emerged from a system based on trust and inconsistent practice to being a worldwide standard and certification system encompassing several products and hundreds of producer groups and companies. As the certification system has formalized, a number of weaknesses have appeared, especially in the area of new product development. FLO's stakeholder model of governance ensures that all actors are represented in standards-setting and decision-making, but may reduce the ability of Fair Trade to move 'at the speed of business'.

Nevertheless, the success of the third-party certification model is undeniable, so much so that it has attracted competitors. Fair Trade education and promotion have raised consumer, retailer and company awareness of the plight of the developing world's farmers and caused competing labels to emerge. These labels represent a threat to the Fair Trade certification system if it is unable to capture more consumer mindshare quickly, a concern to be discussed in the final chapter.

This chapter has set out the Fair Trade certification process in detail. It has also considered the competitive context of such accreditation and has explored how new product development strategies link to certification issues. The establishment of Fair Trade in its marketing context follows on from this.

NOTES

1. TransFair USA, FLO's US member, carries out its own trade audit between producers and importers for some products, notably coffee. FLO-certified coffee farmers submit quarterly reports to TransFair listing their sales to US coffee importers, including container number, ship date, price received and what prefinancing was provided. These data are checked against US importers' reports, who must also provide copies of the contract, proof of wire transfer of payment and the shipment's bill of loading. For other products, TransFair USA collects reports from importers and matches those against the producer reports sent to TransFair by FLO.

7

The Marketing of Fair Trade

This chapter will explore the key marketing issues for Fair Trade and trace the development of marketing communications strategies over the last ten years. There will be a particular focus on the UK market, as this is the most developed in terms of marketing communications, but other European markets and the USA will also be considered. The historical development of Fair Trade marketing to date is broken into three distinct phases and each is explored in detail. Using theory from social network research, the chapter goes on to show how establishing different levels of connectivity between producers and consumers lies at the heart of all successful Fair Trade marketing. The chapter closes by considering some of the options for the future marketing strategy for Fair Trade.

CASE STUDY: TEN YEARS OF FAIR TRADE: 1993–2004

On Monday 1 March 2004 the Fairtrade Foundation announced that sales of products carrying the Fair Trade Mark are running at an annual rate of £100m ($179m). The figures coincided with the official launch of the 10th Birthday year of the FAIR TRADE Mark and of Fair Trade Fortnight (1–14 March 2004). The theme of this Fortnight was 'A Taste for Life', celebrating the quality of life that Fair Trade means for producers and the quality of Fair Trade foods.

'Fair Trade, backed by a vibrant social movement of people throughout the country, is now bedding into the mainstream, giving thousands of producers in developing countries the chance to build a better future and to compete in the all too cut-throat global markets' says Harriet Lamb, Executive Director of the Fairtrade Foundation. 'The rapidly rising sales prove that consumers do care and are prepared to pay the true price for products they know they can trust, guaranteed by the Fair Trade Mark'.

Fair Trade Fortnight celebrations kicked off with a breakfast for 250 stakeholders at the London restaurant Mezzo, part of the Conran Group. Hilary Benn, Secretary of State for International Development, gave a speech and the event was hosted by Fairtrade Foundation patron George Alagiah.

Some 6,000 events were expected to take place around the UK during Fair Trade Fortnight. There was widespread activity around supermarkets – with supporters doing taste tests of Fair Trade foods – and also around high street coffee chains.

As a special focus on the 10th year of the Fair Trade Mark, the Fairtrade Foundation has aimed to persuade the out-of-home sector to switch to Fair Trade. The Office of

Government Commerce issued guidelines on Monday 1 March 2004 on how government procurement offices could source Fair Trade foods.

Other institutions were also launching new buying policies to coincide with the launch of Fair Trade Fortnight. The Salvation Army, the UK's largest care provider after the government, was starting a switch to Fair Trade foods – a move to be rolled out in its 800 centres and supported by TV chef Brian Turner of BBC TV's 'Ready Steady Cook'. The Youth Hostel Association (YHA) was also celebrating Fair Trade Fortnight by beginning the switch to Fair Trade tea and coffee in more than 200 Youth Hostels across England and Wales, as was the British Medical Association.

For Fair Trade Fortnight, a host of towns were also gearing up to gain Fair Trade status. Five pairs of cities such as Oxford and Cambridge and Lancaster and York put aside ancient rivalries to make a joint declaration of Fair Trade status, linked by web-cam, at 1pm on Friday 5 March 2004. Cardiff and Edinburgh also declared themselves as Fair Trade capitals.

Some of the highlights of the 6000 events around the UK were a traditional boat (gaff ketch) bringing a cargo of Fair Trade bananas from the Windward Islands to Southampton for distribution to everyone from the mayor to hospital patients; a Rich/Poor Banquet in Newcastle; a Mad Hatters Tea Party in Glasgow and Jack Ellis from ITV drama 'Bad Girls' joining a Fair Trade quiz at Chelmsford Cathedral. Around 40 cyclists converged on Garstang in Lancashire – the world's first Fair Trade Town – for a 10th Birthday Party. Universities including Edinburgh, Nottingham, Swansea and the London School of Economics declared Fair Trade status during the Fortnight, joining Oxford Brookes and Birmingham which were already Fair Trade universities.

Nearly all of the major supermarkets stock a wide range of Fair Trade products and Sainsbury's, Waitrose, Somerfield and Safeway did major promotional activities for Fair Trade Fortnight. Asda introduced 30 new product lines. Many independent stores also promoted Fair Trade Fortnight.

Source: Fairtrade Foundation at: http://www.fairtrade.org.uk/pr010304.htm

INTRODUCTION

As has already been noted, global sales of all Fair Trade products amounted to approximately £500m ($895m) in 2003 (Vidal, 2004) and have been growing at double-digit annual rates for more than five years. Driven by a widespread increase in 'ethical consumerism' which embraces consumer concerns over environmental issues (for example, packaging and waste, organics, genetically modified produce), animal testing, the human element in the retail supply chain and so on, addressing Fair Trade now sits on the strategic agenda of most major European retailers (Moore, 2004; Nicholls, 2002; Strong, 1996).

However, although consumer research suggests that 84 per cent of UK consumers are willing to pay more for specifically 'ethical' products (Co-operative Group/MORI, 2004) and that more than two thirds are prepared to pay more for Fair Trade products (Retail Week/ICM, 2002), such goods generally account for less than 1 per cent of their individual markets (Cowe and Williams, 2000). This discrepancy can be explained by a number of factors, as outlined by Strong (1997) and Nicholls (2002, 2004):

- The problem of communicating the human element of sustainability to the consumer.
- Difficulties in establishing consumer commitment to Fair Trade purchasing.
- Obstacles in getting more Fair Trade products on to supermarket shelves.
- Perception of low quality because of early negative experience with 'green' or 'ethical/ solidarity' products.
- The ethical aspect is only one of a number of multiple factors in purchase decisions.

Central to the development of Fair Trade in the future is the need for increased consumer education and innovative marketing that builds brands and creates a set of values around the Fair Trade mark that are both ethical and quality-based. Consequently, the sternest challenge facing Fair Trade groups today is how to market their products to a wider audience beyond the naturally sympathetic segment of 'ethically aware' consumers and gain mainstream acceptance. In order to continue to grow, therefore, Fair Trade marketing must move from niche targeting to mass appeal.

At the heart of the marketing of Fair Trade is a set of core values based around a reconfiguration of the traditional neo-liberal model of a profitable supplier-consumer relationship and centred on the concept of common global citizenship encompassing producers and consumers alike (Raynolds, 2002a; Whatmore and Thorne, 1997). In simple terms these values can be expressed as connectivity and fairness. The Fair Trade model is based on partnership exchanges that create strong linkages between consumers and (often quite specific) producers – the commercial relationship is built on respect and understanding rather than exploitation. Thus, the Fair Trade supply chain is 'shortened' by the values it articulates (see Marsden et al., 2000). Producer and consumer are brought closer together by the information flows that serve to bridge the spatial distance that separates them. The marketing process plays a central role in developing these connections.

For the consumer to engage with Fair Trade these core values must be clearly and effectively communicated, particularly since Fair Trade products generally occupy a premium price position within their individual markets. The central issue behind this is the development of a range of recognized Fair Trade brands. However, for marketing communications to work the consumer must also trust the Fair Trade message to deliver what it states – namely improvement in the development of producer groups. One key element in establishing this trust has been the Fair Trade certification mark and its promise of a third-party guarantee that Fair Trade standards were met for that particular product. This is discussed further below.

Despite the fact that Fair Trade marketing centres on explicitly ethical issues, it needs to be seen as quite distinct from either cause-related marketing or what is broadly known as socially responsible marketing. Fair Trade is not about charity or aid and, consequently, does not fit within the cause-related marketing paradigm (see Pracejus and Olsen, 2004; Webb and Mohr, 1998). Similarly, although it is clearly socially responsible in its outcomes, Fair Trade marketing does not aim to adapt an existing commercial model to a new Corporate Social Responsibility agenda (see Hilton and Gibbons, 2002; Schlegelmilch, 1998). Rather, Fair Trade marketing aims to articulate the social and economic interconnectedness between producer and consumer in a commercially viable way (see Table 7.1 on the next page). The ethical element here is the core product rather than the marketing process (although this should, of course, be ethical also).

Fair Trade marketing is, thus, a new model of consumer communications developing fully Kotler et al.'s (1999: 61–4) 'enlightened marketing' concept to embrace the social and

Table 7.1 *Dimensions of ethical marketing*

Marketing approach	Key issue	Example
Cause-related marketing	Congruence with core business image	Safeway: Computers for Schools
Socially responsible marketing	Congruence with public perception of Corporate Social Responsibility	Co-operative Bank
Marketing ethical products	Consumer trust in ethics of product offered to market	Body Shop; Cafédirect

moral dimensions of supply chain relationships. In this sense, it represents a vertically integrated marketing model in which producers, wholesalers and retailers act as a unified system with the significant addition of the end-consumer being a key actor in the operation of the distribution channel. Real and perceived linkages are vital: interconnections and a sense of global community imbue Fair Trade marketing. Fair Trade thus embraces an holistic view of marketing that Young and Welford described as 'a wide array of disciplines from the inception and creation of new products, cost management and the pricing of goods, through sourcing, procurement and logistics management to promotion, sales and after-service' (2002: 51). McDonagh (2002) terms this 'sustainable communication'. The central model here is that of a network of relationships, discussed in detail below.

Furthermore, Fair Trade marketing communications can function both to promote specific Fair Trade goods and to raise issue literacy in general. Successful Fair Trade marketing both satisfies an immediate market demand and, over time, increases the size of this market through education and campaigning.

POSITIONING FAIR TRADE PRODUCTS

Fair Trade products may be seen as 'social goods', combining both functional and ethical values (Kotler et al., 1999: 55). Consequently, the marketing of Fair Trade goods largely avoids many of the usual criticisms of marketing in general. Because Fair Trade fits within a broadly consumerist agenda, developing in parallel with the 'green' tradition of sustainability and environmental awareness (Strong, 1996), its marketing is generally not perceived as being irresponsible, wasteful, manipulative or overly materialistic (McDonagh, 2002). Nevertheless, there is a tension between the objectives of Fair Trade and the traditional marketing communications approach that focuses on consumer rather than producer needs, wants and demands.

These two dimensions of ethical value and consumer satisfaction are conceptualized in Figure 7.1. Quadrant 1 shows the products that generate low levels of consumer satisfaction and have little ethical value. Typically these are low-involvement commodity products such as household goods or other fast-moving consumer goods.

Products with low ethical value but high consumer satisfaction lie in quadrant 2. Fashion products are located here as these are often high-involvement self-actualizing goods that engage consumers' emotions and connect with their self-concept and lifestyle choices, but do not generate an ethical 'feel good' factor. Interestingly, many fashion houses are increasingly

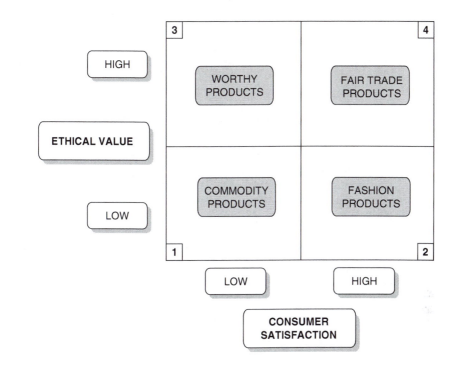

Figure 7.1 *Ethical classification of products*

trying to co-opt the emotional value of ethical behaviour into their brand meanings via explicit codes of conduct or public statements on issues such as banning sweatshop labour from their supply chain. However, many consumers remain cynical, as true ethical value can only be generated by the development of trust in supply chain statements and many so-called 'ethical' brands have been caught out in breach of their own codes. Nike is, perhaps, the best example of this. This quadrant also offers a valuable market opportunity to fashion products that are genuinely ethical and which can move towards quadrant 4. People Tree is one Fair Trade fashion business that is grasping this opportunity. Starting as a catalogue retailer, the business is growing fast and now also has a high street presence in Selfridge's department store (see below).

CASE STUDY: 'SHOP WITH PEOPLE TREE TO CHANGE THE WORLD!'

In 1991, Safia Minney founded People Tree in Tokyo, Japan. The first collection was the result of working with Bangladeshi women's groups to produce a range of hand-woven products using only natural dyes. This was sold via a 32-page catalogue featuring bags, dresses and 'eco-clogs' that was sold on newsstands. In 1999, People Tree's catalogue business was launched in Britain and later moved into the high street in partnership with the Co-operative Group. In 2004, the business turned over nearly £1m ($1.79m) across 20 countries. By 2004, People Tree employed a team of 34 working in a small office in Tokyo's Jiyugaoka district.

People Tree works with 70 Fair Trade groups in 20 developing countries giving design and technical assistance to help producers overcome the barriers of selling their products in Northern markets. People Tree pays its producers a fair price, offers advance payment when needed, provides technical assistance with product design and quality control and commits to ordering regularly. People Tree also funds village welfare projects such as schools and hospitals and supports the continuation of traditional skills and the use of local materials, thus helping to keep threatened rural communities and cultures alive.

People Tree's collections are made with organic cotton and hand-woven fabrics to promote natural farming that is safe to the environment and to the wearer, and creates much-needed income in rural areas. Fair Trade delivers benefit to where it's most needed and helps empower the producer and the consumer. People Tree is a member of The International Federation of Alternative Trade (IFAT).

In August 2004, People Tree launched a Fair Trade and organic cotton collection at Selfridge's department store in London's Oxford Street. The new collection subsequently became available in all four Selfridge's stores across the UK. The clothes in this collection are made by a Fair Trade project in India that employs 150 young women from poor families, many with hearing and speech problems.

Source: http://www.ptree.co.uk

Quadrant 3 contains products that have high ethical value, but low consumer satisfaction. These 'worthy' goods are typified by the outdated image of a charity shop offer as being of poor quality and indifferent design. One of the key initial objectives of Fair Trade marketing has been to distance Fair Trade goods from this negative stereotype and a 'guilt' marketing strategy that encourages purchase as an ethical gesture, rather than this being based upon any attractive product characteristics.

Finally, in quadrant 4 lie Fair Trade products that are successfully marketed to emphasize both their genuine ethical credentials and uniqueness as quality purchases. Either via a certification mark or through the use of other established Fair Trade brand names (such as Traidcraft or the Co-operative Group), consumer trust is established. Other marketing messages can then be overlaid, creating product values such as exoticness, exclusivity and premium quality. Fair Trade marketing has been particularly focussed on developing these twin dimensions in the last five years.

THE FAIR TRADE MARKETING PROCESS

A further distinction between Fair Trade marketing strategy and traditional models may be discerned by an analysis of their relative marketing processes (see Table 7.2). Whereas the traditional process begins with an analysis of market opportunities centred on consumer demand and competitor activity (Kotler et al., 1999), the Fair Trade process starts with identifying the market failures that damage suppliers. Thus, coffee was recognized early on as a commodity that was being traded below cost, in many cases with disastrous consequences for small producers. Both the Max Havelaar initiative and Cafédirect were explicitly established to address this by guaranteeing a fair and liveable price for coffee

Table 7.2 *The Fair Trade marketing process*

Traditional marketing process	Fair Trade marketing process
Analyse market opportunities	Analyse market failures
Select target markets and positioning strategy	Select suppliers/products most affected by market failures
Develop marketing mix	Develop Fair Trade marketing mix
Manage marketing effort	Manage marketing effort
Seek competitive advantage	Encourage competition

carrying their labels. TransFair USA has also followed a similar path, concentrating most of its efforts to date on coffee.

In the second stage of the marketing process, the conventional marketer selects the most appropriate and profitable target markets within the already identified market opportunity and develops a positioning strategy for business communication that maximizes competitive advantage. On the other hand, with Fair Trade marketing the process again focuses not solely on the consumer, but also on the supplier, selecting those cases most in need of assistance and best suited to a Fair Trade approach (for example, to date small co-operatives have been seen as more suitable than large estates). In one instance, when the UK Co-operative Group was looking to develop a Fair Trade wine it worked in conjunction with Traidcraft to identify a small co-operative in Chile – Vinos Los Robles – that functioned independent of the larger businesses that dominate Chilean wine production (Nicholls, 2004).

The third stage of the marketing process is to develop a strategic marketing mix (typically conceptualized as addressing the '4Ps' of 'product, price, place and promotion': see Kotler et al., 1999). Here, again, Fair Trade functions differently from most companies. Of particular importance in Fair Trade marketing is the extended marketing mix (Booms and Bitner, 1981) since this encompasses the additional elements of 'process, people and physical evidence', in addition to the basic '4Ps' (see Table 7.3). The core of the Fair Trade marketing mix lies in the bundle of ethical and economic values inherent in the end product as the developmental focus of the supply chain process aligned with identifiable producers (whose stories are often told in product packaging). Once again the Fair Trade approach to the marketing process is typically centred on the producer, not the end consumer. However, in common with traditional marketing, at the product level Fair Trade is also increasingly emphasizing quality and uniqueness as well as ethical value. This allows

Table 7.3 *The Fair Trade marketing mix*

	Traditional marketing strategy	Fair Trade marketing strategy
Product	Fit with target segment	Uniqueness, quality
Price	Minimize cost price	Social premium
Place	Efficient logistics	'Fair' supply chain
Promotion	Competitive positioning	Ethical issues/education
People	Customer interface	Identifiable producers
Process	Customer service	Developmental focus
Physical evidence	Branding	Fair Trade mark

Fair Trade products to occupy multiple areas of consumer 'mind-space' and opens up potential target segments beyond those where purchase behaviour is clearly driven by ethical imperatives – the 'ethicals' (Cowe and Williams, 2000).

With the price element of the marketing mix, Fair Trade again stresses the producer by highlighting both the 'fair' original commodity price and the social premium that is often added in to the Fair Trade value chain (Porter, 1998: 76–83). The shelf price of Fair Trade goods is typically not as low as that of their competitors, nor is the cost fixed with the aim of maximizing company profits. However, Fair Trade's premium pricing may be changing as supermarkets increasingly introduce own-label Fair Trade products at more competitive prices and Fair Trade composite products are developed that reduce the final shelf-price by mixing Fair Trade and non-Fair Trade ingredients (Nicholls, 2004).

Branding

The development of the Fair Trade 'brand' to date has largely been a decentralized and unstrategic process that has presented a significant challenge in creating effective overall marketing communications. There are several reasons for this. First, Fair Trade as a brand is offered to the market by a wide range of different groups. These include the national labelling initiatives, such as the Fairtrade Foundation and TransFair USA, who are responsible for awarding the certification mark and policing its use. In addition, individual Fair Trade businesses such as Equal Exchange, Cafédirect or Day Chocolate are creating their own brand values in which the Fair Trade mark is only part of the message. Furthermore, with the increasing shelf-presence of supermarket own-label Fair Trade products, another set of brand meanings is also being added to the mix. An example would be Tesco's tagline 'Every Little Helps'. To date there has been no attempt to co-ordinate the range of brand meanings associated with Fair Trade. This issue is discussed further at the conclusion of this chapter.

Despite this wide range of marketing approaches to Fair Trade, some unifying brand values have emerged. It is evident that a moral and ethical message is at the core of the brand, but further elements have been developed through subsequent communications campaigns. Most important of these is the concept of quality, framed in its broadest sense to include not only the nature of the consumer's experience of the product, but also their contribution to the quality of the producer's life and their environment through that purchase choice. The fact that Fair Trade coffee is positioned as a speciality product also emphasizes the brand's contribution to diversity and uniqueness of supply – another quality dimension akin to that offered by organic produce or speciality cheese. Indeed, the clear identification of the source of a Fair Trade product combines both the concepts of fairness and quality through the establishment of producer/consumer connectivity. This is returned to below.

As has already been noted, the Fair Trade certification mark functions as a central element in communicating Fair Trade values and establishing consumer trust. In many ways the mark acts as a brand signifier, encompassing a group of meanings in a risk-reducing logo. The establishment of the Fairtrade Labelling Organisations International (FLO) in 1997 represented an important step towards consolidating various national initiatives into a global marketing approach and helped to project Fair Trade to a wider audience. Furthermore, the re-branding of all European national logos into one universal mark in October 2002 also addressed this issue.

However, there remains the problem of the time lag between Fair Trade goods being developed and the awarding of the mark to an appropriate product category (Nicholls, 2004). This can lead to many genuine Fair Trade products being unable to display the mark. For example, the majority of Traidcraft's or People Tree's Fair Trade ranges do not bear the official mark, but rather leverage their own brand values as reassurance of the true nature of their products. There is a potential tension between the development of such manufacturer Fair Trade brands and the role of the FLO mark, as multiple expressions of Fair Trade branding may well confuse consumers and diminish overall the public trust in Fair Trade that the FLO is attempting to foster. To complicate matters further, as discussed in Chapter 6, alternative non-FLO-endorsed direct trademarks are also beginning to appear, such as Utz Kapeh which was first developed as an own label by the Netherlands' Ahold retail group.

One option may be to draw up legislation that determines exactly what Fair Trade criteria are and how they can be described on product packaging (MacMaolin, 2002). In the USA incorporation of organic standards into a single legal definition and label by the US Department of Agriculture in 2002 has led to increased consumer trust in organic product claims and may underlie the increasingly widespread adoption of organic foods by mainstream consumers. However, despite some lobbying from interest groups, no similar initiative for Fair Trade criteria is yet under discussion in any national or supra-national (such as the European Union) parliaments.

In terms of developing the Fair Trade brand in general, some clear progress has been made. Brand awareness of the Fair Trade mark shows good growth across most developed countries and is as high as 42 per cent of the population in Switzerland (2002), 40 per cent in Germany (2002) and 39 per cent in the UK (2004). Awareness in the USA is also growing: it reached 12 per cent of coffee drinkers in 2004. Since there is reason to believe that the USA has the potential to become the largest market for Fair Trade goods in the next five years, managing brand awareness there will clearly be very important. Fair Trade brand awareness will be discussed in more detail in Chapter 8.

FAIR TRADE MARKETING COMMUNICATIONS

Over the past ten years, Fair Trade marketing has engaged with the majority of traditional marketing communication channels from advertising to public relations to direct marketing (see Table 7.4). These have included conventional media placements for Cafédirect's brands, extensive use of press releases to the newspapers by national Fair Trade-labelling initiatives and catalogue selling from Traidcraft and others. The Internet is also being increasingly employed to disseminate information and develop campaigns. However, the available budget for Fair Trade marketing communications is typically very small, so campaigns tend to be highly focussed on a particular positioning effort or educational agenda. Pro bono work from advertising agencies has also proved to be important, as have celebrity endorsements from the likes of Martin Sheen in the USA and Emma Thompson and Coldplay in the UK.

The main focus for Fair Trade marketing in the UK has been the annual Fair Trade Fortnight event held in March each year (see Fairtrade Foundation, 2003c). This has proved to be highly successful both for raising awareness and increasing sales, although its

Table 7.4   *Fair Trade marketing communication channels*

Communications Channel	Example
Advertising	Poster/newspaper campaign for Cafédirect 5065 (2002)
Sales Promotion	Fair Trade Fortnight (annual)
Celebrity Endorsement	Emma Thompson, Coldplay (UK), Martin Sheen (USA)
Branding	FLO mark; manufacturer brands (Equal Exchange etc.); supermarket own-label products
PR	Cafédirect sponsorship of Edinburgh Fringe Arts Festival (2002)
Internet	www.Ethical-Junction.org; e-marketing (People Tree, national Fair Trade labelling initiatives)
Direct Marketing	Catalogues (Traidcraft, People Tree, etc.)

effect on the latter tends to tail away fairly sharply. Fair Trade Fortnight brings together retailers and campaign groups in various events to present Fair Trade goods and propagate the Fair Trade proposition. The number of activities and participants involved in Fair Trade Fortnight has increased dramatically in the last five years and all the major supermarket chains now engage with the event as a promotional opportunity. In 2004, the UK celebrated the tenth birthday of Fair Trade with a whole series of events throughout the year, but with the Fair Trade Fortnight as its principal focus. In a similar approach in the USA, 2004 has seen the development of a Fair Trade Month to promote products and raise awareness.

Finally, the importance of support networks in marketing communications cannot be overstated. Whether through grass-roots events in churches or town halls, educational input into local schools (such as the Reading International Solidarity Centre's involvement with schools in their area), or co-ordinated action such as the Fair Trade Town campaigns (see further below), committed local groups have played a major role in raising awareness at a community level.

As has already been suggested, there has been a discernible shift in the focus of Fair Trade marketing activities over the past ten years in the most developed markets, such as the UK and continental Europe. Historically, this development can be seen as moving through three phases that can be conceptualized as follows: a focus on process; a focus on product; a focus on place (see Table 7.5).

The progress of marketing communications in less well-developed Fair Trade markets, such as the USA, is generally not as advanced as in Europe. Thus, the approach to marketing communications in the USA is currently between stages 1 and 2. The progression can be shown in the development of the TransFair USA website which was repositioned in 2002 from a more alternative trade left-wing feel to a more upscale gourmet focus to emphasize Fair Trade product quality (see Images 7.1 and 7.2). It should also be noted that future marketing communications across all markets are likely to reflect further stages of development yet to be identified (although some of the possible directions are noted at end of this chapter).

Table 7.5 *Developing Fair Trade marketing communications*

	Phase 1: process	Phase 2: product	Phase 3: place
Target customer (Cowe and Williams, 2000)	Global watchdog	Conscientious consumers	Do what I can
Marketing approach	Supplier driven	Market driven	Society driven
Marketing values	Solidarity and trust	Quality and lifestyle	Community and social linkages
Market size	Niche	Multiple segments	Mass market
Distribution channel	ATOs	National multiples	Local SMEs and multiples, new Fair Trade businesses, websites
Marketing strategy	Raise issue awareness, establish core image	Increase product ranges	Localize PR/communications strategy
Marketing actions	Educational campaigns, establish Fair Trade mark	New product development, increase supermarket listings	Local educational campaigns, generate 'word-of-mouth' interest

It will be argued below that this three-phase transition fits within an analytical framework that is best informed by a range of social exchange concepts moving from commodity chain theory (process focus) to commodity network theory (product) and finally to actor network theory (place). Central to an understanding of how Fair Trade marketing connects producer and consumer is the concept of a network. Therefore, before embarking on a detailed analysis of each of these three phases the theoretical framework that is employed needs to be presented via a discussion of social network theory.

Marketing and Social Network Theory

The application of social network theory to the marketing process is largely absent from the extant literature, at least in terms of business to consumer situations (alternatively, see Iacobucci and Hopkins, 1992). Whilst social network theory has incorporated a variety of research into the cultural and consumption elements of commodity networks, there has yet to be any significant consideration of the marketing impact of such theorizations. This is, perhaps, surprising as there would seem to be a natural link to be made between the information and 'meaning' knowledge flows between the producer and consumer nodes mapped in social exchange network theory and conceptualizations of the strategic marketing communications that delineate the transmission of marketing information between marketer and consumer with resultant effects. Nevertheless, at least in business-to-consumer contexts, such linkages have not yet been made.

Image 7.1   *TransFair USA website, 1998–2002*

Image 7.2   *TransFair USA website, 2002–present*

The IMP group, based mainly in Sweden, pioneered research into markets as networks (MAN) but looked primarily at business-to-business relationships (see for example Hakansson and Ostberg, 1975; Hakansson et al., 1976; for an overview, see McLouglin and Horan, 2002). This research rejected the established uni-directional marketing paradigm based on a behavioural psychology model in favour of an approach built around social exchange theory (Blau, 1964; Cook, 1977; Cook and Emerson, 1984) which conceptualized marketing interactions as a network that was multi-directional in structure (Hakansson and Johanson, 1992). The IMP group thus proposed that research into business-to-business marketing relationships should focus on mapping out the mutual connectedness of actors, rejecting the more traditional dyadic marketing model in favour of a network structure that recognizes power symmetries between buyers and sellers who are linked by a variety of information flows. Moreover, MAN research suggests that marketing networks are not *a priori* structures, but rather that they are dynamically (re)created by the variety of relationships built by their actors and controlled by outside resources and activities (Hakansson and Snehota, 1995).

In the description of the development of Fair Trade marketing below it is suggested that a social network model, similar in its root concept to that used in the MAN literature, also offers an explanatory and analytical mechanism fully appropriate to a business-to-consumer situation. A number of key points of contact between the Fair Trade marketing paradigm and social network theory can be discerned:

- The definitional centrality of connectivity between separate 'nodes' or key 'actants' that constitute the multi-directional network.
- Dynamism and the changing structures of key network relationships.
- Information flows defining meanings across the entire network.
- The importance in the network of both human and non-human actants.

The analytical value of these factors is further elaborated below.

FAIR TRADE AND SOCIAL NETWORK THEORY

Social network theory delineates the supremacy of social relationships over the normalized attributes of individual actors (Araujo, 1999; Araujo and Easton, 1996), relying on an 'anti-categorical imperative' that avoids explaining behaviours through methodological individualism and focuses instead on the links within the network as the foundation of analysis. Since Fair Trade is, by definition, a network construct defined by the nature of the network itself, it fits well into this theorization (Raynolds, 2002a).

Furthermore, social network analysis has been used to examine power relationships via the connectivities in dyadic exchange networks (Cook, 1977; Cook and Emerson, 1984). The concept of contingent exchange relationships elaborated here is also relevant in exploring Fair Trade networks, although it will be argued below that Fair Trade exchange is perhaps best fully conceptualized in terms of multi-directional network theory, rather than in terms of uni-directional commodity chains.

In previous research there have been attempts to use a commodity network approach to analyse the Fair Trade movement (Raynolds, 2002a; Renard, 1999; Whatmore and Thorne, 1997). This research has built upon world commodity chain theory (Gereffi, 1994) to explore the structures around this alternative agri-food network. This work recognizes the value of a commodity chain analysis that reconnects production, distribution and consumption in interpreting the meanings of Fair Trade. From a campaigning perspective this model allows the exposure of unethical production practices to be reconnected to the consumer and, thus, Fair Trade to be offered as a distinct alternative economic mechanism for transnational agri-trade.

Other research can be seen to be highly relevant in understanding the symbolic meanings of Fair Trade from the consumption perspective. For example, Leslie and Reimer (1999) engaged commodity chain theory with consumption to elucidate the informational movements within the chain that accompany the physical displacement of products. Appadurai (1986) provided a consumption focus to the commodity chain by noting the symbolic meanings embedded in goods via the discursive as well as material flows that move across commodity networks: the 'social life of things'. Lockie et al. (2002) noted the importance of consumer knowledge structures in developing trends towards organic consumption.

Clearly, the central point of contact between Fair Trade and social network theory lies in the issue of information flow and embeddedness within a commodity network structure (Murdoch et al., 2000). As Raynolds noted, 'Connections between consumers and Fair Trade organizations are rooted largely in flows of information. Fair Trade networks socially re-embed commodities, so that items arrive at the point of consumption replete with information regarding the social and environmental conditions under which they were produced and traded' (2002a: 415).

FAIR TRADE MARKETING COMMUNICATIONS: A NETWORK PERSPECTIVE

Having established that social network theory has much to offer in terms of analytical approaches to Fair Trade, the next section takes an historical perspective on the growth of Fair Trade marketing in existing markets and applies social network conceptualizations to deepen understanding of the developments involved. As has already been noted above, three distinct stages in the development of Fair Trade marketing can be discerned, each building on what has gone before. With each phase of marketing communications strategy a new and larger customer segment is targeted. In network terms, these phases represent the gradual recognition as regards marketing of the full potentialities of the Fair Trade network. The marketing approach thus begins with a simple conceptualization of Fair Trade as a commodity chain (process), then exploits its structure as a commodity network (product) and finally embraces the marketing opportunities inherent in an actor network analysis of Fair Trade relationships (place). Each of these developmental phases is now treated in turn.

Phase One: Process Focus

Importers of goods who aimed to provide access to developed markets for producers in the developing world at a 'fair' source price have been operating in Europe since Oxfam began trading in the UK after the Second World War. However, it was not until the early 1970s that Alternative Trading Organizations (ATOs) began to proliferate, widening the retail network for 'fairly traded' products. Traidcraft represents one of the more substantial ATOs within a UK sector that also includes Twin Trading and several faith-based organizations such as CAFOD. In this first stage, little external marketing activity could be financed by ATOs and, consequently, products were largely marketed in stores within an 'ethnic' or charity shop merchandising environment such as Ten Thousand Villages in the USA. New product development was patchy and quality control uneven. This stereotypical legacy of poor quality continues to dog Fair Trade goods today.

Recognizing the need to reach a larger audience for Fair Trade by offering a quality brand that could be sold in more mainstream outlets, Oxfam Trading, Traidcraft, Twin Trading and Equal Exchange UK set up Cafédirect in the early 1990s (Bird and Hughes, 1997). Cafédirect launched it first product on the UK market in 1991 (roast and ground coffee) and always aimed to compete directly with mainstream coffee suppliers. To this end, it was run as a for-profit company. Recognizing the reality of the competitive market in which it was situated, Cafédirect was the first Fair Trade company to engage in major marketing campaigns. However, in keeping with its positioning as 'in and against the market', Cafédirect used its marketing communications to highlight the key differences in the Fair Trade process when compared with the existing coffee supply chain and did this through a particular emphasis on individual suppliers' stories (see Image 7.3).

Image 7.3   *Cafédirect's advertising imagery 1993–1995*

Cafédirect's marketing objective was to connect the consumer more closely to the producer and thus combine both a rational (Fair Trade actually helps real people) and emotional (the supply chain is more 'fair') impetus for purchase behaviour. As Raynolds (2002a) noted, Fair Trade labels combine trust and knowledge for the consumer such that purchasing Fair Trade goods can become an act of self-symbolic construction (Elliott and Wattanasuwan, 1998). Indeed, as Zadek et al. (1998, and quoted in Raynolds, 2002a: 415) commented, Fair Trade labels 'function as a mirror for the consumer in securing the benefits of self-expression and positive social identity', thus generating an ethical 'feel-good factor'.

Therefore, the first marketing objective was to raise issue-awareness with the most naturally sympathetic consumer segment, identified by Mintel (1999) as 'strongly ethical' consumers. These are the 'global watchdogs' defined by Cowe and Williams as 'ethical hardliners ... they are, and feel, powerful, but want more information on which to base their decisions' (2000: 23). This segment is affluent, educated, 'values-led', predominantly middle-aged and runs across the whole political spectrum (although with a bias to the left). This group accounts for about 5 per cent of the UK population, although Mintel (1999) effectively combined the two most ethical of Cowe and Williams's groups – Global Watchdogs and Conscientious Consumers – to measure the 'strongly ethical' group as 25 per cent of the total population. Similarly in the USA the LOHAS (Lifestyles of Health and Sustainability) market segment was estimated to be 26 per cent of the adult population, has been identified as the consumer profile most interested in purchasing Fair Trade (Nachman-Hunt, 2003). LOHAS consumers, or 'Cultural Creatives', base their buying decisions in part on social and environmental criteria (Ray, 2000) and are thus sympathetic to the Fair Trade message.

Establishing Fair Trade issue awareness was (and still is) primarily an act of education. As Young and Welford noted in this area 'there is a very thin dividing line between marketing, education and campaigning' (2002: 59). In conventional marketing terms the initial strategy was to move the target segment along the Hierarchy of Effects model from unawareness of Fair Trade to awareness, comprehension, conviction and ultimately purchase behaviour action (Ghosh, 1994). Providing clear and credible process information to the consumer was central to the initial success of Fair Trade marketing; as Marsden et al. noted, 'It is not the number of times a product is handled or the distance over which it is ultimately transported which is necessarily critical, but the fact that the product reaches the consumer embedded with information' (2000: 425).

In addition to building issue awareness amongst consumers, the first phase of Fair Trade marketing focussed on establishing trust in the authenticity of the Fair Trade process. Therefore, beginning in 1989, independent national Fair Trade labels began to appear in Europe, the USA, Canada and Japan, to provide a third-party verification of Fair Trade claims. In 1994, the Fairtrade Foundation, a consortium of Traidcraft, Oxfam, Christian Aid, CAFOD, the World Development Movement and The New Consumer, launched the Fair Trade audit mark in the UK. The Fairtrade Foundation's certification mark aimed to reassure the consumer by representing proof of a defined social audit of all accredited Fair Trade products. This made a guarantee to the consumer that what they were buying was genuinely Fair Trade. Similar marks were launched in other consuming countries.

The Fair Trade mark was applied to all of Cafédirect's products as well as to other ranges and today there are over 100 Fair Trade-marked goods on UK shelves. The Fair Trade mark acts as a brand encompassing the range of ethical meanings incorporated in the Fair Trade supply chain process – it reduces the risk for the consumer and promotes top-of-mind awareness across category groups. The mark serves the need for credible and clear information that confirms production practices (McDonagh, 2002), a need which was central to the early success of Fair Trade. However, as has been noted above, the majority of non-food Fair Trade products have yet to be awarded the Fair Trade mark (and may never be) with clear implications for the integrity of the 'brand' as a whole (Nicholls, 2004).

FLO, the umbrella agency which unites national Fair Trade labels, also aims to continue to increase issue awareness through a number of means, including: widening the range of products to which the Fair Trade mark has been awarded; offering extensive educational resources to interested parties; supporting and encouraging local campaigning and lobbying groups; establishing an on-line presence (www.fairtrade.net) and acting as a press agency to the national medias for Fair Trade. In addition, the national Fair Trade-labelling initiatives coordinate local events such as the UK Fairtrade Foundation's work on the annual Fair Trade Fortnight. As Terry Hudgton, Corporate Marketing Manager for the UK Co-operative Group, commented when interviewed in 2001, 'the more consumer awareness is heightened, the greater propensity there is to buy Fair Trade'.

This first phase of Fair Trade marketing was supplier-driven and aimed to attract only those for whom a process focus was the key purchase decision variable. The central marketing message was one of solidarity with farmers in the developing world and small-scale growers. As such, Fair Trade products found a natural home in ATO retailers, but did not justify listings in national multiples. Similarly, this niche marketing approach worked well with the 'strongly ethicals' but left the remaining 95 per cent of the market relatively untouched: to expand further a more market-driven approach would be needed.

A commodity chain analysis can usefully be employed to explore this first phase of Fair Trade marketing. Commodity chain analysis connects producers and consumers by identifying the network of labour that generates these linkages (Hopkins and Wallerstein, 1986; Leslie and Reimer, 1999). This approach introduces the concept of consumption into otherwise static supply chain structures. There are three main models in this area: Global Commodity Chains, Systems of Provision and Circuits of Consumption.

The Global Commodity Chain (GCC) approach focuses on the connections between production and consumption at a global level within a system of production. However, consumption is often treated simply as a starting point from which to trace back relations to the point of production. This analysis often aims to reveal the exploitative nature of these systemic relationships (see for example, Hopkins and Wallenstein, 1986). The GCC analysis takes a 'horizontal' approach to conceptualizing commodity movements, looking to identify a particular element in the chain and then generalizing its influence across the wider economy (for example, the growing power of retailers over suppliers). From a Fair Trade marketing perspective the GCC approach highlights the primary marketing message that neo-liberal economic structures have left many producers in the developing world disenfranchized within the supply chain. The GCC thus supports the central image of Fair Trade communications but is limited by its uni-directional causality and lack of product/producer specificity to providing only an activist agenda for developing marketing as campaigning (Oxfam, 2002).

More revealing in business-to-consumer contexts is Systems of Provision analysis. This approach uses a 'vertical' focus analysing the linkages in the producer-consumer chain for individual commodity groups and thus identifies particular differences across commodities (Fine and Leopold, 1993). The aim is to 'thicken' the relationship between producer and consumer. Such an approach is more dynamic and recognizes the variable impact of the consumption/demand element within a chain dependent on the particular commodity in question. The introduction of the consumption dimension to the commodity chain is important in normalizing its application to a marketing context. Fair Trade aims explicitly to reconnect producer and consumer through chain-specific information flows: its marketing aims to expose the vertical realities of the commodity chain, in contrast to a conventional framing that deliberately separates the marketing meanings of a commodity from the reality of its production and supply via advertising. This is the 'commodity fetishism' explored by Hudson and Hudson (2003).

Equally applicable to this stage of Fair Trade marketing is the concept of 'short' food supply chains developed by Marsden et al. (2000) within a discussion of alternative food chains that bypass traditional agribusiness supply chains (see also Renting and Marsden, 2003). These short food supply chains generate new relationships between producer and consumer based on a clear understanding of the origins of the produce. Central to the short food supply chain concept is an emphasis upon 'the type of relationship between the producer and the consumer … and the role of this relationship in constructing value and meaning, rather than solely the type of product itself' (Marsden et al., 2000: 425). Critical to the short food supply chain concept is the information embedded within a given product representing its production history and spatial identity – an interpretation which during consumption often gives the good its value added dimension. Again, information flows and embeddedness are crucial to the marketing of the Fair Trade concept.

The final commodity chain paradigm, Commodity Circuits, looks to develop a model that explores the development of meaning associated with a commodity. This theorization is less interested in exploring the causal flow of the chain of production explanatory model, but rather aims to uncover how an understanding of the nature of production may alter the consumption meanings associated with a good (Crang, 1996). The theory acknowledges that the very meaning of a commodity's origin is in itself an artificial and variable construct.

Chocolate demonstrates an interesting example of this paradigm. Whilst most consumers think of chocolate as 'Swiss' or 'Belgian', linking the product to the countries where fine chocolate is processed, the cocoa beans that are the key ingredient in chocolate manufacture are of course grown in developing countries. The Day Chocolate Company, a Fair Trade firm operating in the UK, has attempted to introduce the idea of the cocoa grower into the psyche of British chocolate consumers in order to demonstrate the impact consumers can make when they buy a Fair Trade chocolate bar. As Day Chocolate's Managing Director Sophi Tranchell explains, 'What we have done by telling people the story of chocolate is that it comes from cocoa and that cocoa is grown in places like Africa. Once people know that, they cannot un-know that' (in Davies and Crane, 2003: 83). Day Chocolate has used innovative means to educate their consumer base about cocoa farming, including schools educational packets and setting up pen-friend programs between British school children and their Ghanaian counterparts in cocoa-growing regions.

The flow of knowledge that defines a product is thus circular, moving from producer to consumer and back, growing in 'thickness' as it moves. Ironically, however, despite aiming to bring into the consumption arena the true meanings of (sometimes exploitative) production situations, the rejection of the causality of the commodity chain conceptualization also dilutes the political critique of production in a commodity circuit analysis, as it fails to acknowledge that there are particular forces driving production. Thus, whilst this theory can be used to explore the deepening marketing relationship between the consumer and producer of Fair Trade products that information flows engender, it obscures the socio-political raison d'être behind Fair Trade. Nevertheless, a circuit of consumption reading of this first phase of Fair Trade marketing serves to highlight the critical role played by demand side agents in establishing a Fair Trade market and the initial set of consumer meanings which were then translated into communication by interaction with producer narratives. The circularity of the theory is a valuable pointer towards the next stage of Fair Trade marketing that sought to bring new consumer perspectives to producers which were centred around product elements (that could in turn be reinterpreted back around the circuit to consumers).

Image 7.4 *Cafédirect's advertising imagery 1996–1998*

Phase Two: Product Focus

The first phase of Fair Trade marketing that focussed on process and communicating issue awareness was highly successful in growing the Fair Trade market amongst the '(strongly) ethical' target customer segment. For example, by 2003, Fair Trade coffee accounted for 14 per cent of the total UK roast and ground coffee market. However, it became apparent that to grow Fair Trade market shares beyond the 3–5 per cent of the population that are its 'natural' consumers, the marketing focus needed to broaden. The shift came in a move from communicating process information to product values. Four related marketing communications objectives lay behind this overall change of strategy:

- To reposition Fair Trade products on quality and differentiation.
- To broaden the Fair Trade brand message to include the lifestyle characteristics of new market segments.
- To focus Fair Trade new product development on consumer as well as producer demands.
- To increase the retail availability of Fair Trade products beyond ATOs and into national multiples.

For example, from 2000, Cafédirect repositioned its marketing communications to stress the quality, range, and differentiation of its products. As Diana Gayle, Marketing Officer at the Fairtrade Foundation noted when interviewed in 2003,

> When we started – even as the range got better – it was about conscience, it was still about the producers. And it is still about the producers, but the products taste good too. If people are going to choose Fair Trade products they may do it once in a while, but the only way you will keep them as regular purchasers is if they like the product and the only way you do that is if it is good quality.

Fair Trade marketing communications targeted the 'conscientious consumer' segment as well as the 'global watchdogs' (Cowe and Williams, 2000). This new target group is 'upmarket', concerned about ethical issues, but also sensitive to quality: 'these are the suburban Joneses, keeping up but not ahead of the times' (p. 32). This segment accounts for approximately 18 per cent of the UK population and capturing this group would significantly expand the Fair Trade market. Market research suggested that 'conscientious consumers' were attracted to differentiation and quality in their purchase choices and were also receptive to a message that appealed to their ethical sensitivities without compromising on other product features or values. This segment is driven by a sense of themselves as, at least in part, active consumers whose consumption decisions help define and complement their personalities.

Therefore, Phase Two of the Fair Trade marketing communications began to develop lifestyle messages that appealed to this new 'self-actualizing' group. The immediate consumer experience of Fair Trade products was moved from a largely rational to an emotional appeal as producer information on packaging or in advertisements was reframed by a new emphasis on lush and romantic visions of the country in which the product was grown (see Images 7.4 and 7.5). A new strategic approach to brand building also emerged as its significance in increasing loyalty and encouraging repurchase behaviour was recognized. Alistaire Menzies of Traidcraft, interviewed in 2001, said, 'It's all about developing the brand as a Fair Trade brand and then putting products under that brand'.

Image 7.5   *Cafédirect's advertising imagery 1999–2001*

However, the brand meanings associated with Fair Trade were now more complex, combining both ethical values and statements of unique and premium quality. These meanings reflected a divergence of marketing messaging between the FLO certifiers and wholesalers. As Diana Gayle of the Fairtrade Foundation noted in 2003, 'If you ask Cafédirect they would say that the Fair Trade mark represents the independent consumer guarantee and that the quality messaging should be left to them'.

Many Fair Trade goods thus became positioned as 'exclusive' and 'best quality' as much as 'fairly traded'. The aim was not only to leverage an appeal to consumers' ethical sensibilities or guilt, but also to use brand glamour and consumer escapism to capture a broader market driven by self-referential consumption. As Alistaire Menzies put it, 'In our experience market-driven products do better than product-driven products' (Interview, 2001). This shift also helped support the reality of a value chain that demanded premium-end pricing because it included both above market commodity pricing and, usually, an additional 10 per cent social premium.

However, this move away from a product focus has been controversial amongst many activists and campaigners, as it suggests a diminution of producer importance and handing marketing primacy instead to the consumption process. Wright analysed Cafédirect's print advertising campaigns from 1999 to 2002 and questioned the power relationships suggested in their imagery:

> Privileging and legitimating consumer pleasure may be an essential strategy of going mainstream ... However, a prominent reading is that minority world consumers can 'redeem' majority world producers by perpetuating consumer lifestyles prioritising self-gratification. Moreover, that the lives and landscapes of the majority world are consumables in their own right, alongside cash crops. (2004: 678)

The use of lush landscapes that only suggest the humanity of the producers in these campaigns illustrates this tension (see Image 7.5). Wright also noted that the producer stories used to reinforce consumer-producer connectivity in all phases of Fair Trade marketing are 'visual, virtual, and entirely one-way' (2004: 672) and, as such, are really only representative ciphers for producers as a whole. Indeed, the producer profiles may not even have any direct connection to the actual product on which they appear.

The third objective underpinning Phase Two of Fair Trade marketing was new product development. From 1999–2004 the number of Fair Trade certified products more than doubled (Nicholls, 2004). This included new 'composite' products that combined Fair Trade and non-Fair Trade ingredients (with the proviso that at least 20–50 per cent of the final product was Fair Trade). The most successful example to date has been Traidcraft's Geobar. This fruit bar helped introduce Fair Trade commodities (honey, sugar and so on) to a mass price-sensitive market with a mid-range shelf price made possible by mixing Fair Trade and non-Fair Trade elements. This expansion brought Fair Trade to a wider audience without necessarily weakening the integrity of the Fair Trade guarantee, as most of the non-Fair Trade ingredients were Northern-sourced. Developing more composites and other processed (and thus more value-added) Fair Trade goods is a key objective for new Fair Trade product development in the future.

The final element in the second phase of Fair Trade's marketing strategy was to increase the retail availability of its products. The specific aim was both to win new listings and consolidate existing ones (through the addition of multi-packs of Fair Trade products) in multiple supermarket chains. All of the big four British supermarkets (Tesco, Sainsbury's, Asda and Safeway) were offering Fair Trade products by 2001 and general Fair Trade products are now widely available in supermarkets throughout Europe, including Migros and the Co-op in Switzerland, Ahold in the Netherlands and Carrefour and Monoprix in France. In the USA, natural food and speciality chains like Wild Oats Markets and Starbucks carry Fair Trade products, with larger supermarket chains gradually introducing them. Retail distribution is discussed further in Chapter 8.

Social network theory offers insights into this second phase of Fair Trade marketing via the commodity network literature (Hughes, 2000; Leslie and Reimer, 1999; Raynolds,

2002a). Hughes, for instance, in her examination of the power of UK retailers to drive change in the Kenyan cut flower trade, suggests that conceptualizing around the network overcomes limitations of uni-directionality and linearity present in commodity chain studies. She notes:

> While still recognising the existence of sets of actors (or nodes), whose work it is to shape the circulation of a particular commodity, the connections between these actors are seen as 'complex webs of interdependence' rather than fixed vertical and uni-directional relationships. (2000: 178)

Combining the perspective of networks with that of circuits of knowledge, she concludes, enables a better understanding of retailer power and the influence generated by their capitalization of knowledge (Hughes, 2000: 188). The integration of consumer variables (such as concepts of quality and lifestyle) into the information flows driving marketing communications in this second phase of Fair Trade marketing creates a marketing network similar to that developed in the MAN literature, where industrial buyers and sellers have a symbiotic relationship driven by mutual information exchange. The move from a uni-directional process focus for Fair Trade marketing towards a multi-dimensional product emphasis engaging the consumer mirrors the difference between commodity chains and commodity networks.

Arce and Marsden (1993) also acknowledge the limitations of commodity chain theory as being too structuralist and uni-directional by introducing consumption as a key element. Thus, the focus shifts to a theory that recognizes the importance of cultural and knowledge issues in defining the meanings of food. These consumption dynamics embrace issues regarding the healthiness of food as well as determinations of quality and value linked to the social and ethical actualities of agro-production. This approach also parallels the marketing developments noted above.

Finally, within a commodity network analysis it is interesting to note that, following Marsden (1992), Renard pointed out that 'quality, with its multiple dimensions and meanings, is the factor linking consumers, distributors and industrial and agricultural producers' (1999: 490), making explicit its role in creating the commodity network. Indeed, the search for quality and authenticity has generally been one of the demand-side drivers of alternative food networks (Whatmore, 1994; Whatmore et al., 2003).

Phase Three: Place Focus

The third phase of Fair Trade marketing communications in the UK aimed to broaden the target market yet further by addressing nearly half the population (49 per cent) in the segment described by Cowe and Williams (2000) as the 'do what I can' group. These consumers are typified by weak ethical concerns, but are still engaged with social and environmental issues, particularly those that affect their local area.

The marketing approach to this large segment represented a departure from the more conventional marketing communications discussed above and focussed instead on encouraging consumers to connect their local community with their ethical concerns. Market research demonstrated that many in this segment felt they lacked the power to change things as individuals, so it made logical sense to foster group action as a marketing strategy (Cowe and Williams, 2000). The marketing mechanism behind this new approach came in the form of developing criteria for activists thus gaining accreditation for their local area as a 'Fair Trade Town'. Starting in the small Lancashire town of Garstang in 2002, over 100 UK towns had gained accredited status by 2004 and several others were actively pursuing the goal (see Image 7.6). The Fair Trade Town phenomenon is also found in France and is being explored in Japan and Australia.

The accreditation criteria for a Fair Trade Town are defined as follows (Fairtrade Foundation, 2004c):

- The local council to pass a resolution supporting Fair Trade.
- A range of Fair Trade products to be made available in local shops and sold in at least two restaurants.
- Fair Trade products to be used by at least ten local businesses.
- Being able to attract local media coverage and support for the campaign.
- Being able to convene a local Fair Trade steering group to maintain an on-going commitment to Fair Trade.

Image 7.6 *Bruce Crowther (back left) celebrates Garstang's status as the world's first Fair Trade Town*

These guidelines encompass both educative and commercial aims and, above all, have a community dimension. This initiative aims to generate mass-market interest in Fair Trade through local organic growth and consumer 'word of mouth' activity. The Fair Trade Town campaign also specifically engages both multiple retailers and local small- and medium-sized enterprises (SMEs).

Subsequent to the success of the Fair Trade Towns campaign, a number of other community-based accreditation initiatives have been set in motion, including Fair Trade villages, Fair Trade churches and Fair Trade universities. The latter provides a marketing strategy to target the younger – often brand aware – consumers who can be very difficult to engage with on ethical issues (the 'brand generation' in Cowe and Williams's taxonomy, 2000).

The emergence of the Fair Trade Town concept, which ties the movement's ethical marketing stance to particular places, is of inherent interest. Moreover, while not indicative of typical urban marketing, it is instructive to consider its emergence in the context of more recent changes in place marketing thought and practice. Indeed, it has been suggested that developments in the practice of social marketing removed many of the objections and obstacles that place marketing might otherwise have faced (Ashworth and Voogd, 1990). Three issues, broadly concerned with questions about what is being marketed, by whom and to whom, are worthy of note here.

Firstly, it is important to recognize that the inspiration for Fair Trade Towns came not from the Fairtrade Foundation or one of the large ATOs, but from a local group in a small market town in Lancashire, England in 2001. The townspeople's initiative had its roots in a phase one marketing campaign to raise issue awareness of Fair Trade in their local area, seeking support from local politicians and business leaders. Only when the activities in Garstang gained wider notoriety did the Fairtrade Foundation launch a set of Fair Trade Town Goals and an Action Guide to encourage others to follow in Garstang's footsteps.

Secondly, promotion of the Fair Trade Town represents the use of place branding in a bid to attain social as well as economic goals. Whilst there is sometimes a (healthy) element of civic pride and local and regional competition driving the Fair Trade Towns, the message is primarily concerned with a social redistributive cause. The crucial community element comes from linkages with the producers themselves via the Fair Trade concept. This further reflects the notion of short supply chains mentioned above. Importantly, the community involvement encouraged by the Fair Trade Town initiative is not geographically limited, rather it embraces a model of social capital creation across national boundaries.

Putnam (2000) has explored the concept of social capital as being measurable benefits derived from human connectivity and community activity. Central to the idea of social capital is that economic and other advantages can be a consequence of improved social interaction. Putnam's research discerns a direct correlation between the popularity of group activities (clubs, societies, community events and so on) and other social trends such as voting patterns, education standards, health metrics and the like. The conclusion is that social linkages are beneficial to society as a whole. However, Putnam's work focuses on the relationship between such activities in individual countries. Through a commodity network analysis of Fair Trade community initiatives, social capital can be understood in a wider global context. Namely, local activities can resonate throughout the network to generate social capital not only in the local community, but also in the far distant producer community as well. This is Putnam's 'briding' social capital writ large.

Thirdly, the promotion of Fair Trade Towns is potentially complicated by difficulties in defining the urban product. This issue is common to many place marketing and branding exercises (Ashworth and Voogd, 1990; Warnaby, 1998). A number of factors are relevant here. For instance, the city 'product' comprises both the holistic entity and the specific services, attributes and facilities therein; the consumer assembles the urban product from the variety of services and experiences available; places are multi-sold in different ways and to different consumers, often simultaneously (Ashworth and Voogd, 1990). The Fair Trade message, like others, is in danger of being lost or at least diluted by competing communications (images of Garstang vs. Ghana, for instance) and perceptions. Consequently, care must be taken to avoid an unmanaged profusion of Fair Trade symbols and branding, leading to a loss of consumer interest and trust (Renard, 2002).

The targets of place marketing are typically considered to include business investors, new residents and tourists. The Fair Trade Town initiative epitomizes the town as a place of consumption, albeit of a particular type. Whilst attracting additional tourist and shopper spend may provide some limited economic motive for Fair Trade Towns, the place marketing message's main target would appear to be local citizens. Healy (1994) noted that citizens can represent an important target of place marketing, with objectives including the obtaining of support for a cause and changing their behaviour. This would seem to be the case here. Additionally, as accounts of Fair Trade Towns implicitly suggest, it is important not to underestimate the significance of the reflexive nature of the consumption process in generating a noted 'feel-good factor' (see further, Fairtrade Foundation, 2004). Here also Fair Trade brands 'function as a "mirror" for the consumer in securing the benefits of self-expression and positive social identity' (Zadek et al., 1998; quoted in Raynolds, 2002a: 415).

Actor Network Theory (ANT) provides a useful theorization of this third phase of Fair Trade marketing. This model focuses on the process of exchange, not the structure of exchange relationships – it is not concerned with the relationships between identified entities but rather about how relationships define the entities themselves (Callon, 1986, 1991, 1999; Latour, 1993; Law, 1986, 1992, 1994). These entities include both human (people) and non-human actants (money, texts, machines) that act as intermediaries in constructing the network. In the Fair Trade Town example, non-human actants such as geographical spaces and identities become interwoven into the network of meanings that define Fair Trade marketing at a civic level (see below, Example of a Council Motion Supporting Fair Trade).

Example of a Council Motion Supporting Fair Trade

WHY

[Name of council], as an important consumer and opinion leader, should research, develop, and support a strategy to facilitate the promotion and purchase of foods with the Fair Trade Mark as part of its commitment to [document/advice paper] and in pursuit of sustainable development and to give marginalized producers a fair deal.

AIM

To be recognized by the residents and business community of [name of city/town], suppliers, employees and other local authorities, as a city/town that actively supports and promotes Fair Trade and to increase the sale of products with the Fair Trade Mark. [Name of council] resolves to contribute to the campaign to increase sales of products with the Fair Trade Mark by striving to achieve Fair Trade status for [name of council] as detailed in the Fairtrade Foundation's Fair Trade Towns Initiative.

The initiative involves a commitment to:

- Widely offer Fair Trade Marked food and drink options internally and make them available for internal meetings.
- Promote the Fair Trade Mark using Fairtrade Foundation materials in refreshment areas and promoting the Fair Trade Towns initiative in internal communications and external newsletters.

- Use influence to urge local retailers to provide Fair Trade options for residents.
- Use influence to urge local business to offer Fair Trade options to their staff and promote the Fair Trade Mark internally.
- Engage in a media campaign to publicize the Fair Trade Town initiative.
- Allocate responsibility for progression of the Fair Trade Town initiative to a member or group of staff.
- Organize events and publicity during national Fair Trade Fortnight – the annual national campaign to promote sales of products with the Fair Trade Mark.

Source: http://www.fairtrade.org.uk/downloads/pdf/towns_council_motion.pdf

Power within the actor network goes beyond the simple determinism of structural sociology and is contingent on the network effect itself creating patterns of agency (Araujo and Easton, 1996). Thus, the Fair Trade Town defines itself in its connectedness with Fair Trade values, but also contributes to them as a marketing communications agent. Crucially, both share a social dimension, although ANT rejects the concept of social embeddedness (Granovetter, 1985) as providing a stable background to economic activity, arguing instead that social and economic relations are mutually implicit and symmetrically linked (Law, 1994). Thus, Fair Trade economics provides a good example of the social redefining the economic (something shared with convention theory; Renard, 2002).

Callon and Law's (1992) concept of network intermediaries created by the interactions of network actors and defining and ordering the networks they describe also defines the marketing information flows so crucial to Fair Trade communications concretized in certification, labelling and supplier narratives, as well as civic signage and Fair Trade events. As has been noted above, it is significant that the Fair Trade Town marketing initiative grew up from grass-roots activism and, thus, represents a good example of a marketing 'network intermediary' process. The local dynamism that drives these campaigns fits well with Whatmore and Thorne's description of an ANT approach to analysis that elaborates 'an understanding of global networks as performative orderings (always in the making), rather than as systemic entities (always already constituted)' (1997: 289). Furthermore, the same paper's ANT analysis of Fair Trade supply chains also clearly applies to the place-marketing of the end products: 'alternative geographies of food are located in the political competence and social agency of individuals, institutions, and alliances, enacting a variety of partial knowledges and strategic interests through networks which simultaneously involve a "lengthening" of spatial and institutional reach and a "strengthening" of environmental and social embeddedness' (1997: 294–5).

ANTs are often built around 'modes of ordering of connectivity' rather than causal links: Fair Trade offers just such a patterning, being 'explicitly oriented towards enacting an alternative commodity network' (p. 295). In their case study on Cafédirect, Whatmore and Thorne explore the importance of strengthening the connectivities across a Fair Trade network to empower the formerly passive actants in the network (that is, growers and producers), noting that this is achieved by Fair Trade organizations, which 'must make concrete the telling and performing of connectivity and fairness in the hybrid network' (1997: 299). Again, Fair Trade Towns show powerful network effects in their enactment of the linkages between producer and consumer via both human and non-human nodes, intermediaries and the interactions between them (this parallels an ANT analysis of organic products that are sensitive to the interactions between human society and Nature).

Indeed, within ANT, Callon (1991) proposed that a network 'heavy with norms' may become assimilated into a 'black box' that reduces its complexity and serves to 'shed its history'. Thus a complex agri-food network encompassing many actors may be reduced to a simple commodity network structure, 'if a network acts as a single block, then it disappears, to be replaced by the action itself and the seemingly simple author of that action' (Law, 1992: 382). Goodman (1999) suggests that the black box of modern agri-networks has been exploded by the public demand for supply chain information resultant from food scares such as the outbreak of Bovine Spongiform Encephalopathy (BSE) in the UK. The same approach can be taken in understanding Fair Trade marketing.

Similarly, Goodman also notes that the marketing of organic food deliberately exposes the 'constituent metabolic relations' that make up its production network, in stark contrast to the 'black boxing' of traditional agribusiness. This serves to give 'transparency to the complex material, eco-social, and discursive practices that bring food from the land to the table in the routine context of everyday life' (1999: 33) and allows consumers to make personal and political choices in their food consumption. Whilst Goodman is primarily interested in reuniting society and nature via an ANT theorization, the same approach also allows Fair Trade to be understood as a retranslation of the industrial agri-network paradigm into a network that redefines the economic and power directionality of its connectivities from uni- to multi-directional. Developmental agendas form a key node in the Fair Trade network via which financial as well as informational flows link producer and consumer. That many Fair Trade products are also organic underlines the validity of an ANT analytical approach.

It is striking how closely social exchange models fit the developmental pattern of Fair Trade marketing to date. In network terms, there has been a marketing shift from the dominant node in network being the producer (encapsulated in a focus on process) and the approach being driven by a reliance on a commodity chain conceptualization, to the dominant node being the retailer/consumer (a product focus) within a commodity network model and then to the dominant node being the consumer/retailer (a place focus) best seen in an actor network context. This shift can be explained by the development of target markets that have redefined at each stage what the key information flows are and who the key network actants may be. Fair Trade marketing has developed as the full scope and potential of the Fair Trade commodity network has been understood. An ANT reading of the development of Fair Trade marketing thus far suggests that the core concept of consumer-producer connectivity has been extended to fresh market segments by identifying new nodes within the extant, but emergent, network and making strategic use of the information flows across them.

CONCLUSION

This chapter has argued that Fair Trade marketing has at its core the reconnection of producer and consumer via the communication of information flows. The key differences between Fair Trade and conventional marketing have been demonstrated in terms of positioning, the marketing process, branding and marketing communications. This chapter has suggested that, in its most developed markets, Fair Trade has gone through three discernible phases focussed on process, product and place, as it has grown its target markets (for a summary, see Table 7.5). A variety of approaches within social network theory have been used to explore these three phases and to illuminate the functional attributes of individual marketing strategies.

For all the significant differences between Fair Trade and conventional marketing, both share a need for constant innovation and sensitivity to consumer demand. In the former case, an ethical agenda that brings the world closer together through a new form of trade provides a compelling case for driving the marketing concept forward.

The first three chapters of this book introduced the concept of Fair Trade and placed its development as an economic model within the broader ethical consumer movement. This second part has examined how the Fair Trade system works in practice, focusing on how its structures and strategies, including certification, have changed to accommodate growth and the entry of new players, as well as examining challenges to that growth such as access to finance. This chapter has set out the marketing context for Fair Trade and concludes Part Two of this book.

The final part of this book looks at the increasing impact of Fair Trade globally and outlines important future issues. Chapter 8 builds on the strategic overview given here and considers the Fair Trade customer in more detail. It then goes on to set out the global markets for Fair Trade products.

PART THREE

The Impact of Fair Trade

8

The Fair Trade Market

Part Three of this book considers the growing impact of Fair Trade and plots its likely onward course, including a discussion of the important challenges facing it in the next ten years. This chapter begins by considering the significant shift towards ethical consumption that is evident in many developed countries. As part of this analysis it identifies who are the ethical consumers and how the Fair Trade consumer fits within this larger grouping. The chapter goes on to outline the extent of global Fair Trade sales and then conducts a country-by-country survey of the key markets. Next, the structure of the distribution channels for Fair Trade retailing is set out with a particular note on retailer end-pricing. The chapter ends with a short look at future market growth.

INTRODUCTION: THE RISE OF ETHICAL CONSUMPTION

The idea of 'ethical' consumption is not new. Lang and Hines (1993) identified three waves of consumerism culminating in ethical awareness. The first wave focussed on value for money, basic product information and reliable labelling. The second concentrated on consumer safety and manufacturer accountability. The third, and most recent, introduced environmental and ethical issues linked to notions of corporate citizenship and social responsibility. This latter wave is characterized by consumer awareness of animal welfare, environmental degradation and human working conditions and trade justice.

In another historical survey, Cowe and Williams (2000) identified four streams of ethical innovation emerging in the UK from 1800 to the present day (in roughly chronological order): human rights; animal rights; consumer protection; and environmentalism. Each of these four themes has had a major impact on the practice of retail exchange.

In 1844 the 'Rochdale Pioneers' developed the first operational model of co-operative retailing in Northern England that clearly recognized the need for an approach to business exchange that was not driven solely by the demands of capital but also by human rights and social justice. The co-operative organizational form subsequently went on to become the most widely distributed business structure in the world, ranging from retail giants like the John Lewis Partnership, to tiny producer groups in developing countries.

The Royal Society for the Prevention of Cruelty to Animals (RSPCA) came into being in 1840 and effectively sensitized the public to an issue that would lead directly to the anti-animal testing agenda championed with great commercial success by the Body Shop in the 1980s and 1990s. Such has been the public engagement with animal welfare that the majority of cosmetics firms now completely avoid testing their products on animals.

Indeed, the effect of RSPCA campaigning also encouraged significant changes in livestock husbandry, something accelerated by public demand for free-range and organic products.

In the 1960s, with the rise of the 'consumerist' movement, the power relationship between retailer and shopper, typically tilted heavily towards the former, began to balance out. Critical analyses of retail marketing, notably Vance Packard's seminal work *The Hidden Persuaders* (1957), further encouraged consumers to question the authenticity of what was presented to them in advertising and to demand to know more of the 'truth' about goods and services. As more information about these aspects has become available through third party campaigners and news providers (often via the Internet), manufacturers and retailers have increasingly lost control of their carefully-bounded marketing positioning of products. In many cases, the result has been a move towards more values-driven marketing that acknowledges the consumer as an informed and involved participant in the exchange process. Ironically, however, much of this shift has been achieved through more sophisticated lifestyle branding that, when successful, often allows manufacturers and retailers to develop customer loyalty to a point where the consumer's control of the terms of the exchange agenda actually diminishes. A good example is Nike, a company that has received significant criticism for its use of child labour in third-party suppliers, but which has, nevertheless, created a sufficiently strong brand largely to survive such bad press.

Finally, the environmentalism that was evident in the Victorian passion for parks (the UK Open Spaces and Footpaths Preservation Society was founded in 1865) later evolved into a retail agenda with the foundation of the Soil Association in 1946. The latter encouraged the production and sale of organic produce through campaigning and, more recently, the development of a widely recognized certification system to reassure consumers of the authenticity of organic products. The growth in sales of organic produce had been prodigious in recent years such that, in 2003, the world organic market amounted to over £17.5bn ($31.3bn) (Guardian/ICM, 2004).

Today, the total market for ethical goods and services is growing across all developed countries, in some regions by as much as 20 per cent per annum (NEF, 2001, 2004a) and a recent UK survey suggested that 65 per cent of consumers now judge themselves 'green or ethical consumers' (Guardian/ICM, 2004). Such products may be defined as supporting one of the four ethical themes suggested by Cowe and Williams and may include ethical banking, responsible tourism, recyclable or 'green' goods and developmental aid/poverty reduction through Fair Trade. According to the Co-operative Bank/NEF (2003), the UK ethical market was valued at £19.9bn ($35.6bn) in 2002 with products specifically marketed as 'ethical' accounting for £6.9bn ($12.4bn) (a 13 per cent increase on 2001). As an example, free range eggs accounted for 40 per cent of all UK retail egg sales in 2002. Consumer guides to ethical shopping are also becoming popular (see for example, Elkington and Hailes, 1989; Young and Welford, 2002).

Increasingly, the focus for the consumer is now on the production processes involved for final goods and services, as well as their more traditional selling points of quality and value (see Chapter 7 for a wider discussion of the development of Fair Trade marketing). Whether it be the clothes they wear, the food they eat, or the money they invest, consumers want to know more about the context and history of their consumption choices and are increasingly prepared to vote via their custom against unethical or opaque providers. In the 1980s 'green' or environmentally friendly products and services gained notoriety and market share. In the 1990s sales of organic and non-genetically modified produce grew exponentially, particularly in Europe; the USA has seen a 21 per cent increase in organic sales from 1997 to 2002 and growth is projected to continue at that rate through to 2007 (Organic Trade Association, 2004). However, since the mid-1990s it has been Fair Trade goods that have dominated the ethical consumption discussion (Strong, 1996).

UK consumer surveys show an increasing concern for the plight of producers in developing countries. The Co-operative Group/MORI survey, 'Shopping with Attitude' (Co-operative Group/MORI, 2004), consulted over 30,000 consumers and found that 80 per cent of the sample felt that retailers should help growers in developing countries (up from 55 per cent in the same survey from 1994). Indeed, six out of ten said that they would actively boycott unethical products. Respondents particularly highlighted the importance of complete product information on food labels (96 per cent felt that such information was needed) – something clearly supported by the Soil Association label for organic products and the Fairtrade Foundation mark.

The survey also showed that 43 per cent of those questioned put 'ensuring a fair deal for growers in developing countries' as one of their top three priorities from a super-market (13 per cent put it as their number one priority), with eight out of ten support-ing the specific proposition that retailers should stock more products that help people in developing countries improve their standard of living. Furthermore, there has also been a significant increase in the willingness of consumers to pay more for such ethical prod-ucts (84 per cent of the sample in 2004, up from 62 per cent in 1994). From the evi-dence obtained by this extensive piece of market research it is clear that there is a growing market opportunity both for the development of more Fair Trade products and for supermarkets to engage with Fair Trade more extensively through increased listings and the development of own-label options (see the Tesco case study).

CASE STUDY: THE DEVELOPMENT OF TESCO'S FAIR TRADE OWN-LABEL

Tesco PLC is currently the leading supermarket in the UK, with over 13 million customers coming through its doors each week. In March 2004, to coincide with the tenth anniversary of the first Fair Trade Fortnight in the UK, Tesco launched its own-label range of Fair Trade products in 500 supermarkets, adding 20 new lines to its overall offer. This completed a process of broadening the company's commitment to Fair Trade that had seen 60 new lines added since March 2003 (to a market-leading total of 91 lines). This strategy grew Tesco's share of the UK Fair Trade market from 12 per cent to 32 per cent in a year, making them the largest Fair Trade retailer in the country. Tesco's annual Fair Trade sales for 2003–4 amounted to £24.7m ($44m).

The results of the own-label launch were spectacular: sales for the two weeks of Fair Trade Fortnight were £1.3m ($2.3m), an 86 per cent increase on 2003 and 161 per cent on 2002. Sales of Fair Trade roses – a category Tesco created in the UK – were £323,000 alone ($578,000) during the fortnight, amounting to 800,000 stems nation-ally. The promotional strategy during Fair Trade Fortnight 2004 also reflected the higher strategic value of the range, as it shifted from a '20 per cent off' mechanic with no fixture end displays in 2003 to a 'multi-buy' approach exploiting fixture end 'hot spots' in 2004.

Tesco's decision to develop a range of own-label Fair Trade products can be seen as a major step forward in the Fair Trade movement's scaling strategy. According to Hamish Renton, Product Manager for Fair Trade at the chain, the move to increase Tesco's commitment to Fair Trade (and particularly to develop an own-label range) was driven by three sound business factors: customer demand, a commercial opportunity and brand value.

As far as customer demand is concerned there were two issues. Firstly, Tesco identified a growing interest in Fair Trade from its existing customers buying manufacturer-branded merchandise and wanted to offer this group the best range on the high street. Secondly, developing Tesco own-label Fair Trade offered the middle market and less affluent customers product choices that would grow the overall market (lower pricing leading to larger volumes). The latter was firmly underlined by customer research that demonstrated a 60 per cent growth in first-time buyers of Fair Trade during Fair Trade Fortnight 2004. Furthermore, the move to own-label allowed Tesco to outperform the overall Fair Trade market in value growth by 53 per cent during this period and by 40 per cent subsequently.

The commercial opportunity reflected Tesco's strategic commitment to serve all its customers better than its retail competitors. Thus, winning and maintaining loyalty could be achieved through the differentiation of service and product offers. Furthermore, history demonstrated that following its customers into new product areas had been a successful policy for growing the business overall in the UK (examples included segmenting the extremes of the market with Tesco's *finest and Value ranges and niche opportunities in organic, gluten-free and 'healthy living' ranges). In the 18 weeks prior to May 2004, Tesco's own-label Fair Trade products sold over a million units and were purchased by over 700,000 customers. Overall customer penetration was around five per cent.

Finally, Tesco believed that developing own-label Fair Trade products in tandem with the Fairtrade Foundation offered an opportunity to reinforce the firm's commitment to their Corporate Social Responsibility (CSR) policy and to highlight their ethical credentials. Such a move represented a proactive approach to CSR that complemented other Tesco initiatives (for example, its 'Computers for Schools' voucher programme).

In terms of positioning, the marketing of Fair Trade own-label reflected a similar demographic to the *finest range, aiming primarily at AB1 customers. Indeed, its packaging deliberately mirrored the look of *finest, reversing its colour scheme of black print on silver. The promotional material that accompanied the launch focussed on quality and exclusivity whilst also emphasizing the geographical origins of the products with a stylized 'product map'. The meaning of Fair Trade was explained in information boxes, and producer stories and photographs were also included to highlight the human dimension of Fair Trade purchases.

The initial impact of Tesco own-label in Fair Trade Fortnight was considerable and the subsequent sales picture is equally encouraging. For example, sales of own-label roast and ground coffee have continued to maintain the same level of performance achieved during the promotional period of Fair Trade Fortnight. It would seem, therefore, that new Fair Trade customers are being converted into regular Fair Trade customers. Furthermore, there is no evidence that own label has cannibalized sales from manufacturer brands such as Cafédirect (indeed, Cafédirect outperformed the overall sales growth of all Fair Trade products in Fair Trade Fortnight 2004).

Tesco clearly views the expansion of its Fair Trade range as a success. However, a number of issues have arisen for the future. Tesco plans to expand its own-label offer (and to aim for more 'exclusives' beyond cut flowers), but is constrained by the relative slowness of the Fairtrade Labelling Organizations' international certification process. Thus, current market opportunities in other categories such as fish, spirits and rice may well be missed. Furthermore, in order to expand the customer base beyond the traditional Fair Trade customer there would need to be some flexibility in the mechanics of the price floor for producers, to allow for lower-quality lower-priced Fair Trade goods (whilst still delivering to producers a fair price for the given quality). However, any attempt to flex FLO's minimum prices would be highly controversial (witness Ahold's approach in its Utz Kapeh brand) and is unlikely to be supported by the FLO in the short term. Finally, there is currently some evidence of double-auditing costs for growers attached to Fair Trade lines that are also organic – this adds unnecessarily to the final price. Tesco's have encouraged FLO and the Soil Association to begin a dialogue to explore collaboration on auditing.

Tesco's involvement in Fair Trade has grown the UK market significantly. However, their role has also been controversial. As a powerful multinational Tesco are seen as the problem, rather than the solution, by some activists and campaigners. The corporate buying policies of the big supermarkets have been widely cited as one of the key contributory factors in driving down producer prices worldwide. The reach and power of multinational buyers has undoubtedly increased over the last twenty years and price deflation has become an accepted part of the UK grocery landscape (although costs have also decreased through greater IT and logistical efficiencies). Nevertheless, multinational retailers today offer unprecedented market access to those with whom they trade as well as the benefit of their overall brand values. Working with rather than against them is certainly the fastest way to grow Fair Trade sales.

Whilst the retail price of Fair Trade goods has no influence on the fixed payments that the growers and workers receive at the start of the supply chain, a second damaging criticism was voiced most recently by *The Wall Street Journal* (Stecklow and White, 2004) when it criticized retailers for exploiting ethical consumers by pushing up their margins on organic and Fair Trade lines where there is significant price elasticity. The article pointed out that Tesco Fair Trade decaffeinated coffee sold at a 46 per cent premium against conventional decaff: this translated into an additional cost to the consumer of $3.46 (£1.94) per pound for the Fair Trade coffee which cost only $0.44 (£0.30) per pound extra to buy (that is, the Fair Trade premium to the producer).

However, Tesco's Fair Trade pricing on manufacturer lines and non-labelled products (such as fruit) remains the cheapest in the UK marketplace and includes significant margin flexibility to reflect competitive forces. Tesco aims to make a return to shareholders across the balance of the groceries that it sells and does not reveal data on individual lines. The position on own-label, however, is less clear. For example, the UK Co-operative Group's own-label coffee undersells Tesco's significantly (see Table 8.10). Nevertheless, according to Renton, Tesco Fair Trade lines generally do not attract a margin premium at all. Indeed, there is evidence that the Co-operative Group's pricing of Fair Trade deliberately cross-subsidizes the range using other full margin lines as part of a strategic decision to support the growth of ethical shopping (Nicholls, 2004).

Source: Interview with Hamish Renton (2004)

THE ETHICAL CONSUMER

It is evident that the market for ethical goods and services is growing fast, with this rise largely demand-driven. Nevertheless for the future development of the ethical market more strategic supply-oriented decisions will need to be made. Therefore, the key questions for the Fair Trade movement are: who are the ethical consumers that are driving growth, and how can they be segmented to generate future growth opportunities? Cowe and Williams (2000) specifically addressed the first question through research that combined qualitative data from four focus groups and quantitative data from an intercept survey of 2,000 people in the UK. Their survey unearthed five consumer segments, three of which offer significant opportunities for ethical products and Fair Trade (see Table 8.1). What is, perhaps, most interesting is that all five groups cut across most conventional socio-political boundaries and to some extent are made up of a mix of supporters from all the main political parties.

The two most promising segments for future growth are Global Watchdogs and Conscientious Consumers, accounting for 23 per cent of the total sample. These figures broadly agree with data from the USA that suggest that 32 per cent of consumers may be categorized as 'LOHAS' or 'lifestyles of health and sustainability' (McLaughlin, 2004). This group has been one of the targets for US Fair Traders. However, the largest grouping – 'Do What I Can' (49 per cent) – also has some potential. In total, therefore, ethical products could reasonably target a possible market of up to 72 per cent of the population in developed countries.

Table 8.1   *Who are ethical consumers?*

Segment	Characteristics	Total market share (%)
Global watchdogs	Ethical hardliners. Affluent professionals typically 35–55 years old, well-educated, metropolitan and mainly South East based (particularly London), feel powerful as consumers.	5
Brand generation	Ethical issues secondary to brand, but can augment brand value. Young (one third are under 25), often students, tend to rent housing, Midlands/North based, aware of their power as consumers, but only occasionally use it.	6
Conscientious consumers	Driven primarily by value and quality (defined to include ethics as one variable). Relatively up-market, not brand aware, conservative. Midlands and South East based (not London), feel some power as consumers.	18
'Look after my own'	Little ethical motivation. Young, on low incomes, typically live in the North and Scotland, high percentage of unemployed, often feel powerless as consumers.	22
'Do what I can'	Weak ethical motivation (but still present). Older (a quarter over 65), home owners, typically live outside London, sometimes feel powerless as consumers.	49

Source: Cowe and Williams (2000)

Cowe and Williams (2000) note that although their survey evidence suggests that approximately 30 per cent of the population is particularly motivated to buy ethical goods and services, such products typically account for only 1–3 per cent of their individual markets. Consequently, an 'ethical gap' may be discerned between consumer preference and action. Cowe and Williams (2000) term this the '30:3 syndrome'. They go on to propose that the main reason behind this is a pervading sense of powerlessness, felt by many consumers, in terms of making a real difference to the world through their consumption choices (only 11 per cent of their sample strongly believed that they could effect change).

However, a range of other key issues may be discerned here. For example, an equally significant driver behind the '30:3 syndrome' is the lack of co-ordinated ranges of easily available ethical products priced for mass-market consumption (see further Nicholls, 2002). Thus, although Mintel (2004) research suggested that in 2003 28.3 per cent of consumers bought Fair Trade products when available, such purchases are not always straightforward. For example, for several years supporting Fair Trade by buying certified products was very difficult for UK consumers who did not drink tea or coffee. Moreover, it is only in the last three years that all the major supermarkets have listings for Fair Trade items. Indeed, even as Fair Trade ranges and retail availability have grown, the premium price of most products has effectively excluded many consumers. However, this may be changing as a recent survey reported that 74 per cent of their sample said they would pay more for Fair Trade products (Guardian/ICM, 2004).

Furthermore, ethical goods and services are rarely supported by extensive marketing communications and, therefore, often fail to build any competitive brand presence (Cafédirect is a notable exception). In the face of both incessant marketing noise from competing products and increasingly marketing literate consumers, this becomes a major disadvantage in growing the ethical market.

Finally, an important caveat for Fair Trade marketing communications lies in questioning the assumption of a linear relationship between awareness and action in the ethical decision-making process. In reality, there is a very complex series of connections between awareness, concern and action that are shaped by many internal (personality, attitudes) and external (peer group, competitive marketing 'noise') influences (Tallontire et al., 2001: 19–21). For example, Newholm (1999) identified three categories of ethical consumer:

- *Distancers*: these consumers adopt a negative screening approach and avoid or boycott products they perceive to be unethical.

- *Integrators*: these consumers attempt to integrate ethical purchase behaviour fully into their lifestyle and have an holistic view of their own ethical actions.

- *Rationalizers*: these consumers limit their ethical purchases to extreme cases and distinct parts of their life and, whilst showing concern for issues, rarely sacrifice quality, choice or pleasure.

Such research questions assumptions about a single normative and rational 'ethical' consumer. Furthermore, in a largely qualitative study, Shaw and Clarke (1999) suggested that belief formation was the key to understanding ethical purchase behaviours. Their research also highlighted the complexity of the ethical decision-making process and how contingent it is on multiple variables beyond the control of marketing communications.

In conclusion, what is clear from the survey work done so far is that there is a substantial market for ethical goods in the UK, possibly representing up to three quarters of the population. However, as has been discussed in Chapter 7, accessing the full commercial potential of this market remains difficult and will require co-ordinated and strategic thinking from the supply side to counter competitive forces that may ultimately impede continued exponential growth.

THE FAIR TRADE CONSUMER

There is currently a limited amount of research on the profile of the 'typical' Fair Trade consumer. Furthermore, what is available is largely based on surveys of British consumers only. Consequently, this section will focus mainly on the UK. Nevertheless, the broad characteristics identified below are clearly applicable across most developed countries, albeit with certain cultural biases (such as the UK's curious attachment to the concept of 'fair play').

The general profile of a typical UK Fair Trade consumer – at least in terms of awareness of the certification mark – fits closely with the characteristics of Cowe and Williams's (2000) 'Global Watchdogs' segment. According to a recent Fairtrade Foundation/MORI weighted survey of over 2000 consumers (Fairtrade Foundation/MORI, 2004), UK Fair Trade awareness remains highest amongst the 'AB1' demographic group (at 54 per cent) characterized by well-educated and affluent consumers. Awareness is also highest amongst 45–54-year-olds (47 per cent). In common with other survey work on ethical consumption generally (Mintel, 1999, 2001, 2004), women (42 per cent) are more likely than men (35 per cent) to be aware of the Fair Trade mark. Thus, the idealized Fair Trade composite consumer is a middle-aged, affluent and degree-educated woman. It is, therefore, unsurprising that Waitrose was the first major supermarket to engage with Fair Trade (after the naturally sympathetic Co-operative Group) given that this profile also fits its main target customer.

However, there is also good evidence that awareness is growing amongst younger people and consumers on lower incomes. Amongst the former are many students advocating the exclusive use of Fair Trade on their campuses. In the UK, Oxford Brookes University became the first 'Fair Trade University' in 2003, certified as such by the Fairtrade Foundation with criteria based around its highly successful Fair Trade Towns initiative (see Oxford Brookes University, 2004). The University of Birmingham soon followed and ten others are currently applying for Fair Trade status. Similarly, in the USA two students from Harvard and New York University founded United Students for Fair Trade in 2003. This organization now has over 100 affiliated universities (Capone, 2004).

The Fairtrade Foundation (2003b) identified four levels of target consumer: core Fair Trade supporters; partial adopters; occasional conscience buyers; well-wishing bystanders. These correspond to three of Cowe and Williams's (2000) segments (see Table 8.2), suggesting that they amount to approximately 72 per cent of the total market (the maximum reach of ethical products already noted above).

This analysis confirms that there will also be a group of other consumers who may never be prepared to engage with Fair Trade (probably amounting to roughly 30 per cent of the

Table 8.2   *Fair Trade consumers*

Fairtrade Foundation (2003)	Cowe and Williams (2000)
Core supporters	Global watchdogs
Partial adopters	Conscientious consumers
Occasional conscience buyers	Conscientious consumers
Well-wishing bystanders	'Do what I can'

Table 8.3   *Public responses to the Fair Trade mark*

	2001	2002	2003	2004
Recognizes Fair Trade mark	16%	20%	25%	39%
Understands meaning of the Fair Trade mark				
(of the proportion who recognize the mark)	19%	24%	33%	42%

Source: Fairtrade Foundation/MORI (2004)

population), even if it gains mainstream acceptance. Key reasons for this segment to reject Fair Trade might include its price premium or the influence of individual attitudinal variants (such as a personal or political objection to, or mistrust of, Fair Trade principles).

Despite good evidence of the '30:3 syndrome' continuing today across the broad ethical market, there is some suggestion that at least in terms of Fair Trade things are changing. A Guardian/ICM (2004) poll recently demonstrated that 41 per cent of their sample reported that they have bought Fair Trade food 'in the past month'. One of the key strategic aims of the Fair Trade movement had been to employ marketing communications aimed at raising awareness of Fair Trade products, rather than specifically brand building. This targeted approach appears to be having a demonstrably positive effect on sales, with coffee particularly moving beyond the 30:3 watershed.

The Fairtrade Foundation has focussed on the raising awareness agenda through various marketing channels, perhaps most successfully in the annual Fair Trade Fortnight promotion. As a result of such activities in the UK over the past ten years, recognition of the Fair Trade mark in 2004 has grown to 39 per cent of the population from 25 per cent in 2003 (see Table 8.3). Furthermore, of those who recognized the mark, the proportion understanding that it represents the statement 'Fair Trade guarantees a better deal for Third World producers' also grew to 42 per cent (from 33 per cent in 2003). It would appear, therefore, that two of the prime aims of Fair Trade marketing communications – to raise issues awareness and to build the Fair Trade mark as a brand symbol – are gradually proving to be effective.

According to research by Leatherhead Food International (2003), other Fair Trade Labelling Organization members (for example, Max Havelaar in Switzerland) have also made good progress in raising awareness levels in several other European countries (see Table 8.4).

In the USA, there is also some evidence of a growth in consumer awareness of Fair Trade. The US National Coffee Association reported that awareness of Fair Trade brands amongst coffee consumers aged 18 and over had risen to 12 per cent in 2004 (from 7 per cent in 2003). With those who are aware of Fair Trade, purchase rates also increased, from 38 per cent in 2003 to 45 per cent in 2004 (Coelho, 2004).

Maria Elustondo, Consumer Goods Analyst at Mintel market research, confirms this general trend:

Table 8.4   *Fair Trade awareness levels in Europe (2002)*

Country	Percentage of population aware of Fair Trade
Switzerland	42%
Germany	40%
Austria	38%
France	34%
UK	24%

Source: Leatherhead Food International (2003)

> It is clear that an increasing number of consumers are thinking more about their relationship with the primary producers of the food they eat and about the conditions in which the food is prepared. This concern also implies that media and PR campaigns have succeeded in raising awareness to a point that consumers now feel confident in exercising their economic power over ethical issues. (*Gazette*, 2004)

There is a process of 'normalization' in evidence for Fair Trade as consumer perception has changed from seeing Fair Trade products as marginal and poor quality to viewing them as mainstream and high quality. Perceptions of the natural locus of Fair Trade have fuelled this change as products have grown out of charity shop/alternative trading organization/church contexts into high street supermarkets and up-market coffee houses such as Costa Coffee and Starbucks which opened in 2000, and Prêt à Manger which opened in 2002. In tandem with this, growing public awareness of the impact and meaning of Fair Trade has also widened its acceptance. However, in order to capture the majority of the market, Fair Trade must continue to convert consumer good intentions into purchase behaviour. For the future, there are several marketing strategies for Fair Trade to pursue in order to maintain current levels of growth and exploit the significant untapped market represented by the 'Well Wishing Bystander/Do What I Can' consumer segment (see further Nicholls, 2002, 2004). Some of these are considered in the final chapter.

Having considered the context for the rise of Fair Trade consumption and outlined the profile of a typical consumer, this chapter will now set out the current market performance for Fair Trade products around the world.

THE GLOBAL FAIR TRADE MARKET

Global sales of all Fair Trade products amounted to approximately £500m ($895m) in 2003 (Vidal, 2004), up from an estimated £335m ($600m) in 2002 (Leatherhead Food International, 2003). This figure is projected to grow to over £1b ($1.79bn) by 2007 (Demetriou, 2003). Global sales of labelled Fair Trade goods grew by 42.3 per cent between 2002 and 2003 (IFAT, 2004a), up from £250m ($448m) (PWC, 2002) to £355m ($636m). Fair Trade now spans more than 390 producer organizations in 58 countries in Asia, Africa and Latin America, representing over 800,000 farmers and workers and their families. There are over 100 Fair Trade import organizations working with producer groups providing goods to consumers via over 45,000 sales outlets worldwide (PWC, 2002; Raynolds, 2002a). Today there are 5000 to 7000 Fair Trade products available in developed countries, although only 250 of these currently carry the Fair Trade certification mark (up from 130 in 2003). The bulk of the uncertified products are handicrafts. It is estimated that over 5 million people are benefiting from Fair Trade globally (Fairtrade Foundation, 2004a). In 2002, the Fair Trade price of coffee alone returned an additional £17m ($30m) to producers worldwide (FLO, 2003).

The European market grew to almost £400m ($716m) in 2003 (Vidal, 2004), a 30 per cent increase on 2002. The largest single market for Fair Trade is currently the UK, which generated £92.3m ($165m) of sales in 2003, a 450 per cent increase since 1998 (Fairtrade Foundation, 2004a). Switzerland, with a £50m ($90m) market in 2002 (Leatherhead Food International, 2003) moved nearly as much product in terms of volume (23,336 MT) as the UK (24,212 MT) (FLO, 2004). Other important markets in 2002 included Germany, with £49.4m ($88.4m) in sales, and the Netherlands, with £27m ($48m) (Leatherhead Food International, 2003). The fastest growing markets are Belgium, France and Italy (IFAT, 2004a). The USA and Japan, whilst offering significant market opportunities for Fair Trade, currently remain at an early stage of development. However, the USA is emerging as potentially the most important national market. Estimated total sales for 2003 in the USA will match the UK and at current growth rates should move ahead by 2004.

According to Leatherhead Food International (2003), globally, the most important Fair Trade product by volume has been bananas (62 per cent of the market in 2002) and by value has been coffee (worth £100m–140m [$179m–$251m] in 2002 or about a quarter of all sales). In terms of market share, the highest is the banana market in Switzerland (predicted to grow to over 50 per cent by 2004). In addition, Fair Trade roast and ground coffee has captured 18 per cent of the UK market and Fair Trade coffee in total currently has 3 per cent of the UK market (McCarthy, 2004). Cafédirect roast and ground coffee alone has now captured a notable 10 per cent of its market (Cafédirect, 2004). However, in general, Fair Trade products only account for between 1 and 4 per cent of their respective markets.

However, there has been a significant shift over the last five years in the product mix underpinning the overall global expansion of Fair Trade. According to Carol Wills, Executive Director of the International Federation of Alternative Trade (IFAT), whilst sales in Fair Trade crafts have remained steady, the overall market has expanded dramatically driven largely by commodity food lines. Ten years ago a sales value ratio of 80 per cent crafts/textiles to 20 per cent food was the norm, but these figures have now effectively reversed. Figures from the European Fair Trade Association (EFTA, 2001) confirm this. In a survey of its 11 constituent members, EFTA noted that handicrafts represented only 25.4 per cent of total sales value compared with 69.4 per cent for food (the balance is made up by Fair Trade literature and Northern products). The effect of this trend has been to encourage producers to move into commodity food lines where possible and to improve and consolidate their own marketing of craft products where a change is impractical. As Carol Wills noted when interviewed in 2004:

> So producers are organizing themselves ... for example, in Asia, the Asia Fair Trade Forum has now organized four Fair Trade pavilions at the Bangkok International Gift Fair, which is the biggest international gift fair in Asia – similar to Birmingham. So they have a Fair Trade pavilion funded by Oxfam in Asia or partly funded by Oxfam in Asia, which has been a good partnership. A huge Fair Trade pavilion in which maybe 12 or 16 organizations exhibit, and they decide between themselves who should be there, exhibit their work together with design help

to get it looking coherent, getting the colour co-ordinated and so on, and they are getting really good orders from commercial buyers.

Another strategy has been to re-examine the potential of local Southern hemisphere markets to reduce producer reliance on export markets. Wills commented:

> They are also doing much more in their own countries to sell locally to the growing middle classes and are looking for much more Southern trade.

Targeting local markets for Fair Trade offers an innovative grass-roots strategy to maximize the Fair Trade supplier base in a highly cost-effective way, as it does not rely on the intervention of Northern hemisphere wholesalers or retailers. Regional Fair Trade partnerships such as the Asia Fair Trade Forum have an important role to play in supporting a dual track approach to market development that both engages with the Fairtrade Labelling Organizations International's (FLO) registration and grows demand closer to home. IFAT is also actively supporting this empowerment of its considerable producer network.

NATIONAL SURVEY

The following section gives details of the main Fair Trade markets in the world (see Table 8.5). All the figures quoted in the country-by-country survey relate to sales of certified Fair Trade products only, unless otherwise stated. This clearly plays down total sales of Fair Trade products, but provides the most reliable data.

United Kingdom

The United Kingdom is currently the largest national market for Fair Trade in the world. In 1994, the total retail value of Fair Trade products was £2.75 m ($4.9m). This grew to

Table 8.5 *Largest national markets for Fair Trade 2001–2002*

Country	Sales 2001 (£m/US$m)	Sales 2002 (£m/US$m)	Number of shops (2001)	Per cent change
Austria	2.1/3.8	6.7–10.1/12–18.1	3000	219–381
Belgium	3.4/6.1	6.7–10.1/12–18.1	1700	94–197
Canada	3.7/6.6	5.5/9.9	N/A	67
Denmark	5.4/9.7	6.7/11.9	2750	24
France	12.1/21.7	18.8/33.7	9700	55
Germany	44.9/80.4	49.4/88.4	26200	10
Italy	4.5/8.1	6.0/10.7	3200	30
Netherlands	22.8/40.8	26.8/47.9	5400	17
Japan	25.9/46.4	32.4/57.9	N/A	25
Switzerland	35.1/62.8	50.4/90.2	2760	33
UK	50.5/90.4	63.0/112.8	8270	25
USA	38.3/68.3	58.5/104.5	8000	53

Source: Leatherhead Food International (2003) and Krier (2001)

Table 8.6 *UK retail sales of Fair Trade-labelled goods 1998–2002*

Product	Year					
	1998	**1999**	**2000**	**2001**	**2002**	**2003**
Coffee	13.7	15.0	15.5	18.6	23.1	34.3
Tea	2.0	4.5	5.1	5.9	7.2	9.5
Chocolate/Cocoa	1.0	2.3	3.6	6.0	7.0	10.9
Honey	n/a	<0.1	0.9	3.2	4.9	6.1
Bananas	n/a	n/a	7.8	14.6	17.3	24.3
Other (snacks, etc.)	n/a	n/a	n/a	2.2	3.5	7.2
Total (£m)	**16.7**	**21.8**	**32.9**	**50.5**	**63.0**	**92.3**
Total (US$m)	**29.9**	**39.0**	**58.9**	**90.4**	**112.8**	**165.2**

Source: Fairtrade Foundation (2004a)

£92.3m ($165m) by 2003, a rise of over 3000 per cent in nine years. Today, over 250 products from 100 companies carry the Fair Trade mark in the UK. It is estimated that UK Fair Trade sales in 2004 are running at over £100m per annum and have grown by over 300 per cent in five years (McCarthy, 2004). The most important categories are coffee, bananas and cocoa (see Table 8.6).

The Fair Trade market in the UK started out through a network of world shops and other ATOs offering fairly-traded handicrafts, coffee, tea and dried fruit. In 1979 Traidcraft launched a catalogue retail operation, but remained small-scale for a number of years. Nicaraguan Fair Trade coffee was consumed in the 1980s in support of the socialist and co-operative revolutionary activities in that country, but Fair Trade remained a fringe market until CAFOD, Christian Aid, Oxfam, Traidcraft Exchange and the World Development Movement formed the Fairtrade Foundation in the early 1990s. Green & Black's 'Maya Gold' chocolate became the first certified Fair Trade product in the UK in 1994; Clipper tea and Cafédirect roast and ground coffee and freeze dried instant coffee followed later the same year. Specialist Fair Trade suppliers continue to dominate the UK market today. There is little evidence yet of multinational players entering the market, although Nestlé has clearly been sounding out consumers by floating the possibility of launching an 'ethical' coffee to storms of protest from the Fairtrade Foundation (Drinks Business Review, 2004).

The Co-operative Group has been in the vanguard of UK supermarkets in supporting Fair Trade, introducing the first supermarket own-label Fair Trade product in the UK (milk chocolate) in 2000 and, with much fanfare, converting all its own-label coffee (2002) and then chocolate (2003) to Fair Trade. All four of the major UK supermarkets now offer Fair Trade products and two – Sainsbury's (since 2002) and Tesco (since 2004) – also offer own-label ranges (see further Jones et al., 2003). According to Vanessa Watson, Assistant to the Central Buyer of Fruit at Waitrose:

> Consumers are growing more and more interested in who produces the food they buy, as well as how it is produced, and the Fair Trade mark reassures the consumer that the producer has received a fair price. We are hoping to add more Fair Trade farmers to our supplier base as we believe it is a successful way of supporting producers, especially the smaller ones. (*Gazette*, 2004)

Maria Elustondo, Consumer Goods Analyst at Mintel market research, also highlighted the importance of UK supermarket support in the growth of Fair Trade:

Support for organic and Fair Trade food from leading retailers has been significant in stimulating the market. Ethical choices are now easier and more convenient for consumers to make. (*Gazette*, 2004)

In addition, more than 300 UK catering suppliers now offer Fair Trade products. Several large organizations such as the Salvation Army, the Youth Hostel Association and the British Medical Association have converted to Fair Trade. Political bodies have become interested as well. In 2004, the Office of Government Commerce issued guidelines on how government departments could procure Fair Trade foods.

According to research carried out by Leatherhead Food International (2003), UK penetration rates were particularly high in coffee (with 40 per cent of customers claiming to have bought Fair Trade at some point and 8 per cent claiming to buy it regularly) and bananas (36 per cent and 9 per cent). The strong support for Fair Trade in the UK would appear to be a product of cultural and historical factors. Amongst the former may be cited the UK's liberal and philanthropic traditions and concern for the poor. Amongst the latter, it should be noted that Fair Trade retailers, for instance ATOs and charities such as Oxfam, have been present on the UK high street for a generation and have a clearly defined position (although this is changing). Indeed, so strong is the British support for Fair Trade that 28 per cent of Leatherhead Food International's sample supported the notion that 'all products should be Fair Trade'.

The United States

The United States represent an important current and – more significantly – a potentially huge future market for Fair Trade. Certified sales for 2002 amounted to $105 million (£58.8m), a 53 per cent increase on 2001, making it the largest single national market in the world after the UK. Estimated sales for 2003 are $134m (£75m: see Table 8.7).

Until 1998, the Fair Trade movement in the USA consisted of a few alternative trading retailers such as Ten Thousand Villages – a chain of craft stores operated by the Mennonite Central Committee – and socially conscious coffee roasters who had been to visit coffee farmers in Latin America and had started direct relationships paying co-operatives internationally-recognized Fair Trade prices. The pioneering and most successful of these 'alternative' coffee roasters was Equal Exchange, founded in 1986. Equal Exchange, a worker-owned co-operative based just outside Boston, succeeded in selling Fair Trade coffee into hundreds of natural food stores in the USA and eventually launched a line of Fair Trade teas from co-operatives in Asia.

Third-party certification and labelling for Fair Trade practices, however, remained non-existent in the USA until 1998, when Paul Rice was made Executive Director of TransFair USA, the only FLO member and labelling initiative in the USA. Rice had co-founded Prodecoop, a 3000-member coffee co-operative in northern Nicaragua and had seen the benefit to coffee-farming communities of Fair Trade sales to Europe. Upon returning to the USA, Rice served on the board of TransFair USA and wrote a business plan for the organization, proposing that TransFair USA be spun out from the Institute for Agriculture and Trade Policy, where it was then being housed. The Board made him Executive Director and, soon after, TransFair received its first funding from the Ford Foundation in Mexico.

Table 8.7 *US retail outlets selling labelled Fair Trade*

Year	Sales (US$m/£m)	Number of shops	Comments
1999	N/A	<1,000	Fair Trade label adopted on existing Fair Trade coffee in natural food stores.
2000	51.3/28.7	3,000	Starbucks launches Fair Trade coffee in company-owned stores.
2001	68.3/38.3	8,000	Safeway introduces Fair Trade coffee into over 100 of its stores; several Exxon Mobil and Border's Book Stores offer Fair Trade; Starbucks offers Fair Trade in all new company-owned locations.
2002	104.5/58.5	12,000	Regional supermarket chains and divisions of large supermarket chains such as Albertson's and Kroger start to offer Fair Trade coffee.
2003	133.9/74.9	18,000	Fair Trade products move into retail mainstream, e.g. five flavors of Fair Trade coffee were launched in grocery store chains, including: Publix in the Southeast (776 stores), Harris Teeter in the mid-Atlantic region (143 stores), and D'Agostino's and Wegman's in the NY region (123 and 60 stores respectively). This year also saw a broadening of the Fair Trade category within mainstream retailers: e.g. Green & Black's 'Maya Gold' chocolate bar and Choice Fair Trade teas were picked up by several retailers who already carried Fair Trade coffee.
2004	N/A	>25,000	Continued retail mainstreaming: Ahold Group launched five flavours of own-label Fair Trade coffee in over 800 stores; Dunkin' Donuts launched Fair Trade espresso in all stores; Procter & Gamble introduced a Fair Trade blend of its Millstone brand coffee in hundreds of stores, including WalMart. The launch of Fair Trade fruit in over 300 stores nationwide brought the Fair Trade label into a new part of the store and incorporated a new consumer segment – children (Fair Trade chocolate being positioned toward the gourmet consumer).

Source: TransFair USA (2004); Fair Trade Federation (2002, 2003)

Rice convinced Equal Exchange and other pioneering Fair Trade companies to adopt the TransFair USA label and third-party certification, and TransFair USA started to solicit new coffee roasters to carry Fair Trade certified coffee with the TransFair logo. In 2001 TransFair started certifying tea; they launched Fair Trade cocoa in 2002 (the first product being a hot cocoa from Equal Exchange) and tropical fruit (bananas, mangoes, pineapples and grapes) in early 2004. The number of companies gaining Fair Trade certification through TransFair for at least one product grew from 33 in 1999 to over 300 by 2004 (TransFair USA, 2001, 2004). Similarly, the number of retail outlets offering labelled Fair Trade products has also increased dramatically from fewer than 1000 in 1999 to over 25,000 by 2004.

As a potential market, the USA can be seen as a 'sleeping giant' – if typical market shares in Europe could be replicated in the USA then the global Fair Trade market would increase by up to a factor of 20, perhaps approaching £20bn ($35.8bn) per annum.

Clearly, then, developing the US market must represent one of the key strategic aims for the Fair Trade movement.

Switzerland

Switzerland represents a well-developed Fair Trade market and is the third most important after the UK and the USA. Switzerland was one of the first countries to introduce Fair Trade certified goods (under the Max Havelaar mark) in 1992. Fair Trade sales amounted to £50.4m ($90m) in 2002, an increase of 33 per cent on 2001. This equated to a per capita spend of about £6 ($11) per annum – by far the largest in the world (Leatherhead Food International, 2003).

The most important product is bananas, with sales of £23m ($41m) in 2002. Next came coffee, with sales of £9m ($16m) and a 5 per cent total market share, and chocolate, with sales of £7m ($12.5m), but only 1 per cent of the market. Honey represented a notable 10 per cent of the market.

In terms of retailers, the Claro Weltladen ATO chain of more than 150 stores offers a broad range of Fair Trade products across seven categories. Both the Co-op and Migros – two of the largest supermarket multiples – offer own-label Fair Trade products. The former chain switched to 100 per cent Fair Trade bananas in 2004 and, as a result, it has been predicted that Fair Trade will achieve a 50 per cent market share in bananas in 2004. The Co-op offers Fair Trade own-label in a further eight categories, including coffee, tea, honey and rice. Migros offers ten own-label Fair Trade product groups including coffee, tea, orange juice and bananas and accounted for £20m ($35.8m) of Fair Trade sales in 2002 (or about 40 per cent of the Swiss total).

Germany

The TransFair certification mark was first introduced to Germany in 1992, and there are currently eight product groups available, including coffee, tea, bananas and honey. Fair Trade sales in Germany amounted to £49.4m ($88.4m) in 2002, an increase of 10 per cent on 2001. Coffee is again the most important single commodity but in Germany, as in the Netherlands, sales appear to have reached a plateau, recording a 6.1 per cent drop in 2002.

There are over 70 Fair Trade supplier organizations in Germany, including Gepa (the largest ATO in Europe, with a turnover of £20m or $35.8m) and El Puente. Fair Trade products are retailed in over 22,000 supermarkets and ATOs. Fair Trade week in 2004 saw nearly 1000 events hosted by German retailers, churches and community groups.

Japan

The Japanese market is also emerging as an important source of Fair Trade sales growth. As the second largest economy in the world and in common with the USA, Japan offers a potentially enormous new market for Fair Trade. In 2002 Fair Trade sales amounted to £32.4m ($58m), an increase of 25 per cent on 2001 (Fair Trade Federation, 2003). Sales for 2003 are estimated at £59.1m ($106m), which would make Japan the fourth most important Fair Trade market in the world.

The Netherlands

The Netherlands has the longest tradition of certified Fair Trade retailing, since the Dutch Max Havelaar mark was the first Fair Trade certification label in the world, introduced here in 1988. Fair Trade sales amounted to £26.8m ($48m) in 2002, a 17 per cent increase on 2001. As with elsewhere, coffee is the most significant product in the Netherlands with a 3 per cent market share, although recently sales appear to have flattened out (Leatherhead Food International, 2003). Perhaps surprisingly, only five other Fair Trade certified categories exist: bananas, honey, orange juice, tea and chocolate/cocoa.

The distribution of Fair Trade products is fragmented in the Netherlands, although AgroFair and Neuteboom are two notable suppliers. Ahold, the main retail group in the Netherlands, stocks a range of Fair Trade goods and under its Albert Heijn fascia offers own label coffee (Café Honesta). Otherwise there is no own-label provision. Ahold has also developed the Utz Kapeh range of 'ethically' traded products that do not conform to Fair Trade standards, but clearly represent something of a competitive threat and, consequently, remain controversial within the Fair Trade movement.

STRUCTURE OF FAIR TRADE DISTRIBUTION

Fair Trade products are distributed through four main channels: high street shops, catering, mail order and the Internet (see Table 8.8). High street distribution may be further broken down into: ATOs, charity and world shops; health and natural food shops; and supermarkets. The first of these three represents the traditional home of Fair Trade, reflecting its charity/campaigning origins and typified by Oxfam shops in the UK. The second group of specialist health food shops treats Fair Trade as an example of sustainable development. Because many Fair Trade products are also organic, they can easily fit into a health food retail context such as Wild Oats Markets in the USA. A third grouping of multiple supermarkets is the most recent to engage with Fair Trade and reflects the increasing mainstreaming of demand for such products. The development of supermarket Fair Trade own-label has been another very significant distribution development. Smaller-scale supermarkets or convenience stores also stock Fair Trade, most obviously the Co-operative Group in the UK.

Table 8.8 *Fair Trade distribution*

Distribution channel	Example
High street:	
ATO	Oxfam (UK); Eza 3 Welt (Austria); Gepa (Germany)
Health food shop	Fresh and Wild (UK); Wild Oats Markets (USA)
Supermarket	Co-operative Group (UK); Migros (Switzerland); Albert Heijn (Netherlands); Monoprix (France); Albertson's (USA)
Catering/out-of-home	Costa Coffee (UK); Starbucks (USA); Houses of Parliament (UK); Alliance and Leicester Building Society (UK)
Mail order	Traidcraft (UK), Equal Exchange (UK and USA), People Tree (Japan)
Internet	Fair Trade On-line (UK) (www.store.yahoo.com/fairtradeonline-uk)

Catering distribution of Fair Trade is growing in importance. Indeed, the Fairtrade Foundation in the UK views the out-of-home catering market as a major opportunity for future sales growth. This market includes not only coffee shops and restaurants, but also institutional contexts such as public buildings and workplace canteens. In the USA, this market has been especially important, as speciality coffee companies (the drivers behind Fair Trade sales growth) sell product largely through cafés. Costa Coffee (UK) and Starbucks (worldwide) both offer Fair Trade options, and one of the first actions by the incoming Labour government in the UK in 1997 was to switch all tea and coffee at the Houses of Parliament to Fair Trade. Furthermore, a range of large UK businesses now offers Fair Trade beverages to their workers including the Alliance and Leicester and Woolwich Building Societies, Jarvis and Lucas Varity. In addition, as a result of the Fair Trade Town, Village, and University campaigns, many caterers on the smaller scale are now also offering Fair Trade to their customers.

Mail order distribution has a long history in connection with Fair Trade, dating back to the foundation of Traidcraft in 1979. Other notable players include Oxfam and Equal Exchange in the UK, and SERRV in the USA. Many mail order distributors also have transactional web sites, such as Traidcraft and Equal Exchange. An interesting development on the Internet has been the emergence of ethical shopping portals such as Ethical Junction (www.ethicaljunction.org) and Ethical Shopper (www.ethicalshopper.co.uk). In 2004 Traidcraft and Oxfam combined to establish the Fair Trade On-line Marketplace. These portals not only give on-line consumers access to Fair Trade, but also act as low-cost marketing tools for the idea of Fair Trade, combining product information with raising awareness and educational material.

RETAILER PRICING

Perhaps the most controversial aspect of the mainstreaming of Fair Trade into supermarket multiples across countries has been retailer pricing. Fair Trade products generally retail at a premium as a result of their high quality and more expensive producer costs, including an above-market producer price and, in most cases, an additional 10 per cent social premium.

However, *The Wall Street Journal* (Stecklow and White, 2004) investigated the pricing structure of Fair Trade products in supermarkets in the UK and USA and suggested that there was strong evidence that some retailers were exploiting ethical consumers' willingness to pay more for goods that they believed were doing good. For example, according to the article, in the UK Sainsbury's Fair Trade bananas were found to be around four times more expensive pound for pound than non-Fair Trade (typically a 70 per cent difference). This contrasts with Migros – the Swiss supermarket – that offered both types of banana at almost the same price. Furthermore, with tea a price differential of 25 per cent is usually found in France, but again, in the UK it can be up to 70 per cent (Leatherhead Food International, 2003).

However, when direct price comparisons are made across countries for similar Fair Trade products it appears that pricing is roughly the same (see Table 8.9), with the only exceptions reflecting local market issues such as high tea sales in the UK generally or high

Table 8.9   *Fair Trade prices across Europe (£ per kilo/£ per litre)*

Product	UK	Switzerland	France	Germany
Orange Juice	1.09	0.80–1.40	1.16	1.15
Coffee (instant)	15–30	6–10	8–10	14–30
Tea	7–8	–	40	30

Source: Leatherhead Food International (2003)

Table 8.10   *Coffee pricing in UK supermarkets 2004 (in £)*

Product	Tesco's	Sainsbury's	Asda	Cooperative Group
Nestlé Gold Blend Freeze Dried Coffee 100 gms	2.14	2.14	2.14	2.25
Own-label Freeze Dried Coffee 100 gms	1.40	2.09	1.98	–
Cafedirect 5065 Freeze Dried Coffee 100 gms	2.57	2.57	2.57	2.83
Own-label Fair Trade Freeze Dried Coffee 100 gms	2.39	–	–	1.49

coffee sales in France. Therefore, the price differentials between Fair Trade and non-Fair Trade goods are, in fact, largely a product of price differences in the non-Fair Trade products and there is generally price consistency within local markets (see Table 8.10). Thus, Fair Trade bananas are generally priced roughly the same across Europe (approximately €2 to €3 per kilo), but in the UK non-Fair Trade bananas are far cheaper than in Switzerland. The concentration and maturity of retail markets for non-Fair Trade lines, rather than exploitative retailers, appear to be driving these often dramatic differences.

An important retail pricing issue that has yet to be properly explored is the opportunity for more competitive pricing of some Fair Trade lines to broaden the price structure of Fair Trade and thus access new market segments. As *The Guardian* noted

> Since only a few percent at most of the retail price ends up in the hands of the growers, British consumers have to pay just a fraction more per jar to make a real difference to the life of a peasant farmer … The Co-op added the negligible sum of 1p to the price of a standard coffee jar when it went Fair Trade – but that more than doubled the amount per lb received by its suppliers. (*Spark*, 2004: 10)

There are clear marketing benefits to be had by maintaining Fair Trade products as premium-priced, since this positioning reinforces quality associations and makes them attractive to supermarkets. However, if Fair Trade is to continue to grow beyond the current 'AB1' demographic groups that represent its most loyal supporters, there may well be a case for offering lower-priced products such as has been pioneered by the Co-operative Group own-brand ranges in the UK. In this case, the retailer took the commercial decision to exchange margin for volume (as well as to support an ethical agenda). Is there any reason why other own-label Fair Trade products should not follow suit?

CONCLUSION

The rate of growth of the Fair Trade market in developed countries over the last ten years has been striking. As Fair Trade has moved beyond ATOs and into mainstream super-markets it has reached an audience well beyond the 5 per cent of highly ethical consumers identified in much market research. The mainstreaming of Fair Trade has generated a number of contested issues ranging from the danger of 'mission drift' or selling out, to the lack of supply for quick scaling up or the time lag behind new product development. A number of these points will be revisited in the final chapter of this book.

This chapter has explored the growing market for Fair Trade goods. It has identified who are Fair Trade consumers within the broader segment of 'ethical' consumers and has outlined the exponential growth in Fair Trade sales evident in recent years. The chapter then carried out a national survey of the most important Fair Trade markets and con-cluded by discussing the structure of Fair Trade retail distribution and pricing. Having established the economic scale of Fair Trade sales in this chapter, the next will outline the impact of Fair Trade on producer groups and how this can best be measured.

9

Measuring Impact

This chapter sets out the metrical landscape for Fair Trade. It begins by summarizing the existing research on the impact of Fair Trade and then continues by exploring the direct and indirect social impacts accruing to producers from selling to the Fair Trade market. Next, the chapter addresses the various models that may be used to measure the social impact of Fair Trade. Finally, it examines the social return on investment methodology in some detail.

INTRODUCTION

Fair Trade has two fundamental drivers: the need to be sustainable, which it achieves by working with for-profit businesses, and the need to have a developmental impact on producers. Consumers buy Fair Trade products because they believe that their purchase means an improvement in the lives of Third World producers. Without a demonstrable impact on poor producers, consumer brand loyalty in the Fair Trade model would disappear and the entire system would fall apart.

Demonstrating developmental impact on Fair Trade producers is also important for the Fair Trade movement as a whole in order to continue to receive investment and support from the international development community. Every pound, dollar, or yen of support that non-governmental organizations (NGOs) and government agencies give the Fair Trade movement could be spent on other development projects. Fair Trade actors must prove that their system provides the best return to the world's poorest farmers (see for example, Udomkit and Winnett, 2002). In this way, Fair Trade legitimizes its model and can attract more investment.

Furthermore, effective impact measurement allows not only retrospective analysis of projects, but can also inform future strategic decision making. Convincing impact metrics both justify and critique past actions and also form the basis of subsequent planning. This approach is particularly valuable in resource allocation decisions.

Measuring the extra income earned by farmers through sales of Fair Trade certified products is fairly straightforward. The Fairtrade Labelling Organizations International (FLO) determines the income benefit of Fair Trade by calculating the difference between Fair Trade floor and market prices per Fair Trade product, and then multiplying by the volumes traded. In 2002, FLO estimated the income benefit to Fair Trade coffee, tea, cocoa, sugar, rice, fruit, honey and juice producers at \$37m (£21m), of which \$30m (£17m) was attributable to sales of Fair Trade-certified coffee.[1]

Yet extra income is just one of the benefits accrued to producers through Fair Trade and may not even be the most important aspect to producers (Kocken, 2002). Fair Trade producers gain value from long-term relationships, direct trade and credit provision, all of which help them in their non-Fair Trade sales negotiations. The communities in which Fair Trade producers operate benefit from development projects funded by Fair Trade co-operatives and farm worker organizations. Even self-esteem and self-confidence are improved as Fair Trade farmers identify with an international alternative trading movement.

All of these external benefits must somehow be measured if the true impact of Fair Trade is to be properly assessed. Attaching a monetary value to these social and intangible benefits, however, is highly subjective. Furthermore, attribution is not straightforward. Marketing organic coffee, for instance, has required producers to have direct trade channels and access to professional technical organizations, all of which have contributed to higher prices for farmers (Bacon, 2004). Development agencies have implemented myriad projects that support Fair Trade producer groups with finance, quality improvement programs and technical management assistance (Mayoux, 2001b; Ronchi, 2003). Because of overlapping market opportunities and development agency involvement, separating Fair Trade's unique contribution to producer social benefits is extremely difficult (Raynolds, 2002b).

Existing Research

Recognizing the need to measure the impact of Fair Trade as its popularity as a development strategy increases, several case studies have come out in recent years focusing on Fair Trade producers. The Natural Resources Institute at the University of Greenwich in the UK and Colorado State University in the USA have produced several Fair Trade impact assessments, funded by the UK's Department for International Development and the Ford Foundation respectively. Some alternative trading organizations (ATOs), most notably Traidcraft and Oxfam in the UK, have assessed the impact of some of the Fair Trade projects they support. Traidcraft, a pioneer in social impact reporting in the UK, conducts in-depth assessments with its sourcing partners to determine the progress Fair Trade partners are making through selling to Traidcraft. There are even summaries of studies which aggregate data from several studies.

All Fair Trade impact studies recognize that Fair Trade benefits farmers in several ways beyond increasing income and most include detailed descriptions of non-income benefits. The 11 studies used in this chapter, outlined in Table 9.1, consist of in-depth assessments of the impact of Fair Trade on coffee, cocoa and fruit producers, as well as summary surveys which look at several impact studies. They represent diverse geographies and are comprehensive in attempting to address the social impacts of Fair Trade. Some of the projects studied have been in operation since long before a FLO-certified supply chain existed, thus the impacts of Fair Trade can be seen to be the result of interactions with ATOs first, with the benefits of certification being realized later.

Several limitations exist to the current research. Firstly, very few impact studies exist which focus on how Fair Trade affects workers on plantations. The European Fair Trade Association's (EFTA) list of Fair Trade impact studies (2004) lists none. Some studies (for instance, Wilshaw, 2002) examine the impact of Fair Trade on hired workers producing handicrafts, but for FLO-certified products comprehensive impact studies are very

Table 9.1 Summary of Fair Trade producer impact studies

Author(s)	Date	Country	Product(s)	Name of producer group(s)	Methodology
Bacon	2004	Nicaragua	Coffee	Several	Interviews with 228 farmers
Blowfield and Gallet	1998	Ghana	Bananas	VREL	Not given
Kocken	2002	Several	Handicrafts, honey, coffee, cocoa, other	Several	Summary of existing impact studies
Lyon	2002	Guatemala	Coffee	La Voz	Interviews with La Voz members and leaders, other co-op leaders, industry reps
Malins and Blowfield	2000	Uganda	Dried fruit (e.g. mangoes, pineapples)	Fruits of the Nile	Not given
Mayoux	2001a	Ghana	Cocoa	Kuapa Kokoo	Summary of existing impact studies
Mayoux	2001b	Several	Cocoa, dried fruit, bananas, brazil nuts	Several	Summary of existing impact studies
Nelson and Galvez	2000	Ecuador	Cocoa	MCCH	Consultative field research
Ronchi	2002	Costa Rica	Coffee	Coocafé	Interviews with co-op members and leadership, industry reps
Ronchi	2003	Ghana	Cocoa	Kuapa Kokoo	Participant observation with producers
Taylor	2002	Guatemala, Mexico, El Salvador	Coffee	Seven different co-operatives	Summary of seven case studies of small-farmer co-operatives

limited. One exception is Blowfield and Gallet's research (2000). Their work for the Natural Resources Institute outlined the impacts of Fair Trade on Volta River Estates Ltd (VREL), a FLO-certified banana plantation in Ghana employing 900 full-time workers.

Furthermore, existing studies do not always compare changes in the livelihoods of Fair Trade participants to similar producers who do not have access to Fair Trade markets. The vast majority of impact reports have been case studies rather than comparative assessments. Most studies list non-monetary benefits from Fair Trade and attempt to track progress through time – for instance with questions comparing education levels of parents *vs.* their children, asking if producers feel that their quality of life has been improving, and so on – but rarely compare these answers to non-Fair Trade producers in order to track a difference. Many studies compare income received by Fair Trade *vs.* non-Fair Trade farmers, but few compare the impact of Fair Trade on social development with non-Fair Trade farms and communities.[2]

There are several possible reasons for this. Social impacts are notoriously difficult to quantify (although an attempt will be made to do so in the SROI calculations below), especially such development goals as female and worker empowerment. Longitudinal studies assessing changes in educational levels, nutrition, civic participation and other potential social impacts of Fair Trade are expensive. Finally, even if benefits are found, it is difficult to causally attribute these to farmer participation in Fair Trade (Raynolds, 2002b).

Nevertheless, the impact studies summarized in this chapter do provide a picture of the potential social impacts of Fair Trade. These are varied, so as a framework for analysis this chapter will draw from Ronchi (2002), who divides the impacts of Fair Trade into direct impacts on producers and their organizations (through increased income and credit provision), and the indirect impact that Fair Trade's support of co-operatives has on co-operative members, non-member producers, other co-operatives and other organizations. To summarize:

Direct impacts of Fair Trade on producer groups include:

- Increase in income (Fair Trade market premium and social premium);
- Improved education;
- Female empowerment;
- Preserving indigenous cultures; and
- Psychological effects such as producer empowerment and its effects on civic participation.

Indirect impacts of Fair Trade on producer groups include:

- Positive externalities which derive from support for co-operatives and progressive plantations; and
- Benefits accrued to Fair Trade groups through direct trade relationships.

Impacts of Fair Trade on non-Fair Trade producers include:

- Access to market and price information;
- Impacts on the broader communities where Fair Trade producers operate; and
- Isolation of non-Fair Trade producers.

DIRECT IMPACTS OF FAIR TRADE ON PARTICIPANTS

Whilst the most direct and easily measurable impact of Fair Trade is an increase in income to producers, the Fair Trade system has several non-monetary direct impacts on Fair Trade producers and their organizations. According to Murray et al. (2003), Fair Trade's contributions to the viability of the social systems present in coffee-farming communities have been largely overlooked. The authors identify several benefits beyond income increases enjoyed by farming families involved in the Fair Trade system, including improved self-esteem, family and community stability, and even cultural revival. Other direct impacts of Fair Trade on farmers include gender empowerment and an increase in investments in education. These direct benefits, including income, will be assessed in turn below.

Income

Fair Trade certification guarantees a higher-than-market price to producers, thus it should come as no surprise that every study found income to be higher for producers selling to the Fair Trade market. Taylor (2002) found that the difference Fair Trade made to Majomut, a coffee co-operative, was marked: sales of organic Fair Trade coffee returned on average $1700/year (£952) as opposed to $550 (£308) selling through middlemen. The average Majomut member's income has grown 100–200 per cent in recent years. Ronchi (2002) found that Fair Trade coffee co-operative members earned on average 39 per cent more than non-co-operative members, and 25–60 per cent more than they would have earned from local middlemen operating in the region.

In the extremely impoverished conditions in which many Fair Trade producers operate, incremental income that appears small by Northern standards can nevertheless represent a significant difference. The $225 (£126) in extra income earned by Ugandan small-scale fruit-drying operators selling to the Fair Trade market (Malins and Blowfield, 2000) nearly doubles the average Ugandan per capita income of $236 (£132) (IBRD, 2002).

Many producer groups return the extra income through Fair Trade to producer members, but as Table 9.2 shows, co-operatives vote to retain income to be used on health, education and other community projects, as well as such business development activities as co-operative capitalization and debt repayment, organic conversion and technical training for quality improvements. By amassing increased income at the co-operative level rather than distributing it all to producer members, co-operatives can implement larger projects. Ronchi (2002), for instance, measured several income benefits from ten years of Fair Trade with the Coocafé coffee export co-operative in Costa Rica. These included a $25,200 (£14,112) investment in organic fertilizer production facilities and $3.5m (£1.9m) invested in environmental improvements, including organic conversion and certification. The Kuapa Kokoo impact assessment undertaken by Ronchi (2003) found that income effects on farmers were negligible, but when taken together they amounted to approximately $1m (£0.56m) over eight years, equivalent to annual primary school costs for 245,000 children.

Benefits to Women

It must be recognized, however, that providing extra income to the (usually male) head of a household or wage earner on a Fair Trade plantation does not necessarily guarantee

Table 9.2 *Use of Fair Trade social premia*

Producer group	Health	Education	Extra income for producers	Women's projects	Quality improvements	Organic production	Co-op capitalization & credit	Source
UCIRI	X		X			X		Taylor (2002)
Majomut			X	X	X	X	X	Taylor (2002)
La Selva			X					Taylor (2002)
Las Colinas							X	Taylor (2002)
La Voz							X	Taylor (2002)
Kuapa Kokoo	X	X	X (but negligible, see Berlan (2004) and Ronchi (2003))	X			X (US $467,000/£261,520, in first 4 years)	Mayoux (2001a, 2001b); Ronchi (2003); Page and Slater (2003)
Coocafé		X	X			X	X ($1m/£0.56m)	Ronchi (2002)
Fruits of the Nile	X	X	X				X	Malins and Blowfield (2000)
Nicaraguan coffee (2 co-ops)							X (pay down debt)	Bacon (2004)

that income will trickle across at the intra-household level (Nelson and Galvez, 2000). Women produce 70 per cent of food in developing countries and several Fair Trade handicraft projects focus on female producers, but Fair Trade cash crops like coffee and cocoa, and the income generated from them, are generally controlled by male household members (Redfern and Snedker, 2002). Land ownership can be a requirement for co-operative membership, thus in communities with paternalistic land inheritance practices Fair Trade co-op members are generally men (Tallontire, 2000).

Women and children are often the most vulnerable of household members (Blowfield and Gallet, 2000) and because women generally control household nutrition, extra income in their hands often means better-fed children. Ensuring that women earn extra income from Fair Trade would therefore benefit the poorest members of Fair Trade networks (Bowen, 2001: 26). Whilst female empowerment and direct female income transfers are not specific FLO requirements for Fair Trade certification, improving women's livelihood is increasingly seen as having beneficial effects on development (for example Sunde and Kleinbooi, 1999). Several case studies looked at the impact of Fair Trade on the livelihoods of women.

Mayoux (2001b) did find that payments to Fair Trade smallholders and co-operative members usually go to men, although women may be participating more in Fair Trade production. Blowfield and Gallet (2000) questioned the benefits of VREL on social groups outside of the workforce and noted that women only held 16 per cent of jobs. This indicated that women would benefit relatively less from Fair Trade on the VREL plantation if benefits do stay with the workforce.

Malins and Blowfield (2000), however, found that 70 per cent of Fruits of the Nile producers were women who would otherwise not have been cash-earners. Because Fruits of the Nile works with small-scale producers rather than large co-operatives, groups of marginalized producers who share similar characteristics (for instance, women) can form more easily. And because Fruits of the Nile introduced a new technology (solar fruit drying), there were perhaps fewer pre-existing gender norms, allowing women to more freely engage in a new income-generating activity.

The evidence for direct income increases for women through participation in Fair Trade is thus quite varied. Mayoux (2001b) noted that women's involvement with Fair Trade agricultural production can be a mixed blessing: their participation does not usually exempt them from household duties and a woman's workload can often increase after she becomes involved with export cash crops. Ensuring that women earn extra income through Fair Trade production outside of their normal productive activities, therefore, may not be the best way to improve the livelihoods of women and children.

What about development opportunities for women outside of Fair Trade cash crop production? Lyon (2002) found that many female coffee co-operative members viewed coffee as men's work and many expressed the wish that the co-operative would help market women's products (for instance, weaving and textiles) as well. Some Fair Trade co-operatives have started projects that focus specifically on women, for instance women's savings groups, and have diversified their income sources through marketing products created solely by women. The women's projects instituted by coffee co-operatives studied in Murray et al. (2003) are generally focussed on activities outside the coffee sector, both income-generating (for example, textile production and marketing) and non-commercial (for example, organic farming projects).

Kuapa Kokoo has specific affirmative requirements regarding women's participation in governance; two out of the seven members of the village-level management committees must be women, for instance, and at least one out of three representatives to the regional council (Mayoux, 2001a). Coocafé also has affirmative action policies in place in its scholarship program, but Ronchi (2002) found no evidence that the gender-based initiatives undertaken by the export co-operative had any effect on the everyday reality of producers. Taylor (2002) found that the Latin American coffee co-operatives included in the Colorado State University study were committed to addressing gender issues because international certifiers and donors required it, not necessarily because of indigenous interest in gender issues. Taylor found no cases in which gender was an important internal issue and women did not play an important role in governance in any of the seven co-operatives studied. Similarly, Tallontire's (2000) study of the KNCU coffee co-operative in Tanzania could find no attempts to challenge gender biases or analyse gender relations on the part of KNCU or Twin Trading, one of its Fair Trade importers.

It would appear, then, that Fair Trade's role in increasing female empowerment and improving the livelihoods of women is not significant. FLO's Fair Trade standards protect women from discrimination in the workplace and in obtaining co-operative membership, but do not require pro-active female empowerment initiatives, thus Fair Trade certification itself cannot be a powerful force for gender-specific development. If FLO stakeholders did want to make female empowerment a specific goal of Fair Trade, FLO could choose to focus new Fair Trade product development on those products which are relatively produced more by women, for instance handicrafts and other products which can be made whilst women are performing such household activities as child-minding. Alternatively, FLO could incorporate a gender-development progress component as part of its Fair Trade standards.

Education

Whilst increasing income to women is one way that Fair Trade could expand the direct benefits to children, extra spending on education would also indicate beneficial direct impacts of Fair Trade on vulnerable members of the community. Lyon (2002) found that the higher Fair Trade price allowed the majority of co-operative members, who for the most part have less than a fourth grade education, to pay workers to harvest their crops, freeing their children to attend school. Ronchi's (2002) study found that the Fair Trade coffee co-operative in Costa Rica funded 574 scholarships valued at $105 (£59) each and 96 university scholarships worth $250 (£140), all for a total of $84,270 (£47,191) in educational funding. Fair Trade accounted for 52 per cent of export volume and 67 per cent of export revenue during the time these scholarships were funded. With no Fair Trade income, Coocafé would have had to sell all of its production at market prices, reducing overall income by 31 per cent and overall educational spending by $26,123 (£14,629).

Berlan's study of child labour in Ghana, however, questions whether rural schools are worth the investment by Fair Trade cocoa farming families. She notes that 'some schools record a zero per cent success rate in final examinations. One farmer ... said he refused to carry on paying school fees and sending his children to school as they had attended school for many years and were still almost illiterate' (2004: 164). Nevertheless, most impact studies showed that Fair Trade beneficiaries highly value their children's education and many choose to spend their income on school fees, or vote to create scholarship funds with Fair Trade social premia (see for example, Wilshaw, 2002). Unfortunately, whilst there are several anecdotal examples of Fair Trade producer groups spending Fair Trade income on education, there are no longitudinal studies of educational attainment by Fair Trade participants that would enable real measurements of its impact on education.

Indigenous Culture

Fair Trade in indigenous handicrafts can certainly contribute to the preservation of cultural traditions (LeClair, 2002), although it must be noted that these handicrafts are intended for Western markets and are thus not unaffected by the culture of the end user. Within the realm of Fair Trade-certified agricultural products, Murray et al. (2003) found that Fair Trade contributed to cultural revival in the coffee communities they studied by supporting ancestral farming practices such as inter-cropping and organic production methods (Lyon, 2002).

Fair Trade could have a significant impact on the preservation of rural ways of life by ensuring enough income for farming families to stay on their lands. Anecdotal evidence, however, would suggest that the progress of urbanization is alive and well in Fair Trade communities. Especially in Central America, young men leave rural villages to seek work in cities and in the USA. Spending a few years in the USA has become part of the culture, part of the ritual of becoming a man, and even as Fair Trade income grows and young family members might not have to leave the farm to earn money, the ritual may persist. As Raymond Kimaro, a Tanzanian coffee co-operative member explained: 'We have very few young people in my co-operative. All the young people leave and go to the cities to find jobs; they don't want to work the land anymore. Even if we got 100 per cent Fair Trade prices for our coffee, I still don't think they would stay' (Interview with Kimaro, 2004). At best Fair Trade may stem the flow of rural agricultural labourers to cities, but it is unlikely that it can turn the tide of what may be inevitable urbanization.

Psychological Benefits

Several studies found that Fair Trade had a beneficial impact on self-esteem, feelings of economic security and the pride of farmers involved in Fair Trade networks. According to Murray et al. 'in case after case, farmers reported that the increased attention to their farming – including the visits of Fair Trade and organic inspectors, buyers, and even visiting Northern consumers – promoted renewed pride in coffee farming' (2003: 8). Ronchi also found from her study of a Costa Rican coffee co-operative that 'from annual reports to interview responses, evidence of an increased sense of confidence through association with the Fair Trade market surfaces' (2002: 17).

Taylor (2002) found that being part of a Fair Trade network increased pride and self-esteem amongst producers and resulted in increased participation in public assemblies. According to Mayoux (2001b), Kuapa Kokoo farmers also take great pride in the strength of their co-operative and feel empowered by controlling the cocoa production and marketing chain. Nelson and Galvez (2000) report that Ecuadorian cocoa farmers believed that they had developed self-esteem through their relationship with MCCH, their Fair Trade exporter.

The psychological benefits of extra Fair Trade income and credit provision were also evident. Bacon (2004) found that farmers selling to co-operatives that were not connected to alternative markets were four times as likely to perceive a risk of losing their farms because of low coffee prices than farmers connected to Fair Trade, organic and other alternative markets. According to Taylor, 'knowing that in bad times pre-financing is available from Fair Trade sources is an important source of stability' (2002: 19). One farmer told Bacon: 'We have a little help, a little room to breathe, with the 50 per cent the co-op buys as Fair Trade' (2004: 19). Ronchi (2003) found that Kuapa Kokoo farmers felt more secure being in control of the scales used to weigh their product – the perception that they were being cheated was dissipated, so farmers felt less anxiety.

Where farmers were aware of the Fair Trade market, they expressed pride in taking part in an international alternative trade movement. Blowfield and Gallet (2000) found that workers on the VREL banana plantation in Ghana were very aware of Fair Trade and felt a positive sense of identity with the international Fair Trade movement. Several studies, however, found that producers were not necessarily aware of the importance Fair Trade markets played in their lives. As noted in Lyon: 'Overall, members of La Voz exhibit a complete lack of understanding of the Fair Trade market. The vast majority of interviewed members stared at me blankly when asked if they knew what Fair Trade was' (2002: 24).

This lack of awareness of Fair Trade amongst primary producers is intriguing. Co-operative management may choose to present higher incomes and direct relationships as measures of the co-operative's success, rather than emphasizing to members the role of the Fair Trade market, to increase member loyalty to the co-operative (Taylor, 2002). Because income from Fair Trade sales is lumped with payment for non-Fair Trade sales when the co-operative returns income to produce members, the latter are not always able to easily measure the impact of Fair Trade (Murray et al., 2003).

Taylor's (2002) summary of seven case studies found that producers grasped organic production impacts more easily than Fair Trade impacts because organic production related more to their farming activities. Understanding of Fair Trade was lowest at the primary- or village-level co-operatives, increasing with delegate participation in second- and third-level. Fair Trade certifiers were rarely distinguished from organic certifiers. Nelson and Galvez (2000), however, found many cocoa farmers able to identify, without prompting, with the idea of an alternative trade movement. Because these farmers are not necessarily part of an organized co-operative, they were comparing their experience of trading with MCCH (their Fair Trade exporter) to that of selling to *coyote* middlemen operating in the region, thus the importance of Fair Trade was easily recognizable. Co-operative members, on the other hand, may attribute higher prices to the operation of the co-operative and not alternative traders in the North.

In summary, it would seem that Fair Trade has positive effects on the self-esteem, pride and sense of economic security and power amongst participants. Whilst farmer beneficiaries do not necessarily separate the income and credit provision impacts of Fair Trade from the benefits of being in a co-operative, there is some evidence that farmers in general feel positive about being part of an international alternative trade movement.

SUMMARY OF DIRECT IMPACTS

It is not surprising that Fair Trade was found to have a positive impact on producer income levels. Whether or not the benefits of higher incomes trickle across to all members of producers' families remains to be seen – the anecdotal evidence of Fair Trade beneficiaries placing a priority on education would seem to indicate that children do gain from higher Fair Trade incomes. Women may benefit from participating in Fair Trade production and women-oriented projects implemented by Fair Trade co-operatives, but because their workload may increase this benefit can be lessened. The evidence regarding Fair Trade support of indigenous cultures is limited and the influence Fair Trade networks can have on these cultural factors, especially in agriculture, is most likely negligible. Fair Trade does seem to have positive effects on producer self-esteem and psychological health.

INDIRECT IMPACTS OF FAIR TRADE ON PARTICIPANTS

Fair Trade directly benefits producer well-being through increased income and connections to an international alternative trade movement. But several impact assessments note some indirect benefits from Fair Trade by empowering community members and co-operatives, as well as by supporting co-operatives and plantations with progressive labour relations and thus wider benefits result. It is to these indirect impacts that this chapter now turns.

Relationships With Northern Organizations

By requiring direct relationships between producer groups and their customers in the North, Fair Trade provides producers with market information and contacts that can put them in a better negotiating position for non-Fair Trade sales. Taylor (2002) found that direct ties enabled co-operatives to bargain more effectively with large buyers such as Starbucks and Carrefour. Visits from Northern buyers created positive impacts on self-esteem and stimulated improvements in non-Fair Trade market relations. Coocafé also felt that market information obtained from Fair Trade contacts made them more confident in dealing with non-Fair Trade buyers (Ronchi, 2002).

Co-operatives were also better able to access development funds and relief assistance through improved organizational structures and reputation enhancement. Three of the seven co-operatives examined by Taylor (2002) felt that they had had an easier time accessing bank credit because of the credibility they acquired from being associated with Fair Trade and its external monitoring of their organizations. VREL is able to access development funding and loans at 2 per cent interest rather than the 50 per cent local Ghanaian market rate (Blowfield and Gallet, 2000). Involvement in Fair Trade thus created a positive feedback cycle of informational and reputational benefits which spilled over into non-Fair Trade relationships.

Support for Co-operatives and Progressive Plantations

The Fair Trade certification system requires small farmers to be organized into co-operatives and farm workers to form a democratically-elected committee to decide on the use of the Fair Trade social premia. Whilst these requirements are beneficial from a certification and export perspective (it is much more efficient to deal with a co-operative of small producers than with each farmer individually), there also appears to be significant indirect benefits to working with these organizations by allowing marginalized producers to express their voices collectively. Co-operatives typically consist of an administrative council including a president, secretary and treasurer, with a democratically-elected oversight council or board of directors (Taylor, 2002). Subcommittees often exist to oversee technical education, certification, social projects and marketing. There are thus many opportunities for individual growth through civic participation and leadership development.

Several studies gave evidence of increased civic engagement and individual empowerment through the existence of co-operatives. Taylor (2002) found that many of the Mexican Fair Trade co-operatives had become involved in national coffee, credit and small business associations. Coocafé felt that the association with Fair Trade and FLO as an international movement supported them when asserting their concerns in a local context that was not usually friendly towards small producers (Ronchi, 2002).

Fair Trade's support of the co-operative movement has some spillover benefits into the broader communities in which Fair Trade farmers live, which spreads the positive impacts of Fair Trade beyond just the direct participants. One Mexican Fair Trade coffee co-operative emphasized community-level participation in issues far beyond coffee. Members discussed more general concerns regarding government programs, land tenure, religious festivals and other civic activities (Taylor, 2002). The La Voz co-operative in Guatemala pointed out the environmental and health hazards of waste accumulation and helped the town government organize a rubbish collection program (Lyon, 2002). Interestingly, Taylor (2002) found several examples of co-operation amongst competing co-operatives. Groups shared commercial opportunities and exchanged contacts and information.

But is Fair Trade correct to support the co-operative movement as part of its social development agenda? Mendoza and Bastiaensen argue that co-operatives are inherently inefficient: their structure 'involves an expensive, top-heavy entrepreneurial hierarchy, including a large administrative staff and substantial representation costs for its leaders' (2003: 42). The authors found the Nicaraguan coffee co-operative they studied to copy the 'vertical and clientelistic modes of organization that form the institutional-cultural core of Nicaraguan underdevelopment and injustice' (2003: 43). They caution the Fair Trade movement to not assume that the existence of co-operatives is inherently advantageous for their small family farmer members.

Indeed, the evidence from impact studies regarding co-operative success in empowering members is mixed. Lyon (2002) found that co-operative members did not compete intensively for positions in the co-operative management. Even in a democratically-elected group, leadership can become entrenched which often leads to allegations of corruption and mismanagement. The manager of the La Voz co-operative had his power further strengthened by contact with importers and exporters who preferred to deal with one co-operative representative rather than an ever-changing management board (Lyon, 2002). But excessive turnover was also found by Taylor to lead to inefficiencies as 'elected leaders leave office just as they are becoming experienced and competent' (2002: 11).

Taylor also points out that many of the problems reported with co-operative governance and operations 'are problems found with co-operatives and democratic decision-making more generally. They cannot be viewed as weaknesses specific to Fair Trade or other coffee producers' organizations' (2002: 12). Case studies of Mexican, Salvadoran and Guatemalan coffee producers indicate that Fair Trade certification actually addresses the weaknesses in the participating co-operatives' democratic processes (Murray et al., 2003), presumably by requiring transparency in co-operative finances and governance. But it remains to be seen whether or not supporting the co-operative movement is an appropriate development tool for the Fair Trade movement. This section has listed some potential indirect benefits of supporting co-operatives to members and non-members, but a systematic study of the benefits of co-operatives would strengthen FLO's case for supporting this model of small farmer empowerment.

Finally, Fair Trade also supports plantations with progressive labour relations. Plantations which enter the Fair Trade certification system are most likely self-selecting – any plantation owner wishing to pass Fair Trade certification must be willing to allow his or her workers to organize in a democratic group to receive the Fair Trade premium, something which an exploitative owner might not be willing to allow. According to Blowfield and Gallet (2000), VREL's dialogue with Fair Trade certification organizations 'has probably fine-tuned rather than instigated many of the practices employed on the estate' (2000: 19). While Fair Trade is not the cause of these producer benefits, it lends legitimacy to estates that practice progressive labour relations. Supporting these socially progressive plantations through Fair Trade certification might also provide a demonstrative effect for neighbouring plantations.

SUMMARY OF INDIRECT IMPACTS OF FAIR TRADE

In working exclusively with co-operatives and progressive plantations, Fair Trade has an indirect impact on producers by supporting groups that have other benefits for small farmers and farm workers. In the case of plantations, Fair Trade provides an internationally approved symbol of recognition for those that treat their workers exceptionally well, including a guaranteed export price adjusted to meet labour standards and provide extra social premia to the workers. Co-operatives, whilst far from perfect, do appear to have beneficial effects on social capital development and civic participation. Fair Trade inspections and a certification process can help address their weaknesses. Finally, Fair Trade networks appear to benefit producers in their non-Fair Trade transactions through access to information and reputation enhancement by being involved with the Fair Trade movement.

IMPACTS OF FAIR TRADE ON NON-PARTICIPANTS

Do non-Fair Trade farmers in the broader communy benefit from their neighbours' participation in Fair Trade? Unless their interests differ greatly, non-Fair Trade actors will most likely benefit from the increased civic engagement and social networking of organized Fair Trade farmers (see for instance, Putnam, 2000). Social capital investments made by Fair Trade farmers (for instance, in education) will also likely provide benefits to non-participants. Income multiplier effects would include job creation, increase in tax revenues and other benefits which accrue to an individual's community and government when income increases.

Fair Trade farmers' access to market and price information can also have beneficial spillover effects on non-Fair Trade farmers in the same region. Ronchi (2002) reported that higher wages paid to Coocafé workers caused labour unrest at non-Fair Trade farms until neighbouring farms finally had to raise wages commensurately. Nelson and Galvez found that the high prices offered by MCCH, the Fair Trade cocoa buyer in Ecuador, pushed up prices offered by other middlemen: 'Paradoxically, on the routes in which MCCH operate the difference in prices is minimal, precisely because MCCH is operating as a regulator of prices in the area, and the farmers are in a stronger position to negotiate' (2000: 21). MCCH weighs the farmers' beans and pays them based on humidity calculations – information which the farmers then use to negotiate better terms with the *coyote* middlemen who visit their farms.

These benefits aside, many studies found that the Fair Trade label seems to lend legitimacy to certain groups, giving them access to credit and loans and distancing them from non-Fair Trade farmers. Lyon's (2002) research found that development and lending agencies prefer to give large donations and loans to successful well-established co-operatives rather than new groups. According to the manager of La Selva Co-operative in Mexico, 'Fair Trade is having its impact on an elite group of producers … this is not what the rules of Fair Trade are supposed to strive for. The fair market should have tried to incorporate also the dispossessed into the system' (in Taylor, 2002: 25).

These and other studies found that Fair Trade did not necessarily benefit the poorest producers who were excluded from Fair Trade networks. Nelson and Galvez (2000) found that the poorest and most remote cocoa producers in Ecuador did not benefit from Fair Trade because the Fair Trade exporter found it too difficult to access them. Malins and Blowfield (2000), however, found that the Fruits of the Nile solar fruit-drying project was accessible to many poor and marginalized people (including some impoverished women, widows, young people and refugees) because of the low start-up capital requirements. Fruit drying does not require processors to own land, rather they can buy fresh fruit and use the small driers in their family compounds.

Finally, the standards themselves may limit the benefits that Fair Trade has on the poorest producers and exclude the most vulnerable from the benefits of Fair Trade. According to Bacon (2004), rural landless coffee picking families, specifically the women and children in these families, are the most vulnerable population in Nicaragua. But in the case of coffee, FLO standards require that at least 50 per cent of a certified group's production must be grown by small family farmers not 'structurally dependent' on hired labour. Because the international Fair Trade standards specifically limit the participation of plantations (and thus coffee pickers) from the Fair Trade certification system, the poorest families involved in coffee exports are not benefiting from the Fair Trade system except through indirect means as discussed above.

In summary, non-Fair Trade producers do benefit from the social capital, trade linkages and market information networks created and supported by Fair Trade. Unorganized farmers and farm workers are obviously excluded, however, from the direct benefits of Fair Trade, including higher incomes, direct relationships, social networking and empowerment acquired through being part of an organized co-operative or farm worker organization. Furthermore, substantial anecdotal evidence exists to suggest that Fair Trade does not access the poorest producers in export crop production. Because Fair Trade products must be sold on Northern markets, it is to be expected that only those farmers who can produce export-quality crops can participate in Fair Trade, which might exclude the poorest and most marginalized farmers who cannot invest in quality improvements. However, it must also be noted that Fair Trade standards require the producer group to have the potential to improve the social development of its members and that the intended and actual beneficiaries are indeed 'poor', if not 'the poorest'. No impact study as yet has found that Fair Trade was addressing wealthy populations, or that there were not significant benefits to poor producers from accessing Fair Trade markets.

QUANTIFYING THE IMPACTS OF FAIR TRADE

Over the last ten years, writers and policy makers have explored the role of civil society in generating value. Drawing on a range of empirical and conceptual material, Putnam (2000) encapsulated this new thinking in a wide-ranging analysis of the impact of 'social capital' – namely the value added to a community by associational behaviour. Such social value was acknowledged as being hard to measure, given that it does not typically take the form of transactional commerce. Indeed, social capital creation is difficult even to identify accurately, since it often takes the form of unexpected externalities. For example, the benefits to a community of setting up a local activity and training centre for unemployed young people may have immediate benefits in terms of reducing vandalism or petty crime, but may also have its greatest impact in more longitudinal values, such as improving the long-term economy of the area or restoring family cohesion.

Whilst Putnam's work is an important contribution towards a better understanding of the nature of social value, it does not engage with social impact metrics. In order to comprehend the full impact of Fair Trade, a variety of approaches to quantifying social returns are needed.

The potential value of social impact metrics for Fair Trade is considerable. Firstly, they provide a measure of mission success or failure and, thus, help inform future resource allocation. This could include new product development. Secondly, rigorously derived metrics add credibility to social ventures and help inform stakeholders of progress towards social mission objectives. This may also increase access to resources to support future growth. Thirdly, they help to create models and benchmarks that generate best practice across sectors. This is particularly important to leverage the full benefit of Fair Trade networks such as those supported by the International Federation of Alternative Trade (IFAT).

The key question is, however, what to measure? There are a variety of possible impacts to consider. The simplest are quantifiable outputs, such as the volume of sales of Fair Trade goods by weight or money. However, these figures alone are of limited value. Their main contribution is in longitudinal tracking of organizational performance over time. More useful is data on the social outcomes of Fair Trade, including the generation of social value added impacts. These data might include not only a measure of the increase in a producer's income, but also the improvement in his or her family's standard of living or the overall well-being of his or her community. The public sector value should also be considered. This may involve welfare cost savings by reducing reliance on social services support, as well as increased government revenue through higher tax revenues (potentially in both producing and consuming countries). Furthermore, social value added would include other positive externalities such as the benefits of increasing the social capital in a community via the creation of connections to other producers or producer groups and community building in general. However, the latter is notoriously difficult to calculate.

A second key question is how will the data be measured? Attempting accurately to ascertain individual human impacts is problematic, since they will inevitably be highly personal and individualized and may include multiple unique variables. It is likely, therefore, that aggregated data will be needed that will inevitably lose some of the nuances in each case. Moreover, the most appropriate timescales for measurement are also often unclear.

Some of the impacts of Fair Trade will be almost immediate (such as improved income levels), whilst others (such as greater confidence and success in negotiating situations) may only pay off after several years.

Nevertheless, despite these considerable challenges, there are a number of approaches that may be used to quantify Fair Trade impacts that are emerging. These are explored in the following sections.

SIMPLE RATIOS

The simple ratio of the financial return on investment for Fair Trade represents a useful starting-point. In terms of strategic planning and future fundraising, it is of value to calculate the return on National Fair Trade Labelling Initiative (NI) and FLO expenditures, measured in terms of income return to producers. Unfortunately, NI budget data are only publicly available for Austria, Canada, France, Germany, Switzerland, the UK and the USA. These countries account for about 76 per cent of total FLO-certified product turnover. The total 2002 expenditure for these countries, plus 76 per cent of FLO expenditure, was $9.3m (£5.2m). Dividing this total into 76 per cent of FLO-estimated farmer benefit yields a benefit-cost ratio of 2.8:1. Thus every dollar spent by FLO or a member National Initiative yields $2.80 in increased farmer income.

These expenditure figures do not, of course, include the potentially millions of dollars spent worldwide by non-profit organizations on Fair Trade advocacy and education. As only FLO and its members dedicate their entire budgets to the promotion of Fair Trade-certified products, only their budgets could be taken into account.[3] It would have been impossible to isolate the expenditures of Oxfam, IFAT, the Network of European World Shops, EFTA, the Fair Trade Federation, Global Exchange, church groups, community groups and other Fair Trade advocacy groups on promoting Fair Trade-labelled products. Similarly, there are dozens of non-profits in origin countries that help Fair Trade producer groups with credit provision, preparing for FLO inspections, quality improvements and so on. Neither does this ratio estimate the significant non-income benefits accrued to Fair Trade producers and their communities, or increases in income gained by Fair Trade producers' access to market information and direct trade relationships.

QUALITATIVE MODELS

The first group of metrical models are qualitative in approach. This means that they focus on social impact measurement through capturing specific, and often partial, descriptive outcomes of strategic action. Such metrics are typically human in scale, looking at individual or community level changes or developments and are largely non-comparative. Qualitative metrics have an organizational focus, addressing the issue of 'what is it we do?' One of the most problematic areas for such metrics is defining the appropriate value of each unit of measurement. For example, in one venture it may be the number of wells sunk with developmental money, for another it may be the number of homeless people given shelter. Clearly, such reporting is highly contextualized and rarely comparative.

Triple Bottom Line

The simplest of the qualitative social metrics is the triple bottom line (Elkington, 1997, 2001). This model requires an enterprise's accounting system to incorporate not only the traditional measures of financial performance, but also social and environmental outcomes. However, unlike financial accounts the social and environmental audits are typically descriptive, rather than quantitative, and partial and subjective rather than complete and objective. Any external comparative dimension is also typically lacking (although internal longitudinal comparison is possible). This is primarily a consequence of the lack of agreed social and environmental performance benchmarks. Finally, in this model, the three bottom lines are not weighted or integrated into any final statement of performance.

The triple bottom line is very useful for conventional businesses, as it reminds them to consider the social and environmental outcomes of their commercial behaviour and to audit their progress in all three areas. However, for a Fair Trade venture the model has little value. Since Fair Trade is intrinsically concerned with generating social and environmental outcomes, as well as commercial returns, there is little need to encourage an acknowledgement of the role of all three of these in assessing business performance.

Social Accounting

Social accounting expands the social element of the triple bottom line model through greater qualitative detail of specific outcomes. It also aims for more rigour. In his study of business accountability and ethical performance, Zadek noted eight principles of social accounting (1998: 1436–8):

- *Inclusivity*: social accounts must reflect the views and inputs of all stakeholders, and not just those who have a formal influence over strategic planning, as well as other externalities such as environmental impact.

- *Comparability*: social accounts must be designed in conjunction with relevant external benchmarks and must be methodologically consistent over time.

- *Completeness*: social accounts must not cherry-pick results or 'spin' data to provide a false picture.

- *Regularity and evolution*: social accounts should be published at predetermined intervals and support strategy by helping set and measure positive (or negative) progress towards social aims and objectives.

- *Embeddedness*: the areas of assessment in social accounts need to reflect the strategic issues for a venture and must be incorporated back into future planning through feedback mechanisms.

- *Communication*: social accounts must be transparent and easily available as the aim is for full public disclosure to generate a dialogue on performance with stakeholders.

- *Externally verified*: social accounts must be accurate and impartial.

- *Continuous improvement*: social accounts must aim to contribute to a larger organizational process of continuous assessment and development.

Social accounting reports typically act as longitudinal assessments of internal performance and tend to use descriptive metrics, such as profiles of target populations or stakeholder characteristics, as well as some financial information. Currently, a number of Fair Trade organizations such as Traidcraft (see case study below) and Cafédirect publish social accounts that largely conform to Zadek's principles. This information provides a valuable narrative of particular actions and objectives and can be used to demonstrate progress over time. Such accounts would typically include not only information about sales levels, but also about the level of developmental assistance that was generated for producers and often some description of specific local impacts (the building of a school or funding for grain silos). Again, however, social accounting is largely an internally driven marketing strategy for stakeholders lacking comparative value and is, thus, a generally poor measure of overall performance.

CASE STUDY: TRAIDCRAFT

Traidcraft has been fighting poverty through trade since 1979. As the UK's leading Fair Trade organization, Traidcraft works with more than 100 producer groups in over 30 countries around the world. Traidcraft aims to help the poor to trade more effectively by breaking down the barriers that prevent them gaining access to markets. The company works with in-country partners to develop producers' business skills and capacity and to create the environment needed to help poor producers engage in sustainable trade. Furthermore, Traidcraft works at national and international levels advocating changes in trade rules to make them work in the interests of the poor and they mobilize public opinion to support fairer trade practices.

Traidcraft has a unique structure that combines a trading company (Traidcraft PLC) with a development charity (Traidcraft Exchange) overseen by a Foundation. This gives the company many opportunities to influence opinion and behaviour in the charitable, business and public sectors.

The three main organizations that make up Traidcraft are bound together by a Deed of Mutual Covenant, which enshrines Traidcraft's Foundation principles and sets out the basis for mutual co-operation. The Traidcraft Foundation holds a Guardian Share in Traidcraft PLC to enable it to protect the vision and mission of the organization. It is also the Founder member of the charity, Traidcraft Exchange, and appoints all its directors. Traidcraft PLC and Traidcraft Exchange work closely wherever possible and share the same senior management team and support services. The two boards share many of the same members and all their meetings are held jointly.

In 2003–4, sales in the Traidcraft PLC trading company grew by 15 per cent to £13.8 million ($24.7m). Gross profit for the year was £4.97 million ($8.9m), compared with £4.37 million ($7.8m) in 2002. Profit after tax was £348,000 ($622,920) in 2003 compared to £321,000 ($574,590) in 2002. The total income received by

Traidcraft Exchange increased again during 2003 to reach £2.52 million ($4.5m) compared to £2.43 million ($4.3m) in 2002.

Traidcraft PLC's activities can be broken down into four catagories: crafts (handicrafts and similar items bought by the plc for re-sale); food (food commodities and beverages bought by the plc either directly or through European partners, for re-sale); Teadirect (tea sourced whilst the plc acted as a sourcing agent for Cafédirect's brand Teadirect, an activity which ended in 2003); licenced goods (Fair Trade purchases attributable to sales of wine, fruit juice and other lines, where the PLC does not buy/sell the stock, but earns a licence fee for carrying out the supply chain verification).

Social Accounting

Social accounting is a systematic means of accounting for the social impact of an organization. It can be compared to the way that financial accounting provides the means to account for an organization's financial performance. Traidcraft is one of the pioneers of social accounting in the UK, having published its first independently audited report in 1993. Since then Traidcraft has further developed its methodology in collaboration with the New Economics Foundation. Traidcraft's social accounts are based on the following step-by-step approach:

- Define the social objectives and ethical values of the organization.
- Be clear about who are the stakeholders of the organization.
- Establish indicators by which performance against the objectives and values can be measured.
- Measure performance against indicators.
- Gain the views of stakeholders about how they perceive the organization's performance.
- Report all of the above in as balanced a manner as possible.
- Submit the report to independent audit.
- Publish the report.
- Gain feedback from stakeholders on the report's findings.

Source: Traidcraft (2002, 2003, 2004)

Balanced Scorecard

Another common qualitative approach to performance measurement is the Balanced Scorecard, first developed by Kaplan and Norton (1996). Kaplan adapted the Scorecard (2002) for use by not-for profit organizations (see Figure 9.1). The approach he recommended provided a clear framework for defining a causal link between non-financial performance measures and the achievement of mission. The adapted Balanced Scorecard involved defining mission success by setting and then testing organizational objectives with respect to a range of stakeholders aligned to a business analysis that considered internal business process and organizational learning.

When this model is applied to Fair Trade (see Figure 9.2), the mission is two-fold: maximizing returns to producers and advocating greater trade justice. The 'customers'

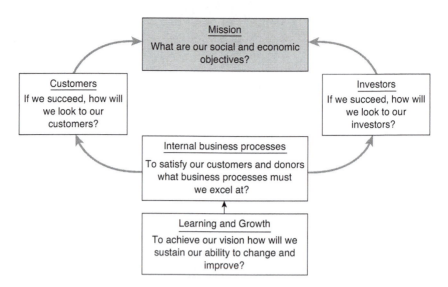

Figure 9.1   *The Balanced Scorecard for Not-For-Profits (Kaplan, 2002)*

become producers and the 'investors' become consumers. Key objectives for the former would be developmental improvements and for the latter these would be sales and awareness levels. The internal business processes require Fair Trade organizations to develop commercial skills and capacity whilst still creating strategies for campaigning and raising awareness. Combining these two objectives is difficult: the reality is that they tend to be divided within Fair Trade into advocacy groups (FLO members, IFAT, EFTA) and commercial operators (Traidcraft, Cafédirect, People Tree). Indeed Oxfam, one of the few organizations to combine commercial Fair Trade and advocacy, recently moved out of the former to concentrate on the latter. Finally, the organizational learning input centres on the various Fair Trade networks to encourage information flows and innovations. The Asia Fair Trade Centre of Excellence is one example of such a dynamic learning organization.

Family of Measures

As a reaction to the perceived lack of focus in existing social metrics, Sawhill and Williamson (2001) developed the Family of Measures model to better articulate a venture's progress towards its mission objectives. As they commented, 'Every nonprofit organization should measure its progress towards fulfilling its mission, its success in mobilizing its resources, and its staff's effectiveness on the job' (2001: 98). The key point they made was that not-for-profit organizations needed to devise metrics that reflected the detail of their mission objectives, rather than their organizational performance overall. Thus, a Fair Trade venture would need to focus less on general level of sales growth or profitability and concentrate more on the producer impact it was achieving.

The model was built around three sets of linked metrics: impact measures, activity measures and capacity measures. Impact measures aim to map the progress towards fulfilling the organization's mission and the long-term objectives that drive it. For these to work, the elements of the mission must be broken down into quantifiable and specific

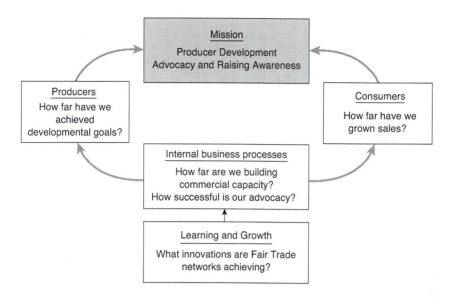

Figure 9.2 *The Balanced Scorecard for Fair Trade (adapted from Kaplan, 2002)*

objectives. It may be that detailed research is required for this to be effective. Activity measures chart the progress towards goals and programme implementation that drive organizational behaviour. These would include the success or otherwise of mobilizing resources toward program implementations. Capacity measures capture the effectiveness and progress of all the levels of an organization that keep it operational. These might include resource allocation and fundraising or market share.

If applied to a Fair Trade venture this model would allow an analysis of its organizational features and performance. The impact measures would be quantified by specific data on producer development (in economic and social units) and possibly advocacy (such as awareness levels). The activity measures would correspond to the number of producer projects underway. The capacity measures would indicate staff levels, productivity, use of income and so on.

Sawhill and Williamson (2001; see Figure 9.3) linked each of these three sets of measurements in an organizational diagram that mapped the operational flow of a social venture as it moved from mission (impact) via vision and goals (activities) to strategy and tactics (capacity). This model is inherently both more sophisticated (by having a dynamic element) and rigorous (by aiming for more specific objectives) than the other descriptive models described above. However, as with the others it is essentially an internal tool that fails to offer a comparative set of performance metrics and is thus limited in terms of its strategic value.

QUANTITATIVE MODEL: SOCIAL RETURN ON INVESTMENT

To date the only rigorously quantitative model of social impact measurement is the Social Return on Investment (SROI) framework devised by Emerson and the Roberts Enterprise Development Fund (Emerson, 1999, 2003; REDF, 2000) and, more recently, extended by

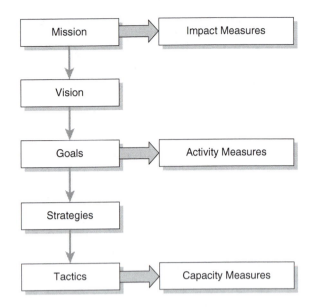

Figure 9.3   *Family of Measures (Sawhill and Williamson, 2001)*

the New Economics Foundation (NEF, 2004b). It represents the most sophisticated attempt yet to measure the impact of social ventures. The NEF commented:

> Social Return on Investment mirrors the standard financial measure of economic return but shows how organizations of all kinds create value beyond the economic. This is particularly true for those organizations in the social economy that may search for either economic and social value, or just social value. When compared to mainstream businesses, they may or may not achieve similar levels of financial return, but even if they do not, the value to society of the social or environmental returns that they create may well be equal or higher. (2004b: 3)

SROI methodology allows social ventures to answer the following questions more effectively:

- How do we know whether we are accomplishing what we set out to do?
- How can we make informed decisions about the ongoing use of resources?
- How can we test and convince others of what we have achieved and show the value of our social outputs in terms that would be understood by those financing social ventures? (2004b: 6)

SROI develops a quantitative approach that uses the fundamentals of Cost Benefit Analysis reporting on return on investment as its starting-point. This approach is very different from the more qualitative approach of Social Accounting, for example. SROI aims to guide future investment decisions and justify past decision making, whereas Social Accounting demonstrates accountability and generates stakeholder engagement. Both models are clearly useful and, in best practice, should be used in tandem.

The SROI model is in three parts: the first calculates the full blended value of a social venture (combing its enterprise value and social purpose value); the second establishes the investment in the project; the third then calculates the blended return on investment (combining the enterprise and social returns). For a given venture or project the model works as follows:

- To measure value:

  - Calculate the enterprise value
    - Discount this figure by an appropriate rate, taking into account the WACC, where relevant
  - Calculate the monetized social purpose value, taking into account the direct social costs of the project
    - Discount this figure by an appropriate rate, taking into account the WACC, where relevant
  - Calculate the blended value
    - Add enterprise and social venture values together

- To measure investment:

  - Calculate the total costs of supporting the social venture (in many, but not all, cases this is a philanthropic grant or donation)
    - Discount this figure by the weighted average of the discount rates for the enterprise and social venture values already worked out

- To measure return:

  - Calculate the enterprise index of return
    - Divide the enterprise value by the total investment
  - Calculate the social purpose index of return
    - Divide the social purpose value by the total investment
  - Calculate the blended index of return
    - Divide the blended value by the total investment

In order to follow the SROI methodology effectively a number of other issues must also be considered (NEF, 2004b: 11). Firstly, the organizational boundaries of the social venture must be set as this allows a clearer picture of the range of stakeholders to be established and the key social objectives to be identified. Secondly, an 'impact map' should be drawn as this clarifies how social impact is intended to be achieved. Typically, this process is conceptualized as linking inputs to outputs to outcomes to impacts. In this model, inputs represent the total costs of the social venture, outputs the simple quantitative effects (such as sales, number of jobs created and so on), outcomes the direct and indirect changes in target stakeholders and their communities (improved education, better levels of health, longitudinal factors) and impacts the changes discounted by a 'deadweight analysis' (the extent to which outcomes would have happened without any interventions by the social venture). Finally, appropriate indicators must be identified to capture the elements within the impact map and monetized values for them determined.

The enterprise value of a social venture is calculated, as with any traditional business project, as the present value of its predicted total future cash flows (typically measured over a ten-year period), discounted by a risk premium. This is the project's output. At the beginning, then, the future income from a social venture must be established. In the case of Fair Trade projects this is calculated as the total income to producers from their Fair Trade sales. In order to project the long-term growth of Fair Trade sales it seems sensible for a modest figure of 10 per cent to be used rather than the 20–50 per cent 'start up' rates that have typically been the case so far.

Next, the future cash flows must be discounted at an appropriate rate that allows the total value to be compared with the baseline return expected from such an investment in a similar project. The discount rate is typically calculated by first using the Capital Asset Pricing Model (CAPM). This financial model calculates the risk of a given sector or project based on its historical level of variance from the basic market return on an investment. In other words, it estimates what additional return on an investment should be expected for a particular project using its risk profile. In terms of social ventures there is often an additional small business risk premium added to this. For a Fair Trade business the CAPM would reflect both its sector (typically retail) and its size (typically small).

Finally, the Weighted Average Cost of Capital (WACC) process is used to adjust the CAPM discount rate. The WACC recognizes the different risk profiles of businesses according to their financial structure, namely their balance of debt and equity. The WACC is typically weighted according to the average finance structure for the sector in which the particular social venture operates (for example, health, education or retail). Since most Fair Trade businesses are financed by grants alone, the WACC adjustment is probably irrelevant.

The social purpose value of the venture is calculated in the same way as the enterprise value. However, the main innovation here lies in quantifying the various elements that make up these calculations. To begin with, the economic value of the social project must be determined. In the case of an employment project this could be calculated by taking the average public welfare saving per new employee and the average incremental increase in income tax revenue per new employee and then multiplying the total by the projected number of employees. In the case of Fair Trade, the various developmental impacts would need to be quantified and monetized. For example, technical assistance may increase productivity by a measurable amount. Alternatively, pre-financing may allow crop diversification that increases the yields for existing planting or, possibly, new high-value commodities (such as a switch to organic). Furthermore, the less obvious social impacts such as better education and health that often follow on from Fair Trade development should also be included in the calculations. This is difficult, but not impossible. One approach is to search for proxies or previously calculated financial values for social impacts. For example, the United Nations Development Programme has developed monetized lifetime values for educational improvement in children in terms of extra productivity compared to a control sample.

The key objective is to attempt to capture and quantify as many of the social impacts of a Fair Trade project as possible. It will probably always be impossible to capture all the benefits, not least because some will effectively be externalities to the main mission (see above). Furthermore, many impacts will only be apparent over time and these are notoriously difficult to track. Nevertheless, such calculations still represent the most systematic and quantifiable approach to social impact currently available.

Having calculated the monetized value of social purpose impact, any directly linked social operating costs must be deducted. In an employment-creation program these would include the cost of additional training or supervision. In the case of Fair Trade such costs could include cross-subsidies across product groups or the real costs of design and technical support that were provided for free.

The total future social purpose value must then also be discounted to a present value, in just the same way as the enterprise value. Typically, a public sector bond rate is used for most not-for-profits (for example, government program-related investments are usually discounted at about 3 per cent). However, for grant-funded programmes the rate would be 0 per cent, because there are typically no opportunity costs in this form of funding. The discounted social purpose value represents the project's outcome. If possible, this should be subject to a deadweight analysis to determine more accurately the real impact of the social venture. Finally, with both the enterprise and the social purpose value of a venture calculated, they can be combined to show the blended value.

In order to calculate the SROI, the total investment in a project must firstly be calculated and then discounted by the weighted average discount rate of the enterprise and social purpose values that have already been worked out. This figure can then be divided into the enterprise, social, or blended values of the project in order to establish the level of return. For a Fair Trade business this would be the cost *differential* of goods bought from a particular producer above the market price, plus any social premium payments. Set out below is an example set of SROI calculations based on a fictitious Fair Trade project. It is important to note that these figures are not intended as benchmarks for any real Fair Trade ventures, but as an example of how to use the methodology. The assumptions made are deliberately simplistic for ease of demonstration and do not attempt to capture all the possible types of value creation. For example, including other social premium-funded projects and externalities such as benefits to non-Fair Trade sales would increase the estimated return several-fold.

CASE STUDY: SOCIAL RETURN ON INVESTMENT (SROI) CALCULATIONS FOR A FAIR TRADE WINE PROJECT IN SOUTH AFRICA

A wine importer in the UK is buying Fair Trade wine from a co-operative in South Africa. In this case, the extra 'investment' in Fair Trade is calculated as the amount the importer paid above and beyond the market price for the wine. The SROI methodology utilized below will approximate the total return on this investment in Fair Trade, including both the income to producers as well as positive social externalities achieved through the development projects in which the farmers invest.

Assumptions:
- Sales will start at 7000 bottles a year and grow by 10 per cent per annum.
- The co-operative will receive a floor price of £1.50 per bottle, representing a Fair Trade premium above the market price of 20p per bottle. Cost of goods (including bottles and equipment rental) is £1 per bottle, representing a net producer enterprise income of £0.50 per bottle.
- In addition, the co-operative will receive a social premium of 10 per cent of the cost price, or 15p per bottle.

Step 1: Calculate the enterprise value

This is the present value (PV) of all future net income.

Assumptions: • The discount rate is 8 per cent for the duration of the project, calculated as the standard small retailer risk premium, unadjusted by the WACC because the investment can be considered a grant (as the importer is not expecting a financial return).

Year	0	1	2	3	4	...	8	9
Sales (bottles)	7000	7700	8470	9317	10248	...	15005	16505
Producer income	£3,500	£3,850	£14,235	£14,659	£5,124	...	£7,503	£8,253
Discount rate	8%							
Enterprise value	£38,065							

Step 2: Calculate the social purpose value

This is the present value (PV) of all future social impacts.

Assumptions: • The social purpose costs are £300 per year for technical support and planning.
• The co-operative votes to use the social premium funds to renovate the community school in the fifth year. The cost of the renovation will be £5,000.
• The co-operative, now an empowered group of family farmers, lobbies its local government to provide an extra teacher for the school.
• The impact of the renovation and an extra teacher will be the improvement of learning levels for 50 children in the community.
• It is estimated that their improved learning levels will increase the average productivity of the children by 20 per cent over their economic lifetime.
• The average economic contribution of a citizen of this community during their working life is currently £40,000. It is therefore estimated that the improvements to the school will be worth an additional £8,000 per pupil or a total of £400,000 by year five.
• The discount rate is 5 per cent, a typical government bond rate for public improvement projects.

Year	0	1	2	3	4	...	8	9
Social premium	£1,050	£1,155	£1,271	£1,398	£1,537	...	£2,251	£2,476
Social purpose costs	£300	£300	£300	£300	£5300	...	£300	£300
Social premium account balance		£750	£1,905	£3,176	£4,573	£1,110		£13,958	£16,434
Schooling benefits						£400,000			
Social purpose value PV (5% discount rate)	£339,675							

The Social Purpose Value is calculated as the present value (PV) of social projects plus any remaining unspent social premium funds.

Step 3: Calculate the Blended Value by adding together Enterprise and Social Purpose values

Enterprise Value	£38,065
Social Purpose Value	£339,675
Blended Value	£377,740

Step 4: Calculate Social Return on Investment

Assumptions:
- The investment to date by importers is calculated as the cost of sales above the market price plus the costs of the social premium, at a total of £0.35 per bottle.
- In addition, the Fair Trade wine importer paid for a media visit to the wine co-operative which resulted in a newspaper article that directly contributed to sales growth. The cost of this trip at £3,000 is added to the social operating costs.

The weighted discount rate is equal to: (enterprise value/blended value per cent) × 8 per cent + (social purpose value/blended value per cent) × 5 per cent = (£38,065/£377,740)*8% + £339,675/£377,740)*5% = 5.3%.

This discount rate is used to calculate the present value (PV) of the social operating costs.

Year	0	1	2	3	4	...	8	9
Social operating costs (extra spend on Fair Trade wine by importers)	£2,450	£2,695	£2,965	£3,261	£3,587	...	£5,252	£5,777
Cost of trip	£3,000					...		
Discount rate	5.3%							
Social operating costs (PV)	£54,811							

Social return ratio = (enterprise value + social purpose value)/present value of social operating costs = £377,740/£54,811 = 6.89.

Thus, for every £1 spent on Fair Trade wine (at the import level), a value of £6.89 was returned to the community.

Despite its quantitative rigour, there remains a number of problems with the SROI methodology as it currently stands. Firstly, there are as yet no reliable SROI benchmarks or industry standards. This makes credible comparative analysis of rates of return impossible.

Secondly, there are a limited number of accepted proxies by which to monetize social value. Thirdly, social operating costs may be difficult to extract from core costs. Finally, the typical grant finance structure of many not-for-profits, including Fair Trade ventures, distorts discount rates and may undermine the accuracy of present value calculations.

Nevertheless, for all these caveats, the SROI still represents both a promising model of quantitative social impact measurement and, more generally, an important demonstration of a new and more rigorous approach to performance measurement and accountability for the social sector. For both reasons its value should be carefully considered by all Fair Trade ventures.

CONCLUSION

This chapter has explored the impact of Fair Trade. The summary of the studies to date at its beginning clearly indicated the need for more research in this area. Next, the complexity of Fair Trade's social impacts was exposed in an analysis of its direct and indirect effects on producers and their communities. Finally, the available methodologies for measuring social impact were explored. The chapter concluded by suggesting that, although problematic, the SROI model offers an excellent opportunity to begin a process of more thorough impact measurement for Fair Trade.

Providing convincing and accurate measures of the impact of Fair Trade has considerable value. Such figures can add legitimacy to the claims made by Fair Trade organizations that not only are they helping disenfranchised producers, but that they are doing it more effectively than the conventional trade model. In addition, reliable figures offer key stakeholders a better view on the successes and failures of Fair Trade ventures and this could have a positive marketing and brand value. And lastly, rigorous impact metrics should help improve Fair Trade performance by signalling where successful strategies and structures lie and giving access to new investment and other resources.

The next chapter concludes the third and final part of this book by addressing the key future strategic issues for Fair Trade.

NOTES

1. One adjustment was made from FLO's 2002 Annual Report numbers. For cocoa, an average of the FLO 2002 Annual Report number ($180,504; £101,082) and $150 (£84)/MT Fair Trade social premium times FLO bean turnover of 1618 MT ($242,700; £135,912) was taken, for a total Fair Trade benefit to cocoa farmers of $211,602 (£118,497).

2. Bacon (2004) did ask some qualitative questions to assess indirect benefits, especially psychological kinds, as enjoyed by Fair Trade *vs.* non-Fair Trade producers, but this comparative focus is the exception rather than the norm.

3. TransFair Germany's budget also includes expenditures on the Rugmark label, which were taken out of TransFair Germany's numbers to reflect only TransFair's expenditures on Fair Trade-labelled products.

10

Fair Trade Futures

The Fair Trade movement finds itself at a turning point. After years of functioning as an effective alternative trading mechanism, Fair Trade is now entering the mainstream, trying to balance being 'in and against' the market. The engagement of multinationals like Procter & Gamble and Starbucks and major retailers such as Tesco and Carrefour clearly signals the commercial opportunity represented by Fair Trade (Welford et al., 2003). However, future development remains highly contested. This chapter begins by summarizing the key points of the book thus far to provide a context for the broader discussion of future issues that follows. It then lays out some of the strategic opportunities to grow Fair Trade and identifies the challenges in obtaining those objectives. After discussing competitive threats to Fair Trade certification, the chapter will conclude with a discussion of Fair Trade governance in order to define a structure that will best perpetuate and grow the Fair Trade revolution worldwide.

INTRODUCTION: FAIR TRADE TODAY

The previous chapters have explored the phenomenon of Fair Trade from many different angles and through a number of theoretical lenses ranging from orthodox economic theory, via finance, operations and marketing, to business ethics. Some key strengths of the Fair Trade movement and market have emerged from the discussion:

- Fair Trade sales are growing fast globally to over £500m ($895m) in 2003 and this growth looks set to continue.
- If the potentially huge US market matches the growth rates in more established markets, Fair Trade sales could increase by a factor of 20 or more in the next few years.
- Fair Trade is now in the mainstream in many countries with increasing levels of public awareness and multinational company involvement.
- Fair Trade is not about charity or aid, but about using trade relationships to achieve economic development and empowerment.
- Fair Trade addresses economic and social market failures effectively.
- Fair Trade reconfigures the value chain to the advantage of producers, often via reducing multiple mark-up inefficiencies and cutting out exploitative middlemen.
- Fair Trade delivers genuine and measurable benefits to producers around the world.
- The Fair Trade model has proven to be financially sustainable and Fair Trade companies are now attractive to a range of investors.

- Certification and audit mechanisms ensure the integrity of the Fair Trade process and have built up consumer trust.
- The success of Fair Trade is helping to catalyze a significant shift towards more ethical trading across many sectors.
- Fair Trade is increasingly consumer-driven as well as activist-led and producer-focussed.

All of the above give good grounds for an optimistic analysis of the Fair Trade future. However, if growth is to continue at its current exponential rates key actors cannot become complacent. Indeed, the Fair Trade movement as a whole is only at the beginning:

- Fair Trade still only represents approximately 0.01 per cent of all goods exchanged internationally (Vidal, 2004).
- Several previous 'ethical' consumer movements – particularly environmentalism in the 1980s – have proved to be short-lived commercial fads.
- The largest markets for Fair Trade (European) may be approaching saturation point, especially in heavily branded products like coffee.

Nevertheless, new opportunities for growth are emerging and it will be crucial to devise the best strategies and structures to exploit these. In fact, the more problematic issues that have also emerged in this book largely reflect the challenges of growth, namely:

- If the Fair Trade market is to continue to grow, significant infusions of capital are needed for marketing and certification (especially new product development).
- The current structures of Fair Trade governance are not well suited to fast growth.
- The definition and characteristics of Fair Trade change as mainstream actors enter, which can lead to fissures in the movement.
- As consumer awareness of producer realities grows, mainstream companies may adopt other lower-cost non-Fair Trade certification systems to address consumer concerns.
- There is no legal definition of Fair Trade and no protection against 'counterfeit' Fair Trade products.

Before discussing the various future issues confronting Fair Trade, it will be helpful to recap the development of the market to date in order to take stock of where Fair Trade is today. So far, the strategic development of Fair Trade as a business in the North can be seen as following a trajectory in three broad stages: grassroots, new institutions and mainstreaming.

Stage One: Grassroots (1970–1990)

Activist-led campaigning drove the first wave of Fair Trade sales. Growth came via increased listings in alternative trading organizations (ATOs) such as Oxfam and world shops. Sales relied on a loyal core segment of ethical consumers and, thus, this stage was highly process-focussed and supply rather than demand driven. Any development of Fair Trade as a business was largely organic, unplanned and relatively unstrategic. Nevertheless, this campaigning approach effectively established a market for Fair Trade in the North and played an important role in raising awareness of trade injustice more generally. The fact that social justice and social value-added are consumer issues at all owes much to the pioneering work of activists and Fair Trade non-governmental organizations (NGOs).

Stage Two: New Institutions (1990–1999)

In the second stage, macro-level Fair Trade organizations began to emerge. The need for an agreed certification process and mark was one of the key drivers behind this. Consequently, from the late 1980s a range of national labelling and certification initiatives began to appear that were later consolidated into the Fair Trade Labelling Organizations International (FLO). At the same time, more strategic groups began to emerge such as the International Federation of Alternative Trade (IFAT), the European Fair Trade Association (EFTA) and in the USA, the Fair Trade Federation. These organizations typically functioned as trade associations that aimed, firstly, to network smaller Fair Trade groups to leverage shared skills and knowledge and, secondly, to address key strategic issues for the Fair Trade movement as a whole.

In addition to recognizing the importance of a consistent Fair Trade mark and message (rationalized across European national initiatives in 2003), these macro-level groups also addressed the issue of engagement with more conventional retailers. This strategy effectively acknowledged that to grow Fair Trade sales beyond a core group of supporters, there was a need to reposition Fair Trade products. Thus, many Fair Trade products began to emphasize issues of quality and exclusivity as well as ethical value. In this way, Fair Trade became more product focussed and increasingly demand rather than supply driven. At this stage, new companies such as Cafédirect and the Day Chocolate Company secured listings in high street retailers for the first time. Sympathetic retailers such as the Co-operative Group in the UK also grew their Fair Trade offer. Finally, institutions such as the Fairtrade Foundation in the UK ramped up promotion and awareness-raising activities through new initiatives such as Fair Trade Fortnight.

Stage 3: Mainstreaming (2000–)

From the late 1990s, building on the activities described in Stage 2, Fair Trade began to enter the mainstream in many developed markets. An exception to this is the US which developed later than markets in Europe and is working through Stage 2. The path to the mainstream evolved through two channels: firstly, increasing activities to include large-scale non-Fair Trade businesses; secondly, broadening the range of consumer-facing promotional and educational activities. In the former, key strategic achievements included the development of a broad range of supermarket own-label products and the pursuit of co-branding opportunities, such as the collaboration between Traidcraft and the Co-operative Group in the case of Carmenere wine. In terms of consumer engagement, creative and opportunistic responses to grassroots' initiatives such as Fair Trade Towns allowed FLO members to leverage new approaches to raising involvement and awareness to great effect. As has already been noted, this mainstreaming strategy has worked well for certified food products, but has yet to be addressed by non-certified handicrafts.

Given the development thus far, what does the future hold for Fair Trade?

Strategic Opportunities

Fair Trade has been extremely successful to date and is increasingly entering the mainstream. The following section will outline several strategies that will ensure that growth of Fair Trade continues, including building brand equity in the Fair Trade concept, continuing to build market share, consolidating and strengthening Fair Trade advocacy in the international political arena and examining new Fair Trade opportunities such as developing Southern markets. Whilst a range of strategic opportunities can be discerned, the concerns and challenges facing each potential growth path must also be acknowledged. Tallontire (2002) outlined some of the significant demands that face Fair Trade as it proceeds further. These included:

- Producer dependency.
- Impact measurement.
- Increasing competition in the ethical marketplace.
- Mainstreaming.
- Linking consumer awareness to action.
- Engagement with private companies.

In the course of this book many of these issues have already been addressed. However, after this section outlining strategic opportunities, the most important threats to the continued success of Fair Trade will be identified. These include potential fissures within the movement and competitive threats from other systems.

Strategic Marketing Opportunities: Building the Fair Trade Brand

One major issue for Fair Trade is the possibility that consumer-driven growth will decline if Fair Trade proves simply to be a fashionable rather than a sustainable trend. The analogy here is with the boom and bust of 'green' products like Ecover household goods in the 1980s. Guarding against such faddishness will be an important objective for Fair Trade groups in the future. The best strategy is clearly to continue to raise awareness and build the 'brand' of Fair Trade. The strategic marketing initiatives noted below will help protect Fair Trade from a shortened business life cycle, with new product introductions also being a way to reduce brand fatigue. In this way a more appropriate comparison could be made with organic produce, which has secured a strong, sustainable and growing market based on clear positioning and an appeal to the consumer's sense of quality and lifestyle.

Since brand awareness is a necessary precursor to brand loyalty, the first priority for the national certification initiatives and other Fair Trade groups must be to continue to increase consumer marketing literacy about Fair Trade generally and the Fair Trade mark specifically. Ensuring that a growing number of consumers understand and identify with Fair Trade objectives and processes will underpin all future market growth in developed countries. Such a strategy will also be important to defend the Fair Trade certification mark from copycat labelling such as 'fairly traded' or the Utz Kapeh 'Certified Responsible' range at Ahold (see further below). Therefore, the Fair Trade movement must continue to devote considerable energy and resources to consumer education as a commercial as well as an advocacy strategy. Ranges should be broadened when a market opportunity presents itself and there should be a relentless search for marketing innovation supported by creative thinking (see Nicholls, 2004). Given limited resources, key Fair Trade actors must concentrate on using various creative means to avoid brand fatigue amongst mainstream audiences and grassroots supporters and must strengthen the brand messaging through Fair Trade's association with quality and the launching of new Fair Trade products.

Continual Rejuvenation of Communications to Mass-market Audiences

In common with all business-to-consumer marketing, Fair Trade marketers (led by the national Fair Trade labelling initiatives such as TransFair, Max Havelaar and the Fairtrade Foundation) need to engage in a constant process of evaluation and renewal as regards their communication strategies. For example, with its Big Noise Music download website, Oxfam has exploited the growing interest in Fair Trade amongst young people by mobilizing support by various bands in order to generate income that will further support its campaigning (10% of all sales from this site go to Oxfam). Similarly, the Fairtrade Foundation developed a relationship with the organizers of the UK's Glastonbury Music Festival 2004 to ensure that the hot beverages sold at the Festival were all Fair Trade. It also co-sponsored a CD of unsigned bands performing at the festival and shared the proceeds with the bands themselves. Another example is the Triodos Bank's Fair Trade current account which offers competitive rates of interest to personal investors and uses their savings to support such businesses as Cafédirect. Cross-sectoral partnerships like these offer significant commercial opportunities to enhance core retail or wholesale Fair Trade businesses.

Fair Trade has been increasingly successful in terms of raising consumer awareness across a variety of national markets in recent years. The proven success of events such as Fair Trade Fortnight (in the UK) or Fair Trade Month (in the USA) should continue to be leveraged to generate effective media interest and positive public relations activity. Creating consumer involvement is vital. There should also be more promotional events organized, for example, the UK Cooperative Group ran a successful Christmas Fair Trade advertising campaign.

The growing involvement of supermarkets (often via own-label initiatives) should be exploited to help support Fair Trade messaging both inside and outside of any timetable of promotional events. Wholesalers would benefit by building active partnerships with retailers to secure the best shelf positioning for Fair Trade products.

Furthermore, all Fair Trade ventures should seek *pro bono* marketing and advertising support from top-tier professional service organizations to produce more impactful mass-marketing communications. Fair Trade will need a greater share of marketing voice in going forward if it is to successfully resist the likely development of low-bar non-Fair Trade (but ethically positioned) competition from such companies as Nestlé and Kraft. The *quid pro quo* here is the valuable boost in terms of social responsibility offered by Fair Trade to an advertising agency's profile. Fundraising should focus on consumer marketing opportunities such as advertising. Indeed, Cafédirect has acknowledged this by allocating a significant proportion of new income from its 2004 initial public offering to fresh advertising and promotion campaigns.

Continue Grassroots Campaigning

Another way for Fair Trade marketers to leverage limited resources is to ensure that grassroots Fair Trade support remains strong. The role of traditional advocates of Fair Trade should be enhanced through creative campaigning and the use of multiple channels. For example, Oxfam's campaign to 'Make a Big Noise' for trade justice has made innovative use of the Internet, e-mail, celebrity endorsement and events to raise Fair Trade awareness within the younger population. The value of word-of-mouth communications should be developed through sponsoring Fair Trade coffee groups, debating societies or other community activities.

Following the enormous success of the UK's Fair Trade Towns campaign, other national Fair Trade-labelling initiatives should look to spin out the concept in their markets. The USA, in particular, should offer significant potential here since, at a local level, it often demonstrates a strong sense of community and typically values good civic behaviour. Using word-of-mouth marketing communications to tap into civic values and thus connect US towns to producer groups around the world could prove to be a very low-cost way of networking out Fair Trade messages across the USA and ramping up sales quickly.

The more recent 'Fair Trade' University, Village and Church successes in the UK could also lead to the scaling up of awarding criteria to be applied to other geographically centred campaigns, perhaps including Fair Trade Counties and, even, Countries! The USA has already seen success with student activists converting university campuses to Fair Trade coffee (Capone, 2004).

Finally, the importance of children in future Fair Trade campaigns must be fully recognized. Children represent three markets in one (McNeal, 1992, 1999): a current market (particularly for pocket-money level goods such as confectionery), an influencing market on peers and family and a future market as brand-loyal adults. Educational campaigns designed for children should be developed going forward in order to appeal to children's innate sense of fairness and give them a more informed view of the realities of their purchase decisions. The success of the Day Chocolate Company's Dubble bar and its tie-in with the UK's charity event Red Nose Day is a good example of how to reach the children's market.

As with all Fair Trade marketing, the key is to establish connections between producer and consumer. Fair Trade classroom lessons in UK schools have become part of the citizenship element in the National Curriculum. Anecdotal evidence to date suggests that such teaching works well to raise awareness, but has limited immediate success in terms of changing brand loyalty or purchase behaviour. This underlines the importance of growing Fair Trade's overall share of marketing voice.

Position Fair Trade to be Associated with Quality

In order to continue Fair Trade's progress into the mainstream, the move away from charity shop marketing and towards lifestyle presentation is likely to continue. Although this has been controversial, it has clearly yielded a significant lift in sales. Therefore, a move away from negative 'guilt' or 'do good' marketing positioning (something you should do) towards more positive quality and aspirational/lifestyle statements (something you want to do) should be sought. This may encourage consumers to seek out Fair Trade and build loyalty and repeat purchases. Clearly, for many consumers ethical motivation/positioning alone is not enough to break many strongly held brand loyalties (for example, to Nescafé, Cadbury's, Typhoo Tea and so on).

To achieve this repositioning, the national Fair Trade labelling initiatives should consider adding more marketing authority to the Fair Trade mark by broadening its set of meanings to include explicit quality statements about the nature of production. This would parallel the successful work done by the Soil Association in the UK in promoting organic food as both healthier *and* better quality. Such an approach would strengthen the mark by transforming it from being more than just an ethical proposition to a sophisticated statement about controlling the premium quality of goods as part of a unique and empowering production process. TransFair USA has started to move towards this positioning with their tagline, 'Quality fruit for you. Quality of life for farmers'.

This repositioning will be difficult, given the lack of consistency across packaging communications by Fair Trade wholesalers and manufacturers that typically overwhelm the impact of the certification mark. The huge variety of marketing messages sent to consumers by the range of products certified by TransFair USA demonstrates this clearly. Each product has its own distinct manufacturer brand packaging style with which the TransFair logo simply cannot compete for consumer attention. Another example would be to compare the lavish styling of a Divine chocolate bar with its sister product the Dubble bar, which aims to create a fun image aimed at children.

Consequently, there is a case to be made for FLO and its member national initiatives to take the lead in building a consistent brand image for Fair Trade as a whole. This would require national initiatives to establish a house style for Fair Trade products to which manufacturers wishing to use the Fair Trade mark would have to conform. FLO's members could then build a strong and coherent brand personality that would address current fragmentation across packaging styles in Fair Trade ranges. Such an approach would significantly increase the marketing impact of Fair Trade as a unifying feature for many products and could enhance the effectiveness of the supermarket shelf presentation of Fair Trade. However, it is certain that there would be strong opposition to this from manufacturers who are keen to promote their own identity in their packaging.

Brand Extensions: Launching New Products

A final way to avoid brand fatigue is to continually innovate and introduce new Fair Trade products. As will be discussed later, this brand extension strategy has the added advantage of positioning Fair Trade well vis-à-vis competitive certification systems, including company or industry self-certification, by broadening the Fair Trade offer and making it difficult to replicate. Having the Fair Trade mark appear on a wide variety of products will also increase consumer awareness by repeating brand impressions, as noted by Paul Rice of TransFair USA when interviewed in 2004:

> I think that [new Fair Trade product development] addresses the resource shortage that we have in terms of raising consumer awareness because people are just going to come into contact with more and more products that have our label or concept attached to them, and those products are our advertising vehicle themselves, and we give industry more of an incentive to invest in it because it becomes, particularly in retail, a more significant part of what they do.

Generally speaking, there should be continuous investment in innovative Fair Trade new product development, particularly in processed or composite goods. The latter, best exemplified to date by Traidcraft's Geobar, offers the chance to carry the Fair Trade mark on more products, educate more consumers and allow them to adopt more of a Fair Trade 'lifestyle', creating a virtuous circle in which they look for the Fair Trade mark on more and more products because this mark is on more and more products. The development of more Fair Trade fashion products would also contribute significantly here. Also the ranges of non-branded goods, particularly fruit and vegetables, could be expanded to avoid competition with the huge marketing voice of many multinational manufacturers such as Nestlé and Unilever.

Innovative new product development and greater market responsiveness are essential if Fair Trade businesses are to exploit emerging demands to their fullest extent. The first aspect of successful new product development is product selection and to be successful this requires a clear understanding of the emerging demands of the key target segments that drive the selection process. To date Fair Trade has been slow to recognize such opportunities, focusing largely on producer-driven product development instead. Nevertheless, today, a range of important market opportunities for Fair Trade does exist and should be explored. According to Luuk Zonneveld of FLO, the most promising categories include: textiles that do not have limited price elasticities (such as bedlinen or children's clothes); household and kitchen products (such as glassware) and partly processed commodities. The latter has particular potential for exponential growth, although Luuk Zonneveld added a caveat when recently interviewed on the subject:

> I also see potential – if you can get the major companies interested – in semi-finished products: washing powder, detergents. The core requirement there is that you get the biggest companies on board. The core elements are palm oil, soy – things that are imported. Products that are mass-produced in Southern countries and then enter into products that we use here – people don't even know that there are core Southern ingredients in them. But if you don't get Procter & Gamble to work with you on it, there's no use. It's not a market where you start with a 1 per cent market segment. Either you have 25 per cent market share or you don't do Fair Trade. But potentially, right away you reach hundreds of thousands of people. (Interview, 2004)

There is also a huge market opportunity in rethinking the development and distribution patterns of handicrafts and in considering applying the Fair Trade mark to these products. According to Watson (2004) the European market for Fair Trade handicrafts amounted to roughly £60m ($107m) in 2003. These are non-certified products typically sourced by IFAT members. All of these products are distributed through a network of 2,870 world shops run as not-for-profits by NGOs. This translates to only about £21,000 ($37,590) per shop per year – a figure that in traditional retail terms would be considered unsustainable and which only allows shops to survive due to use of voluntary labour.

On the other hand, the European market for 'exotic gifts' is estimated to be worth about £3.5 billion ($6.3 billion). These are typically sold through private sector companies. There is currently no strategy for Fair Trade producers to address this huge segment, largely due to their historical business structures. This is in stark contrast to Fair Trade food which has grown rapidly both in sales and value-added, by working closely with a range of private sector retailers. There would, therefore, seem to be a great opportunity for Fair Trade handicrafts to enter the mainstream by following the lead set by food. The key will be firstly to understand the needs of the 'premium' gifts market and then fit the design and quality control process to target this which will involve a systematic approach to raising skill levels amongst Fair Trade producers. This is already being addressed by initiatives such as the Asia Fair Trade Centre of Excellence. Next, new distribution networks will need to be created in partnership with sympathetic private sector businesses. Certainly, entering the mainstream presents many challenges not least that it is a much less forgiving competitive environment than world shops, but this should be seen as a valuable developmental challenge rather than a threat. Furthermore, the market opportunity is huge.

Once the product selection process becomes more responsive to the market, the second important issue is a review of the new product development process (Nicholls, 2004). Currently, the speed of development of certified products is severely restricted by the FLO's auditing mechanism. Large supermarkets such as Tesco that wish to engage with Fair Trade more actively have found the current governance structures difficult to deal with in conventional commercial terms, largely due to the lack of a centralized strategic decision-making body. As Hamish Renton, responsible for the development of Fair Trade at Tesco UK commented in 2003:

> I am not in the business of poking fingers at particular institutions because, frankly, we understand how the system works, but I don't understand the intricacies of it. All I know is that, from a practitioner's point of view, trying to get product on the shelf and trying to get outcomes on the ground, well, the system frustrates both. Because we have an appetite to do a whole number of other categories and we can't, because there are no marks. Fair Trade prawns – not a real example – but it could be. They have to hire a PhD to go and look at the prawn market. 'What's a fair wage? What's a fair price?' Three years later we have forgotten about it, I've moved on two jobs and they've missed the boat.
>
> The issue is that the governance of the system is such that it's such a decentralized and diffuse system … there's no Central Body, no Council of Ministers, there's no Executive President. It is what you would expect from activists … I think that what we're doing – and what hopefully will be matched by our competition – will expose the fault-lines within Fair Trade that will lead to an enhanced system that leads to better outcomes. (Interview, 2003)

The issue of standards is discussed further below, but the basic point of Renton's comments underlines the need for Fair Trade to develop its business-facing structure better to fit the mainstream market into which it is rapidly moving. The NGO-to-NGO supply and distribution chain that once characterized Fair Trade is rapidly evolving into a series of partnerships with private companies as well as NGOs. If these new relationships are to deliver the maximum benefit back to suppliers then a new interface with private companies will need to be created, one that can discuss commercial strategy and deliver on agreed objectives.

To support this, the certification process should be rethought and streamlined through partnerships, new investment and more use of outsourced auditors. Such an approach should also be employed to ramp up volumes of existing certified products where necessary by bringing new suppliers on board quickly. One way to do this would be to combine forces with IFAT, a coalition of ATOs in the North and Fair Trade producers in the South, many of whom produce handicrafts for which no FLO standards exist. In 2004 Carol Wills, Chief Executive of IFAT, explained the perceived marketing value of such a move in a personal interview:

> At our AGM last year, we were asked by our membership across the world to not only investigate the possibility of a product mark for all the products that our members produce, which include a broad range of handicrafts as well as coffee, but also to look at integrating with FLO as well. (Interview, 2004)

As part of this larger investigation, a discussion paper was disseminated at IFAT's 2004 regional meetings that sets out the options for providing a product-level Fair Trade mark for its members (IFAT, 2004b). Three options were offered for consideration:

Option One

To develop a joint IFAT/FLO mark. This would effectively be a single unified mark for all Fair Trade products whether accredited by FLO or IFAT. It is likely that this would continue to be the existing FLO mark. The objective would be 'To use the IFAT system of self-assessment and mutual review of its member Fair Trade Organizations (FTOs) as a means to allow FTOs complying with the relevant standards to sell products to retailers wishing to Fair Trade Mark those products in order to signal to consumers that there has been independent certification of compliance with Standards' (IFAT, 2004b: 1).

Option Two

To develop an exclusive IFAT product level mark to be awarded to its member organizations based upon their FTO registration. Such a mark would, effectively, compete with the FLO mark and would lack authority and therefore be open to abuse. A new external verification process would be required and would inevitably add to producers' costs.

Option Three

To develop an IFAT product registration website for FTO-accredited members to place their products. This would feature a new IFAT Fair Trade product mark and would act as an on-line catalogue for FTOs wishing to add legitimacy to their offer and increase their market reach. However, whilst having marketing value as a new distribution channel, this option may not create a strong new mark, but rather be perceived as an internal IFAT mark in competition with FLO mark. There would also be associated costs from establishing and maintaining the website.

Of the three options under discussion, options two and three represent a departure from the FLO label and will be discussed with other competitive threats to the Fair Trade certification system below. Only option one effectively integrates the FLO label into existing practices with handicraft producers – effectively this would be a unified label for Fair Trade. Integrating the FLO and IFAT standards would allow FLO to quickly bring on several new product groups and extend the Fair Trade label, an effective brand extension. This would have the added benefit of developing a unified and strategic marketing outlook to maximize the impact of campaigns and to avoid consumer confusion. As Carol Wills noted:

> Consumers like to have things presented to them in a very straightforward sort of way. I hate supermarket shopping. I hate being faced with all these different sorts of brands. If I want to buy something Fair Trade, I don't want to have to choose different kinds of Fair Trade, I just want to do it and my vision is that in five years' time, we will have one Fair Trade mission, one Fair Trade movement and one Fair Trade market. Effectively we are one Fair Trade movement, but in a way I think the label is moving away from it a little bit because of the market. (Interview, 2004)

The administration of a unified mark would involve adapting the existing IFAT standards for FTOs to the format for FLO standards, or vice versa. As the standards are quite different, implications for the FLO label are significant. IFAT members self-report their Fair Trade practices, enforced only by peer review and an IFAT inspection of a certain percentage of members each year. FLO inspects every producer group each year. Furthermore, unlike FLO, IFAT requires its members to pay 'fair prices' but does not set price floors.

Reconciling the IFAT/FTO accreditation system and FLO standards would thus be complex, but FLO should consider the option as a low-cost high-speed way to increase the breadth of Fair Trade products and maintain its competitive positioning. IFAT's option one, however, still keeps the Fair Trade mark at the product level rather than the organizational level. It seems, therefore, that a fourth strategic option is needed. This strategy could develop an umbrella product mark to accommodate both FLO-registered and FTO-accredited producers, as well as being able to communicate the message of a 'Fair Trade company' that the FTO mark signifies. The mark would act as a statement of audited Fair Trade quality control which would encompass both FLO and IFAT approaches to Fair Trade. The meanings attached to the mark would, thus, reflect the concept that this was a premium quality product and that its purchase would deliver quality of life back to a producer, with the result that the company importing and trading the product would be viewed as a social-mission driven company committed to Fair Trade. This would have the added benefit of helping key ATOs consolidate their position as larger mainstream brands enter the Fair Trade market. As regards packaging, the new mark could be used in tandem with the existing FLO mark in much the same way as organic Fair Trade products feature both FLO/TransFair and organic certification marks.

STRATEGIC COMMERCIAL OPPORTUNITIES

This section considers a variety of growth strategies for Fair Trade. To date Fair Trade commercial strategy has achieved considerable success in mainstreaming Fair Trade products and growing sales across a range of national markets. However, for growth to continue, constant innovation and creative strategic thinking will be required. As Fair Trade moves from niche to mainstream markets it will need to approach growth in a more strategic manner. To date much of the increase in Fair Trade sales has been opportunistic and the result of *ad hoc* partnerships. To achieve significant scale in future, the Fair Trade system will need to develop an infrastructure that can support producers to ramp up production and certify new producer groups, without compromising product quality or compliance with Fair Trade standards. As the market grows, the Fair Trade model may need to increase in flexibility to allow it to capture differentiated market segments. Such flexibility will have significant implications for the future direction of Fair Trade standards and certification (see further below).

Growing Volumes in Existing Lines

The first approach to bringing Fair Trade to scale lies with developing effective strategies to ramp up volumes of existing products quickly where demand outstrips supply. The structure of the Fair Trade business model makes this inherently difficult since it is typically based around aggregating small-scale producers who often lack technical expertise, resources and even effective communication systems. Nevertheless, new strategies can be discerned that would facilitate more rapid supply side growth when necessary. Such planning should have two objectives: to enhance the productivity and flexibility of existing producers and to bring new producers swiftly on-line when the opportunity for growth emerges.

In the case of existing producers several strategies are needed. Firstly, increasing the developmental support for small-scale producers through training and technical assistance would allow them to prepare more effectively for growth. This would include management consultancy to develop a more entrepreneurial mindset in traditionally risk-averse producers that would lead to increased productivity and preparedness for scaling up. As Roopa Mehta of Sasha Exports of India commented when interviewed in 2004:

The biggest challenge is to guide small producers towards an entrepreneurial outlook that grasps every opportunity. We want to ensure that our producers can respond to the new product demands of the market quickly and at a consistent quality level through training and support. But it is ongoing work.

The Asia Fair Trade Centre of Excellence is already exploring such management and leadership training programmes.

Secondly, producers should be encouraged to improve their product mixes, primarily to develop both high-volume (safe) and high-growth (risky) lines. By blending their product portfolio and diversifying some of their risk, producers are more likely to be able to respond to sudden market demand. By the same token, producers should be trained to monitor their product lifecycles carefully so that they constantly look to weed out failures and bring on stream products with more potential.

In reality, however, to achieve success such strategic planning must be combined with concentrated management education and continuous support to ensure that producers both understand and fully buy into new processes and change in operational objectives. For the very poorest and most marginalized small-scale producers the business speak of high level strategic planning will seem alien and highly risky; nevertheless, practices must gradually change if every growth opportunity is to be exploited. This business capacity building represents a key development need that is currently underfinanced in the cash-strapped Fair Trade system.

The second approach to growing volumes from existing lines involves bringing new producers into the Fair Trade system quickly when market demand is there. To achieve this, the Fair Trade movement needs to design new systems that speed up the registration of incoming producers whilst ensuring that overall quality control is not compromised. The main brake on such a system is likely to be lack of resources rather than a dearth of available producers. Charging the latter for certification, introduced by FLO in 2004, is one way to help capitalize on the Fair Trade certification system. This certification service could eventually even be spun out from FLO. Indeed, Paul Rice from TransFair USA is not averse to introducing profit-driven companies into the certification system:

> I don't know whether the current model is the best model for scaling this thing to the level of a standard because we have a monopoly on this service and we're a non-profit, so we can't attract equity and capital. Maybe if there were a financial incentive out there for investors to put money into taking this to scale to get to the endpoint ... I'm not wed to the idea of Fair Trade certification being a non-profit model; I don't see that as a core value that we have to cling to. The organics people do a great job of transforming industries, albeit on a slower time horizon than we feel comfortable with, but they're all for-profit. (Interview, 2004)

Increasing Flexibility in Fair Trade Standards to Capture More Market Segments

Whilst positioning Fair Trade products as high-quality will allow the capture of a lucrative segment of up-market consumers, this positioning sets a natural limit to the size of market share which Fair Trade can address. Furthermore, in certain products (notably coffee) the current Fair Trade standards proscribe potential market size by limiting Fair Trade certification only to small-scale producers. Arguments can be made for liberalizing the current pricing structure of Fair Trade and opening the system up to farms of all sizes.

Thus, a further opportunity lies in a reconfiguration of the price positioning of Fair Trade products. As things currently stand Fair Trade ranges are generally positioned as 'premium' products. This pricing reflects the reality of the Fair Trade value chain and also helps reinforce marketing messages about the premium quality of Fair Trade. However, it also excludes a significant proportion of the consumer market. If the price architecture of Fair Trade were broadened to include cheaper products, a true 'democratization' of Fair Trade could occur. One strategy to achieve this would be to develop the Fair Trade equivalent of Tesco's *Value* lines that are of lower, but still quite acceptable, quality but lack any cachet or exclusivity.

Such a move would clearly only make sense once most of the quality-conscious consumer segment had been captured. Some national markets are closer to achieving the penetration rates necessary to move to this next stage than others. The USA has low market share and awareness rate and should, therefore, focus on linking Fair Trade with quality to capture the gourmet segment. The UK, however, may have achieved the brand loyalty necessary to move beyond this high-price high-quality positioning. *Value* Fair Trade lines would, therefore, significantly grow the overall market and offer poorer consumers the ethical purchase options that they currently lack.

This position would require more flexibility in the Fair Trade pricing model, either by introducing new price floors for differentiated quality, or by abandoning the price floor model altogether. The price floor will most likely need to be re-thought anyway as higher market share levels are achieved and the Fair Trade market becomes price-setting, although, as Paul Rice of TransFair USA noted in 2004, demand for low-priced coffee may decrease with consumer awareness:

> You know, we talk a lot about Fair Trade becoming the standard, and yet I don't know that we've really brought in the brainpower or outside expertise to think about what happens to supply if everyone in the world can make $1.26 per pound. Does that mean that lots of new entrants go into coffee? Does it mean that supply grows dramatically? That is certainly a fear, and a plausible scenario, but I don't know that it's necessarily that mechanical, the way that neo-classical economists like to portray it – that we're contributing to the problem because we're keeping people in business who by rights should just get out. Because what we're doing is also creating demand for high-priced coffee, or we're upgrading existing demand for feel-good coffee. So I don't know what that does to supply and demand curves, and how they intersect. (Interview, 2004)

Yet even if the demand curves did change with consumer awareness of producer needs, in oligopolistic vertically integrated industries (for example, bananas) price floors would likely be deemed anti-competitive and illegal. It is probable, then, that flexibility will eventually need to be introduced into the Fair Trade pricing model.

A further challenge as Fair Trade grows is to ensure that it empowers stakeholders and does not simply create producer dependency. Producer dependency is two-fold. Firstly, producers can become dependent on a particular Fair Trade buyer, which is a risky position as buyers move on, companies go out of business and so on. Tallontire (2002) noted that according to a study of producers working with what was then the Oxfam Fair Trade Company, 44 per cent sold more than half of their output solely to Oxfam (Hopkins, 2000). Secondly, producers can also become dependent on one crop, a phenomenon that is of course already present in the developing world but which might be exacerbated by the Fair Trade guarantee of high prices for that particular commodity. Dependency on one income source leaves producers vulnerable to bad weather risk and change in consumer trends.

Recognizing the issue of producer dependency on a particular buyer, some Fair Trade companies, such as Traidcraft, are actively pursuing development strategies that will enable producers to better engage with the mainstream (Humphrey, 2000). Companies sometimes limit themselves to purchasing only a certain percentage of a group's products, to force that group into diversifying its buyers, or to working with producers for a defined period of time only until they 'graduate' from the system and go on to form relationships with more mainstream companies on a better footing. FLO might even consider adopting some of these practices and changing the Fair Trade standards to require producer groups to diversify their customer base in order to remain within the system. Of course, this would go against one of the key Fair Trade principles which is to encourage long-term relationships.

Dependency on one customer base is not something that is specific to the South. Any Northern supplier to an oligopolistic industry (for example, mass-market retail, automobile manufacture) is faced with the same situation. The real issue is whether or not producers in developing countries are able to recognize and assess the risks associated with such a strategy and if they have other options to turn to if they suddenly lose their key client(s). The empowerment and development of business capacity amongst producers that is a requirement of Fair Trade certification should ensure that producers are well equipped to assess these risks. Furthermore, as the Fair Trade market grows the number of interested buyers will increase and producer groups will in turn have more options to sell to.

Beyond dependency on one buyer, producer dependency on one *product* as the main source of income is another major concern for all developing countries, even outside of the Fair Trade context. FLO would be best placed to advise co-operatives and farm worker organizations to implement income diversification projects by making this objective compulsory amongst the 'progress standards' included in the Fair Trade requirements. Many producer groups have already recognized the dangers of this dependency and have started micro-credit funds to encourage community members to consider other businesses outside of the main Fair Trade income generator. Nelson and Galvez (2000) found that one approach by MCCH, a Fair Trade cocoa bean exporter in Ecuador, had led cocoa farmers to try marketing oranges and vegetables, having learned more about negotiation and price information from working with MCCH. The Coocafé Fair Trade Coffee Co-operative in Costa Rica also diversified from coffee into the export of yucca and plantain chips (Ronchi, 2002).

Whichever combination of these growth strategies is adopted by Fair Trade ventures, it is of critical importance that implementation is put into a context of the overall mission of Fair Trade, which is to empower the world's poorest producers. A constant effort must be made to ensure that the most marginalized producers are not excluded from the Fair Trade system because of poor quality product or business skills. One way to make this happen would be to set aside some certification fees to be spent on integrating marginalized producers into the Fair Trade supply chain.

Encouraging South-South Fair Trade

The current focus on Northern markets needs to be balanced by recognition of the opportunities offered by Southern markets, many of which are producer-local. These markets can be accessed without significant shipping costs or wholesaler intervention and would permit a re-engineering of the value chain to offer end pricing that is suitable for consumers in developing countries. This is already the case with many Fair Trade handicrafts such as baskets (see Craft Link case study). In order to sell commodity food or processed products, package sizes may need to be redesigned to suit poorer consumers who cannot afford the one-off cost of bulk purchase, or innovative credit mechanisms could be developed. A huge market opportunity is clearly emerging for many new goods in developing countries (see Prahalad, 2004) and Fair Trade products should be well placed to grow sales here also. There is already a significant middle class emerging in many developing countries: for example, India alone has more middle-income consumers than all of Europe. Consequently, emerging Asian markets offer particularly attractive market opportunities for Fair Trade.

However, the marketing and development of products targeted for South-South trade may well be different from those aimed at Northern markets. For example, in China handicrafts do not have the cachet they attract in the North and time spent on manufacturing is given less value. Therefore, the positioning of Fair Trade handicrafts cannot rest on premium exclusivity. Instead, it should aim to understand the culture of its local market. In China's case, there is a large business-to-business 'gift-giving' market opportunity where consistent quality and price are valued. The development of successful local markets not only adds to overall sales but also diversifies risk, particularly of currency fluctuations. The establishment of the first national Fair Trade-labelling initiative in a producing country (Mexico in 2004) is another interesting development in South-South Fair Trade.

CASE STUDY: CRAFT LINK

Craft Link is a Vietnamese not-for-profit organization that seeks to assist small Vietnamese craft producers to develop their businesses and find market opportunities in a changing economy. Craft Link runs a shop in Hanoi, Vietnam, hosts two to three handicraft bazaars a year and offers wholesale and export sales.

Craft Link was started by a local non-governmental organization interested in the production and sale of handicrafts as a means of generating income for poor and marginalized local people. Whilst some people were benefiting from the new economy in Vietnam, others were being left behind. One approach to this problem involves handicraft projects that develop new skills, design new products and organize production groups.

All producer groups with which Craft Link works meet the basic Fair Trade criteria in terms of fair wages, environmental sensitivity and employee working conditions. Craft Link does not work with state-owned factories, but gives preference to producers who are marginalized or disadvantaged. These include ethnic minority people in remote areas, street children and people with disabilities. Groups that invest in handicraft producers' social welfare are given preference. Projects include training in new design developments in traditional embroidery and weaving produced within the Black Thai, Nung and Ta Qi minorities. Another group, Mai Handicraft, was initiated by a group of Vietnamese social workers to create employment opportunities for street children and disadvantaged women. This group alone sold over $25,000 (£14,000) through Craft Link-initiated market opportunities. Craft Link also develops its own products. For example, it purchases handmade paper from traditional paper-makers north of Hanoi and manufactures stationery sets and boxes on their behalf.

Despite its not-for-profit status, Craft Link is profitable and commercially minded. This ensures that it remains sustainable.

Source: Craft Link promotional flyer, 2004

POLITICAL STRATEGIES: ADVOCACY

Whilst pursuing commercial strategies such as increasing market share and building brand awareness will doubtless have a positive impact on the lives of Fair Trade producers, they would also benefit from lobbying to influence policy at both national and supra national levels (Page and Slater, 2003). In both cases there is a great need for all the various Fair Trade players to co-ordinate their activities in a strategic fashion. Thus, national initiatives under the umbrella of FLO and others such as IFAT should work together towards clear advocacy objectives via agreed tactics. The importance of such co-ordination is discussed further below.

In contrast to the considerable achievement in raising consumer awareness of the issues, Fair Trade has had only limited success in changing government policy. For example, whilst the incoming UK Labour government was quick to support Fair Trade by switching all beverages at the palace of Westminster (1997) and has subsequently helped to develop a larger market in public sector organizations more generally, there have been no significant unilateral policy concessions to the Fair Trade agenda. Nevertheless, Fair Trade is increasingly well placed to harness growing consumer concern for trade injustice and therefore lobby for specific trade liberalization objectives. A precursor to this must be greater agreement on what the headline objectives should be.

The Fair Trade movement needs to address both national governments and supra-national bodies such as the European Union and the World Trade Organization (WTO) to reassess macro-governance trade issues and structures. In the latter there has been some success with the Doha round of WTO negotiations (2004) suggesting that the developing world's lobbying for a reduction in Northern agricultural subsidies may finally starting to be heard. Whilst any reduction in the hugely distorting tariffs currently in place must be valuable, Fair Trade activists must also lobby with others for a reduction in these same tariffs on processed as well as commodity products to ensure that producers can really begin to benefit from the value chain. In addition, developing countries should be encouraged to reduce their own South-South tariffs.

Key Fair Trade organizations should continue to work to gain positions of influence in the major supra-national bodies worldwide for themselves or the producers they represent. Some progress is being made here. For example, Euro Co-op, EFTA and NEWS! sponsored a Fair Trade conference at the European Parliament in 2004 that included contributions from European Commissioners Pascal Lamy and Paul Nielson. Another success was the Symposium on Fair Trade at the UNCTAD (the United Nation's agency concerned with trade and development) XI annual meeting in São Paolo which took place in June 2004. This led to a declaration of intent presented to UNCTAD. Nevertheless, as public support for Fair Trade grows the opportunities to participate in policy discussions will also increase and it is of great importance that such engagements are effectively exploited (see pages 26–9).

A potential threat to pursuing an advocacy strategy centres upon the balance of global versus local perspectives. Two examples of this are the position of Northern producers with respect to Fair Trade and the distribution of Fair Trade income. In the first case – and often driven by media stories – some consumers feel that their local farmers are as needy of support as Southern growers, arguing that the buying power of supermarkets is driving farm-gate prices in their respective areas down below subsistence levels. This may be particularly true in rural communities. Indeed, the first Fair Trade Town initiative in Garstang specifically linked Fair Trade with support for local produce in its campaigning. However, the case for Northern farmers is clearly very different from that of those in the South, not least because the former still benefit from large subsidies and favourable trade tariffs as well as a social security safety net should their incomes fall too low. Nevertheless, Fair Trade will need to be sensitive to local issues in future new product development. For example, introducing Fair Trade apples from South Africa that were in direct competition with British apples proved to be controversial.

Furthermore, as discussed in Chapter 2, the majority of extra dollars (or pounds) spent on Fair Trade products actually stays with Northern businesses. This is because most Fair Trade companies are incorporated in the North and thus pay taxes and employ local workers there. Furthermore, most of the 'value added' happens in the North, even if it simply reflects margin-based costing for retailers and distributors. This has little to do with inefficiencies in the Fair Trade supply chain (especially as the traded volume grows and inefficiencies are weeded out) but rather with the value chain of manufacturing and retailing more generally. Unfortunately, consumers may not easily understand this reality and instead attribute the low return to farmers as being due to faults within the Fair Trade system.

Whilst it is the case that the bulk of financial benefits for Fair Trade do accrue to Northern governments through taxation and to Northern businesses through trade in higher-priced products, there are several reasons why rational consumers should buy Fair Trade products and why the national initiatives, Fair Trade businesses and FLO should be ready to answer critics. Firstly, Fair Trade provides several benefits to farmers beyond extra income, including improved market information, market access and even self-esteem. Secondly, by interacting with producers in a business relationship, Fair Trade preserves the dignity of farmers who want to provide high-quality products and earn a decent living. 'These hands were made for farming, not begging' is a common sentiment heard at Fair Trade producer gatherings. Finally, by voting with their pockets consumers can send a signal to mainstream retailers and politicians that they believe in fair returns to the world's poorest producers. Fair Trade purchases thus become acts of advocacy and solidarity as well as consumption choices.

COMPETITIVE THREATS TO FAIR TRADE

By following the strategies outlined above, the Fair Trade movement can continue to grow and position itself as the 'gold standard' for how business should treat the poorest participants in the supply chain. However, there are a number of threats to Fair Trade becoming the dominant trading model. These come both from inside and outside the Fair Trade movement. In the former case, mission-driven companies may become unhappy with the widening of participation in Fair Trade that includes those companies that see Fair Trade only as a market opportunity and are not necessarily interested in long-term change in the world trading systems (such is the case with many multinational brand owners). With the latter, non-mission-driven companies may decide not to adopt more expensive Fair Trade practices and instead develop 'low-bar' less expensive standards to placate consumers who have been made aware of problems facing producers. Examples of this include Utz Kapeh (see Chapter 6) or Nestlé's threatened 'fairly-traded' statement (Sweney, 2004).

THREATS FROM WITHIN THE FAIR TRADE MOVEMENT

The Fair Trade mechanism represents a highly innovative approach both to improving global social justice and to addressing economic market failures through trade. The Fair Trade proposition therefore sits in an unusual position articulated both as an activist-led advocacy campaign and as a consumer-driven commercial venture. For the moment, Fair Trade market growth is such that new entrants can be easily accommodated. Indeed, many in the Fair Trade movement would welcome more players in the marketplace, since any increase in overall volume can only benefit producers. This approach contrasts strikingly with traditional competitive theory in which the move to monopoly is every company's aim. However, as Fair Trade continues to grow and expand into the mainstream, there is a danger that the activists and campaigners that drove the movement in its infancy will become disaffected. This may come about as a reaction to commercial partnerships with multinationals hitherto seen as 'the enemy'.

As noted in Chapter 6, a few mission-driven companies have become so disillusioned with the Fair Trade certification system that they have dropped out of it altogether. Whilst this does not seem to be a significant trend, there is a clear tension between the twin roles of advocacy and commercial growth best encapsulated in the move towards mainstreaming Fair Trade, which shows success in sales terms whilst also attracting grassroots' criticism. Continuing to manage these two roles effectively will be crucial to the future growth and long-term success of Fair Trade.

Another potentially divisive issue is the criteria for Fair Trade certification. Effectively, there are two sets of Fair Trade products and thus two sets of Fair Trade producers: those with FLO accreditation and those without. Therefore, one important goal for Fair Trade certification could be to bring all participants under the same umbrella mark. Indeed, under the auspices of the FINE collaboration (see further below), discussion of a common Fair Trade mark is already underway.

As consumer awareness of the Fair Trade mark continues to grow it seems likely that in order to benefit from the Fair Trade proposition accreditation may, in fact, become a *sine qua non* of packaging. A single mark encompassing the many Fair Trade crafts would significantly enhance retailer access for non-food products where food is already present and have advocacy as well as commercial value, since it will give more market space to Fair Trade products. Sales should rise long term and awareness levels should be enhanced.

However, the situation is complex. Despite the strong case for a single Fair Trade mark, there remains a number of objections to unifying under the FLO logo. IFAT activists have raised a number of concerns as voiced by Carol Wills in 2004:

> The integrated monitoring system is incredibly difficult because not all Fair Trade organizations are sure they want to be associated with the FLO certification mark because it's carried by the likes of Starbucks and others and our members say, 'We are not Starbucks and we don't want to be associated in the minds of consumers with the Starbucks of this world. We believe that those organizations giving the impression that they are Fair Trade somehow dilute Fair Trade.

Indeed, there may well be commercial arguments against the case for a single mark. As Luuk Zonneveld, Managing Director of FLO, noted:

For many handicrafts, Fair Trade labelling doesn't make sense. Those handicrafts already have a market – gift shops, world shops, etc. – you don't need to stick a label on it. The consumers are buying it and the label's not going to make a difference. The extra costs and energy that you have to put into getting the label on the product will not be offset by a similar increase in sales. From a marketing perspective, regarding handicraft products that IFAT members produce, Fair Trade labelling only makes sense for 10–15 per cent of those producers. For the rest, from a market/financial perspective, it doesn't make sense. So that's a tough one. If you're going to do it any-way, then you're back to either external funding or one product subsidizing the other, or a solidarity type of system where the producers themselves pay. (Interview, 2004)

Carol Wills concurred:

So maybe all things should not be marked, maybe it's best for certain types of Fair Trade pro-duction to be sold through the niche markets in the world shops which have always provided a fantastic market for Fair Trade and, you know, small gift shops with quite a strong brand on them. (Interview, 2004)

Fair Trade groups must work together to avoid consumer confusion, however, espe-cially in the face of serious competition from non-Fair Trade actors competing for eth-ical spend. These external threats are serious and will be discussed in the next section.

THREATS FROM OUTSIDE THE FAIR TRADE MOVEMENT

As successful commercial ventures, Fair Trade marketers can expect increasing competition as the consumer market grows. Non-Fair Trade companies can choose to promote their own company charity or self-certification programs, or alternatively to adopt low-cost industry codes of conduct that do not involve floor-price calculations. As consumers and retailers become more concerned about working conditions in developing countries, com-panies may also choose to adopt lower-cost third party certification systems and then use the funds saved to promote these systems. Such systems will not have the same degree of impact on producers as the Fair Trade model, but may still generate positive marketing spin.

Self-Certification/Codes of Conduct

As long as the Fair Trade certification mark and its attendant mechanisms remain unpro-tected by law, there will always be the possibility that an opportunistic business with far greater marketing voice than the members of FLO will launch a 'fair trade' or 'fairly-traded' range that does not follow FLO guidelines and will thus directly compete with existing Fair Trade lines. Such products would confuse consumers and potentially threaten the integrity of the Fair Trade mark (see for example, Sweney, 2004).
   As Luuk Zonneveld of FLO noted:

I'm not worried about codes (of conduct) as such. I'm worried about codes that are being trans-formed into a label. And not so much about the label itself, because the market has a tendency to weed out the credible labels from the non-credible labels. Any system that does not have a minimum level of transparency, an external verification of standards, etc. won't last. But the major danger for me is that this confuses consumers. So in the end, the (industry) label might not work, and usually doesn't, but the damage it does in the eyes of consumers to the other labelling schemes like ours – I am very worried about this. (Interview, 2004)

One natural conclusion would be that the Fair Trade movement should aim for international legal status for its certification criteria and mark. The legal standardization of the organic certification label in the USA has been largely successful, helping to reduce consumer confusion and increase sales. Attempts on Capitol Hill to weaken the legal definition of 'organic' have been stopped by lobbying on the part of organic-loyal consumers and businesses with strong organic brands.

The counter argument, however, suggests that any legal framework for Fair Trade, as defined by FLO, would be harmful to thousands of small-scale uncertified Fair Trade producers. These are typically members of IFAT who either produce goods for which no certification criteria exist or who cannot afford the licence for certification. In the case of this constituency, despite conforming to the spirit of Fair Trade, more formal Fair Trade criteria may exclude them from the movement.

Either way, developing the breadth of available Fair Trade products will certainly help protect the FLO system from industry or company-specific labels. It is unlikely that the coffee, cocoa, tea, fruit and other industries will join forces to create a broad umbrella label to compete with the FLO label. Furthermore, by continuing to work with grassroots activist groups, FLO can rely on a variety of watchdogs to expose non-credible labels. Finally, promoting and certifying own-company codes does cost money, and as the FLO label becomes more popular companies (especially medium-sized companies) may find it more efficient to adopt FLO standards rather than creating their own systems.

Low-cost Independent Certification

Media and NGO attentions focussed on trade justice issues and, particularly, Fair Trade producers have contributed to a widespread interest in social responsibility amongst consumers and retailers. The growth of Fair Trade has also led to the entry of new players into the arena of socially responsible certification offering lower cost options than FLO. The two most significant new arrivals are Utz Kapeh and the Rainforest Alliance. Both have appeared in recent years to take advantage of the growing market for 'ethically' traded coffee without taking on board the full cost of FLO accreditation. Utz Kapeh and the Rainforest Alliance do not incorporate price floors and, thus, represent significantly cheaper options than Fair Trade. Both models started off outside the sphere of social responsibility (Utz Kapeh was originally developed as a product safety traceability system for the Ahold retail group and the Rainforest Alliance was primarily an environmental seal) but have repositioned themselves to be more socially oriented to be able to respond to market demand.

In response to these competitors, FLO and its members must rely on their own marketing efforts and partnerships with grassroots educational organizations to promote the FLO system as the 'gold standard' and continue to highlight the key differences between FLO's mechanism and other models. Furthermore, FLO must also continue to improve its standards in the face of competition. Certain aspects of the FLO system open it up to criticism: for instance, the fact that Fair Trade coffee standards do not allow for the case of estate-farm worker models effectively isolates 50 per cent of the world's production and leaves a space for other certification systems that do work with large plantations to find a way in. These weaknesses should be addressed in the face of competitive threats from lower-cost systems.

Another criticism of the FLO model is that its price floor mechanism is not scalable or 'mainstream' because it is price-setting. As discussed here and in Chapter 2, market share of the FLO system is not high enough today to be considered as price-setting, and as long as the system remains flexible standards can be changed if the system ever did become anti-competitive. FLO and its members should emphasize the flexibility yet integrity of the standard-setting model as a multi-stakeholder system that is continually redefining itself in the face of producer realities and changing market contexts.

So far, this chapter has summarized the key market opportunities and competitive threats to the Fair Trade system that are emerging. But, moving forward, who is going to take advantage of these opportunities and address perceived threats? This book will now conclude with a discussion of Fair Trade governance and will identify the players who will determine the Fair Trade future.

GOVERNANCE OF FAIR TRADE

As its global growth continues, the Fair Trade movement faces a series of institutional challenges. Firstly, Fair Trade is presented with several critical governance issues: namely, to develop a more effective and transparent approach to governance that both demonstrates and operationalizes its accountability to all its stakeholders. Secondly, and in tandem with this, Fair Trade needs to develop new structures at both macro- and micro-levels to extend its effectiveness and impact. This final section will address these issues.

New Approaches

Conventional socio-political accounts of modern society in developed countries typically identify three interrelated spheres of activity: the public sector, the private sector and the 'third' or social sector (Edwards, 2003). The first is the domain of government, the second of the commercial market and the third of associational citizenship. Despite these distinctions it is accepted that these three sectors are closely related and inter-reliant and as such they interact on multiple levels in successfully functioning societies. For example, government distributes a proportion of business profits as public goods through taxation whilst providing a legal and regulatory context that enables business to function effectively (such as property rights). Similarly, charities often provide public goods in situations where government and sometimes the private sector has failed, but are also reliant for funding from public grants and corporate or individual donations generated by the actions of the market. In situations of dysfunctional polity (such as totalitarian dictatorships) the relationship between the three sectors is often strikingly unbalanced, with power concentrated in one or two sectors alone. This thinking also underpins some anti-globalization rhetoric that characterizes Anglo-American society as being dominated by the commercial market in tandem with a quiescent government to the detriment of individual citizens.

In recent years the arena in which these three sectors play out their complex relationships has been increasingly conceptualized as 'civil society' (Chambers and Kymlicka, 2002; Cohen and Arato, 1992; Ehrenberg, 1999; Geremek, 1992; Hall, 1995; Keane, 2003; Putnam, 2000; Salamon and Anheier, 1999). Characterized as a 'universal expression of the collective life of individuals' (Edwards, 2003: 3), civil society remains a contested and developing idea, claimed in various guises by both left and right, yet there is broad agreement that it is best defined as being both associational and focussed on the citizen. The nature of these sectoral interactions has been conceptualized as dynamic and evolving, a process largely normalized in the development and critique of the 'Third Way' philosophy (Giddens, 1998, 2000) which argues that the traditional boundaries between public, private and social sectors are arbitrary, contingent and largely unnecessary. The progressive thinking and policy making of the current New Labour government in the UK and the Clinton administration in the USA, as well as the Republicans' 'compassionate conservatism' that followed, each offer good examples of this evolving notion of a new civil society responsive to both the private and public (in particular). Examples include the Public-Private Finance Initiatives brokered in the UK to rejuvenate public goods with private capital connected to returns (and, therefore, risk) underwritten by the government, as well as the outsourcing of public sector service contracts to NGOs such as charities.

A team of researchers led by Lester Salamon at Johns Hopkins University mapped the dimensions of global NGO activity in a wide-ranging survey of 35 countries (Salamon et al., 2003). They calculated that the total Gross Domestic Product (GDP) value (that is, aggregate expenditures, 1999) of the global civil sector 'industry' was $1.3 trillion (£0.72 trillion), or 5.1 per cent of the total combined GDP of the countries surveyed. This made NGO's the seventh largest global 'economy' above Italy, Russia, Turkey and many others. Salamon and his team also suggested that NGOs employ 39.5 million full-time equivalent staff globally, equal to 4.4 per cent of the total economically active population. In addition there are 190 million unpaid volunteers. The main sectors in which the NGOs were active were identified as: education; social services; culture; health; development.

Central to the development of recent ideas around the concept of civil society has been a renewed focus on the role and social impact of NGOs as an embodiment of the rights and responsibilities of the citizenry in the context of the globalization of markets. NGOs do not represent new organizational forms – indeed, some date back to the nineteenth century – but they are now taking on new roles and are increasingly visible and influential actors in the interplay between government, business and society. However, as the significance of NGO activity has grown, a number of critiques have emerged. What are particularly pressing are issues of accountability and good governance. *The Economist* has been particularly critical of NGOs adopting new roles:

> Citizens' groups are increasingly powerful at the corporate, national and international level … Are citizens' groups, as many of their supporters claim, the first step towards an 'international civil society'? Or do they represent a dangerous shift of power to unelected and unaccountable special interest groups? (1999: 12)

Or further:

> Non-governmental organizations, as many charities are pompously described these days, often escape the sort of scrutiny that they, themselves, like to apply to governments and companies. (2003: 53)

For example, it could be that NGO funding may be diverted from its social mission towards institutional survival and self-interested issues, all of which would be hidden to donors and other activists due to a lack of transparency or accountability in NGO activities.

The Fair Trade movement represents a good example of the evolution of a modern NGO. Starting as a traditional campaigning and advocacy group, Fair Trade now encompasses certifiers (Fairtrade Foundation), not-for-profit organizations (Oxfam), co-operatives (many producer groups) and more conventional 'social' businesses limited by liability (Cafédirect).

The ownership structure of Fair Trade bodies provides the first governance challenge. All the major Fair Trade groups are either owned by charities or have traditionally relied on grants for a significant part of their funding. Consequently, there is a complete absence of conventional (financial) market discipline in terms of either punishing poor performance (by withholding resources) or rewarding success (with the allocation of additional resources). Cafédirect's 2004 share offer represented an innovative way to draw a Fair Trade business closer to the financial markets, but this was a highly unconventional initial public offering that restricted access to shares and did not offer shareholders the possibility of wresting control of the business. Whilst there is little that can or, perhaps, should be done in terms of Fair Trade ownership structures, reform of their relationships with key stakeholders would be highly valuable. Central to this is a review of the existing governance structures. There are three interlocking objectives through which this can be achieved.

To begin with, such a body would clearly need to identify the stakeholders to whom it is accountable. These would include not only the producers, but also funding bodies (parent charities, governments and, in the case of Cafédirect, shareholders), consumers and other NGOs. The responsibilities towards each stakeholder should be recognized and addressed in strategic planning. Currently, most Fair Trade organizations do demonstrate a sound understanding of their range of stakeholders, but the mechanisms by which they may be included in the planning process are partial and sometimes opaque.

Therefore, the second objective of good governance is to ensure that Fair Trade organizations are fully accountable for their actions through transparent reporting of their objectives and impacts. The issue of impact measurement was discussed in detail in Chapter 9, but it is worth reasserting the crucial importance of using sound metrics to justify the use of resources and to support the strategic value of chosen paths of action. Currently, many Fair Trade organizations provide limited accounts of their impacts, chiefly in internal qualitative social accounts. For the future, external social auditing should become the norm with a full account of both successful and failed objectives put at the centre of a credible statement of performance. Of particular importance here would be a measurement of social return on investment to demonstrate the level of productivity and efficiency achieved by the venture.

Finally, new accessible mechanisms need to be developed through which Fair Trade's performance can be held accountable. Whilst it is crucial that Fair Trade becomes more accountable, rigorous and objective in its performance assessment, such progress will be meaningless without a transparent and effective mechanism through which any external party may access performance criteria. Such a mechanism should mirror the accessibility, if not the spirit, of traditional financial accounts and allow for stakeholder feedback. Fair Trade has much to be proud about, but currently its reporting and governance structures neither deliver the full benefit of its achievements back to it (via positive marketing) nor encourage better future performance.

New Structures

Whilst, by many measures, the growth of Fair Trade sales has been impressive to date, in order to maintain growth there is a need for a more co-ordinated and strategic view of Fair Trade as a whole. As the Fair Trade movement continues to grow, its current organizational structures will also need to develop. This is the case at both the macro- and micro-levels.

At the macro-level there will be the need for more co-ordination across the various groups that effectively govern Fair Trade. This is already beginning to happen with the publication in 2001 of a collaborative document under the auspices of FINE, a joint working group involving the Fair Trade Labelling Organizations International (FLO), the International Federation of Alternative Trade (IFAT), the Network of European World Shops (NEWS) and the European Fair Trade Association (EFTA). Carol Wills of IFAT outlined the thinking behind FINE:

> We decided that we could do more together on an integrated harmonized monitoring system, advocacy and information. Advocacy is where we have really moved ahead. Earlier this year we appointed an Advocacy Co-ordinator who has an office in Brussels. I manage the person so she is employed by IFAT, but there is a steering committee made up of each of the four (FINE) bodies. (Interview, 2004)

However, it is as yet unclear what authority will ultimately be invested in FINE. Given that each of its members come to it from different strategic trajectories representing a number of stakeholder groups there will, inevitably, be many internal political hurdles to be surmounted before it can function as the unified 'voice' of Fair Trade. Wills clearly articulated one such issue:

> I think the perception that came out of a recent (IFAT) producer meeting in São Paolo is that Fair Trade – and by that they mean the labelled Fair Trade – is something that happens to them from the North, something alongside IFAT. So they are looking at the IFAT discussions with FLO and it may be that we cannot do anything. But that would be a real pity, because we come out of the same stable. For the sake of broad Fair Trade, we ought to be able to agree. But IFAT will never agree to something that it believes will let down the small producer, and I guess it's something to do with the strategic direction of FLO and FLO being able to say it's not just about the label and the market but it is truly about the marginalized producer. I think their problem is that they say quite categorically at the moment that they will not work in certain sectors with plantations, but in others they do, and they need to be clearer about their social criteria. (Interview, 2004)

Whether such a role is appropriate for a FINE-like organization or not, a single governing body is clearly needed to tackle the global co-ordination of the strategic future direction of Fair Trade. Hamish Renton, responsible for the development of Fair Trade at Tesco UK, found the current structure of the Fair Trade movement frustrating. In his view, unless the structural diversity of Fair Trade organizations is addressed the movement will fail to maximize its impacts:

> Where's the manifestation of the thought leadership, where's the manifestation of the direction? I think that's what we found most disappointing. I really like the Fair Trade guys in the UK, but the trouble is they're a local office of a global organization that has no central power. So it's everywhere and nowhere … There are three things that need to be addressed: scalability; the speed of response; the structural vacuum of decision-making. And it's also the fact that it seems to be very much about where they've come from, rather than where they are going. (Interview, 2003)

The advantages of establishing a single governing body for Fair Trade are many. Firstly, such an organization would be able to leverage greater impact in its lobbying and advocacy activities addressed to political and supra-political bodies. By clearly speaking for all its constituents across many nations a Fair Trade governing body would have far greater influence than the range of multiple initiatives and representative groups currently talking to the World Trade Organization, United Nations or local government. Secondly, a single voice for Fair Trade would be able to act strategically for all its stakeholders by developing a planned set of objectives to co-ordinate its Fair Trade activities and messages more effectively than is the case to day. This would include both policy and market development.

Nevertheless, despite the undoubted need to reform the macro-level Fair Trade institutions, the development of the micro-level structures underpinning the Fair Trade movement is also essential. For example, there is an urgent need to address the lack of Southern participation in the strategic development of Fair Trade. Carol Wills, Executive Director of IFAT, commented:

> I have had it reported to me from two sources that Latin American Fair Traders see Fair Trade as something that happens in the North, they don't feel any real sense of ownership in the process: it is something that is imposed on them from the North ... One of the things that we are trying to do in IFAT is to build the movement globally and I think we have done that, but, funnily enough, as we work to make the regions stronger, we risk fragmentation. (Interview, 2004)

FLO has recently been addressing this issue by opening up membership on its board and key committees (including Standards and Policy and Certification) to FLO-certified producers. Yet FLO's member national labelling initiatives still hold the majority of positions on the board, and many key negotiations and meetings still take place in the North. There is a real danger that Southern stakeholders, relatively isolated from the decision-making process and governance mechanisms of Fair Trade, may grow to feel isolated and dislocated from the very process that aims to empower them. It may even be the case that producers benefiting from Fair Trade become so distanced from its aims that they do not want to fully understand its policies and objectives at all, but rather prefer to focus on the positive economic benefits in isolation. As Sutcliffe noted from interviewing a cocoa farmer in Belize:

> His understanding of Fair Trade is only sketchy, and his comprehension of the extent to which his economic situation would be altered if he were left to the mercy of market forces is non-existent. He is proud of what he grows. As to the price he gets for it, he seems to feel that this is simply beyond him. (2004: 20)

Given the broader aims of Fair Trade to address the power and social justice discrepancies in global trade relationships, such a sense of dislocation between producer and process must clearly be addressed. Many local Fair Trade organizations are playing a crucial role in educating producers to understand the benefits and strictures of the Fair Trade process. Such organizations may act as local co-ordinators for producers, such as the TARA projects in India, or Craft Link in Vietnam, or through larger umbrella groups such as the Asia Fair Trade Forum or Oxfam.

IFAT is also playing an important role in setting up and connecting Fair Trade organizations worldwide that do not have formal FLO accreditation. In January 2004, IFAT launched a Fair Trade Organization (FTO) mark that audited Fair Trade at an organizational, rather than a product, level to recognize its constituents who mainly trade in non-certified handicrafts. Furthermore, the continuing work of IFAT to encourage producers to orga-nize themselves into co-operatives and also to bring together a wide range of disparate Fair Trade groups worldwide will play an important part in addressing producer disloca-tion. As Wills commented on the IFAT network:

> It's being in an international voluntary membership association of like-minded organizations and having opportunities to meet and share experiences and learn from each other, to learn from special workshops that are put on all over the world all the time, to be part of your national and regional set up, to meet people from other parts of the world. Even today it's so important to meet people and be friends with people and talk about the same sort of things together. It's very diffi-cult to say what networks really bring, but I think the value of networks has been grossly under-estimated by a lot of people. We can be in touch with each other in a matter of seconds round the world; it's very self-supportive, self-sustaining and people help each other out in all kinds of situa-tions – producers and importers. It's almost like the Fair Trade Trade Association, I guess, and we produce information, newsletters, electronic updates, commercial contacts; we have a very close link with Shared Interest's credit facility and other financial instruments that are available to our members. So we have all sorts of things going on all over the world all the time. (Interview, 2004)

NEWS is also addressing the need to better connect all Fair Trade stakeholders through its Fair Trade Global Communication System project launched in 2000 (www. fairtradeforum.net). This web-based initiative aims to offer a forum to encourage infor-mation flows and richer communication between Fair Trade groups in order to leverage knowledge and share resources across geographical boundaries.

Nevertheless, despite the work of IFAT, NEWS and others, there must continue to be a co-ordinated approach to ensuring that producers, particularly in the South, are fully integrated into Fair Trade policy-making and truly feel connected both to the economic benefits of Fair Trade and its broader social justice aims and objectives.

CONCLUSION

This chapter has attempted to set out the range of strategic issues that will ultimately determine the Fair Trade future. It has considered the ongoing opportunities open to Fair Trade and the threats that it will most likely have to counter. The chapter concluded with a strategic review of future governance issues that may confront the movement.

Despite all the grounds for optimism in the story so far, it is important to remember the limitations of Fair Trade. It is not a solution to all trade problems. Fair Trade can help many marginalized producers and greatly contribute to the process of improving trade justice, but it cannot address alone the structural issues in world trade generally. Neither does it aim to reduce global consumption, nor reduce the air miles travelled by imported products (see for example, Johnston, 2002). Luuk Zonneveld, Managing Director of FLO Fair Trade Labelling Organizations International, articulated the *realpolitik* of Fair Trade:

> One of the challenges for Fair Trade is to understand where the development needs and poten-tial lie and where the market needs and potential lie ... to try and combine and balance those is difficult. Not everything that the market asks to sell as Fair Trade could make a difference

without impossibly expensive investments. There are lots of poor producers that should have the right to a much better life, but maybe Fair Trade is not the adequate answer to it. It's finding that balance that is a challenge. (Interview, 2004)

As long as Fair Trade continues to grow there remains the question of how large Fair Trade market shares can ultimately get. Again Zonneveld has a realistic view:

> I don't think Fair Trade was ever meant to be 100 per cent mainstream, and it cannot be, because its specific target group is the poorest producers, and depending on how many those are, that sort of proscribes that maximum size of the market that you're going to have. But I must say, I do believe it's a bit of a theoretical debate for almost all products. Eighty per cent of agricultural products imported from the South are produced by poor producers, and Fair Trade might have 1 to 2 per cent of that market for the time being, so by the time we're getting anywhere near that type of percentage, we can always raise the question again. (Interview, 2004)

In the meantime, for many businesses, the Fair Trade model is increasingly recognized as offering a valuable contribution towards maintaining international competitiveness (see for example, Welford et al., 2003). The commercial attractiveness of Fair Trade as both a defensive and proactive marketing tool should not be underestimated.

Furthermore, there is still an enormous opportunity to grow demand and to contribute more to the process of improving social justice worldwide. In many product categories there is a real chance that Fair Trade may, one day, become the industry standard. This is clearly already beginning to be the case for premium coffee. Once Fair Trade's share gets to be the majority of a market it seems likely that the whole industry will then move to become Fair Trade. At this point the Fair Trade concept effectively becomes irrelevant, because other mechanisms would most likely be put into place that would effectively replace it, namely legislation or industry codes of conduct. This must be the curious ultimate commercial goal of Fair Trade – to put itself out of business.

Fair Trade is both a developmental tool and commercial proposition. Whilst it may one day reach a terminal point in its growth, Fair Trade has to date pioneered a sea change in consumer attitudes to trade justice that will surely endure. UK Fair Trade Towns Co-ordinator Bruce Crowther summed up the essence of Fair Trade:

> In the end I don't really care about councils or governments giving me a pat on the back, although we do need them to support Fair Trade. But when somebody from Ghana comes to me and says 'thank you for what you've done' – and I don't mean that in a condescending way – it means a lot to me. If I can really feel that Fair Trade is making a difference to that person's life it fills me up. Because that is what it is about. (Interview, 2003)

Fair Trade is a phenomenon of our time. A benign manifestation of globalization, it unites consumers and producers across the globe in a new trade partnership that addresses market failures by being market driven. As this book closes, the Fair Trade story is still only in its opening chapters. Nevertheless, what is abundantly clear is that the impact and influence of Fair Trade can only grow as more and more consumers engage with its progressive, global narrative. Today more than ever, the Fair Trade future is our future.

References

AgroFair (2004) 'The Co-op in Switzerland goes for 100% Fair Trade bananas and AgroFair', press release, 2 February. Available at: www.fairtradefruit.com/Press Releases.

AlterEco (2003) 'Coopérative de Eswatini Swazi'. Available at: www.altereco.com/produits/autreproduc/swazitexte.htm.

Annan, K. (2001) 'A route out of poverty', *The Financial Times*, 5 March: 12.

Appadurai, A. (1986) 'Introduction: commodities and the politics of value', in A. Appadurai (ed.), *The Social Life of Things*. Cambridge: Cambridge University Press. pp. 1–7.

Aranda, J. and Morales, C. (2002) *Poverty Alleviation Through Participation in Fair Trade Coffee: The Case of CEPCO, Oaxaca, Mexico*. Fort Collins, CO: Colorado State University. Available at: www.colostate.edu/Depts/Sociology/FairTradeResearchGroup.

Araujo, L. (1999) 'Exchange, institutions and time', in D. Brownlie, M. Saren and R. Whittington (eds), *Rethinking Marketing: Towards Critical Marketing Accountings*. London: Sage. pp. 84–105.

Araujo, L. and Easton, G. (1996) 'Networks in socio-economic systems', in D. Iacobucci (ed.), *Networks in Marketing*. London: Sage. pp. 63–107.

Arce, A. and Marsden, T. (1993) 'The social construction of international food: a new research agenda', *Economic Geography*, 69: 291–311.

Arias, P., Dankers, C., Liu, P. and Pilkauskas, P. (2003), *The world banana economy 1985–2002*. Rome: Food and Agriculture Organization of the United Nations; Raw Materials, Tropical and Horticultural Products Service (ESCR), Commodity and Trade Division.

Ashworth, G. and Voogd, H. (1990) *Selling the City: Marketing Approaches in Public Sector Urban Planning*. London: Belhaven.

Bacon, C. (2004) '*Small-scale coffee farmers use of Fair Trade networks to negotiate globalization, crisis and sustainability*', unpublished doctoral dissertation. University of Santa Cruz, CA.

Barratt Brown, M. (1993) *Fair Trade: Reform and Realities in the International Trading System*. London: Zed.

Barrientos, S. (2000) 'Globalisation and ethical trade: assessing the implications for development', *Journal of International Development*, 12: 559–70.

Batsell, J. (2003) 'Fair chance at Starbucks', *The Seattle Times*, 10 June: C1.

Beck, L. (1959) *Immanuel Kant: Foundations of the Metaphysics of Morals*. New York: Bobbs-Merrill.

Berlan, A. (2004) 'Child labour, education and child rights among cocoa producers in Ghana', in C. van den Anker (ed.), *The Political Economy of Slavery*. New York: Palgrave Macmillan. pp. 158–78.

Bhagwati, J. (1995) 'Trade liberalisation and "Fair Trade" demands: Addressing the environmental and labour standard issues', *World Economy*, 18(6): 745–59.

Bird, K. and Hughes, D. (1997) 'Ethical consumerism: the case of "fair trade" coffee', *Business Ethics: A European Review*, 6(3): 159–67.

Bishop, T. (1992) 'Integrating business ethics into an undergraduate curriculum', *Journal of Business Ethics*, 11: 291–9.

Blau, P. (1964) *Exchange and Power in Social Life*. London: Wiley.

Blow, M. (1999) 'Ethical trade: a review of developments and issues', *Third World Quarterly*, 20: 753–70.

Blowfield, M. (2002) 'ETI: a multi-stakeholder approach', in R. Jenkins, R. Pearson and G. Seyfang (eds) *Corporate Responsibility and Labour Rights: Codes of Conduct in the Global Economy*. London: Earthscan. pp. 184–95.

Blowfield, M. and Gallet, S. (2000) *Volta River Estates Fair Trade Bananas Case Study*. University of Greenwich: Ethical Trade and Sustainable Livelihoods Case Studies Series. Available at: http://www.nri.org/NRET/csvrel.pdf.

Booms, B. and Bitner, M.-J. (1981) 'Marketing strategies and organisation structures for service firms', in J. Donnelly and W. George (eds), *Marketing of Services*. Chicago: American Marketing Association. pp. 32–50.

Bornstein, D. (2004) *How to Change the World*. Oxford: Oxford University Press.

Bowen, B. (2001) 'Let's go fair!', *Fair Trade Yearbook*. Brussels: European Fair Trade Association. pp. 21–41.

Bowie, N. (1999) *Business Ethics: A Kantian Perspective*. Oxford: Blackwell.

Braverman, A. and Guasch, J. (1989) *Rural Credit in Developing Countries*, Working Papers. Washington, DC: World Bank, Agriculture and Rural Development Department.

Burke, M. and Berry, L. (1974) 'Do social actions of a corporation influence store image and profits?', *Journal of Retailing*, 50(4): 62–72.

Cafédirect (2004) available at: http://www.Cafédirect.co.uk/news.php/000084.html.

Callon, M. (1986) 'The sociology of an actor-network: The case of the electric vehicle', in M. Callon, J. Law and A. Rip (eds), *Mapping the Dynamics of Science and Technology*. Basingstoke: Macmillan, pp. 19–34.

Callon, M. (1991) 'Techno-economic networks and irreversability', in J. Law (ed.), *A Sociology of Monsters: Power, Technology and Domination*. London: Routledge. pp. 132–61.

Callon, M. (1999) 'Actor-network theory – the market test', in J. Law and J. Hassard (eds), *Actor Network Theory and After*. Oxford: Blackwell. pp. 35–49.

Callon, M. and Law, J. (1992) 'Agency and the hybrid collectif', *South Atlantic Quarterly*, 94(2): 481–507.

Capone, L. (2004) 'There is a new cause brewing on campuses', *Boston Globe*, 2 Feb: 13.

Carslaw, N. (2002) 'UK stores beacon for Fair Trade', BBC News, 26 Nov. Available at: http://news.bbc.co.uk/1/hi/business/2512921.stm.

Chambers, S. and Kymlicka, W. (2002) *Alternative Conceptions of Civil Society*. Princeton, NJ: Princeton University Press.

Chambron, A. (1999) *Bananas: The Green Gold of the TNCs'*. London: UK Food Group.

Chambron, A. and Smith, S. (1997) *Bananas: Towards Sustainable Production and Trade*. Paris: Charles Léopold Mayer.

Chiquita Brands International (2002) *Corporate Social Responsibility Report – Executive Summary*. Available at: http://www.chiquita.com/corpres/CR2002/2002-CRExecSummary-FINAL. pdf.

Chiquita Brands International (2004) 'Chiquita and Migros establish nature reserves in Costa Rica', press release, 8 June. Available at: www.chiquita.com/Press Releases.

Chryssides, G. and Kaler, J. (1993) *An Introduction to Business Ethics*. London: Thomson Business.

CIA (2004) Central Intelligence Agency, *World Factbook*. Available at: http://www.cia.gov/cia/publications/factbook.

Clifton, R. (2001) 'The future of the brand', Retail Week Conference, London, 6 March.

Coelho, J. (2004) 'Fair trade on the rise', *Reuters New York*, 22 August.

Cohen, J. and Arato, A. (1992) *Civil Society and Political Theory*. Cambridge, MA: MIT Press.

Collier, P. and Gunning, J.W. (1994) 'Trade and development: protection, shocks and liberalisation', in D. Greenaway and L. Winters (eds), *Surveys in International Trade*. Oxford: Blackwell. pp. 206–33.

Concise Oxford Dictionary of Current English, 8th edn. (1990). Oxford: Clarendon.

Cook, K. (1977) 'Exchange and power in networks of interorganisational relations', *Sociological Quarterly*, 18: 62–82.

Cook, K. and Emerson, R. (1984) 'Exchange networks and the analysis of complex organisations', *Research into the Sociology of Organisations*, 3: 1–30.

Co-operative Bank/NEF (2003) *The Ethical Consumption Report 2003*. Available at: www.co-operativebank.co.uk/epi.

Co-operative Group (2004) 'Co-op on target to double Fair Trade range', press release, 2 June. Available at: www.co-op.co.uk/Media Centre/News Releases.

Co-operative Group/MORI (2004) *Shopping with Attitude*. Available at: www.co-op.co.uk/ext_1/Development.nsf1014ac97bcc96820a980256c7c004937d6?Opendocument.

Cowe, R. (2000) 'Black hole in MBA curriculum', *The Guardian*, 19 Feb: 43.

Cowe, R. and Williams, S. (2000) *Who are the Ethical Consumers?* Manchester: Co-operative Bank/MORI.

Crang, P. (1996) 'Displacement, consumption and identity', *Environment and Planning A*, 28: 47–67.

Curtis, J. (2004) 'Brand Builders: Divine Chocolate', *Marketing,* 16 June: 29.

Cycon, D. (2004) *The Fair Trade Road Map.* Available at: www.deansbeans.com/ic/fair_trade_roadmap.html.

Davies, I. and Crane, A. (2003) 'Ethical decision making in Fair Trade companies', *Journal of Business Ethics*, 45(1): 79–90.

De George, R. (1999) *Business Ethics*, 5th edn. London: Prentice-Hall.

Demetriou, D. (2003) 'Consumers embrace ethical sales, costing firms £2.6bn a year', *The Independent*, 9 Dec: 7.

deSoto, H. (2000) *The Mystery of Capital: Why Capitalism Triumphs in the West and Fails Everywhere Else*. London: Basic.

DFID (2002) Department for International Development, *British Consumer Attitudes Survey*. Available at: http://62.189.42.51/DFIDstage/Pubs/files/omnibus2002_tables.pdf.

Dikhanov, Y. and Ward, M. (2001) *Measuring the Distribution of Global Income.* Washington, DC: World Bank.

Diller, J. (1999) 'A social conscience in the global marketplace? Labour dimensions of codes of conduct, social labelling and investor initiatives', *International Labour Review*, 138: 183–97.

Dorward, A., Poulton, C. and Kydd, J. (2001) 'Rural and farmer finance: an international perspective (with particular reference to sub-Saharan Africa)', paper presented at Rural Finance Agricultural Economics Association of South Africa Conference, Imperial College at Wye, 19 September. Available at: http://www.imperial.ac.uk/agriculturalsciences/research/sections/aebm/projects/diverse_downloads/levsapap.pdf.

Drinks Business Review (2004) 'Nestlé: Fair Trade?', 10 May. Available at: www.drinks-business-review.com/article_feature.asp?guid=4F14BCE7–C18E-4F01–A966–9685A239 B249.

Dworkin, R. (1977) *Taking Rights Seriously*. London: Duckworth.

Economist (1999) 'The non-governmental order', 9 Dec: 12.

Economist (2003) 'Who guards the guardians?', 18 Sept: 53.

Edwards, M. (2003) *Civil Society*. London: Polity Press.

EFTA (2001) European Fair Trade Association, *Fair Trade in Europe 2001*. Available at: www.eftafairtrade.net.

EFTA (2004) European Fair Trade Association, *Research on the impact of Fair Trade*. Maastricht: EFTA.

Ehrenberg, J. (1999) *Civil Society: The Critical History of An Idea*. New York: New York University Press.

EIU (2003) Economist Intelligence Unit, 'UK food: price war going bananas', executive briefing, London, 4 August.

Elkington, J. (1997) *Cannibals with Forks: The Triple Bottom Line of 21st Century Business*. London: Capstone.

Elkington, J. (2001) 'The triple bottom line for 21st century business', in R. Strakely and R. Welford (eds), *Business and Sustainable Development*. London: Earthscan. pp. 20–43.

Elkington, J. and Hailes, J. (1989) *The Green Consumer's Supermarket Shopping Guide*. London: Gollancz.

Elliott, R. and Wattanasuwan, K. (1998) 'Brands as resources for the symbolic construction of identity', *International Journal of Advertising*, 17: 131–44.

Emerson, J. (1999) 'Social return on investment: exploring aspects of value creation', Roberts Enterprise Development Foundation Vol. 2. San Francisco: Roberts Enterprise Development Foundation. pp. 132–45.

Emerson, J. (2003) 'The Blended Value Proposition: integrating social and financial returns', *California Management Review*, 45(4): 35–51.

Enders, A. (1997) 'Fair trade and domestic policy harmonisation', *World Economy*, 20(3): 369–76.

Equal Exchange (1999) 'Equal Exchange "Conscious Coffee" joins top ranks of nation's ethical businesses', press release 15 November. Available at: http://www.equalexchange.com/news_info/prbizethics.html.

Equal Exchange (2000) 'Fair trade coffee pioneers welcome competitors to their niche', press release, 21 September. Available at: http://www.equalexchange.com/news_info/pr9.00. html.

Equal Exchange (2002) *2002 Annual Report*. Canton, MA: Equal Exchange.

Equal Exchange (2003) *2003 Annual Report*. Canton, MA: Equal Exchange.

ETI (2004) Ethical Trade Initiative. Available at: www.ethicaltrade.org/pub/about/eti/faq/content.shtml.

European Commission (1997) *Attitudes of European Union Consumers to Fair Trade Bananas*. Brussels: Directorate-General for Agriculture.

Fair Trade Federation (2002) *Report on Fair Trade Trends in the US & Canada*.

Fair Trade Federation (2003) *Report on Fair Trade Trends in the US & Canada*.

Fair Trade Federation and IFAT (2003) *2003 Report on. Fair Trade Trends*, p. 15. Also available at www.ifat.org/downloads/2003_trends_report.pdf.

Fairtrade Foundation (2002) *2001 Annual Report and Financial Statements*. London: Fairtrade.

Fairtrade Foundation (2003a) *2002 Annual Report and Financial Statements*. London: Fairtrade.

Fairtrade Foundation (2003b) Personal correspondence with the Fairtrade Foundation, October 2003.

Fairtrade Foundation (2003c) *Fairtrade Fortnight Briefing 2003*. London: Fairtrade.

Fairtrade Foundation (2004a) Available at: http://www.fairtrade.org.uk/about_sales.htm.

Fairtrade Foundation (2004b) *Ten Years of Fair Trade Fortnight*. Available at: http://www.fairtrade.org.uk/pr010304.htm.

Fairtrade Foundation (2004c) Available at: http://www.fairtrade.org.uk/get_involved_fairtrade_towns.htm.

Fairtrade Foundation (2004d) 'Response to Marks and Spencer's switch to 100% Fairtrade coffee in Café Revive'. Available at: http://www.fairtrade.org.uk/downloads/pdf/marksandspencer.pdf.

Fairtrade Foundation/MORI (2004) *Consumer Awareness of Fair Trade Survey*. Available at: www.fairtrade.org.uk/pr150504.htm.

FAO/GTZ (1998) Food and Agriculture Organization of the United Nations (FAO) and Deutsche Gesellschaft für Technische Zusammenarbeit (GTZ), *Agricultural Finance Revisited: Why?* Available at: http://www.gtz.de/themen/economic-development/download/afr_why.pdf.

FAO/GTZ (1999) Food and Agriculture Organization of the United Nations (FAO) and Deutsche Gesellschaft für Technische Zusammenarbeit (GTZ), *Better Practices in Agricultural Lending*. Available at: http://www.gtz.de/themen/economic-development/download/afr_ 3.pdf.

Fine, B. and Leopold, E. (1993) *The World of Consumption*. London: Routledge.

Fisher, C. and Lovell, A. (2003) *Business Ethics and Values*. Harlow: FT Prentice Hall.

Fletcher, F. (1990) 'Caring sharing consumers', *What's New in Marketing*, Oct: 30–2.

FLO (2002) Fairtrade Labelling Organisations International, *FLO Annual Report 2002*. Bonn: Fairtrade Labelling Organisations International. Available at: www.fairtrade.net.

FLO (2003) Fairtrade Labelling Organisations International, *FLO Annual Report 2003*. Bonn: Fairtrade Labelling Organisations International. Available at: www.fairtrade.net.

FLO (2004) Fairtrade Labelling Organisations International, *Generic Standards for Hired Labour*. Available at: http://www.fairtrade.net/sites/impact/facts.html.

Fukuyama, F. (1992) *The End of History*. London: Hamish Hamilton.

Gabriel, Y. and Lang, T. (1995) *The Unmangeable Consumer: Contemporary Consumption and Its Fragmentation*. London: Sage.

Gazette, The Magazine of the John Lewis Partnership (2004) 'Rise in ethical trading', 22 May: 4.

Gereffi, G. (1994) 'The organization of buyer-driven global commodity chains', in G. Gereffi and M. Korzeniewicz (eds), *Commodity Chains and Global Capitalism*. Westport, CT: Greenwood. pp. 95–122.

Geremek, B. (1992) *The Idea of Civil Society*. North Carolina: National Humanities Centre.

Ghillani, P. (2002) Interview as part of press file for the King Baudouin International Development Prize. Available at: www.kbs-frb.be/files/db/EN/KBPri.

Ghosh, S. (1994) *Retailing*, 2nd edn. Fort Worth, TX: Dryden Press.

Giddens, A. (1998) *The Third Way: Renewal of Social Democracy (IGN European Country Maps)*. London: Polity.

Giddens, A. (2000) *The Third Way and Its Critics*. London: Polity.

GMCR (2003) Green Mountain Coffee Roasters, *2003 Annual Report*. Waterbury, VT: Green Mountain Coffee Roasters.

Goodman, D. (1999) 'Agro-food studies in the "Age of Ecology": nature, corporeality, bio-politics', *Sociologia Ruralis*, 39(1): 17–38.

Gould, N. (2003) 'Fair Trade and the consumer interest: a personal account', *International Journal of Consumer Studies*, 27(4): 341–5.

Granovetter, M. (1985) 'Economic action and social structure: the problem of embeddedness', *American Journal of Sociology*, 91: 481–510.

Gresser, C. and Tickell, S. (2002) *Mugged: Poverty in Your Coffee Cup*. Oxford: Oxfam.

Grolleau, G. and Ben Abid, S. (2001) 'Fair trading in markets for credence goods: an analysis applied to agri-food products', *Intereconomics*, 36(4): 208–15.

Guardian/ICM (2004) Toyota Prius and Guardian/ICM survey published in The Guardian's *Spark* magazine, 28 Feb: 8–15.

Hakansson, H. and Johanson, J. (1992) 'A model of industrial networks', in B. Axelsson and G. Easton (eds), *Industrial Networks – a New View of Reality*. London: Routledge. pp. 28–34.

Hakansson, H. and Ostberg, C. (1975) 'Industrial marketing – an organisational problem', *Industrial Marketing Management*, 4: 113–23.

Hakansson, H. and Snehota, I. (1995) *Developing Relationships in Business Networks*. London: Routledge.

Hakansson, H., Johanson, J. and Wootz, B. (1976) 'Influence tactics in buyer-seller processes', *Industrial Marketing Management*, 5: 319–32.

Hall, J. (ed.) (1995) *Civil Society: Theory, History, Comparison*. Cambridge: Polity.

Hartwick, E. (2000) 'Towards a geographical politics of consumption', *Environment and Planning A*, 32: 1177–92.

Healy, P. (1994) 'The reasons for a prize to the best urban marketing project', in G. Ave and F. Corsico (eds), *Urban Marketing in Europe*. Torino: Incontra. pp. 3–13.

Hilton, S. and Gibbons, G. (2002) *Good Business*. London: Texere.

Hopkins, R. (2000) *Impact Assessment study of Oxfam Fair Trade*. Oxford: Oxfam.

Hopkins, T. and Wallenstein, I. (1986) 'Commodity chains in the world economy prior to 1800', *Review*, 10: 157–70.

Horowitz, B. (2004) 'Market to sell certified Fair Trade bananas', *USA Today*, 21 Jan: 17.

Howse, R. and Trebilcock, M. (1996) 'The Fair Trade-free trade debate: Trade, labour and the environment', *International Review of Law and Economics*, 16: 61–79.

Hudson, I. and Hudson, M. (2003) 'Removing the veil? Commodity fetishism, Fair Trade and the environment', *Organization and Environment*, 16(4): 413–30.

Hughes, A. (2000) 'Retailers, knowledges and changing commodity networks: the case of the cut flower trade', *Geoforum*, 31: 175–90.

Hughes, A. (2001) 'Multi-stakeholder approaches to ethical trade: towards a reorganisation of UK retailer's global supply chains?', *Journal of Economic Geography*, 1(4): 421–37.

Human Rights Watch (2002) *Tainted Harvest: Child Labour and Obstacles to Organizing on Ecuador's Banana Plantations*. New York: Human Rights Watch.

Humphrey, L. (2000) *Which Way to Market? Exploring Opportunities for Marginalized Producers in Developing Countries to Supply Mainstream Commercial Companies in the UK.* Traidcraft Policy Unit Report Series, 1. London: Traidcraft Exchange.

Hutton, W., MacDougall, A. and Zadek, S. (2001) 'Topics in business ethics – corporate stakeholding, ethical investment, social accounting', *Journal of Business Ethics*, 32: 107–17.

Iacobucci, D. and Hopkins, N. (1992) 'Modelling dyadic interactions and networks in marketing', *Journal of Marketing Research*, 29: 5–17.

IADB (1998) Inter-American Development Bank, *Rural Finance Strategy*, Microenterprise Unit, Sustainable Development Department. Available at: http://www.iadb.org/sds/doc/mic%2Dgn2022e.pdf.

IBRD (2000) International Bank for Reconstruction and Development (World Bank), *Global Economic Prospects and the Developing Countries.* Washington, DC: The World Bank Group.

IBRD (2002) International Bank for Reconstruction and Development (World Bank), *World Development Indicators.* Available at: http://www.worldbank.org/data/wdi2004/ index.htm.

ICO (2004) International Coffee Organization, *World Coffee Export and Price Data, 1986–2003.* Available at: http://www.ico.org/frameset/traset.htm/Historical Data.

IFAT (2004a) International Federation of Alternative Trade, *Impact: Facts and Figures.* Available at: http://www.fairtrade.net/sites/impact/facts.html.

IFAT (2004b) International Federation of Alternative Trade, 'A Fair Trade mark for the products of FTOs', discussion paper for IFAT regional conferences, IFAT Asia Conference, Hanoi, 5–10 September.

IFAT (2004c) International Federation of Alternative Trade, 'What does IFAT do?', http://www. ifat.org/ifatdoes.html.

IFAT (2004d) International Federation of Alternative Trade, 'The FTO mark and Fair Trade labelling', http://www.ifat.org/theftomark/ftomarkftlabelling.html.

International Taskforce on Commodity Risk Volatility in Developing Countries (1999) *Discussion Paper for the Roundtable on Commodity Risk Management in Developing Countries*, 24 September, Washington, DC, available at: http://www.itf-commrisk.org/documents/ dsp73.pdf.

International Trade Centre, UNCTAD/WTO (2001) *Cocoa: A Guide to Trade Practices.* Geneva: UNCTAD/WTO.

Jain, A., Mody, P., Rowell, S. and Yeats, T. (2003) *Are Bananas the New Coffee?*, study prepared for TransFair USA. Palo Alto, CA: Stanford University Business School.

Jenkins, R. (2002) 'Wake up and smell the coffee, Oxfam', *The Guardian*, 7 Oct: 16.

Johnston, J. (2002) 'Consuming global justice: Fair Trade shopping and alternative development', in J. Goodman (ed.), *Protest and Globalisation: Prospects for Transnational Solidarity.* Annandale: Pluto. pp. 113–36.

Jones, L. (2004) 'How Fair Trade hit the mainstream', BBC News, 2 March. Available at: http://news.bbc.co.uk/1/hi/business/3522059.stm.

Jones, P., Comfort, D. and Hillier, D. (2003) 'Retailing Fair Trade food products in the UK', *British Food Journal*, 105(11): 800–10.

Just Coffee (2004) available at: www.justcoffee.net/contracts.asp.

Kaplan, R. (2002) 'The balanced scorecard and nonprofit organizations', *Balanced Scorecard Report*: 2–6.

Kaplan, R. and Norton, D. (1996) *The Balanced Scorecard.* Harvard: Harvard Business School Press.

Keane, J. (2003) *Global Civil Society.* Cambridge: Cambridge University Press.

Kelly, M. (2003) 'The legacy problem: why social mission gets squeezed out of firms when they're sold and what to do about it', *Business Ethics,* Summer: 23–9.

Keynes, J.M. (1946) 'The International control of raw commodity prices', in E. Johnson and D. Moggridge (eds), *The Collected Writings of John Maynard Keynes,* Vol. 27. Cambridge: Cambridge University Press. pp. 27–41.

Klein, N. (2000) *No Logo.* London: Flamingo.

Kocken, M. (2002) *The Impact of Fair Trade.* Maastricht: European Fair Trade Association.

Kocken, M. (2003) *Fifty Years of Fair Trade.* Maastricht: European Fair Trade Association. Available at: http://www.gepa3.de/download/gepa_Fair_Trade_history_en.pdf.

Kotler, P., Armstrong, G., Saunders, J. and Wong, V. (1999) *Principles of Marketing*, 2nd European edn. London: Prentice Hall.

Krier, J.-M. (2001) *Fair Trade in Europe 2001*. Maastricht: European Fair Trade Association.

Krugman, P. and Obstfeld, M. (1997) *International Economics: Theory and Policy*, 4th edn. New York: Addison Wesley.

Lang, T. (2003) 'Food industrialisation and food power: implications for food governance', *Development Policy Review*, 21(5): 555–68.

Lang, T. and Hines, C. (1993) *The New Protectionism*. London: Earthscan.

Latour, B. (1993) *We Have Never Been Modern*. Harvard: Harvard University Press.

Law, J. (1986) 'On methods of long-distance control: vessels, navigation and the Portuguese route to India', in J. Law (ed.), *Power, Action and Belief: A New Sociology of Knowledge?* London: Routledge and Kegan Paul. pp. 122–40.

Law, J. (1992) 'Notes on the theory of actor-network: ordering, strategy and heterogeneity', *Systems Practice*, 5: 379–93.

Law, J. (1994) *Organising Modernity*. Oxford: Blackwell.

Leadbeater, C. (1997) *The Rise of the Social Entrepreneur*. London: Demos.

Leatherhead Food International (2003) *Fair Trade Foods – Market Prospects for the Ethical Option*. London: Leatherhead Food International.

LeClair, M. (2002) 'Fighting the tide: alternative trade organizations in the era of global free trade', *World Development*, 30(6): 949–58.

LeClair, M. (2003) 'Fighting back: the growth of alternative trade', *Society for International Development*, 46(1): 66–73.

LeComte, T. (2003) *Le Pari du Commerce Equitable*. Paris: Editions d'Organisations.

Legrain, P. (2002) *Open World: The Truth about Globalisation*. London: Abacus.

Leholo, T. (1996) *Possibilities in Law of Outlawing the 'Tot' System*. Cape Town: Chennells Albertyn.

Leslie, D. and Reimer, S. (1999) 'Spatializing commodity chains', *Progress in Human Geography*, 23: 401–20.

Levi, M. and Linton, A. (2003) 'Fair Trade: a cup at a time?', *Politics and Society*, 31(3): 407–32.

Lewin, B., Giovannucci, D. and Varangis, P. (2004) 'Coffee markets: new paradigms in global supply and demand', *Agricultural and Rural Development Discussion Paper*, 3. Washington, DC: World Bank. Available at: http://lnweb18.worldbank.org/ESSD/ardext.nsf/11ByDocName/Coffee MarketsNewParadigmsinGlobalSupplyandDemand/$FILE/CoffeeMarkets-ArdDp3.pdf.

Lindsey, B. (2004) *Grounds for Complaint: Fair Trade and the Coffee Crisis*. London: Adam Smith Institute/Cato Institute.

Littrell, M. and Dickson, M. (1997) 'Alternative trading organizations: a shifting paradigm in a culture of social responsibility', *Human Organization*, 563: 344–56.

Littrell, M. and Dickson, M. (1998) 'Fair Trade performance in a competitive market', *Clothing and Textiles Research Journal*, 16(4): 176–89.

Littrell, M. and Dickson, M. (1999) *Social Responsibility in the Global Market: Fair Trade of Cultural Products*. London: Sage.

Lockie, S., Lyons, K., Lawrence, G. and Mummery, W. (2002) 'Eating "green": motivations behind organic food consumption in Australia', *Sociologia Ruralis*, 42(1): 23–40.

Lyon, S. (2002) *Evaluation of the Actual and Potential Benefits for the Alleviation of Poverty through the Participation in Fair Trade Coffee Networks: Guatemalan Case Study*. Available at: www.colostate.edu/Depts/Sociology/FairTradeResearchGroup.

MacIntyre, A. (1982) *After Virtue*. London: Duckworth.

MacMaolain, C. (2002) 'Ethical food labelling: the role of European Union free trade in facilitating international fair trade', *Common Market Law Review*, 39: 1–20.

Malins, A. and Blowfield, M. (2000) *Fruits of the Nile: Fair Trade Processing Case Study*. University of Greenwich, Ethical Trade and Sustainable Livelihoods Case Studies series. Available at: http://www.nri.org/NRET/fruitnil.pdf.

Marsden, T. (1992) 'Exploring a rural sociology for the Fordist transition', *Sociologia Ruralis*, 32(2): 209–29.

Marsden, T., Banks, J. and Bristow, G. (2000) 'Food supply chain approaches: exploring their role in rural development', *Sociologia Ruralis*, 40(4): 424–38.

Maseland, R. and de Vaal, A. (2002) 'How fair is fair trade?', *De Economist*, 150(3): 251–63.

Max Havelaar France (2002) *Comptes Annuels*. Paris: Max Havelaar. Available at: http://www.maxhavelaarfrance.org/documents/RAPPORT%20ANNUEL_MAX.pdf.

Max Havelaar Switzerland (2000) *Comptes/Bilan*. Basel: Max Havelaar Switzerland. Available at: http://www.maxhavelaar.ch/web/havelaar/mainR2.nsf/allbyunid/22A8888BE36BAE4BC1256B7C002E11DD/$file/MH_report_2000.pdf?OpenElement.

Max Havelaar Switzerland (2001) *Comptes/Bilan*. Basel: Max Havelaar Switzerland. Available at: http://www.maxhavelaar.ch/web/havelaar/mainR2.nsf/allbyunid/10A4D409D2F34138C1256E6D002AE5B4/$file/MH_report_03_farb.pdf?OpenElement.

Max Havelaar Switzerland (2003) *Comptes/Bilan*. Basel: Max Havelaar Switzerland. Available at: http://www.maxhavelaar.ch/web/havelaar/mainR2.nsf/allbyunid/10A4D409D2F34138C1256E6D002AE5B4/$file/MH_report_03_farb.pdf?OpenElement.

Mayoux, L. (2001a) *Case Study: Kuapa Kokoo*. Available at: http://www.enterprise-impact.org.uk/informationresources/casestudies/kuapakokoo.shtml.

Mayoux, L. (2001b) *Impact Assessment of Fair Trade and Ethical Enterprise Development*. Available at: www.enterprise-impact.org.uk/word-files/IAofFairTrade-3-Section2.doc.

McCarthy, M. (2004) 'Fair Trade produce tempts the shoppers with a conscience as annual sales surge to £100m', *The Independent*, 1 March: 5.

McDonagh, P. (2002) 'Communicative campaigns to effect anti-slavery and Fair Trade. The cases of Rugmark and Cafédirect', *European Journal of Marketing*, 36(5–6): 642–66.

McLaughlin, K. (2004) 'Food world's new buzzword is "sustainable products": Fair Trade certified mangoes', *Wall Street Journal*, 17 February: A7.

McLouglin, D. and Horan, C. (2002) 'Markets as networks: notes on a unique understanding', *Journal of Business Research*, 55: 535–43.

McNeal, J. (1992) *Kids as Customers: A Handbook of Marketing to Children*. New York: Paramount.

McNeal, J. (1999) *The Kids' Market: Myths and Realities*. New York: Paramount.

Mendoza, R. and Bastiaensen, J. (2003) 'Fair Trade and the coffee crisis in the Nicaraguan Segovias', *Small Enterprise Development*, 14(2): 36–46.

Micklethwait, J. and Wooldridge, A. (2003) *The Company: A Short History of a Revolutionary Idea (Modern Library Chronicles)*. London: Modern Library.

Mintel (1999) *Green and Ethical Consumer Survey*. London: Mintel.

Mintel (2001) *Attitudes Towards Ethical Food Survey*. London: Mintel.

Mintel (2004) *Green and Ethical Consumer Survey*. London: Mintel.

Moore, G. (2004) 'The Fair Trade movement: parameters, issues and future research', *Journal of Business Ethics*, 53: 73–86.

Moore, M. (2001) *Stupid White Men*. London: Penguin.

Moore, M. (2003) *Dude Where's My Country?* London: Penguin.

Morgan, K. and Murdoch, J. (2000) 'Organic vs. conventional agriculture: knowledge, power and innovation in the food chain', *Geoforum* 3: 159–73.

Murdoch, J., Marsden, T. and Banks, J. (2000) 'Quality, nature, and embeddedness: some theoretical considerations in the context of the food sector', *Economic Geography*, 76: 107–25.

Murray, D. and Raynolds, L. (2000) 'Alternative trade in bananas: obstacles and opportunities for progressive social change in the global economy', *Agriculture and Human Values*, 17: 65–74.

Murray, D., Raynolds, L. and Taylor, P. (2003) 'One cup at a time: poverty alleviation and Fair Trade coffee in Latin America'. Colorado State University, Fair Trade Research Group. Available at: http://www.colostate.edu/Depts/Sociology/FairTradeResearchGroup/doc/ fairtrade.pdf.

Nachman-Hunt, N. (2003) 'Will Fair Trade become the next growth wave?', *Natural Foods Merchandiser*, Sep: 22–5.

NEF (2001) New Economics Foundation, *Taking Flight: The Rapid Growth of Ethical Consumerism*, report for the Co-operative Bank. London: NEF.

NEF (2004a) New Economics Foundation, *Ethical Pioneers Project*. Available at: www.neweconomics.org/gen/trans_ethicalwp.aspx.

NEF (2004b) New Economics Foundation, *Social Return on Investment. Valuing What Matters.* Available at: http://www.neweconomics.org/gen/z_sys_PublicationDetail.aspx? PID=180.

Nelson, V. and Galvez, M. (2000) *Social Impact of Ethical and Conventional Cocoa Trading on Forest-Dependent People in Ecuador.* Greenwich, UK: Natural Resources Institute, University of Greenwich, Natural Resources and Ethical Trading Programme.

New, S. (2004) 'The ethical supply chain', in S. New and R. Westbrook (eds), *Understanding Supply Chains: Concepts, Critiques and Futures.* Oxford: Oxford University Press. pp. 253–80.

Newholm, T. (1999) *Considering the Ethical Consumer and Summing Up Case Studies.* Unpublished PhD. University of Greenwich.

Newman, P. (2002) 'Cafédirect – the height of coffee taste', *Cafédirect Annual Report 2001–2.* London: Cafédirect. p. 14.

Nicholls, A. (2002) 'Strategic options in fair trade retailing', *International Journal of Retail and Distribution Management*, 30(1): 6–17.

Nicholls, A. (2004) 'New product development in fair trade retailing', *Service Industries Journal*, 24(2): 102–17.

Nicholls, A. and Alexander, A. (forthcoming) 'Rediscovering consumer-producer involvement: a network perspective on Fair Trade marketing in the UK', *European Journal of Marketing*.

Nozick, R. (1974) *Anarchy, State and Utopia.* London: Basic.

Odak, P. (2003) 'Wild Oats Markets', presentation at WildStock company conference, Las Vegas, April.

Orchard, J. et al. (1998) *Potential for Fair Trade and Organic Bananas from the Caribbean.* Greenwich, UK: Natural Resources Institute, University of Greenwich.

Organic Trade Association (2004) *Industry Statistics and Projected Growth.* Available at: www.ota.com.

Otis, J. (2003) 'Fruitless labor: ruled by fear, banana workers resist unions', *Houston Chronicle*, 14 September: 1A.

Oxfam (2002) *Rigged Rules and Double Standards.* Oxford: Oxfam.

Oxfam (2004) *Trading Away Our Rights.* Available at: http://www.oxfam.org/eng/pdfs/report_042008_labor.pdf.

Oxfam America and TransFair USA (2002) *Fair Trade Coffee: The Time is Now.* Boston, MA: Oxfam America.

Oxford Brookes University (2004) Available at: http://www.brookes.ac.uk/news/other/fairtrade_policy.

Packard, V. (1957) *The Hidden Persuaders.* London: Penguin.

Page, S. and Slater, R. (2003) 'Small producer participation in global food systems: policy opportunities and constraints', *Development Policy Review*, 21(5–6): 641–54.

Petrick, J. and Quinn, J. (1997) *Management Ethics. Integrity at Work.* London: Sage.

Ploetz, R. (2001) 'Black Sigatoka of banana', *The Plant Health Instructor.* Available at: http://www.apsnet.org/education/feature/banana/Top.html.

Porter, M. (1998) *On Competition.* Harvard: Harvard Business School.

Pracejus, J. and Olsen, G. (2004) 'The role of brand/cause fit in the effectiveness of cause-related marketing campaigns', *Journal of Business Research*, 57(6): 635–40.

Prahalad, C.K. (2004) *The Fortune at the Bottom of the Pyramid.* Wharton: Wharton Business School.

Princeton University (2002) 'Daniel Kahneman wins Nobel prize', press release, 9 October. Available at: http://www.princeton.edu/pr/home/02/1009_kahneman/hmcap.html.

Purvis, A. (2003) 'The tribe that survives on chocolate', *Observer Food Monthly, The Observer*, November: 23–32.

Putnam, R. (2000) *Bowling Alone.* New York: Simon and Schuster.

PWC (2002) PriceWaterhouseCoopers, *Governors of the World Economic Forum for Retail and Consumer Goods.* London: PriceWaterhouseCoopers.

Rainforest Alliance (2004) Available at: http://www.ra.org/programs/agriculture/certified-crops/nine-principles.html.

Ransom, D. (2001) *The No-Nonsense Guide to Fair Trade*. London: New Internationalist/ Verso.

Rawls, J. (1971) *A Theory of Justice*. Harvard: Harvard University Press.

Ray, P. (2000) 'Who is the LOHAS consumer?', *LOHAS Journal*, March: 7–14.

Raynolds, L. (1994) 'Institutionalizing flexibility: a comparative analysis of Fordist and post-Fordist models of Third World agro-export production', in G. Gereffi and M. Korzeniewicz (eds), *Commodity Chains and Global Capitalism*. Westport, CT: Greenwood. pp. 143–62.

Raynolds, L. (1997) 'Restructuring national agriculture, agro-food trade, and agrarian livelihoods in the Caribbean', in D. Goodman and M. Watts (eds), *Globalising Food: Agrarian Questions and Global Restructuring*. New York: Routledge. pp. 119–31.

Raynolds, L. (2000) 'Re-embedding global agriculture: the international organic and fair trade movements', *Agriculture and Human Values*, 17: 297–309.

Raynolds, L. (2002a) 'Consumer/producer links in fair trade coffee networks', *Sociologia Ruralis*, 42(4): 404–24.

Raynolds, L. (2002b) *Poverty Alleviation Through Participation in Fair Trade Coffee Networks: Existing Research and Critical Issues*. Available at: www.colostate.edu/Depts/Sociology/FairTrade ResearchGroup.

Raynolds, L. and Murray, D. (1998) 'Yes, we have no bananas: re-regulating global and regional trade', *International Journal of Sociology of Agriculture and Food*, 7: 7–44.

REDF (2000) Roberts Enterprise Development Foundation, *SROI Methodology*. San Francisco: Roberts Enterprise Development Foundation.

Redfern, A. and Snedker, P. (2002) 'Creating market opportunities for small enterprises: experiences of the Fair Trade movement', *SEED Working Paper*, 30. Geneva: International Labour Organisation.

Renard, M.-C. (1999) 'The interstices of globalization: the example of fair trade coffee', *Sociologia Ruralis*, 39(4): 484–500.

Renard, M.-C. (2002) 'Fair trade quality, market and conventions', *Journal of Rural Studies*, 19: 87–96.

Renting, H. and Marsden, T. (2003) 'Understanding alternative food networks: exploring the role of short food supply chains in rural development', *Environment and Planning A*, 35: 393–411.

Retail Week/ICM (2002) 'Public Eye: Fair Trade', 25 October: 6.

Rice, R. (2001) 'Noble goals and challenging terrain: organic and Fair Trade coffee movements in the global marketplace', *Journal of Agricultural and Environmental Ethics*, 14: 39–66.

Rice, P. (2004) address to the Fair Trade Forum at the Speciality Coffee Association of America 2004 conference, TransFair USA, Atlanta, GA, 22 April.

Rice, P. and McLean, J. (1999) *Sustainable Coffee at the Crossroads*. Washington, DC: Consumers' Choice Council.

Rodrik, D. (1992) 'The limits of trade policy reform in developing countries', *Journal of Economic Perspectives*, 6(1): 87–105.

Rogers, T. (2004) 'Small coffee brewers try to redefine fair trade', *Christian Science Monitor,* 13 April: 12–14.

Ronchi, L. (2002) *The Impact of Fair Trade on Producers and Their Organizations: A Case Study with Coocafé in Costa Rica*. University of Sussex, Brighton, UK. Available at: http://www.sussex.ac.uk/Units/PRU/wps/wp11.pdf.

Ronchi, L. (2003) *Monitoring Impact of Fair Trade Initiatives. A Case Study of Kuapa Kokoo and the Day Chocolate Company*. London: Twin Trading.

Roozen, N. and van der Hoff, F. (2003) *Comercio Justo*. Amsterdam: Uitgeverij Van Gennep.

Rosenberg, J. (2000) *The Follies of Globalization*. London: Verso.

Rosenthal, J. (2003) *Sustainable Coffee Trade Finance Options for the US Market*. Report for the Finance Alliance for Sustainable Trade (FAST). Baltimore: Johns Hopkins University.

Roy, A. (2002) *The Algebra of Infinite Justice*. London: Flamingo.

Rugman, A. (2002) *International Business: A Strategic Management Approach*. Harlow: FT/Prentice Hall.

SA8000 (2004) Available at: http://www.cepaa.org/SA8000/SA8000.htm.

Salamon, L. and Anheier, H. (eds) (1999) *Global Civil Society: Dimensions of the Non-Profit Sector.* Baltimore: Johns Hopkins University.

Salamon, L., Sokolowski, S. and List, R. (2003) *Global Civil Society: An Overview.* Baltimore: Johns Hopkins University.

Sawhill, D. and Williamson, D. (2001) 'Measuring what matters in nonprofits', *McKinsey Quarterly*, 2: 98–107.

SCAA (2004) Specialty Coffee Association of America, *Specialty Coffee Facts.* Available at: http://www.scaa.org/pdfs/press-sc_facts.pdf.

Schlegelmilch, B. (1998) *Marketing Ethics.* London: Thomson Business.

SERRV International (2003) Available at: www.serrv.org/catalog/producers/prodpage.php?txfr=ESK,Eswatini%20Swazi%20Kitchen.

Shaw, D. and Clarke, I. (1999) 'Belief formation in ethical consumer groups: an exploratory study', *Marketing and Intelligence Planning*, 17(2): 109–20.

Sheridan, E. (2000) 'Ethics on the march', *The Guardian*, 10 October: 13.

Singer, P. (2002) *One World: The Ethics of Globalization.* Yale, CT: Yale University Press.

Smith, A. (2004) *Marketing Fair Trade Bananas in an Unsustainable Banana Economy.* Norwich: Banana Link.

Social Enterprise Coalition (2003) *There's More to Business Than You Think: A Guide to Social Enterprise.* London: Social Enterprise Coalition.

Spark (2004) *The Guardian, Spark Magazine*, 28 February: 10.

Stecklow, S. and White, E. (2004) 'What price virtue?', *Wall Street Journal*, 8 June: A1–2.

Stiglitz, J. (2002) *Globalization and Its Discontents.* London: Penguin/Allen Lane.

Strong, C. (1996) 'Features contributing to the growth of ethical consumerism – a preliminary investigation', *Marketing Intelligence and Planning*, 14(5): 5–13.

Strong, C. (1997) 'The problems of translating Fair Trade principles into consumer purchase behaviour', *Marketing Intelligence and Planning*, 15(1): 32–7.

Sunde, J. and Kleinbooi, K. (1999) *Promoting Equitable and Sustainable Development for Women Farm Workers in the Western Cape.* Stellenbosch, South Africa: Centre for Rural Legal Studies.

Sutcliffe, W. (2004) 'Counting beans', *Guardian Weekend*, 7 August: 18–23.

Sweney, M. (2004) 'Nescafé plots entry into fair trade coffee market', *Marketing*, 6 May: 1.

Tallontire, A. (2000) 'Partnerships in Fair Trade: reflections from a case study of Cafédirect', *Development in Practice*, 10(2): 166–77.

Tallontire, A. (2002) 'Challenges facing Fair Trade: which way now?', *Small Enterprise Development*, 13(3): 12–24.

Tallontire, A., Rentsendorj, E. and Blowfield, M. (2001) *Ethical Consumers and Ethical Trade: A Review of Current Literature.* Chatham: Natural Resources Institute.

Taylor, P. (2002) *Poverty Alleviation Through Participation in Fair Trade Coffee Networks: Synthesis of Case Study Research Questions and Findings.* Available at: www.colostate.edu/Depts/Sociology/FairTradeResearchGroup.

Thomson, B. (1999) 'Lessons for Fair Trade', *Small Enterprise Development*, 10(4): 56–60.

Thorpe, N. (2004) 'Better than fair', *Developments – The International Development Magazine*, 25: 2–7.

Tickle, L. (2004) 'Raising the bar', *Developments – The International Development Magazine*, 25: 8–15.

Timberlake, L. (1985) *Africa in Crisis: The Causes, the Cures of Environmental Bankruptcy.* London: Earthscan.

Traidcraft Plc (2002) *Traidcraft Plc.* Available at: http://www.traidcraft.co.uk/template2.asp?pageID=1505.

Traidcraft Plc (2003) *2002–3 Annual Report, Traidcraft plc.* Available at: http://www.traidcraft.co.uk/template2.asp?pageID=1597.

Traidcraft Plc (2004) *Social Accounts 2003/04.* Available at: http://www.traidcraft.co.uk/template2.asp?pageID=1500.

TransFair Canada (2003) *Audited Financial Statements.* Ottawa: TransFair Canada. Available at: www.transfair.ca/tfc/financial.html.

TransFair Germany (2001) *Annual Report 2001.* Cologne: TransFair Germany. Available at: http://www.transfair.org/download/pdf/4.pdf.

TransFair Germany (2002) *Annual Report 2002.* Cologne: TransFair Germany.

TransFair USA (2001) *Annual Report 2001.* Oakland, CA: TransFair USA.

TransFair USA (2002a) *Fair Trade Update: Fall 2002.* Oakland, CA: TransFair USA.

TransFair USA (2002b) *Annual Report 2002.* Oakland, CA: TransFair USA.

TransFair USA (2004) *Fair Trade Coffee Fast Facts.* Oakland, CA: TransFair USA. Available at: http://www.transfairusa.org/pdfs/fastfacts_coffee.pdf.

Tropical Wholefoods (2003) *Uganda – Partner Profile – Fruits of the Nile, Kampala.* Available at: http://www.tropicalwholefoods.co.uk/ Partners/Uganda.

Udomkit, N. and Winnett, A. (2002) 'Fair Trade in organic rice: a case study from Thailand', *Small Enterprise Development*, 13(3): 45–53.

Utz Kapeh Foundation (2004) Available at: http://www.utzkapeh.org/utzkapeh/ukenglishwebsite. nsf/codeofconduct/codeofconduct.htm.

Van de Kasteele, A. (1998) *The Banana Chain: The Macro-Economics of the Banana Trade.* Report to the International Union of Food, Agricultural, Hotel, Restaurant, Catering, Tobacco and Allied Workers' Associations (IUF). Available at: http://www.iuf.org.uk.

Varangis, P., Dana, J. and Hess, U. (2004) *Status Report on Commodity Risk Management.* Presentation made at the International Task Force meeting on Commodity Risk management, FAO Rome, 5–6 May. Available at: http://www.itf-commrisk.org/documents/meetings/rome2004/C RM.pdf.

Vidal, J. (2004) 'Fair Trade sales hit £100m a year', *The Guardian*, 28 February: 13.

Walker, R. (2004) 'The joys and perils of attack marketing', *Inc. Magazine*, April: 29.

Warnaby, G. (1998) 'Marketing UK cities as shopping destinations: problems and prospects', *Journal of Retailing and Consumer Services*, 5(1): 55–8.

Watson, L. (2004) *Upgrading Management Skills.* Presentation to the IFAT Asia Conference, Hanoi, 6 September.

Webb, D. and Mohr, L. (1998) 'A typology of consumer responses to cause-related marketing from sceptics to socially concerned', *Journal of Public Policy*, 17(2): 226–38.

Welford, R., Meaton, J. and Young, W. (2003) 'Fair Trade as a strategy for international competitiveness', *International Journal of Sustainable Development and World Ecology*, 10: 1–13.

Whatmore, S. (1994) 'Global agro-food complexes and the refashioning of the rural in Europe', in N. Thrift and A. Amin (eds), *Holding Down the Global.* Oxford: Oxford University Press. pp. 45–61.

Whatmore, S. and Thorne, L. (1997) 'Nourishing networks: alternative geographies of food', in D. Goodman and M. Watts (eds), *Globalising Food: Agrarian Questions and Global Responses.* London: Routledge. pp. 287–304.

Whatmore, S., Stassart, P. and Renting, H. (2003) 'What's alternative about alternative food networks?', *Environment and Planning A*, 35: 389–91.

Whysall, P. (1995) 'Ethics in retailing', *Business Ethics: A European Review*, 4(3): 150–6.

Whysall, P. (1998) 'Ethical relationships in retailing: some cautionary tales', *Business Ethics: A European Review*, 7(2): 103–10.

Whysall, P. (2000a) 'Addressing ethical issues in retailing: a stakeholder perspective', *International Review of Retail Distribution and Consumer Research*, 10(3): 305–18.

Whysall, P. (2000b) 'Retailing and the Internet: a review of ethical issues', *International Journal of Retail and Distribution Management*, 28(11): 481–9.

Whysall, P. (2000c) 'Stakeholder mismanagement in retailing: a British perspective', *Journal of Business Ethics*, 23: 19–28.

Williamson, H. (2004) 'Coffee industry to agree improved standards', *The Financial Times*, 9 September: 13.

Wilshaw, R. (2002) 'Code monitoring in the informal Fair Trade sector: the experience of Oxfam GB', in R. Jenkins, R. Pearson and G. Seyfang (eds), *Corporate Responsibility and Labour Rights: Codes of Conduct in the Global Economy.* London: Earthscan. pp. 209–23.

WorldAware (2002) *The Trade Partners UK Award for Small Businesses in Africa. Runner-up: The Day Chocolate Company.* Available at: www.worldaware.org.uk/awards/awards2002/daychoc.html.

Wright, C. (2004) 'Consuming lives, consuming landscapes: interpreting advertisements for Cafédirect coffees', *Journal of International Development*, 16(5): 665–80.

Young, W. and Welford, R. (2002) *Ethical Shopping.* London: Fusion.

Zadek, S. (1994) 'Trading ethics: auditing the market', *Journal of Economic Issues*, 28(2): 631–46.

Zadek, S. (1998) 'Balancing performance, ethics, and accountability', *Journal of Business Ethics*, 17: 1421–41.

Zadek S., Lingayah, S. and Forstater, M. (1998) *Social Labels: Tools for Ethical Trade.* Luxemburg: Office for Official Publications of the European Communities.

Zazima, K. (2003) 'Helping farmers, a cup of coffee at a time', *New York Times*, 27 December: 41.

INTERVIEWS

Claudia Salazar Lewis, New Product Development Manager, Cafédirect
London, 17 April 2001
Mark Shayler, Environmental Manager, Asda
Leeds, 14 May 2001
Terry Hudgton, Corporate Marketing Manager, the Co-operative Group
Manchester, 23 May 2001
Ian Bretman, Acting Executive Director, Fairtrade Foundation
London, 12 June 2001
Alistaire Menzies, Product Manager [Food], Traidcraft
Gateshead, 14 June 2001
René Ausecha Chaux, Managing Director, Cosurca
Washington, DC, 12 October 2002
José Luis Zárate, Executive Director, Fomcafé
Oaxaca, 14 January 2003
Steve Sellers, Chief Operating Officer, TransFair USA
Oakland, 25 July 2003
Kimberly Easson, Business Affairs Director, TransFair USA
Oakland, 25 July 2003
Tristan LeComte, President, Alter Eco
London, 2 September 2003
Colin Crawford, Operations Director, Shared Interest
London, 22 September 2003
Phil King, Financial Director, Cafédirect
London, 24 September 2003
Sarah Garden, Campaigns Officer, Fairtrade Foundation
London, 24 October 2003
Diana Gayle, Marketing Officer, Fairtrade Foundation
London, 24 October 2003
Stephanie Sturrock, Managing Director, Shared Interest
17 November 2003 and 11 August 2004
Sylvie Barr, Strategic Development Manager, Cafédirect
London, 17 November 2003
Bruce Crowther, Fair Trade Towns Co-ordinator, Fairtrade Foundation
Garstang, 18 November 2003
Hamish Renton, Project Leader, 'Food You Can Trust', Tesco
Cheshunt, 27 November 2003

Luuk Zonneveld, Managing Director, Fair Trade Labelling Organizations International
Oakland, 2 February 2004
Safia Minney, founder of the Fair Trade Company
Japan 10 March 2004
Colin MacDougall, Director of Finance, La Siembra Co-operative
Ottawa, 13 April 2004
Kevin Thomson, Co-Executive Director, La Siembra Co-operative
Ottawa, 13 April 2004
Raymond Kimaro, General Manager, KNCU Cooperative, Arusha, Tanzania
Atlanta, 2 April 2004
Paul Rice, CEO, TransFair USA
Oakland, 17 May 2004
Carol Wills, Executive Director, International Federation of Alternative Trade
Oxford, 28 June 2004
Adam Brett, Company Director, Tropical Wholefoods
London, 8 July 2004
Tristan Lecomte, President, Alter Eco
Paris, 16 July 2004
Pauline Tiffen, Board Member, The Day Chocolate Company
Washington DC (e-mail), 9 August 2004
Sophi Tranchell, Managing Director, The Day Chocolate Company
London (telephone) 10 August 2004
Joe Osman, Sourcing and Development Manager, Traidcraft
E-mail, 17 August 2004
Ben Huyghe, Sourcing Manager, AgroFair Europe
Telephone, 21 August 2004
Rob Everts, Co-Director, Equal Exchange (USA)
E-mail, 21 August 2004
Jeroen Kroezen, Managing Director, AgroFair
E-mail, 1 September 2004
Sue Mayo, Business Development Manager, Shared Interest
London, 1 September 2004

MARKET RESEARCH

Oxfam (1992) *Flocking to Fair Trade.*
Christian Aid/NOP (1993) *Consumer Awareness of Fair Trade.*
Oxfam (1994) *Fair Trade Consumers.*
SuperMarketing/NOP (1994) *Consumer Awareness of Fair Trade.*
Co-operative Wholesale Society/Gallup (1995) *Responsible Retailing Survey.*
Fairtrade Foundation/MORI (1999) *Consumer Awareness of Fair Trade.*
Mintel (1999) *Green and Ethical Consumer Survey.*
Co-operative Bank/MORI (2000) (Cowe and Williams), *Who are the Ethical Consumers?*
Fairtrade Foundation/MORI (2000) *Consumer Awareness of Fair Trade.*
Mintel (2001) *Attitudes Towards Ethical Food Survey.*
Co-operative Bank/NEF (2003) *The Ethical Consumption Report 2003.*
Co-operative Group/MORI (2004) *Shopping with Attitude.*
Fairtrade Foundation/MORI (2004) *Consumer Awareness of Fair Trade.*
Mintel (2004) *Green and Ethical Consumer Survey.*

Some Useful Websites

www.cafédirect.co.uk
www.eftafairtrade.org (European Fair Trade Association)
www.fairtrade.net (Fair Trade Labelling Organisations International)
www.fairtrade.org.uk (UK Fair Trade Foundation)
www.fairtradefederation.org (US based Fair Trade Federation)
www.fairtradeforum.net
www.fairtraderesource.org
www.ifat.org (International Federation of Alternative Trade)
www.maxhavelaar.nl
www.ptree.co.uk
www.traidcraft.org
www.transfairusa.org

Index

New from SAGE Publications

The Ethical Consumer

Edited by **Rob Harrison** *Ethical Consumer Research Association*, **Terry Newholm** *The Open University, Milton Keynes* and **Deirdre Shaw** *Glasgow Caledonian University*

'This book is not simply the best book on the remarkable phenomenon of today's ethical consumer. It is a gift of advice and insight, from the people that know best, to the cause of tomorrow. Many of the writers deserve the plaudits of being pioneers of a new consumer movement. These are the issues of our time' - *Ed Mayo, Chief Executive of the UK's National Consumer Council (NCC)*

Twenty one writers including **Tim Lang** and **Robert Worcester** of MORI contribute their perspectives on this fast-growing new phenomenon.

March 2005 • 280 pages
Cloth (1-4129-0352-1) • £70.00 / Paper (1-4129-0353-X) • £21.99

⑤SAGE Publications
40 Years 1965–2005

www.sagepub.co.uk